The Methods Of Ethics

Sidgwick, Henry

This work has been selected by scholars as being culturally important, and is part of the knowledge base of civilization as we know it. This work was reproduced from the original artifact, and remains as true to the original work as possible. Therefore, you will see the original copyright references, library stamps (as most of these works have been housed in our most important libraries around the world), and other notations in the work.

This work is in the public domain in the United States of America, and possibly other nations. Within the United States, you may freely copy and distribute this work, as no entity (individual or corporate) has a copyright on the body of the work.

As a reproduction of a historical artifact, this work may contain missing or blurred pages, poor pictures, errant marks, etc. Scholars believe, and we concur, that this work is important enough to be preserved, reproduced, and made generally available to the public. We appreciate your support of the preservation process, and thank you for being an important part of keeping this knowledge alive and relevant.

THE
METHODS OF ETHICS

BY

HENRY SIDGWICK,

KNIGHTBRIDGE PROFESSOR OF MORAL PHILOSOPHY IN THE UNIVERSITY OF CAMBRIDGE.

Ἦ οὐ γελοῖον ἐπὶ μὲν ἄλλοις σμικροῦ ἀξίοις πᾶν ποιεῖν συντεινομένους, ὅπως ὅτι ἀκριβέστατα καὶ καθαρώτατα ἕξει, τῶν δὲ μεγίστων μὴ μεγίστας ἀξιοῦν εἶναι καὶ τὰς ἀκριβείας;—PLATO.

THIRD EDITION.

London:
MACMILLAN AND CO.
1884

[The Right of Translation is reserved.]

PREFACE TO THE FIRST EDITION.

In offering to the public a new book upon a subject so trite as Ethics, it seems desirable to indicate clearly at the outset its plan and purpose. Its distinctive characteristics may be first given negatively. It is not, in the main, metaphysical or psychological: at the same time it is not dogmatic or directly practical: it does not deal, except by way of illustration, with the history of ethical thought: in a sense it might be said to be not even critical, since it is only quite incidentally that it offers any criticism of the systems of individual moralists. It claims to be an examination, at once expository and critical, of the different methods of obtaining reasoned convictions as to what ought to be done which are to be found—either explicit or implicit—in the moral consciousness of mankind generally: and which, from time to time, have been developed, either singly or in combination, by individual thinkers, and worked up into the systems now historical.

I have avoided the inquiry into the Origin of the Moral Faculty—which has perhaps occupied a disproportionate amount of the attention of modern moralists—by the simple assumption (which seems to be made implicitly in all ethical reasoning) that there is something[1] under any given circumstances which it is right or reasonable to do, and that this may be known. If it be admitted that we now have the faculty of knowing this, it appears to me that the investigation of the historical antecedents of this cognition, and of its relation to other elements of the mind, no more properly belong to Ethics than the corresponding questions as to the cognition of Space belong to Geometry[2]. I make, however, no further assumption as to the nature of the object of ethical knowledge: and hence my treatise is not dogmatic: all the different methods developed in it are expounded and criticized from a neutral position, and as impartially as possible. And thus, though my treatment of the subject is, in a sense, more practical than that of many moralists, since I am occupied from first to last in considering how conclusions are to be rationally reached in the familiar matter of our common daily life and actual practice; still, my immediate object—to invert Aristotle's phrase—is not Practice but Knowledge. I have thought that the predominance in the minds of moralists of a desire to edify has impeded the real progress of ethical science: and that this would be benefited by an application to it of the same disinterested curiosity to which we chiefly owe the great discoveries of physics. It is in this spirit that I have endeavoured to compose the present work: and with this view I have desired to concentrate the reader's attention, from first to last, not on the practical results to which our methods lead, but on the methods themselves. I have wished to put aside temporarily the

---

[1] I did not mean to exclude the supposition that two or more alternatives might under certain circumstances be equally right (1884).

[2] This statement now appears to me to require a slight modification (1884).

urgent need which we all feel of finding and adopting the true method of determining what we ought to do; and to consider simply what conclusions will be rationally reached if we start with certain ethical premises, and with what degree of certainty and precision.

I ought to mention that Chapter iv. of Book i. has been reprinted (with considerable modifications) from the *Contemporary Review*, in which it originally appeared as an article on "Pleasure and Desire." And I cannot conclude without a tribute of thanks to my friend Mr Venn, to whose kindness in accepting the somewhat laborious task of reading and criticizing my work, both before and during its passage through the press, I am indebted for several improvements in my exposition.

PREFACE TO THE SECOND EDITION.

In preparing this work for the second edition, I have found it desirable to make numerous alterations and additions. Indeed the extent which these have reached is so considerable, that I have thought it well to publish them in a separate form, for the use of purchasers of my first edition. On one or two points I have to acknowledge a certain change of view; which is partly at least due to criticism. For instance, in ch. iv. of Bk. i. (on "Pleasure and Desire"), which has been a good deal criticized by Prof. Bain and others, although I still retain my former opinion on the psychological question at issue, I have been led to take a different view of the relation of this question to Ethics; and in fact § 1 of this chapter as it at present stands directly contradicts the corresponding passage in the former edition. So again, as regards the following chapter, on 'Free-Will,' though I have not exactly found that the comments which it has called forth have removed my difficulties in dealing with this time-honoured problem, I have become convinced that I ought not to have crudely obtruded these difficulties on the reader, while professedly excluding the consideration of them from my subject. In the present edition therefore I have carefully limited myself to explaining and justifying the view that I take of the practical aspect of the question. I have further been led, through study of the Theory of Evolution in its application to practice, to attach somewhat more importance to this theory than I had previously done; and also in several passages of Bks. III. and IV. to substitute 'well-being' for 'happiness,' in my exposition of that implicit reference to some further end and standard which reflection on the Morality of Common Sense continually brings into view. This latter change however (as I explain in the concluding chapter of Book III.) is not ultimately found to have any practical effect. I have also modified my view of 'objective rightness,' as the reader will see by comparing Bk. I. c. i., § 3 with the corresponding passage in the former edition; but here again the alteration has no material importance. In my exposition of the Utilitarian principle (Bk. IV. c. i.) I have shortened the cumbrous phrase 'greatest happiness of the greatest number' by omitting—as its author ultimately advised—the last four words. And finally, I have yielded as far as I could to the objections that have been strongly urged against the concluding chapter of the treatise. The main discussion therein contained still seems to me indispensable to the completeness of the work; but I have endeavoured to give the chapter a new aspect by altering its commencement, and omitting most of the concluding paragraph.

The greater part, however, of the new matter in this edition is merely explanatory and supplementary. I have endeavoured to give a fuller and clearer account of my views on any points on which I either have myself seen them to be ambiguously or inadequately expressed, or have found by experience that they were liable to be misunderstood. Thus in Bk. I. c. ii., I have tried to furnish a rather more instructive account than my first edition contained of the mutual relations of Ethics and Politics. Again, even before the appearance of Mr Leslie Stephen's interesting review in *Fraser* (March, 1875), I had seen the desirability of explaining further my general view of the 'Practical Reason,' and of the fundamental notion signified by the terms 'right,' 'ought,' &c. With this object I have entirely rewritten c. iii. of Book I., and made considerable changes in c. i. Elsewhere, as in cc. vi. and ix. of Book I., and c. 6 of Book II., I have altered chiefly in order to make my expositions more clear and symmetrical. This is partly the case with the considerable changes that I have made in the first three chapters of Book III.; but I have also tried to obviate the objections brought by Professor Calderwood[1] against the first of these chapters. The main part of this Book (cc. iv.—xii.) has been but slightly altered; but in c. xiii. (on 'Philosophical Intuitionism'), which has been suggestively criticized by more than one

[1] Cf. *Mind*, No. II.

writer, I have thought it expedient to give a more direct statement of my own opinions; instead of confining myself (as I did in the first edition) to comments on those of other moralists. Ch. xiv. again has been considerably modified; chiefly in order to introduce into it the substance of certain portions of an article on 'Hedonism and Ultimate Good,' which I published in *Mind* (No. v.). In Book iv. the changes (besides those above mentioned) have been inconsiderable; and have been chiefly made in order to remove a misconception which I shall presently notice, as to my general attitude towards the three Methods which I am principally occupied in examining.

In revising my work, I have endeavoured to profit as much as possible by all the criticisms on it that have been brought to my notice, whether public or private[1]. I have frequently deferred to objections, even when they appeared to me unsound, if I thought I could avoid controversy by alterations to which I was myself indifferent. Where I have been unable to make the changes required, I have usually replied, in the text or the notes, to such criticisms as have appeared to me plausible, or in any way instructive. In so doing, I have sometimes referred by name to opponents, where I thought that, from their recognized position as teachers of the subject, this would give a distinct addition of interest to the discussion; but I have been careful to omit such reference where experience has shewn that it would be likely to cause offence. The book is already more controversial than I could wish; and I have therefore avoided encumbering it with any

[1] Among unpublished criticisms I ought especially to mention the valuable suggestions that I have received from Mr Carveth Read; to whose assistance in revising the present edition many of my corrections are due.

polemics of purely personal interest. For this reason I have generally left unnoticed such criticisms as have been due to mere misapprehensions, against which I thought I could effectually guard in the present edition. There is, however, one fundamental misunderstanding, on which it seems desirable to say a few words. I find that more than one critic has overlooked or disregarded the account of the plan of my treatise, given in the original preface and in § 5 of the introductory chapter: and has consequently supposed me to be writing as an assailant of two of the methods which I chiefly examine, and a defender of the third. Thus one of my reviewers seems to regard Book III. (on Intuitionism) as containing mere hostile criticism from the outside: another has constructed an article on the supposition that my principal object is the 'suppression of Egoism': a third has gone to the length of a pamphlet under the impression (apparently) that the 'main argument' of my treatise is a demonstration of Universalistic Hedonism. I am concerned to have caused so much misdirection of criticism: and I have carefully altered in this edition the passages which I perceive to have contributed to it. The morality that I examine in Book III. is my own morality as much as it is any man's: it is, as I say, the 'Morality of Common Sense,' which I only attempt to represent in so far as I share it; I only place myself outside it either (1) temporarily, for the purpose of impartial criticism, or (2) in so far as I am forced beyond it by a practical consciousness of its incompleteness. I have certainly criticized this morality unsparingly: but I conceive myself to have exposed with equal unreserve the defects and difficulties of the hedonistic method (cf. especially cc. iii, iv. of Bk. II. and c. v. of Bk. IV.).

And as regards the two hedonistic principles, I do not hold the reasonableness of aiming at happiness generally with any stronger conviction than I do that of aiming at one's own. It was no part of my plan to call special attention to this "Dualism of the Practical Reason" as I have elsewhere called it: but I am surprised at the extent to which my view has perplexed even those of my critics who have understood it. I had imagined that they would readily trace it to the source from which I learnt it, Butler's well-known Sermons. I hold with Butler that "Reasonable Self-love and Conscience are the two chief or superior principles in the nature of man," each of which we are under a "manifest obligation" to obey: and I do not (I believe) differ materially from Butler in my view either of reasonable self-love, or—theology apart—of its relation to conscience. Nor, again, do I differ from him in regarding conscience as essentially a function of the practical Reason: "moral precepts", he says in the *Analogy* (pt. II. c. viii.), "are precepts the reason of which we see." My difference only begins when I ask myself, 'What among the precepts of our common conscience do we really see to be ultimately reasonable?' a question which Butler does not seem to have seriously put, and to which, at any rate, he has given no satisfactory answer. The answer that I found to it supplied the rational basis that I had long perceived to be wanting to the Utilitarianism of Bentham, regarded as an ethical doctrine: and thus enabled me to transcend the commonly received antithesis between Intuitionists and Utilitarians.

PREFACE TO THE THIRD EDITION.

In this third edition I have again made extensive alterations, and introduced a considerable amount of new matter. Some of these changes and additions are due to modifications of my own ethical or psychological views; but I do not think that any of these are of great importance in relation to the main subject of the treatise. And by far the largest part of the new matter introduced has been written either (1) to remove obscurities, ambiguities, and minor inconsistencies in the exposition of my views which the criticisms[1] of others or my own reflection have enabled me to discover; or (2) to treat as fully as seemed desirable certain parts or aspects of the subject which I had either passed over altogether or discussed too slightly in my previous editions, and on which it now appears to me important to explain my opinions, either for the greater completeness of my treatise,—according to my own view of the subject,—or for its better adaptation to the present state of ethical thought in England. The most important changes of the first kind have been made in chaps. i. and ix. of Book I., chaps. i.—iii. of Book II. and chaps. i., xiii. and xiv. of Book III.: under the second head I may mention the discussions of the relation of intellect to moral action in Book I. chap. iii.,

---

[1] I must here acknowledge the advantage that I have received from the remarks and questions of my pupils, and from criticisms privately communicated to me by others; among these latter I ought especially to mention an instructive examination of my fundamental doctrines by the Rev. Hastings Rashdall.

of volition in Book I. chap. v., of the causes of pleasure and pain in Book II. chap. vi., of the notion of virtue in the morality of Common Sense in Book III. chap. ii. and of evolutional ethics in Book IV. chap. iv. (chiefly).

I may add that all the important alterations and additions have been published in a separate form, for the use of purchasers of my second edition.

CONTENTS.

BOOK I.

CHAPTER I.

INTRODUCTION.

		PAGES
1.	Ethics is a department of the Science or Study of Practice	1—2
2.	It is the study of what ought to be, so far as this depends upon the voluntary action of individuals . . .	2—4
3.	In deciding what they ought to do, men naturally proceed on different principles, and by different methods . .	4—6
4.	There are two *primâ facie* rational Ends, Perfection and Happiness: of which the latter at least may be sought for oneself or universally. It is also commonly thought that certain Rules are prescribed without reference to ulterior consequences. The Methods corresponding to these different principles reduce themselves in the main to three, Egoism, Intuitionism, Utilitarianism . .	6—10
5.	These methods we are to examine separately, abstracting them from ordinary thought, where we find them in confused synthesis, and developing them as rationally as possible	10—14

CHAPTER II.

ETHICS AND POLITICS.

1.	The relation of Ethics to Politics is determined differently by different ethical schools.	15—20
2.	But at any rate the primary object of Ethics is not to determine what ought to be done in an ideal society: it therefore does not require as a preliminary the construction of the latter, which belongs to Theoretical Politics .	20—24

S. E.   *b*

CHAPTER III.

REASON AND FEELING.

		PAGES
1.	By 'Reasonable' conduct—whether morally or prudentially reasonable—we mean that of which we judge that it 'ought' to be done. The term 'ought,' as used in moral judgments, does not merely signify that the person judging feels a specific emotion:	25—27
2.	nor does it merely signify that the conduct in question is prescribed under penalties:	27—32
3.	it is unanalysable: but judgments in which it is used are assumed to be objectively valid; and when they relate to the future conduct of the person judging, are accompanied by a special kind of impulse to action	32—35
4.	This 'dictate of reason' is also exemplified by merely prudential judgments; and by merely hypothetical imperatives	35—38

CHAPTER IV.

PLEASURE AND DESIRE.

1.	The psychological doctrine, that the object of Desire is always Pleasure, has been thought to conflict with the view of Reason just given: and in any case deserves examination	39—42
2.	If by "pleasure" is meant "agreeable feeling," this doctrine is opposed to experience: for throughout the whole scale of our desires, from the highest to the lowest, we can distinguish impulses directed towards other ends than our own feelings from the desire of pleasure	42—49
3.	as is further shewn by the occasional conflict between the two kinds of impulse	49—51
4.	Nor can the doctrine derive any real support from consideration either of the 'unconscious' or the 'original' aim of human action	51—53

CHAPTER V.

FREE WILL.

1.	The Kantian identification of 'Free' and Rational action is misleading from the ambiguity of the term 'freedom'	54—56
2.	When, by definition and analysis of voluntary action, the issue in the Free Will Controversy has been made clear, it appears that the cumulative argument for Determinism is almost overwhelming:	56—64

3. still it is impossible to me not to regard myself as free to do what I judge to be reasonable: otherwise the question of Free Will does not seem to be generally connected with systematic Ethics: . . . . . . 64—66
4. as becomes more clear if we scrutinize closely the range of volitional effects: . . . . 66—70
5. it seems however to have a special relation to the notion of Justice . . . .

CHAPTER VI.

ETHICAL PRINCIPLES AND METHODS.

1. The Methods indicated in chap. i. have a *primâ facie* claim to proceed on reasonable principles: other principles seem, in so far as they can be made precise, to reduce themselves to these: . . . . . . 71—74
2. especially the principle of "living according to nature" . 74—76
3. In short, all varieties of Method may conveniently be classed under three heads: Intuitionism and the two kinds of Hedonism, Egoistic and Universalistic. The common confusion between the two latter is easily explained, but must be carefully guarded against . . . . 76—82

CHAPTER VII.

EGOISM AND SELF-LOVE.

1. To get a clear idea of what is commonly known as Egoism, we must distinguish and exclude several possible meanings of the term: . . . . 83—87
2. and define its end as an aggregate of pleasures, valued in proportion to their pleasantness . . . . 88—90

CHAPTER VIII.

INTUITIONISM.

1. I apply the term Intuitional—in the narrower of two legitimate senses—to distinguish a method in which the rightness of some kinds of action is assumed to be known without consideration of ulterior consequences . . 91—93

2. The common antithesis between Intuitive and Inductive is inexact, since this method does not necessarily proceed from the universal to the particular. We may distinguish Perceptional Intuitionism, according to which it is always the rightness of some particular action that is held to be immediately known: . . . . . . 93—95
3. Dogmatic Intuitionism, in which the general rules of Common Sense are accepted as axiomatic: and Philosophical Intuitionism, which attempts to find a deeper explanation for these current rules . . . . . 95—97
4. The last of these is historically the earliest in English ethics . . . . 97—100

CHAPTER IX.

GOOD.

1. Another important variety of Intuitionism is constituted by substituting for "right" the wider notion "good." This is illustrated by the Ethical speculation of Greece . 101—103
2. The common judgment that a thing is "good" does not on reflection appear to be equivalent to a judgment that it is directly or indirectly pleasant . . . . 103—106
3. "Good" = "desirable" or "reasonably desired": as applied to conduct, the term does not convey so definite a dictate as "right", and it is not confined to the strictly voluntary 106—109
4. There are many other things commonly judged to be good: but reflection shows that nothing is ultimately good except some mode of human existence . . . 109—111

BOOK II.

EGOISM.

CHAPTER I.

THE PRINCIPLE AND METHOD OF EGOISM.

1. The Principle of Egoistic Hedonism is the widely accepted proposition that the rational end of conduct for each individual is the Maximum of his own Happiness or Pleasure 115–
2. There are several methods of seeking this end: but we may take as primary that which proceeds by Empirical-reflective comparison of pleasures 117

CHAPTER II.

EMPIRICAL HEDONISM.

PAGES

1. In this method it is assumed that all pleasures sought and pains shunned are commensurable; and can be arranged in a certain scale of preferableness: . . . 119—121
2. pleasure being defined as "feeling judged to be desirable considered merely as feeling, according to the judgment of the sentient individual at the time of feeling it" . 121—127

CHAPTER III.

EMPIRICAL HEDONISM (CONTINUED).

1. To get a clearer view of this method, let us consider objections tending to shew its inherent impracticability; as, first, that a "sum of pleasures is nonsense": . . 128—130
2. that transient pleasures cannot satisfy; and that the predominance of self-love tends to defeat its own end . 131—134
3. that the habit of introspectively comparing pleasures is unfavourable to pleasure: . . . . . . 135—136
4. that any quantitative comparison of pleasures and pains is vague and uncertain; even in the case of our own past experiences: . . . . 136—140
5. that it also tends to be different at different times: especially from variations in the present state of the person performing the comparison . . . . 140—142
6. that, in fact, the supposed definite commensurability of pleasures is an unverifiable assumption . . . . 142—143
7. that there is a similar liability to error in appropriating the experience of others; and in inferring future pleasures from past . . . . 143—147

CHAPTER IV.

OBJECTIVE HEDONISM AND COMMON SENSE.

1. It may seem that the judgments of Common Sense respecting the Sources of Happiness offer a refuge from the uncertainties of Empirical Hedonism: but there are several fundamental defects in this refuge: . . . 148—150
2. and these judgments when closely examined are found to be perplexingly inconsistent . . . . . 150—155
3. Still we may derive from them a certain amount of practical guidance . . . . 155—158

CHAPTER V.

HAPPINESS AND DUTY.

		PAGES
1.	It has been thought possible to prove on empirical grounds that one's greatest happiness is always attained by the performance of duty	159—160
2.	But no such complete coincidence seems to result from a consideration either of the Legal Sanctions of Duty:	160—164
3.	or of the Social Sanctions:	164—168
4.	or of the Internal Sanctions: even if we consider not merely isolated acts of duty, but a virtuous life as a whole	168—174

CHAPTER VI.

OTHER METHODS OF EGOISTIC HEDONISM.

1.	Hedonistic Method must ultimately rest on facts of empirical observation: but it might become largely deductive, through scientific knowledge of the causes of pleasure and pain:	175—178
2.	but we have no practically available general theory of these causes, either psychophysical,	178—186
3.	or biological	186—188
4.	Nor can the principle of 'increasing life,' or that of 'aiming at self-development,' or that of 'giving free play to impulse', be so defined as to afford us any practical guidance to this result, without falling back on the empirical comparison of pleasures and pains	188—194

BOOK III.

INTUITIONISM.

CHAPTER I.

PAGES

1. The fundamental assumption of Intuitionism is that we have the power of seeing clearly what actions are in themselves right and reasonable. . . . . . 197—199
2. Intended actions (not motives) are to be taken as the primary object of the intuitive moral judgment; one motive, indeed, the desire to do what is right as such, has been thought an essential condition to right conduct: but the Intuitional method should be treated as not involving this assumption . . . . 199—204
3. It is certainly an essential condition that we should believe the act to be right, which involves the belief that it would be right for all similar persons in similar circumstances: but this belief, though it may supply a valuable practical rule, cannot—as Kant held—furnish a complete criterion of right conduct. . . . . 204—208
4. The *existence* of apparent cognitions of right conduct, intuitively obtained, as distinct from their validity, will scarcely be questioned; and to establish their validity it is not needful to prove their 'originality' . . . . 208—212
5. Both particular and universal intuitions are found in our common moral thought: but it is for the latter that ultimate validity is ordinarily claimed by moralists. We must try, by reflecting on Common Sense, to state these Moral Axioms with clearness and precision . . . 212—214

CHAPTER II.

VIRTUE AND DUTY.

1. Duties are Right acts, for the adequate performance of which a moral motive is at least occasionally necessary. Virtue is manifested in the performance of duties as well as praiseworthy acts that are thought to go beyond strict duty. 215—219
2. Virtues, as commonly recognized, are manifested primarily in volitions to produce particular right effects—which must at least be thought by the agent to be not wrong—: but for the completeness of some virtues the presence of certain emotions seems necessary . . . . . 219—226
3. It may be said that Moral Excellence, like Beauty, eludes definition: but if Ethical Science is to be constituted, we must obtain definite Moral Axioms . . . . . 226—228

CHAPTER III.
THE INTELLECTUAL VIRTUES.

PAGES

1. The common conception of Wisdom assumes a harmony of the ends of different ethical methods: all of which—and not one rather than another—the wise man is thought to choose and attain as far as possible . . . . . 229—231
2. The Will is to some extent involved in forming wise decisions: but more clearly in acting on them—whatever we may call the Virtue thus manifested: . . . . 231—234
3. Of minor intellectual excellences, some are not strictly Virtues: others are, such as Caution and Decision, being in part voluntary . . . . 234—235

CHAPTER IV.
BENEVOLENCE.

1. The Maxim of Benevolence bids us to some extent *cultivate* affections, and confer happiness on . . . . . 236—239
2. sentient, chiefly human, beings; especially in certain circumstances and relations; in which affections—that are hardly virtues—prompt to kind services. Thus rules for the distribution of kindness . . . . . 239—244
3. are needed, as claims may conflict; but are very difficult to obtain in a definite form: . . . . 244—246
4. as is seen when we examine the duties to Kinsmen, as commonly conceived: . . . . 246—249
5. and the wider duties of Neighbourhood, Citizenship, Universal Benevolence; and the duties of cultivating Reverence and Loyalty: . . . . 249—253
6. and those springing from the Conjugal relation: . . . 253—255
7. and those of Friendship: . . . . 255—258
8. and those of Gratitude: and those to which we are prompted by Pity . . . . 258—261

CHAPTER V.
JUSTICE.

1. Justice is especially difficult to define. The Just cannot be identified with the Legal, as laws may be unjust. Again, the Justice of laws does not consist merely in the absence of arbitrary inequality in framing or administering them 262—266
2. One element of Justice seems to consist in the fulfilment of (1) contracts and definite understandings, and (2) expectations arising naturally out of the established order of Society; but the duty of fulfilling these latter is somewhat indefinite: . . . . 266—269

CONTENTS. xxiii

PAGES

3. and this social order may itself, from another point of view, be condemned as unjust; that is, as tried by the standard of Ideal Justice. What then is this Standard? We seem to find various degrees and forms of it . . . . 269—273
4. One view of Ideal Law states Freedom as its absolute End: but the attempt to construct a system of law on this principle involves us in insuperable difficulties . . . 273—277
5. Nor does it express our conception of Ideal Justice. The principle of this is rather 'that Desert should be requited' . . . . 277—282
6. But the application of this principle is again very perplexing: whether we try to determine Good Desert (or the worth of services) . . . . 283—289
7. or Ill Desert, in order to realize Criminal Justice. There remains too the difficulty of reconciling the different kinds or elements of Justice . . . . . 289—293

CHAPTER VI.

LAWS AND PROMISES.

1. The duty of obeying Laws, though it may to a great extent be included under Justice, still requires a separate treatment. We can, however, obtain no *consensus* for any precise definition of it . . . . . . 294—296
2. For we can neither agree as to what kind of government is ideally legitimate, ... 296—298
3. nor as to the criterion of a traditionally legitimate government, or the proper limits of its authority . . 298—302
4. The duty of fulfilling a promise in the sense in which it was understood by both promiser and promisee . . . 302—304
5. (it being admitted that its obligation is relative to the promisee, and may be annulled by him, and that it cannot override strict prior obligations) is thought to be peculiarly stringent and certain . . . . . 304—305
6. But Common Sense seems to doubt how far a promise is binding when it has been obtained by force or fraud: . 305—306
7. or when circumstances have materially altered since it was made—especially if it be a promise to the dead or absent, from which no release can be obtained, or if the performance of the promise will be harmful to the promisee, or inflict a disproportionate sacrifice on the promiser . 306—309
8. Other doubts arise when a promise has been misapprehended: and in the peculiar case where a prescribed form of words has been used . . . . . . 309—312

CHAPTER VII.

CLASSIFICATION OF DUTIES. TRUTH.

PAGES

1. I have not adopted the classification of duties into Social and Self-regarding: as it seems inappropriate to the Intuitional method, of which the characteristic is, that it lays down certain absolute and independent rules: such as the rule of Truth . . . . 313—316
2. But Common Sense after all scarcely seems to prescribe truth-speaking under all circumstances: nor to decide clearly whether the beliefs which we are bound to make true are those directly produced by our words or the immediate inferences from these . . . . 316—318
3. It is said that the general allowance of Unveracity would be suicidal, as no one would believe the falsehood. But this argument, though forcible, is not decisive; for (1) this result may be in special circumstances desirable, or (2) we may have reason to expect that it will not occur . . 318—320

CHAPTER VIII.

OTHER SOCIAL DUTIES AND VIRTUES.

1. Common opinion sometimes condemns sweepingly Malevolent feelings and volitions: but Reflective Common Sense seems to admit some as legitimate, determining the limits of this admission on utilitarian grounds . . . 321—324
2. Other maxims of social duty seem clearly subordinate to those already discussed: as is illustrated by an examination of Liberality and other cognate notions . . . 324—327

CHAPTER IX.

SELF-REGARDING VIRTUES.

1. The general duty of seeking one's own happiness is commonly recognized under the notion of Prudence . . 328—329
2. This as specially applied to the control of bodily appetites is called Temperance: but under this notion a more rigid restraint is sometimes thought to be prescribed: though as to the principle of this there seems no agreement . . . . 329—330
3. Nor is it easy to give a clear definition of the maxim of Purity—but in fact common sense seems averse to attempt this . . . . 330—332

CHAPTER X.

COURAGE, HUMILITY, &c.

		PAGES
1.	The Duty of Courage is subordinate to those already discussed: and in drawing the line between the Excellence of Courage and the Fault of Foolhardiness we seem forced to have recourse to considerations of expediency	333—335
2.	Similarly the maxim of Humility seems either clearly subordinate or not clearly determinate	335—337

CHAPTER XI.

REVIEW OF THE MORALITY OF COMMON SENSE.

1.	We have now to examine the moral maxims that have been defined, to ascertain whether they possess the characteristics of scientific intuitions	338—339
2.	We require of an Axiom that it should be (1) stated in clear and precise terms, (2) really self-evident, (3) not conflicting with any other truth, (4) supported by a complete 'consensus of experts.' These characteristics are not found in the moral maxims of Common Sense	339—344
3.	The maxims of Wisdom and Self-control are only self-evident in so far as they are tautological	344—346
4.	Nor can we state any clear, absolute, universally-admitted axioms for determining the duties of the Affections	346—350
5.	And as for the group of principles that were extracted from the common notion of Justice, we cannot define each singly in a satisfactory manner, still less reconcile them	350—353
6.	And even the Duty of Good Faith, when we consider the numerous qualifications of it more or less doubtfully admitted by Common Sense, seems more like a subordinate rule than an independent First Principle. Still more is this the case with Veracity	353—356
7.	And similarly with other virtues: including even Purity when we force ourselves to examine it rigorously. The common moral maxims are adequate for practical guidance, but do not admit of being elevated into scientific axioms	356—361

CHAPTER XII.

MOTIVES OR SPRINGS OF ACTION AS SUBJECTS OF MORAL JUDGMENT.

1.	It has been held by several moralists (most definitely by Mr Martineau), that the "Universal Conscience" judges primarily not of Rightness of acts, but of Rank of Motives	362—366

2. If, however, we include the Moral Sentiments among these motives, this latter view involves all the difficulties and perplexities of the former . . . . 366—368
3. But even if we leave these out, we still find very little agreement as to Rank of Motives: and there is a special difficulty arising from complexity of motive. Nor, finally, does it seem strictly true that a higher motive is always better than a lower one . . . . . 368—371

CHAPTER XIII.

PHILOSOPHICAL INTUITIONISM.

1. The Philosopher, as such, attempts to penetrate beneath the surface of Common Sense to some deeper principles: 372—373
2. but has too often presented to the world, as the result of his investigation, tautological propositions and vicious circles . . . . 373—378
3. Still there are certain abstract moral principles of real importance, intuitively known; though they are not sufficient by themselves to give complete practical guidance. Thus we can exhibit a self-evident element in the commonly recognized principles of Prudence, Justice and Benevolence . . . . 378—383
4. This is confirmed by a reference to Clarke's system : . . 383—385
5. and also to Kant's: . . . . 385—388
6. and also to Utilitarianism. In fact, the principle of Benevolence, if for 'Good' we substitute the more definite term 'Happiness,' is the First Principle of Utilitarianism . 388—390

CHAPTER XIV.

THE SUMMUM BONUM.

1. The notion of Virtue, as commonly conceived, cannot properly be used in a scientific account of the notion of Ultimate Good: . . . . 391—394
2. what is ultimately good or desirable must be either Happiness, or certain objective relations of the Conscious Mind. 394—398
3. When these alternatives are fairly presented, Common Sense seems disposed to choose the former: especially as we can now explain its instinctive disinclination to admit Pleasure as ultimate end: while the other alternative leaves us without a criterion for determining the comparative value of different elements of 'Good' . . 398—404

BOOK IV.

UTILITARIANISM.

CHAPTER I.

THE MEANING OF UTILITARIANISM.

                                                                       PAGES

1. The ethical theory called Utilitarianism, or Universalistic Hedonism, is to be carefully distinguished from Egoistic Hedonism: and also from any psychological theory as to the nature and origin of the Moral Sentiments . . 407—409

2. The notion of 'Greatest Happiness' has been determined in B. II. c. 1: but the extent and manner of its application require to be further defined. Are we to include all Sentient Beings? and is it Total or Average Happiness that we seek to make a maximum? We also require a supplementary Principle for *Distribution* of Happiness: the principle of Equality is *primâ facie* reasonable . 409—413

CHAPTER II.

THE PROOF OF UTILITARIANISM.

Common Sense demands a Proof of the first Principle of this method, more clearly than it does of those of Egoism and Intuitionism. Such a proof, addressed to the Egoist, was in fact given in B. III. ch. xiii., § 3: where it appeared as an exhibition of this Principle as the most certain of our Intuitions. But it is on several grounds important to examine its relation to other received moral rules . 414—418

CHAPTER III.

THE RELATION OF UTILITARIANISM TO THE MORALITY OF COMMON SENSE.

1. Taking as our basis Hume's exhibition of the Virtues as Felicific qualities of character, we can trace a complex coincidence between Utilitarianism and Common Sense. It is not needful—nor does it even help the argument— to shew this coincidence to be perfect and exact . 419—422

2. We may observe, first, that Dispositions may often be admired (as generally felicific) when the special acts that have resulted from them are infelicific. Again, the maxims of many virtues are found to contain an explicit or implicit reference to Duty conceived as already determinate. Passing over these to examine the more definite among common notions of Duty: . . . . 422—427
3. we observe, first, how the rules that prescribe the distribution of kindness in accordance with normal promptings of Family Affections, Friendship, Gratitude and Pity, have a firm Utilitarian basis: and how Utilitarianism is naturally referred to for an explanation of the difficulties that arise in attempting to define these rules . . . 427—436
4. A similar result is reached by an examination, singly and together, of the different elements into which I analyzed the common notion of Justice: . . . . . 436—445
5. and in the case of other virtues . . . . . 445—447
6. Purity has been thought an exception: but a careful examination of common opinions as to the regulation of sexual relations exhibits a peculiarly complex and delicate correspondence between moral sentiments and social utilities . . . . 447—450
7. The hypothesis that the Moral Sense is 'unconsciously Utilitarian' also accounts for the actual differences in different codes of Duty and estimates of Virtue, either in the same age and country, or when we compare different ages and countries. This does not imply that perception of rightness has always been consciously derived from perception of utility: a view which the evidence of history fails to support . . . . . 450—454

CHAPTER IV.

THE METHOD OF UTILITARIANISM.

1. Ought a Utilitarian, then, to accept the Morality of Common Sense provisionally as a body of Utilitarian doctrine? Not quite; for even accepting the theory that the Moral Sense is derived from Sympathy, we can discern several causes that must have operated to produce a divergence between Common Sense and a perfectly Utilitarian code of morality . . . . 455—462
2. At the same time it seems idle to try to construct such a code in any other way than by taking Positive Morality as our basis . . . . 462—469

CHAPTER V.

THE METHOD OF UTILITARIANISM (CONTINUED).

PAGES

1. It is, then, a Utilitarian's duty at once to support generally, and to rectify in detail, the morality of Common Sense: and the method of pure empirical Hedonism seems to be the only one that he can at present use in the reasonings that finally determine the nature and extent of this rectification . . . . 470—475
2. His innovations may be either negative and destructive, or positive and supplementary. There are certain important general reasons against an innovation of the former kind, which may, in any given case, easily outweigh the special arguments in its favour . . . . 475—480
3. Generally, a Utilitarian in recommending, by example or precept, a deviation from an established rule of conduct, desires his innovation to be generally imitated. But in some cases he may neither expect nor desire such imitation; though cases of this kind are rare and difficult to determine . . . . 480—487
4. There are no similar difficulties in the way of modifying the Ideal of Moral Excellence—as distinguished from the dictates of Moral Duty—in order to render it more perfectly felicific . . . . 487—491

CONCLUDING CHAPTER.

THE MUTUAL RELATIONS OF THE THREE METHODS.

1. It is not difficult to combine the Intuitional and Utilitarian methods into one; but can we reconcile Egoistic and Universalistic Hedonism? . . . . . . 492—494
2. In so far as the latter coincides with Common Sense, we have seen in B. II. c. 5, that no complete reconciliation is possible . . . . 494—495
3. Nor does a fuller consideration of Sympathy, as a specially Utilitarian sanction, lead us to modify this conclusion; in spite of the importance that is undoubtedly to be attached to sympathetic pleasures . . . . . 495—500

		PAGES
4.	The Religious Sanction, if we can shew that it is actually attached to the Utilitarian Code, is of course adequate	500—502
5.	but its existence cannot be demonstrated by ethical arguments alone. We can only shew that, without this or some similar assumption, Ethical Science cannot be constructed	502—505

THE METHODS OF ETHICS.

BOOK I.

CHAPTER I.

INTRODUCTION.

§ 1. The boundaries of the study called Ethics are variously and often vaguely conceived: but they will perhaps be sufficiently defined, at the outset, for the purposes of the present treatise if a 'Method of Ethics' is explained to mean any rational procedure by which we determine Right Conduct or Practice in any particular case. Of the two last terms 'Conduct' is preferable, as the Method of Right Practice might naturally be understood as including Politics also[1]: both Ethics and Politics being, in my view, distinguished from positive sciences by having as their special and primary object to determine what ought to be, and not to ascertain what merely is.

An objection is sometimes taken to the application of the term 'Science' to such studies as these. It is said that a Science must necessarily have some department of actual existence for its subject-matter: and there is no doubt that the term Ethical Science might, according to usage, denote studies that deal with the actually existent: viz. either the department of Psychology that deals with pleasures and pains, desires and volitions, moral sentiments and judgments, as actual phenomena of individual human minds; or the department of Sociology dealing with similar phenomena, as exhibited by the larger organizations of which individual human beings are elements.

[1] I use 'Politics' in its widest signification, to denote the science or study of Right or Good Legislation and Government.

We observe, however, that comparatively few persons pursue these studies from pure curiosity, in order merely to ascertain what actually exists, has existed, or will exist in time. Most men wish not only to understand human action, but also to regulate it; they apply the ideas 'good' and 'bad,' 'right' and 'wrong,' to the conduct or institutions which they describe; and thus pass, as I should say, from the point of view of Psychology or Sociology to the point of view of Ethics or Politics. It is true that the mutual implication of the two kinds of study is, on any theory, very close and complete, though the precise nature and extent of their connexion is very differently conceived in different systems, as will hereafter appear. But, on any theory, our view of what ought to be, must be largely derived, in details, from our apprehension of what is; the means of realizing our ideal can only be thoroughly learnt by a careful study of actual phenomena; and to any individual asking himself 'What ought I to do or aim at?' it is important to examine the answers which his fellow-men have actually given to similar questions. Still it seems clear that an attempt to ascertain the general laws or uniformities by which the varieties of human conduct, and of men's sentiments and judgments respecting conduct, may be *explained*, is essentially different from an attempt to determine which among these varieties of conduct is *right* and which of these divergent judgments *valid*. It is, then, the systematic consideration of these latter questions which constitutes the special and distinct aim of Ethics and Politics: and it is merely a verbal question whether we shall apply the name 'science' to such systematic studies; though it is, of course, important that we should not confound them with the positive inquiries to which they bear respectively so close a relation.

§ 2. In the language of the preceding section I could not avoid taking account of two different forms in which the fundamental problem of Ethics is stated; the difference between which leads, as we shall presently see, to rather important consequences. Ethics is sometimes considered as an investigation of the true Moral laws or rational Rules of Conduct; sometimes as an inquiry into the nature of the ultimate End of reasonable human action, anciently known as the Bonum, or

Summum Bonum. Both these views will have to be carefully considered: but the former seems most easily applicable to ethical systems generally. For the Good that we investigate in Ethics is generally understood to be limited to Good, attainable by human effort; we seek knowledge of the end in order to ascertain what actions are the right means to its attainment. Thus however prominent the notion of an Ultimate Good, other than voluntary action of any kind, may be in our ethical system, and whatever interpretation we may give to this notion, we must still arrive finally, in our ethical conclusions, at the determination of directive rules of conduct.

On the other hand, the conception of Ethics as essentially an investigation of the Summum Bonum of Man and the means of attaining it is not generally applicable, without straining, to the view of Morality which we may conveniently distinguish as the Intuitional view; according to which conduct is held to be right when conformed to certain precepts or principles of Duty, intuitively known to be unconditionally binding. In this case we can only regard the conception of Ultimate Good as fundamentally important in the determination of Right conduct if we identify the two notions and say that Right conduct is itself the sole Ultimate Good for man. But this identification would not, I conceive, accord with the moral common sense of modern Christian communities; nor would it be ordinarily made by those who, in such communities have held the Intuitional view of Ethics. The majority of such persons would consider that the notion of human Good or Well-being must include the attainment of Happiness as well as the performance of Duty; even while denying that it is reasonable for men to make their performance of Duty conditional on their knowledge of its conduciveness to Happiness. Or, to put it otherwise, they would hold that what men ought to take as the *practically* ultimate end of their action is not identical with what we may call its really ultimate or Divine End; the former being often entirely realised in the action itself, while the latter includes ulterior consequences: so that, in such cases, though some conception of these consequences may be indispensable to the completeness of an ethical system, it cannot be important for the methodical determination of Right conduct.

It is on account of the prevalence of the Intuitional view just mentioned, and the prominent place which it consequently occupies in my discussion, that in defining the subject of the present treatise I have avoided the term 'Art of Conduct' which some would regard as its more appropriate designation. For the term Art as properly used seems to signify systematic express knowledge (with or without the implicit knowledge or instinct which we call skill,) of the right means to a given end. Now if we assume that the rightness of action depends on its conduçiveness to some ulterior end, then no doubt the process of determining the right rules of conduct for human beings in different relations and circumstances would naturally come under the notion of Art. But on the view that the practical end of moral action is often the Rightness of the action itself and not any ulterior consequences, and that this is known intuitively in each case or class of cases; we can hardly regard the term 'Art' as properly applicable to the systematization of such knowledge. Hence, as I do not wish to start with any assumption incompatible with this latter view, I prefer to consider Ethics as the science or study of what ought to be, so far as this depends upon the voluntary action of individuals.

§ 3. If, however, this view of the scope of Ethics is accepted, the question arises why it is commonly taken to consist, to a great extent, of psychological discussion as to the 'nature of the moral faculty;' especially as I have myself thought it right to include such a discussion in the present treatise. For it does not at first appear why this should belong to ethics, any more than discussions about the mathematcal faculty or the faculty of sense-perception belong to mathematics and physics respectively. Our judgments 'that 2 and 2 make 4' and 'that every effect has a cause' are no doubt psychical facts: but we do not in mathematics or physics consider these truths in their relation to the thinking subject: we assume and apply them without psychological reflection. It is therefore interesting to inquire why this is not the case in ethics; why we do not similarly start with certain premises as to what ought to be done or sought without considering the faculty by which we apprehend their truth.

One answer is that the moralist has a practical aim: we

desire knowledge of right conduct in order to act on it. Now we cannot help believing what we see to be true, but we can help doing what we see to be right or wise, and in fact often do what we know to be wrong or unwise: thus we are forced to notice the existence in us of irrational springs of action, conflicting with knowledge and preventing its practical realization: and the very imperfectness of the connexion between our practical reason and our will impels us to seek for more precise knowledge as to the nature of that connexion.

But this is not all. Men never ask 'Why should I believe what I see to be true?' but they frequently ask, 'Why should I do what I see to be right?' It is easy to reply that the question is futile, since it could only be answered by a reference to some other recognised principle of right conduct, and the question might just as well be asked as regards that, and so on. But still we do ask the question widely and continually, and therefore this demonstration of its futility is not completely satisfactory; we require besides some explanation of its persistency.

One explanation that may be offered is that, since we are moved to action not by Reason alone but also by desires and inclinations that operate independently of reason, the answer which we really want to the question 'why' is one which does not merely prove a certain action to be right, but also is accompanied by a predominant inclination to do it.

That this explanation is true for some minds in some moods I would not deny. Still I cannot but think that when a man asks 'why he should do' anything, he commonly assumes in himself a determination to pursue whatever conduct may be shown to be reasonable, even though it be very different from that to which his non-rational inclinations may prompt. And we are generally agreed that reasonable conduct in any case has to be determined on principles, in applying which the agent's inclination—as it exists apart from such determination—is only one element among several that have to be considered, and commonly not the most important element. But when we ask what these principles are, the diversity of answers which we find manifestly declared in the systems and fundamental formulæ of professed moralists seems to be really present in the common practical reasoning of men generally; with this difference, that whereas the philosopher seeks unity of principle, and consistency of method at the risk of paradox, the unphilosophic man is apt to hold different principles at once, in more or less confused combination. If this be so, we can offer another explanation of the persistent unsatisfied demand for an ultimate reason, above noticed. For if there are different views of the ultimate reasonableness of conduct, implicit in the thought of ordinary men, though not brought into clear relation to each other: it is easy to see that any single answer to the question 'why' will not be completely satisfactory; as it will be given only from one of these points of view, and will always leave room to ask the questions from some other.

I am myself convinced that this is the main explanation of the phenomenon: and it is on this conviction that the plan of the present treatise is based. I hold that men, in so far as they attempt to make their conduct rational, do so, naturally and habitually, upon different principles and by different methods. I admit, of course, as a fundamental postulate of Ethics, that either these methods must be reconciled and harmonized, or all but one of them rejected. The common sense of men cannot acquiesce in conflicting principles: so there can be but one rational method of Ethics (in the widest sense of the word method). But in setting out to inquire what this is, we ought to recognize the fact that there is more than one natural method.

§ 4. What then are these different methods? what are the different practical principles which the common sense of mankind is *primâ facie* prepared to accept as ultimate? Some care is needed in answering this question: because we frequently prescribe that this or that 'ought' to be done or aimed at without any express reference to an ulterior end, while yet such an end is tacitly presupposed. It is obvious that such prescriptions are merely, what Kant calls them, Hypothetical Imperatives; they are not addressed to any one who has not first accepted the end.

For instance: a teacher of any art assumes that his pupil wants to produce the product of the art, or to produce it excellent in quality: he tells him that he *ought* to hold the awl, the hammer, the brush differently. A physician assumes that his patient wants health: he tells him that he *ought* to rise early, to live plainly, to take hard exercise. If the patient deliberately prefers ease and good living to health, the physician's precepts fall to the ground: they are no longer addressed to him. So, again, a man of the world assumes that his hearers wish to get on in society, when he lays down rules of dress, manner, conversation, habits of life. A similar view may be plausibly taken of many rules that are commonly regarded as rules of morality: of many, for example, that form part of the proverbial code of precepts handed down in an early stage of civilization. It may be said that they are given on the assumption that a man regards his own Happiness as an ultimate end: that if any one should be so exceptional as to disregard it, he does not come within their scope: in short, that the 'ought' in such formulæ is still implicitly relative to an *optional* end.

It does not, however, seem to me that this account of the matter is exhaustive. We do not all look with simple indifference on a man who declines to take the right means to attain his own happiness, on no other ground than that he does not care about happiness. Most men would regard such a refusal as irrational, with a certain disapprobation; they would thus implicitly assent to Butler's statement that "interest, one's own happiness, is a manifest obligation," though the phrase might strike them as unusual. In other words, they would think that he *ought* to seek his own happiness. The word 'ought' thus used is no longer relative: happiness now appears as an end unconditionally prescribed by reason.

Similarly, many Utilitarians hold all the rules of conduct which men prescribe to one another *as moral rules*, to be partly consciously and partly unconsciously prescribed as means to the end of the happiness of the community. But here again it would seem to be the common view that while the rules are relative, the end is unconditionally prescribed. Indeed it seems more obviously held that we *ought* to seek the happiness of the community than that we 'ought' to seek our own; for in the case of a man's own happiness it may be said with a semblance of truth that the idea of 'ought' is inapplicable to that which, according to a psychological law that has no exceptions, is always the end and aim of his voluntary actions[1]. But it is not similarly thought that all men, by a universal law of their nature, are always aiming at the general happiness.

At the same time, it is not necessary, in the methodical investigation of right conduct, considered relatively to the end either of private or of general happiness, to assume that the end itself is determined or prescribed by reason: we only require to assume, in reasoning to cogent practical conclusions, that it is generally or widely adopted as ultimate and paramount. For if a man accepts any end as ultimate and paramount, he accepts implicitly as his "method of ethics" whatever process of reasoning enables us to determine the conduct most conducive to this end. Since, however, to every difference in the end accepted at least some difference in method will generally correspond: if all the ends which men have practically adopted as ultimate, subordinating everything else to the attainment of them (under the influence of 'ruling passions'), were taken as principles for which the student of ethics is called upon to construct rational methods, his task would be very complex and extensive. But if we confine ourselves to such ends as the common sense of mankind appears to accept as reasonable ultimate ends, the task is reduced, I think, within manageable limits; since this criterion will exclude at least many of the objects which men practically seem to regard as paramount. Thus many men sacrifice health, fortune, happiness, to Fame; but no one, so far as I know, has deliberately maintained that Fame is an object which it is reasonable for men to seek for its own sake: it only commends itself to reflective persons either (1) on account of the Happiness derived from it, or (2) because it attests Excellence of some kind already attained by the famous person, and at the same time stimulates him to the attainment of further excellence in the future. Whether there are any ends besides these two, which it is reasonable to regard as ultimate, it will hereafter be an important part of our business to investigate: but we may perhaps say that *primâ facie* the only two ends which clearly claim to be *rational ends*, are the two just mentioned, Happiness and

---

[1] In a subsequent chapter (iii.) I shall try to shew that this objection has really no practical force.

Perfection or Excellence of human nature; identifying with perfect or excellent existence the vaguer terms Wellbeing or Welfare, so far as they are interpreted as meaning something distinct from Happiness. And we must observe that the adoption of the former of these ends leads us to two *primâ facie* distinct methods, according as it is sought to be realized universally, or by each individual for himself alone. For though doubtless a man may often best promote his own happiness by labouring and abstaining for the sake of others, we cannot therefore assume that actions most conducive to the general happiness will always tend also to the greatest happiness of the agent. And among those who hold that "happiness is our being's end and aim" we seem to find a fundamental difference of opinion as to whose happiness it is that it is ultimately reasonable to aim at. For to some it seems that each agent ought, as a rational being, to make his own happiness his ultimate end; whereas others hold that the view of reason is essentially universal, and that it cannot be reasonable to take as an ultimate and paramount end the happiness of any one individual rather than that of any other—at any rate if equally deserving and susceptible of it—so that general happiness must be the true standard of right and wrong, in the field of morals no less than of politics. It is, of course, possible to adopt an end intermediate between the two, and to aim at the happiness of some limited portion of mankind, such as one's family or nation or race: but any such limitation seems arbitrary, and probably no one would maintain it to be reasonable *per se*, but only as the most practicable way of aiming at the general happiness, or of indirectly securing one's own.

The case seems to be otherwise with Perfection. At first sight, indeed, the same alternatives present themselves[1]: it seems that the Perfection aimed at may be taken either individually

---

[1] It may be said that even more divergent views of the reasonable end are possible here than in the case of happiness: for we are not necessarily limited (as in that case) to the consideration of sentient beings: inanimate things also seem to have a perfection and excellence of their own and to be capable of being made better or worse in their kind; and this perfection, or one species of it, appears to be the end of the Fine Arts. But reflection I think shews that neither beauty nor any other quality of inanimate objects can be regarded as good or desirable in itself, out of relation to the perfection or happiness of sentient beings. Cf. *post*, c. ix.

or universally; and circumstances are conceivable in which a man is not unlikely to think that he could best promote the Perfection of others by sacrificing his own. But no moralist has ever approved of such sacrifice, at least so far as Moral Perfection is concerned; no one has ever directed an individual to promote the virtue of others except in so far as this promotion is compatible with, or rather involved in, the complete realization of Virtue in himself[1]. So far, then, there is no *primâ facie* need of separating the method of determining right conduct which takes the Perfection of the individual as the ultimate end from that which aims at the Perfection of the human community. And since Virtue is commonly conceived as the most valuable element of human Perfection or Excellence; while again the realization of Virtue is commonly thought (by those who reject Utilitarianism) to consist mainly in the complete observance of certain absolute rules of Duty, intuitively known; any method which takes Perfection or Excellence of human nature as ultimate End will *primâ facie* coincide to a great extent with that which systematizes and developes what I have before called the Intuitional view: and I have accordingly treated it as a special form of this latter. The two methods which make Happiness an ultimate end it will be convenient to distinguish as Egoistic and Universalistic Hedonism: and as it is the latter of these, as taught by Bentham and his successors, that is more generally understood under the term Utilitarianism, I shall always restrict that word to this signification. For Egoistic Hedonism it is somewhat hard to find a single perfectly appropriate term. I shall often call this simply Egoism: but it may sometimes be convenient to call it Epicureanism: for though this name more properly denotes a particular historical system, it has come to be commonly used in the wider sense in which I wish to employ it.

§ 5. The last sentence suggests one more explanation, which, for clearness' sake, it seems desirable to make: an explanation, however, rather of the plan and purpose of the present treatise, than of the nature and boundaries of the subject of Ethics, as generally understood.

---

[1] Kant roundly denies that it can be my duty to take the Perfection of others for my end: but his argument is not, I think, valid. Cf. *post*, B. III., c. iv. § 1.

There are several recognized ways of treating this subject, none of which I have thought it desirable to adopt. We may start with existing systems, and either study them historically, tracing the changes in thought through the centuries, or compare and classify them according to relations of resemblance, or criticize their internal coherence. Or we may seek to add to the number of these systems: and claim after so many unsuccessful efforts to have at last attained the one true theory of the subject, by which all others may be tested. The present book contains neither the exposition of a system nor a natural or critical history of systems. I have attempted to define and unfold not one Method of Ethics, but several: at the same time these are not here studied historically, as methods that have actually been used or proposed for the regulation of practice: but rather as alternatives between which the human mind seems to me necessarily forced to choose, when it attempts to frame a complete synthesis of practical maxims and to act in a perfectly rational manner. Thus though I have called them natural methods, they might more properly be called natural methods rationalized; because it is perhaps most natural to men to guide themselves by a mixture of different methods, more or less disguised under ambiguities of language. The impulses or principles from which the different methods take their rise, the different claims of different ends to be rational, are admitted, to some extent, by all minds: and as along with these claims is felt the need of harmonizing them—since it is, as was said, a postulate of the Practical Reason, that two conflicting rules of action cannot both be reasonable—the result is ordinarily either a confused blending, or a forced and premature reconciliation, of different principles and methods. Nor have the systems framed by professed moralists been free from similar defects. The writers have usually proceeded to synthesis without adequate analysis; the practical demand for the former being much more urgently felt than the theoretical need of the latter. For in this and other points the development of the theory of Ethics has been much impeded by the preponderance of practical considerations. Although Aristotle has said that "the end of our study is not knowledge, but conduct," it is still true that the peculiar excellence of his own system is due to the pure air of scientific curiosity in which it has been developed. And it would seem that a more complete detachment of the scientific study of right conduct from its practical application is to be desired for the sake even of the latter itself. A treatment which is a compound between the scientific and the hortatory is apt to miss both the results that it would combine: the mixture is bewildering to the brain and not stimulating to the heart. Again, in other sciences, the more distinctly we draw the line between the known and the unknown, the more rapidly the science progresses: for the clear indication of an unsolved problem is an important step to its solution. But in ethical treatises there has been a continual tendency to ignore and keep out of sight the difficulties of the subject; either unconsciously, from a latent conviction that the questions which the writer cannot answer satisfactorily must be questions which ought not to be asked; or consciously, that he may not shake the sway of morality over the minds of his readers. This last amiable precaution frequently defeats itself: the difficulties thus concealed in exposition are liable to reappear in controversy; and then they appear not carefully limited, but magnified for polemical purposes. Thus we get on the one hand vague and hazy reconciliation, on the other loose and random exaggeration of discrepancies: and neither process is effective to dispel the original vagueness and ambiguity which lurks in the fundamental notions of our common practical reasonings. The mists which the dawn of philosophical reflection in Socrates struggled to dispel still hang about the methods of the most highly reputed moralists. To eliminate this indefiniteness and confusion is the sole immediate end that I have proposed to myself in the present work. In order better to execute this task, I have refrained from attempting any such complete and final solution of the chief ethical difficulties and controversies as would convert this exposition of various methods into the development of a harmonious system. At the same time I am not without hope of affording aid towards the construction of such a system; because it seems easier to judge of the conflicting claims of different modes of thought, after an impartial and rigorous investigation of the conclusions to which they logically lead. A humourist once said that he would not admit that two and two made four until he knew what use would be made of the statement; and the paradox is subtle and suggestive: since it is not uncommon to find in reflecting on practical principles, that however unhesitatingly they seem to command our assent at first sight, and however familiar and apparently clear the notions of which they are composed, nevertheless when we have carefully examined the consequences of adopting them they wear a changed and somewhat dubious aspect. The truth seems to be that most of the practical principles that have been seriously put forward are more or less satisfactory to the common sense of mankind, so long as they have the field to themselves. They all find a response in our nature: their fundamental assumptions are all such as we are disposed to accept, and such as we find to govern to a certain extent our habitual conduct. When I am asked, "Are you not continually seeking pleasure and avoiding pain?" "Have you not a moral sense?" "Do you not intuitively pronounce some actions to be right and others wrong?" "Do you not acknowledge the general happiness to be a paramount end?" I answer yes to all questions. My difficulty begins when I have to choose between the different principles. We admit the necessity, when they conflict, of making this choice, and that it is irrational to let sometimes one principle prevail and sometimes another; but the necessity is a painful one. We cannot but hope that all methods may ultimately coincide: and at any rate, before making our election we may reasonably wish to have the completest possible knowledge of each.

My object, then, in the present work, is to expound as clearly and as fully as my limits will allow, the different methods of Ethics that I find implicit in our common moral reasoning; to point out their mutual relations; and where they seem to conflict, to define the issue as much as possible. In the course of this endeavour I am led to discuss the considerations which should, in my opinion, be decisive in determining the adoption of ethical first principles: but it is not my primary aim to establish such principles; nor, again, is it my primary aim to supply a set of rules for conduct. I have wished to keep the reader's attention throughout directed to the processes rather than the results of ethical thought: and have therefore never stated as my own any positive practical conclusions unless by way of illustration: and have never ventured to decide dogmatically any controverted points, except where the controversy seemed to arise from want of precision or clearness in the definition of principles, or want of consistency in reasoning.

CHAPTER II.

THE RELATION OF ETHICS TO POLITICS.

§ 1. IN the last chapter I have spoken of Ethics and Politics as branches of Practical Philosophy, including in the scope of their investigation somewhat that lies outside the sphere of positive sciences: viz. the determination of ends to be sought, or unconditional rules to be obeyed. Before proceeding further, it would naturally seem desirable to determine in outline the limits and mutual relations of these different studies; though it is somewhat difficult to do this satisfactorily at the outset of our inquiry; because generally according as we adopt one method of ethics or another we shall adopt different views as to these limits and relations.

If we define Politics as the theory of what ought to be (in human affairs) as far as this depends on the common action of societies of men; we may subdivide it into (1) the Theory of the *work* of government, of which legislation and enforcement of laws is a chief part; and (2) the Theory of the constitution of government, and its relation to the governed (other than the relation of command and obedience, which is involved in the notion of government).

As regards (1). Since a Theory of Legislation is a Theory of what men ought to be compelled by legal penalties to do or forbear, and since no one ought to be legally forced to do what is wrong or bad, it may seem that the legal code will be included within the moral; and that we should determine first the whole code of rules that should be generally observed, and then cut out of this the body of rules that should be legally enforced. On the other hand, it is clear that the right conduct for any member of society depends to a great extent on what others expect him to do, and what he may reasonably expect them to do; and all such expectations are largely determined by Law. In such cases the definition of moral duty seems to be dependent on and posterior to the determination of legal obligation. But further, from an Egoistic point of view, it may seem that the reasonableness of observing any rules must depend on the consequences to oneself of observing or not observing them; and that legal penalties are likely to be decisive in this consideration; so that egoistic morality will practically depend altogether on Law,—so far as the scope of Law extends— and not *vice versâ* (as in Hobbism). Here, however, we see the need of distinguishing Positive Law and Ideal Law, or Law determined on theoretical principles. For all moralists are agreed that there is a general duty of obeying Positive Laws, even when they are not such as we approve: and few, if any, would maintain this duty to be unlimited, and that it is always reasonable to conform to the worst commands of tyrants. The limits, however, of this duty are hard to fix, and would no doubt be fixed differently by different schools. But as regards Law as it ought to be, Egoism does not seem to offer any principles: for though governors have not unfrequently framed laws and ordinances in their own interest, no speculative person has ever pushed

"the enormous faith of many made for one,"

so far as to construct an ideal social system with a view to the greatest happiness of a single member of it. Thinkers who have held it reasonable for an individual to take his own happiness as the end of his private conduct, have commonly considered the general happiness as the reasonable end of Law.

Let us assume, then, that Ideal Law is to be framed on Utilitarian principles, and consider what its relation will be to Morality similarly constructed. It is evident, in the first place, that the question, what rules of conduct and modes of distributing objects of desire should be legally fixed and enforced, will be determined by the same kind of forecast of consequences as will be used in settling all moral questions: we shall endeavour to estimate and balance against each other the effects of such enforcement on the aggregate pleasures and pains of individuals.

In so far, however, as we divide the Utilitarian theory of private conduct from that of legislation, and ask which is prior, the answer will be different in respect of different parts of the legal code.

1. To a great extent, obviously, a utilitarian code of law will consist of rules, which any man sincerely desirous of promoting the general happiness would observe, even if they were not legally binding: such as the rule of not inflicting any bodily harm or gratuitous annoyance on any one, except in self-defence or retaliation; and the rule of not interfering with another's enjoyment of wealth acquired by his own labour, or the free consent of others, or inheritance from parents; and the rule of fulfilling all engagements freely entered into with any one, at any rate unless the fulfilment were harmful to others, or more harmful to oneself than beneficial to him, or unless there were good grounds for supposing that the other party would not perform his share of a bilateral contract; and the rule of supporting one's children while helpless, and their mother during pregnancy and nursing, and one's parents if decrepit, and of educating one's children suitably to their future life. As regards such rules as these, Ethics seems independent of Politics, and naturally prior to it; we first consider what conduct is right for private individuals, and then to how much of this they ought to be compelled by legal penalties.

2. There are other rules again which it is clearly for the general happiness to observe, if only their observance is enforced on others; *e.g.* abstinence from personal retaliation of injuries, and a more general and unhesitating fulfilment of contracts than would perhaps be expedient if they were not legally enforced.

3. But again, in the complete determination of the mutual claims of members of society to services and forbearances, there are many points on which the utilitarian theory of right private conduct apart from law would lead to a considerable variety of conclusions, from the great difference in the force of the relevant considerations under different circumstances; while at the same time uniformity is either indispensable, to prevent disputes and disappointments, or at least highly desirable, in order to maintain effectively such rules of conduct as are *generally*—though

not *universally*—expedient. Under this head would come the exacter definition of the limits of appropriation, *e.g.* as regards incorporeal property in literary compositions and technical inventions, and much of the law of inheritance, and of the law regulating the family relations. In all these cases, in so far as they are capable of being theoretically determined, Utilitarian Ethics blends with and is indistinguishable from Utilitarian Politics. We cannot determine the right conduct for a private individual in any particular case, without first ascertaining the rule which it would be generally expedient to maintain in the society of which he is a member. When this is settled there remains for the politician the further problem of deciding which of these rules should be enforced by legal penalties, and which should be left to rest on the weaker and less definite sanctions of moral opinion. It would be out of place to discuss here the principles on which this problem should be determined: but we may observe that their application to any concrete case is necessarily complicated by the consideration of the delicate mutual relations of Positive Law and Positive Morality—as we may call the actual moral opinions generally held in a given society at a given time. For on the one hand it is dangerous in legislation to advance beyond Positive Morality, by prohibiting actions (or inactions) that are generally approved or tolerated; on the other hand, up to the point at which this danger becomes serious, legislation is a most effective instrument for modifying or intensifying public opinion, in the direction in which it is desirable that it should progress. Leaving this difficult question of social dynamics, we may say that normally in a well-organized society the most important and indispensable rules of social behaviour will be legally enforced and the less important left to be maintained by Positive Morality. Law will constitute, as it were, the skeleton of social order, clothed upon by the flesh and blood of Morality.

What has been said above of the blending of Ethics and Politics from a utilitarian point of view applies, of course, to the rules which form the second part of Politics (as I define the term). It is obvious that the moral regulation of the relations of governors to the governed, and of the different parts of government to each other, must be theoretically determined in close connexion with the definite quasi-legal code which is called the Constitution.

I have treated this subject first from the utilitarian point of view, because Utilitarianism—at least of a loose and popular sort—seems to be now commonly accepted in Politics to a much greater extent than it is in the sphere of private conduct: many who recognize absolute rules of private duty, to be obeyed without regard to consequences, still hold that it is a question of expediency what actions and abstinences morally right or allowable should be made compulsory under legal penalties; and similarly that the right form of government for any society is to be determined on grounds of expediency only. At the same time, we still find in current political thought—even in England—an Intuitional method of Politics, which lays down *a priori* certain absolute *rights*, which it should be the primary end of civil law in any community to maintain; just as Intuitional Ethics lays down absolute duties for private individuals. And further, since among these 'natural rights' is reckoned the Right to Freedom, limited only by the equal freedom of others—indeed by many (as Kant) the Right to Freedom is held to include all truly natural rights—it is inferred by the same method that no man is originally and 'naturally' bound to obey any other: and thus we get as the fundamental principle of a true constitutional code, that the Right of Government to exist and operate must be derived from the consent of its subjects to a limitation of their natural rights. On this view, the main questions to be asked, in considering the legitimacy of any form of government, are, firstly, how far these natural rights are alienable, and secondly how the consent of the members of any society to their partial alienation may be inferred; we must observe, however, that in more or less distinct opposition to this last view it was once held, and the doctrine still lingers, that the natural right of government in any society is vested, as a kind of heritable though not transferable property, in the persons belonging to a particular line of descent.

But both the theory of hereditary rights of monarchs, and the theory of a Law of Nature by which all persons have rights prior to the social compact that binds them into a community, are regarded as more or less antiquated by most educated Englishmen at the present day. The political views now chiefly opposed to Utilitarianism are those which take the Perfection of Society—or Social Welfare or Wellbeing interpreted otherwise than hedonistically—as the ultimate end in Politics as well as in Ethics. According to any such view, the connexion between Politics and Ethics is naturally very close; since on the one hand the Duty or Virtue of any individual is held to consist essentially in the performance of his function as a member of a 'social organism' in such a manner as to realise or effectively promote the Wellbeing of the whole organism; while on the other hand a certain kind of political order is generally held to be an indispensable condition or constituent of such Wellbeing. The degree, however, of separation between the two studies, and their mutual relations of dependence or priority, can hardly be determined without a clearer conception than I can here attempt to give of that Wellbeing or Welfare which is not Happiness[1].

§ 2. There are, however, thinkers who regard Ethics as dependent on Politics in a manner quite different from any that has yet been discussed: viz. as being an investigation not of what ought to be done here and now, but of what ought to be the rules of behaviour in an ideal society. So that the subject-matter of our science would be doubly ideal: as it would not only prescribe what ought to be done as distinct from what is, but what ought to be done in a society that itself *is* not, but only *ought* to be. Those who take this view[2]

[1] Some further discussion of this question will be found in Book III., chap. xiv.

[2] In writing this section I had primarily in view the doctrine set forth in Mr Spencer's *Social Statics*. As Mr Spencer has restated his view and replied to my arguments in his *Data of Ethics*, it is necessary for me to point out that the first paragraph of this section is not directed against such a view of 'Absolute' and 'Relative' Ethics as is given in the later treatise—which seems to me to differ materially from the doctrine of *Social Statics*. In *Social Statics* it is maintained not merely—as in the *Data of Ethics*—that Absolute Ethics which "formulates normal conduct in an ideal society" ought to "take precedence' of Relative Ethics"; but that Absolute Ethics is the only kind of Ethics with which a philosophical moralist can possibly concern himself. To quote Mr Spencer's words:—"Any proposed system of morals which recognizes existing

adduce the analogy of Geometry to shew that Ethics ought to deal with ideally perfect human relations, just as Geometry treats of ideally straight lines and perfect circles. But the irregular lines which we meet with in experience have spatial relations which Geometry does not ignore altogether; it can and does ascertain them with a sufficient degree of accuracy for practical purposes: though of course they are more complex than those of perfectly straight lines. So in Astronomy, it would be more convenient for purposes of study if the stars moved in circles, as was once believed: but the fact that they move not in circles but in ellipses, and even in imperfect and perturbed ellipses, does not take them out of the sphere of scientific investigation: by patience and industry we have learnt how to reduce to principles and calculate even these more complicated motions. It is, no doubt, a convenient artifice for purposes of instruction to assume that the planets move in perfect ellipses or even—at an earlier stage of study—in circles: we thus allow the individual's knowledge to pass through the same gradations in accuracy as that of the race has done. But what we want, as astronomers, to know is the actual motion of the stars and its causes: and similarly as moralists we naturally inquire what ought to be done in the actual world in which we live. It may be that neither in the former case nor in the latter can we hope to represent in our calculations the full complexity of the actual considerations: but we endeavour to approximate to it as closely as possible. It is only so that we really grapple with the question to which mankind generally require an answer: 'What is a man's duty in his present

---

defects, and countenances acts made needful by them, stands self-condemned .. Moral law...requires as its postulate that human beings be perfect. The philosophical moralist treats solely of the *straight* man. .shews in what relationship he stands to other straight men. a problem in which a *crooked* man forms one of the elements, is insoluble by him". *Social Statics* (c. i.). Still more definitely is Relative Ethics excluded in the following passage of the concluding chapter of the same treatise (the italics are mine):—"It will very likely be urged that, whereas the perfect moral code is confessedly beyond the fulfilment of imperfect men, some other code is needful for our present guidance...to say that the imperfect man requires a moral code which recognizes his imperfection and allows for it, *seems at first sight reasonable. But it is not really so...a system of morals which shall recognize man's present imperfections and allow for them cannot be devised; and would be useless if it could be devised.*"

condition?' For it is too paradoxical to say that the whole duty of man is summed up in the effort to attain a right state of social relations; we must therefore determine our duties to the present world of men somehow: and Ethics seeks to do this in a systematic manner.

This inquiry into the morality of an ideal society can therefore be at best but a preliminary investigation, after which the step from the ideal to the actual, in accordance with reason, remains to be taken. We have to ask, then, how far such a preliminary construction seems desirable. And in answering this we must distinguish the different methods of Ethics. For it is generally held by Intuitionists that true morality prescribes absolutely what is in itself right, under all social conditions; at least as far as determinate duties are concerned: as (*e.g.*) that 'Truth should always be spoken' and 'Justice be done, though the sky should fall.' And so far as this is held it would seem that there can be no fundamental distinction drawn, in the determination of duty, between the actual and an ideal state of society: at any rate the general definition of (*e.g.*) Justice will be the same for both, no less than its absolute stringency—though I suppose even an extreme Intuitionist would admit that the details of this and other duties will vary with social institutions.

It would seem more natural that those methods which propose an ultimate end, which at present we cannot perfectly attain, viz. Happiness (whether individual or universal), should develop this consideration of the ideal conditions under which the end could be more fully realized[1]. And I shall not at present deny that this task might usefully be included in an exhaustive investigation of the particulars of these methods. But it can easily be shewn that it is involved in serious difficulties.

For as in ordinary deliberation we have to consider what is best under certain conditions of human life, internal or ex-

---

[1] I omit, for the present, the consideration of the method which takes Perfection as an ultimate end: since, as has been before observed, it is hardly possible to discuss this satisfactorily, in relation to the present question, until it has been somewhat more clearly distinguished from the ordinary Intuitional Method.

ternal, so we must do this in contemplating the ideal society. We require to contemplate not so much the end supposed to be attained—which is simply the most pleasant consciousness conceivable, lasting as long and as uninterruptedly as possible—but rather some method of realizing it, pursued by human beings; and these, again, must be conceived as existing under conditions not too remote from our own, so that we can at least endeavour to imitate them. And for this we must know how far our present circumstances are modifiable; a very difficult question, as the constructions which have actually been made of such ideal societies shew. For example, the *Republic* of Plato seems in many respects sufficiently divergent from the reality, and yet he contemplates war as a permanent unalterable fact, to be provided for in the ideal state, and indeed such provision seems the predominant aim of his construction; whereas the soberest modern Utopia would certainly include the suppression of war. Indeed the ideal will often seem to diverge in diametrically opposite directions from the actual, according to the line of imagined change which we happen to adopt, in our visionary flight from present evils. For example, permanent marriage-unions now cause some unhappiness, because conjugal affection is not always permanent; but they are thought to be necessary, partly to protect men and women from vagaries of passion pernicious to themselves, but chiefly in order to the better rearing of children. Now it may seem to some that in an ideal state of society we could trust more to parental affections, and require less to control the natural play of emotion between the sexes, and that 'Free Love' is therefore the ideal; while others would maintain that permanence in conjugal affection is natural and normal, and that any exceptions to this rule must be supposed to disappear as we approximate to the ideal. Again, the happiness enjoyed in our actual society seems much diminished by the unequal distribution of the means of happiness, and the division of mankind into rich and poor. But we can conceive this evil removed in two quite different ways; either by an increased disposition on the part of the rich to redistribute their share, or by such social arrangements as would enable the poor to secure more for themselves. In the one case the ideal involves a great extension and systematization of the arbitrary and casual almsgiving that now goes on: in the other case, its extinction.

In short, it seems that when we abandon the firm ground of actual society we have an illimitable cloudland surrounding us on all sides, in which we may construct any variety of pattern states; but no definite ideal to which the actual undeniably approximates, as the straight lines and circles of the actual physical world approximate to those of scientific geometry.

It may be said, however, that we can reduce this variety by studying the past history of mankind, as this will enable us to predict to some extent their future manner of existence. But even so it does not appear that we shall gain much definite guidance for our present conduct. For let us make the most favourable suppositions that we can, and such as soar even above the confidence of the most dogmatic of scientific historians. Let us assume that the process of human history is a progress of mankind towards ever greater happiness. Let us assume further that we can not only fix certain limits within which the future social condition of mankind must lie, but even determine in detail the mutual relations of the different elements of the future community, so as to view in clear outline the rules of behaviour, by observing which they will attain the maximum of happiness. It still remains quite doubtful how far it would be desirable for us to imitate these rules in the circumstances in which we now live. For this foreknown social order is *ex hypothesi* only presented as a more advanced stage in our social progress, and not as a type or pattern which we ought to make a struggle to realize approximately at any earlier stage. How far it should be taken as such a pattern, is a question which would still have to be determined, and in the consideration of it the effects of our actions on the existing generation would after all be the most important element[1].

[1] Some further consideration of this question will be found in a subsequent chapter. Cf. Book IV. c. iv.

CHAPTER III.

REASON AND FEELING.

§ 1. In the first chapter I spoke of actions that we judge to be right and what ought to be done as being "reasonable," or "rational," and similarly of ultimate ends as "prescribed by Reason": and I contrasted the motive to action supplied by the recognition of such reasonableness with "non-rational" desires and inclinations. This manner of speaking is employed by writers of different schools, and seems in accordance with the common view and language on the subject. For we commonly think that wrong conduct is essentially irrational, and can be shewn to be so by argument; and though we do not conceive that it is by reason alone that men are influenced to act rightly, we still hold that appeals to the reason are an essential part of all moral persuasion, and that part which concerns the moralist or moral philosopher as distinct from the preacher or moral rhetorician. On the other hand it is widely maintained that, as Hume says, "Reason, meaning the judgment of truth and falsehood, can never of itself be any motive to the Will"—the motive to action being in all cases some feeling similar to what I have characterized as Non-rational Desire. It seems desirable to examine with some care the grounds of this contention, before we proceed any further.

Let us begin by defining the issue raised, as clearly as possible. Every one, I suppose, has had experience of what is meant by the conflict of non-rational or irrational desires with reason: most of us (*e.g.*) occasionally feel bodily appetite prompting us to indulgences which we judge to be imprudent, and anger prompting us to acts of which we disapprove as unjust or unkind. It is when this conflict occurs that the desires are said to be irrational, as impelling us to volitions opposed to our deliberate judgments: sometimes we yield to such seductive impulses, and sometimes not: and it is perhaps when we do *not* yield, that the impulsive force of such irrational desires is most definitely felt, as we have to exert in resisting them a voluntary effort somewhat analogous to that involved in any muscular exertion. Often, again,—since we are not always thinking either of our duty or of our interest,—desires of this kind take effect in voluntary actions without our having judged such actions to be either right or wrong, either prudent or imprudent; as (*e. g.*) when an ordinary eupeptic person eats his dinner. In such cases it seems most appropriate to call the desires "non-rational" rather than "irrational." Neither term is intended to imply that the desires spoken of—or at least the more important of them—are not normally accompanied by rational or intellectual processes. It is true that some impulses to action seem to take effect "instinctively," as we say, without any definite consciousness either of the end at which the action is aimed, or of the means by which the end is to be attained: but this, I conceive, is only the case with impulses that do not occupy consciousness for an appreciable time, and do not require any but very familiar and habitual actions for the attainment of their proximate ends. In all other cases—that is, in the case of all the actions with which we are chiefly concerned in ethical discussion—the result aimed at, and usually some part at least of the means by which it is to be realized, are more or less distinctly represented in consciousness, previous to the volition that initiates the movements tending to its realization. Hence the resultant forces of what I call "non-rational" desires, and the volitions to which they prompt, are continually modified by intellectual processes in two distinct ways; first by new perceptions or representations of means conducive to the desired ends, and secondly by new presentations or representations of facts—either as actually existing, or as more or less probable consequences of contemplated actions—which rouse new impulses of desire and aversion.

The question, then, is whether this account of the influence of reason on desire and volition is not exhaustive; and whether the experience which is commonly described as a "conflict of desire with reason" is not more properly conceived as a conflict among desires and aversions; the sole function of reason being to bring before the mind ideas of actual or possible facts, which modify in the manner above described the resultant force of our various impulses.

I hold that this is not the case; that the ordinary moral or prudential judgments which, in the case of all or most minds have a certain—though too often not a predominant—influence on volition, cannot legitimately be interpreted as judgments respecting the present or future existence of human feelings or other facts of experience; the notion "ought" or "right," which in some form or other such judgments contain, being essentially different from all notions representing empirical facts. The question is one on which appeal must ultimately be made to the reflection of individuals on their practical judgments and reasonings: and in making this appeal it seems most convenient to begin by shewing the inadequacy of all attempts to explain the practical judgments or propositions in which the notion "ought" is introduced, without recognizing its unique character as above negatively defined. There is an element of truth in such explanations, in so far as they bring into view feelings which undoubtedly accompany moral or prudential judgments, and which ordinarily have more or less effect in determining the will to actions judged to be right; but so far as they profess to be interpretations of what such judgments mean, they appear to me to fail altogether.

In considering this question it will, I think, conduce to clearness to take separately the two species of judgments which I have distinguished as "moral" and "prudential" respectively; since though it is widely held that the ultimate obligation of all rules of duty must be rested on the self-interest of the individual to whom they are addressed—so that all valid moral rules have ultimately a prudential basis—it seems clear that in ordinary thought cognitions or judgments of duty present themselves as *primâ facie* distinct from cognitions or judgments as to what conduces to self-interest.

To begin then with the former, *i. e.* with moral judgments in the narrower sense: it is maintained by some that the judgments or propositions which we commonly call moral really affirm no more than the existence of a specific emotion in the mind of the person who utters them : that when I say 'Truth ought to be spoken' or 'Truthspeaking is right,' I mean no more than that the idea of truthspeaking excites in my mind a feeling of approbation. And probably some degree of such emotion, commonly distinguished as 'moral sentiment,' always or ordinarily accompanies moral judgment. But it is absurd to say that a mere statement of my approbation of truthspeaking is properly given in the proposition 'Truth ought to be spoken'; otherwise the fact of another man's disapprobation might equally be expressed by saying 'Truth ought not to be spoken'; and thus we should have two coexistent facts stated in two mutually contradictory propositions. This is so obvious, that we must suppose that those who hold the view which I am combating do not really intend to deny it: but rather to maintain that the existence of this merely subjective fact is all that there is any *ground* for stating, or perhaps that it is all that any reasonable person is prepared on reflection to affirm. And no doubt there is a large class of statements, in form objective, which yet we are not commonly prepared to maintain as such if their validity is called in question. If I say that 'the air is sweet,' or 'the food disagreeable,' it would not be exactly true to say that I mean no more than that I like the one or dislike the other: but if my statement is challenged, I shall probably content myself with affirming the existence of such feelings in my own mind. But there appears to me to be a fundamental difference between this case and that of moral feelings. The peculiar emotion of moral approbation is, in my experience, inseparably bound up with the conviction, implicit or explicit, that the conduct approved is 'objectively' right—*i.e.* that it cannot, without error, be disapproved by any other mind. If I give up this conviction because others do not share it — which may very likely happen—I may no doubt still retain a strong liking for the conduct in question: but this liking will no longer have the special quality of 'moral sentiment' strictly so called. This difference between the two is often overlooked in ethical discussion: but any experience of a change in moral opinion produced by argument may afford an illustration of it. Suppose (*e.g.*) that any one habitually influenced by the sentiment of Veracity is convinced that under certain peculiar circumstances in which he finds himself, speaking truth is not right but wrong. A certain liking for veracity will probably still remain in his mind: he will feel a repugnance against violating the rule of truthspeaking: but it will be a feeling quite different in kind and degree from that which prompted him to veracity as a department of virtuous action. We might perhaps call the latter a 'moral' and the former a 'quasi-moral' sentiment.

The argument just given holds equally against the view that approbation is not the mere liking of an individual for certain kinds of conduct, but this complicated by a sympathetic representation of similar likings and aversions felt by other human beings. No doubt such sympathy is a normal concomitant of moral emotion, and when the former is absent there is much greater difficulty in maintaining the latter: this, however, is partly because our moral beliefs commonly agree with those of other members of our society, and on this agreement depends to an important extent our confidence in the truth of these beliefs[1]. But if, as in the case just supposed, we are really led by argument to a new moral belief, opposed not only to our own habitual sentiment but also to that of the society in which we live, we have a crucial experiment that proves the existence of the moral sentiment proper, as distinct from the represented sympathies of our fellow-men no less than from our own habitual likings and aversions. And even if we imaginatively extend the sympathies opposed to our convictions until they include those of the whole human race, against whom we imagine ourselves to stand as *Athanasius contra mundum*; still, so long as our conviction of duty is firm, the emotion which we call moral stands out in imagination quite distinct from the complex sympathy opposed to it, however much we extend, complicate and intensify the latter.

§ 2. So far, then, from being prepared to admit that the proposition 'ought to be done' *merely* expresses the existence of a certain sentiment in myself or others, I find it strictly

---

[1] Cf. *post*, Book III. chap. xi. § 1.

impossible so to regard my own moral judgments without eliminating from the concomitant sentiment the peculiar quality signified by the term 'moral.' There is, however, another view in which moral judgments are considered to relate to the likings and aversions that men in general feel for certain kinds of conduct; not as sympathetically represented in the emotion of the person judging, and thus constituting the moral element in it, but as the causes of pain to the person of whom 'ought' is predicated. On this view, when we say that a man 'ought' to do anything, we mean that he is bound under penalties to do it; the particular penalty considered being the pain that will accrue to him directly or indirectly from a kind of conduct which his fellow-creatures dislike.

It cannot be denied that this interpretation has some plausibility. For in using, as we commonly do, the term 'moral obligation' or 'boundness' as equivalent to that contained in the verb 'ought' we imply an analogy between this notion and that of legal obligation: and in the case of positive law the connexion of 'obligation' and 'punishment' seems indissoluble: a law cannot be properly said to be actually established in a society if it is habitually violated with impunity. But a more careful reflection on the relation of Law to Morality, as ordinarily conceived, seems to shew that it really affords no argument for the interpretation of 'ought' that I am now discussing. For the ideal distinction taken in common thought between legal and merely moral rules seems to lie in just this connexion of the former with punishment: we think that there are some things which a man ought to be compelled to do, or forbear, and others which he ought to do or forbear without compulsion, and that the former alone fall properly within the sphere of law. And it is otherwise evident that what we mean when we say that a man is "morally though not legally bound" to do a thing is not merely that he "will be punished by public opinion if he does not": for we often join the two statements, clearly distinguishing their import: and further (since public opinion is known to be eminently fallible) there are many things which we judge men 'ought' to do, while perfectly aware that they will incur no serious social penalties for omitting them. In such cases, indeed, it would be commonly said that social disapprobation 'ought' to follow on immoral conduct; and in this very assertion it is clear that the term 'ought' cannot mean that social penalties are to be feared by those who do not disapprove. Again, all or most men in whom the moral consciousness is strongly developed find themselves from time to time in conflict with the commonly received morality of the society to which they belong: and thus—as was before said—have a crucial experience proving that duty does not mean *to them* what other men will disapprove of them for not doing.

At the same time I admit, as indeed I have already suggested in § 3 of chap. I., that we not unfrequently pass judgments resembling moral judgments in form, and not distinguished from them in ordinary thought, in cases where the obligation affirmed is found, on reflection, to depend on the existence of current opinions and sentiments as such. The members of modern civilised societies are under the sway of a code of Public Opinion, enforced by social penalties, which no reflective person obeying it identifies with the moral code, or regards as unconditionally binding: indeed the code is manifestly fluctuating and variable, different at the same time in different classes, professions, social circles, of the same political community. Such a code always supports to a considerable extent the commonly received code of morality: and most reflective persons think it generally reasonable to conform to the dictates of public opinion—to the Code of Honour, we may say, in graver matters, or the Code of Politeness or Good Breeding in lighter matters—wherever they do not positively conflict with morality; either on grounds of private interest, or because they think it conducive to general happiness or wellbeing to keep as much as possible in harmony with their fellow-men. Hence in the ordinary thought of unreflective persons the duties imposed by either code are often undistinguished from moral duties: and indeed this indistinctness is almost inherent in the common meaning of many terms. For instance, if we say that a man has been 'dishonoured' by a cowardly act, it is not quite clear whether we mean that he has incurred contempt, or that he has deserved it, or both: as becomes evident when we take a case in which the Code of Honour comes into conflict with Morality. If (*e.g.*) a man were to incur social ostracism anywhere for refusing a duel on religious grounds, some would say that he was 'dishonoured,' though he had acted rightly, others that there could be no real dishonour in a virtuous act. A similar ambiguity seems to lurk in the common notion of 'improper' or 'incorrect' behaviour. Still in all such cases the ambiguity becomes evident on reflection: and when discovered, merely serves to illustrate further the distinction between moral 'rightness' or 'goodness' of conduct, strictly so called, and mere conformity to the standard of current opinion.

There is, however, another way of interpreting 'ought' as connoting penalties, which is somewhat less easy to meet by a crucial psychological experiment. The moral imperative may be taken to be a law of God, to the breach of which Divine penalties are annexed; and these, no doubt, in a Christian society, are commonly conceived to be adequate and universally applicable. Still, it can hardly be said that this belief is shared by all the persons whose conduct is influenced by independent moral convictions, occasionally unsupported either by the law or the public opinion of their community. And even in the case of many of those who believe fully in the moral government of the world, the judgment "I ought to do this" cannot be identified with the judgment "God will punish me if I do not"; since the conviction that the former proposition is true is distinctly recognized as an important part of the grounds for believing the latter. Again, when Christians speak—as they commonly do—of the 'justice' (or other moral attributes) of God, as exhibited in punishing sinners and rewarding the righteous, they obviously imply not merely that God *will* thus punish and reward, but that it is 'right'[1] for Him to do so: which, of course, cannot be taken to mean that He is 'bound under penalties.'

§ 3. It seems then that the notion of 'ought' or 'moral obligation,' as used in our common moral judgments, does not merely import (1) that there exists in the mind of the person judging a specific emotion (whether complicated or not by sympathetic representation of similar emotions in other minds);

---

[1] 'Ought' is here inapplicable, for a reason presently explained.

nor (2) that certain rules of conduct are supported by penalties which will follow on their violation (whether such penalties result from the general liking or aversion felt for the conduct prescribed or forbidden, or from some other source). What then, it may be asked, does it import? What definition can we give of 'ought,' 'right,' and other terms expressing the same fundamental notion? To this it may be answered that the notion is too elementary to admit of any formal definition; it can only be made clearer by determining its relation to other notions with which it is connected in ordinary thought, especially to those with which it is liable to be confounded. If however it appears that what the questioner wants is really a complete account of the relation of Morality to other objects of knowledge, we must add that it does not belong to Ethics to furnish this, but to some more comprehensive science: at any rate this task is not undertaken in the present treatise, which only attempts to methodize our practical judgments and reasonings, in which this fundamental notion must, I conceive, be taken as ultimate and unanalysable.

We have, however, to distinguish two different implications with which the term is used; according as the result which we judge 'ought to be' is or is not thought capable of being brought about by the volition of any individual, in the circumstances to which the judgment applies. The former alternative is, I conceive, implied by the strictly ethical 'ought:' in the narrowest ethical sense I cannot conceive that I 'ought' to do anything which at the same time I judge that I cannot do. In a wider sense, however,—which cannot conveniently be discarded in ordinary discourse—I sometimes judge that I 'ought' to know what a wiser man would know, or feel as a better man would feel, in my place, though I may know that I could not directly produce in myself such knowledge or feeling by any effort of will. In this case the word merely implies an ideal or pattern which I 'ought'—in the stricter sense—to seek to imitate as far as possible. And this wider sense seems to be that in which the word is normally used in the precepts of Art generally, and in political judgments: when I judge that the laws and constitution of my country 'ought to be' other than they are, I do not of course imply that my own or any other individual's single volition can directly bring about the change[1]. In either case, however, I imply—as has been before said—that the judgment is objective[2]: *i. e.* that what I judge " right " or " what ought to be " must, unless I am in error, be thought to be so by all rational beings who judge truly of the matter.

In referring such judgments to the 'Reason,' I mean to imply no more than just this 'objectivity.' I do not mean to imply that valid moral judgments can only be attained by a process of reasoning from universal principles, and not by direct intuition of the particular duties of individuals. At the same time it must be admitted that this latter implication would naturally be suggested by the use of the term 'Reason' in other departments of thought. We do not commonly say that particular physical facts are apprehended by the Reason: we consider this faculty to be conversant in its discursive operation with the relation of judgments or propositions: and the intuitive reason (which is here rather in question) we restrict to the apprehension of universal truths, such as the axioms of Logic and Mathematics. Now, as I shall presently observe, it is not uncommonly held that the moral faculty deals primarily with individual cases, applying directly to these the general notion of duty, and deciding intuitively what ought to be done by this person in these particular circumstances. On this view the apprehension of moral truth is more analogous to Sense-perception than to Rational Intuition (as commonly understood): and hence the term Moral Sense might seem more appropriate. But the term sense suggests a capacity for feelings which may vary from *A* to *B* without either being in error, rather than a faculty of objective cognition[3]: hence it has seemed to me better

---

[1] I do not even imply that any combination of individuals could completely realize the state of political relations which I conceive 'ought to' exist. My conception would be futile if it had no relation to practice: but it may merely delineate a pattern to which no more than an approximation is practically possible.

[2] There are certain difficulties or ambiguities involved in the application of the term "objective" to right conduct, which I shall discuss later (Book III., chap. i. § 3). But these do not, in my opinion, necessitate any modification of the simple account of the meaning of the term which I have given in the text.

[3] By cognition I always mean what some would rather call "apparent cognition," that is, I do not mean to affirm the *validity* of the cognition, but only its existence as a psychical fact.

to use the term Reason as above explained, to denote merely such a faculty, without restricting it to universal cognitions[1].

Further, when I speak of the cognition or judgment that 'X ought to be done'—in the stricter ethical sense of the term ought[2]—as a 'dictate' or 'precept' of reason to the persons to whom it relates; I imply that in rational beings as such this cognition gives an impulse or motive to action: though in human beings, of course, this is only one motive among others which are liable to conflict with it, and is not always—perhaps not usually—a predominant motive. In fact, this possible conflict of motives seems to be connoted by the term 'dictate' or 'imperative'; which describes the relation of Reason to mere inclinations or non-rational impulses by comparing it to the relation between the will of a superior and the wills of his subordinates. This conflict seems also to be implied in the terms 'ought,' 'duty,' 'moral obligation,' as used in ordinary moral discourse: and hence these terms cannot be applied to the actions of rational beings to whom we cannot attribute impulses conflicting with reason. We may, however, say of such beings that their actions are 'reasonable,' or (in an absolute sense) 'right.'

§ 4. I am aware that some persons will be disposed to answer all the preceding argument by a simple denial that they can find in their consciousness any such absolute imperative as I have been trying to exhibit. If this is really the final result of self-examination in any case, there is no more to be said. I, at least, do not know how to impart the notion of moral obligation to any one who is entirely devoid of it. I think, however, that many of those who give this denial only mean to deny that they have any consciousness of moral obligation to actions *per se* without reference to their consequences; and would not deny that they recognize some universal end or ends—whether it be the general happiness, or well-being otherwise understood—as that at which it is ultimately reasonable to

---

[1] A further justification for this extended use of the term Reason will be suggested in a subsequent chapter (ch. viii. § 3).

[2] This is the sense in which the term will always be used in the present treatise, except where the context makes it quite clear that only the wider meaning—that of the political 'ought'—is applicable.

aim, subordinating the gratification of personal desires to its attainment. But in this view, as I have before said, it appears to me that the unconditional imperative really comes in as regards the end; it is implicitly recognized as an end at which all men 'ought' to aim; and it can hardly be denied that the recognition of an end as ultimately reasonable involves the recognition of an obligation to do such acts as most conduce to the end. The obligation is not indeed "unconditional," but it does not depend on the existence of any non-rational desires or aversions. And nothing that has been said in the preceding section is intended as an argument in favour of Intuitionism, as against Utilitarianism or any other method that treats moral rules as relative to General Good or Well-being. For instance, nothing that I have said is inconsistent with the view that Truthspeaking is only valuable as a means to the preservation of society: only if it be admitted that it *is* valuable on this ground I should say that it is implied that the preservation of society—or some further end to which this preservation, again, is a means—must be valuable *per se*, and therefore something at which a rational being, as such, ought to aim. If it be granted that we need not look beyond the preservation of society, the primary 'dictate of reason,' in this case would be 'that society *ought* to be preserved:' but reason would also dictate truthspeaking, so far as truthspeaking is recognized as the indispensable or fittest means to this end.

So again, even those who hold that moral rules are only obligatory because it is the individual's interest to conform to them—thus regarding them as a particular species of prudential rules—do not thereby get rid of the 'dictate of reason,' so far as they recognize private interest or happiness as an end at which it is ultimately reasonable to aim. The conflict of Practical Reason with irrational desire remains an indubitable fact of our conscious experience, even if practical reason is interpreted to mean merely self-regarding Prudence. It is, indeed, maintained by Kant and others that it cannot properly be said to be a man's duty to promote his own happiness; since "what every one inevitably wills cannot be brought under the notion of duty." But even granting[1] it to be in some sense true that a

---

[1] As will be seen from the next chapter, I do not grant this.

man's volition is always directed to the attainment of his own happiness: it does not follow that a man always does what he believes will be conducive to his own *greatest* happiness, or his 'good on the whole.' As Butler urges, it is a matter of common experience that men indulge appetite or passion even when, in their own view, the indulgence is as clearly opposed to what they conceive to be their interest as it is to what they conceive to be their duty. "Video meliora proboque, deteriora sequor" is as applicable to the Epicurean as it is to any one else: and in recognizing that he 'chooses the worse,' a man implicitly, if not explicitly, recognizes that he ought to choose something else.

Even, finally, if we discard the belief, that any end of action is unconditionally or "categorically" prescribed by reason, the notion 'ought' as above explained is not thereby eliminated from our practical reasonings: it still remains in the "hypothetical imperative" which prescribes the fittest means to any end that we may have determined to aim at. When (*e.g.*) a physician says, "If you wish to be healthy you ought to rise early," this is not the same thing as saying "early rising is an indispensable condition of the attainment of health." This latter proposition expresses the relation of physiological facts on which the former is founded; but it is not merely this relation of facts that the word "ought" imports: it also implies the unreasonableness of adopting an end and refusing to adopt the means indispensable to its attainment. It may perhaps be argued that this is not only unreasonable but impossible: since adoption of an end means the preponderance of a desire for it, and if aversion to the indispensable means causes them not to be adopted although recognized as indispensable, the desire for the end is *not* preponderant and it ceases to be adopted. But this view is due, in my opinion, to a defective psychological analysis. According to my observation of consciousness, the adoption of an end as paramount—either absolutely or within certain limits—is quite a distinct psychical phenomenon from desire: it is to be classed with volitions, though it is, of course, specifically different from a volition initiating a particular immediate action. As a species intermediate between the two, we may place resolutions to act in a certain way at some future time: we continually make such resolutions, and sometimes when the time comes for carrying them out, we do in fact act otherwise under the influence of passion or mere habit, without consciously cancelling our previous resolve: in this case the act is, I conceive, clearly irrational as inconsistent with a resolution that still persists in thought. Similarly the adoption of an end logically implies a resolution to take whatever means we may see to be indispensable to its attainment: and if when the time comes we do not take them while yet we do not consciously retract our adoption of the end, it must surely be admitted that we 'ought' in consistency to act otherwise than we do. That Reason dictates the avoidance of a contradiction will be allowed even by those who deny that it dictates anything else: and it will hardly be maintained that such a contradiction as I have described, between a general resolution and a particular volition, is not a matter of common experience.

CHAPTER IV.

PLEASURE AND DESIRE.

§ 1. In the preceding chapter I have left undetermined the emotional characteristics of the impulse that prompts us to obey the dictates of Reason. I have done so because these seem to be very different in different minds, and even to vary much and rapidly in the same mind, without any corresponding variation in the volitional direction of the impulse. For instance, in the mind of a rational Egoist the ruling impulse is generally what Butler and Hutcheson call a "calm" or "cool" self-love: whereas in the man who takes universal happiness as the end and standard of right conduct, the desire to do what is judged to be reasonable as such is commonly blended in varying degrees with sympathy and philanthropic enthusiasm. Again, if one conceives the dictating Reason—whatever its dictates may be—as external to oneself, the cognition of rightness is accompanied by a sentiment of Reverence for Authority; which may by some be conceived impersonally, but is more commonly regarded as the authority of a supreme Person, so that the sentiment blends with the affections normally excited by persons in different relations, and becomes Religious. While again, if we identify Reason and Self, Reverence for Authority blends with Self-respect: and again, the antithetical and even more powerful sentiment of Freedom is called in, if we consider the rational Self as liable to be enslaved by the usurping force of sensual impulses. Quite different again are the emotions of Aspiration or Admiration aroused by the conception of Virtue as an ideal of Moral Perfection or Beauty. Other phases of emotion might be mentioned, all having with these the common characteristic that they are inseparable from an apparent cognition,—implicit or explicit, direct or indirect,—of *rightness* in the conduct to which they prompt. So that, although there may be important differences in their moral value owing to differences in their secondary effects or accompaniments, their primary moral effect does not vary without variation in the cognitive element of the moral consciousness. It is then with these cognitions that Ethics is primarily concerned: its object is to free them from doubt and error, and systematize them as far as possible.

There is, however, one view of the feelings which prompt to voluntary action, which is sometimes thought to involve a particular theory of the principles on which such action ought to be regulated, and so to cut short all controversy on the fundamental question of ethical method. I mean the view that volition is always determined by pleasures or pains actual or prospective. This doctrine—which I may distinguish as Psychological Hedonism—is often connected and not seldom confounded with the method of Ethics which I have called Egoistic Hedonism; and no doubt it is plausible to infer that if one end of action—my own pleasure or absence of pain—is definitely determined for me by unvarying psychological laws, another conflicting end cannot be prescribed for me by Reason.

Reflection however shows that this inference involves the unwarranted assumption that my view of my own pleasure is determined independently of any question as to Rightness or Reasonableness of Conduct: whereas it is manifestly possible that our prospect of pleasure resulting from any course of conduct may largely depend on our conception of it as right or otherwise: and in fact this must be normally the case with the conduct of conscientious persons, who habitually act in accordance with their moral convictions, if the psychological theory above-mentioned is sound. Indeed on looking closer it rather appears that the adoption of psychological Hedonism in its extreme quantitative form, is so far from leading logically to Egoistic Hedonism as an ethical doctrine that it is really incompatible with it. If it were true, as Bentham[1] affirms (with

---

[1] *Constitutional Code*, Introduction, § 2.

the verbose precision of his later style) that "on the occasion of every act he exercises, every human being is led to pursue that line of conduct which, according to his view of the case, taken by him at the moment, will be in the highest degree contributory to his own greatest happiness[1]"; the proposition that a man 'ought' to pursue such conduct is incapable of being affirmed with any significance. For a psychological law invariably realized in my conduct does not admit of being conceived as a 'precept' or 'dictate' of reason: this latter must be a rule from which I am conscious of being able to deviate. But I do not think that the proposition quoted from Bentham would be affirmed without qualification by any of the writers who now maintain psychological Hedonism. They would admit, with J. S. Mill[2], that men often, not from merely intellectual deficiencies, but from "infirmity of character, make their election for the nearer good, though they know it to be less valuable: and this no less when the choice is between two bodily pleasures...they pursue sensual indulgences to the injury of health, though perfectly aware that health is the greater good[3]."

It is just because this is so that psychological Hedonism is of some real ethical importance. If it can be shewn that each of us in acting *does* aim at *some* pleasure (or absence of pain) to himself, the demonstration would at least forcibly suggest as an ideal that he *ought* to seek his own *greatest* pleasure[4]. It is important to observe that this is merely a suggestion. There is no inconsistency in holding that the precepts of reason have no reference to pleasure as an end, and yet that they actually operate in producing volition only in so far as they are connected with prospective pleasures and pains of some kind. In fact, not a few moralists seem to have held the two opinions

---

[1] I here, as in chap. i., adopt the exact hedonistic interpretation of 'happiness' which Bentham has made current. This seems to me the most suitable use of the term; but I afterwards (ch. vii. § 1) take note of other uses.

[2] *Utilitarianism*, c. ii., p. 14.

[3] Mr Leslie Stephen, who holds (*Science of Ethics*, p. 50) that "pain and pleasure are the sole determining causes of action" at the same time thinks that it "will be admitted on all hands" that "we are not always determined by a calculation of pleasure to come."

[4] It is convenient to use this term for 'greatest surplus of pleasure over pain,' which would be more exact.

together. Still, though there is no cogent inference possible from the psychological generalization that his own pleasure is what each desires, to the ethical principle that his own greatest pleasure is for each the ultimate end at which it is reasonable to aim, the mind has a natural tendency to pass from the one position to the other: since if we once admit that our actual motives are always our own pleasures and pains of some kind, it seems *primâ facie* reasonable to be moved by them in proportion to their pleasantness and painfulness, and to choose the greatest pleasure or least pain on the whole. And in any case this psychological doctrine conflicts with the ethical proposition widely held by persons whose moral consciousness is highly developed: viz. that an act in the highest sense virtuous must be done for its own sake and not for the sake of the attendant pleasure, even if that be the pleasure of the moral sense: and that if I do an act from the sole desire of obtaining the glow of moral self-approbation which I believe will attend its performance, the act will not be truly virtuous. It is clear that if psychological Hedonism were true this opinion would have to be abandoned.

It seems therefore important to subject this generalization, even in its more indefinite form, to a careful examination.

§ 2. It will be well to begin by defining more precisely the terms used and the question at issue. First, there is no doubt that pleasure is a kind of feeling which stimulates the will to actions tending to sustain or produce it,—to sustain it, if actually present, and to produce it, if it be only represented in idea—; and similarly pain is a kind of feeling which stimulates as to actions tending to remove or avert it. These statements, in fact, may be given as adequate[1] definitions of Pleasure and Pain. It seems convenient to call the volitional stimulus in the two cases respectively Desire and Aversion; though it should be observed that the former term is ordinarily restricted to the impulse felt when pleasure is not actually present, but only represented in idea. The question at issue, then, is not whether pleasure, present or represented, is normally accom-

---

[1] Adequate, that is, for the purpose of *distinction*—whether they are adequate for the *measurement* that Ethical Hedonism requires is a question that we shall have subsequently to consider. Cf. *post*, Book II. chap. ii. § 2.

panied by desire for itself, and pain by aversion: but whether there are no desires and aversions which have not pleasures and pains for their objects—no conscious impulses to produce or avert results other than the agent's own feelings. In the treatise to which I have referred, Mill explains that "desiring a thing, and finding it pleasant, are, in the strictness of language, two modes of naming the same psychological fact." If this be the case, it is hard to see how the proposition we are discussing requires to be determined by "practised self-consciousness and self-observation;" as the denial of it would involve a contradiction in terms. The truth is that there is an ambiguity in the word Pleasure, which has always tended seriously to confuse the discussion of this question[1]. When we speak of a man doing something at his own "pleasure," or as he "pleases," we usually signify the mere fact of choice or preference; the mere determination of the will in a certain direction. Now, if by "pleasant" we mean that which influences choice, exercises a certain attractive force on the will, it is an assertion incontrovertible because tautological, to say that we desire what is pleasant—or even that we desire a thing in proportion as it appears pleasant. But if we take "pleasure" to denote the kind of feelings above defined, it then becomes a really debateable question whether our desires are always consciously directed towards the attainment by ourselves of such feelings. And this is what we must understand Mr Mill to consider "so obvious, that it will hardly be disputed."

It is rather curious to find that one of the best-known of English moralists regards the exact opposite of what Mr Mill thinks so obvious, as being not merely a universal fact of our conscious experience, but even a necessary truth. Butler, as is well known, distinguishes self-love, or the impulse towards our own pleasure, from "particular movements towards particular external objects—honour, power, the harm or good of another;" the actions proceeding from which are "no otherwise interested than as every action of every creature must

---

[1] The confusion occurs in the most singular form in Hobbes, who actually identifies Pleasure and Appetite, "this motion in which consisteth pleasure, is a solicitation to draw near to the thing that pleaseth."

from the nature of the case be; for no one can act but from a desire, or choice, or preference of his own." Such particular passions or appetites are, he goes on to say, "*necessarily presupposed by the very idea* of an interested pursuit; since the very idea of interest or happiness consists in this, that an appetite or affection enjoys its object." We could not pursue pleasure at all, unless we had desires for something else than pleasure; for pleasure consists in the satisfaction of just these "disinterested" impulses.

Butler has certainly over-stated his case[1], so far as my own experience goes; for many pleasures,—especially those of sight, hearing and smell, together with many emotional pleasures,—occur to me without any relation to previous desires, and it seems quite *conceivable* that our primary desires might be entirely directed towards such pleasures as these. But as a matter of fact, it appears to me that throughout the whole scale of my impulses, sensual, emotional, and intellectual alike, I can distinguish desires of which the object is something other than my own pleasure.

I will begin by taking an illustration of this from the impulses commonly placed lowest in the scale. Hunger, so far as I can observe, is a direct impulse to the eating of food. Such eating is no doubt commonly attended with an agreeable feeling of more or less intensity: but it cannot, I think, be strictly said that this agreeable feeling is the object of hunger, and that it is the representation of this pleasure which stimulates the will of the hungry man as such. Of course hunger, is frequently and naturally accompanied with anticipation of the pleasure of eating: but careful introspection seems to show that the two are by means inseparable. And even when they occur together the pleasure seems properly the object not of the primary appetite, but of a secondary desire which can be distinguished from the former; since the *gourmand*, in whom this secondary desire is strong, is often prompted by it to actions designed to stimulate hunger, and often, again, is led to control the primary impulse, in order to prolong and vary the process of satisfying it.

[1] The same argument is put in a more guarded, and, I think, unexceptionable form by Hutcheson.

Indeed it is so obvious that hunger is something different from the desire for anticipated pleasure, that some writers have regarded its volitional stimulus (and that of appetite generally) as a case of aversion from present pain. This, however, seems to me a distinct mistake in psychological classification. In my ordinary experience, the feeling of hunger is usually what Mr Bain distinguishes as a neutral excitement; it only becomes definitely painful in the case of exceptionally prolonged abstinence from food. No doubt hunger, and desire generally, is a state of consciousness so far similar to pain, that in both we feel a stimulus prompting us to pass from the present state into a different one. But aversion from pain is an impulse to get out of the present state and pass into some other state which is only negatively represented as different from the present: whereas in desire as such, the primary impulse is towards the realization of some positive future result—the desire itself being often not distinctly either pleasurable or painful, even when it reaches a high degree of intensity, but rather tending to assume either quality according to the nature of its concomitants. When a strong desire is, for any reason, baulked of its effect in causing action, it is generally painful in some degree: and so a secondary aversion to the state of desire is generated, which blends itself with the desire and may easily be confounded with it. But here, again, we may distinguish the two impulses by observing the different kinds of conduct to which they occasionally prompt: for the aversion to the pain of ungratified desire, though it may act as an additional stimulus towards the gratification of the desire, may also (and often does) prompt us to get rid of the pain by suppressing the desire. We may observe also that desire, even when it has become a pain or uneasiness, is often but very slightly painful: so that the mere aversion to it as pain is clearly but a small part of the total volitional stimulus of which we are conscious.

When, however, a desire is having its natural effect in causing the actions which tend to the attainment of its object, it seems to be commonly a more or less pleasurable consciousness: even when this attainment is still remote. Or at least the consciousness of eager activity, in which this desire is an essential element, is highly pleasurable: and in fact such pleasures, which we may call generally the pleasures of Pursuit, constitute a considerable item in the total enjoyment of life. Indeed it is almost a commonplace to say that they are more important than the pleasures of Attainment: and in many cases it is the prospect of the former rather than of the latter that induces us to engage in a pursuit. In such cases it is peculiarly easy to distinguish the desire of the object pursued from a desire of the pleasure of attaining it: as in fact attainment is not originally represented in the mind as a source of pleasure, but only becomes pleasant in prospect because the pursuit itself stimulates a desire for what is pursued. Take, for example, the case of any game which involves—as most games do—a contest for victory. No ordinary player before entering on such a contest, has any desire for victory in it: indeed he often finds it difficult to imagine himself deriving gratification from such victory, before he has actually engaged in the competition. What he deliberately, before the game begins, desires is not victory, but the pleasant excitement of the struggle for it; only for the full development of this pleasure a transient desire to win the game is generally indispensable. This desire, which does not exist at first, is stimulated to considerable intensity by the competition itself: and in proportion as it is thus stimulated both the mere contest becomes more pleasurable, and the victory, which was originally indifferent, comes to afford a keen enjoyment.

The same phenomenon is exhibited in the case of more important kinds of pursuit. Thus it often happens that a man, feeling his life languid and devoid of interests, begins to occupy himself in the prosecution of some scientific or socially useful work, for the sake not of the end but of the occupation. At first, very likely, the occupation is irksome: but soon, as he foresaw, his sustained exercise of voluntary effort in one direction reacts on his involuntary emotions; so that his pursuit becoming eager becomes also a source of pleasure. Here, again, it is no doubt true that in proportion as his desire for the end becomes strong, the attainment of it becomes pleasant in prospect: but it would be inverting cause and effect to say that it is this prospective pleasure that he desires.

When we compare these pleasures with those previously discussed, another important observation suggests itself. In the former case, though we could distinguish appetite, as it appears in consciousness, from the desire of the pleasure attending the satisfaction of appetite, there appeared to be no incompatibility between the two. The fact that the gourmand is dominated by the desire of the pleasures of eating in no way impedes the development in him of the appetite which is a necessary condition of these pleasures. But when we turn to the pleasures of pursuit, we seem to perceive this incompatibility to a certain extent: a certain degree of disinterestedness seems to be necessary in order to obtain full enjoyment. A man who maintains throughout an epicurean mood, fixing his aim on his own pleasure, does not catch the full spirit of the chase; his eagerness never gets just the sharpness of edge which imparts to the pleasure its highest zest. Here comes into view what we may call the fundamental paradox of Hedonism, that the impulse towards pleasure, if too predominant, defeats its own aim. This effect is not visible, or at any rate is scarcely visible, in the case of passive sensual pleasures. But of our active enjoyments generally, whether the activities on which they attend are classed as 'bodily' or as 'intellectual' (as well as of many emotional pleasures), it may certainly be said that we cannot attain them, at least in their highest degree, so long as we concentrate our aim on them. Nor is it only that the exercise of our faculties is insufficiently stimulated by the mere desire of the pleasure attending it, and requires the presence of other more objective, 'extra-regarding,' impulses, in order to be fully developed: we may go further and say that these other impulses must be temporarily predominant and absorbing, if the exercise and its attendant gratification are to attain their full height. Many middle-aged Englishmen would maintain the doctrine that business is more agreeable than amusement; but they would hardly find it so, if they transacted the business with a perpetual conscious aim at the attendant pleasure. Similarly, the pleasures of thought and study can only be enjoyed in the highest degree by those who have an ardour of curiosity which carries the mind temporarily away from self and its sensations. In all kinds of Art, again, the exercise of the creative faculty is attended by intense and exquisite pleasures: but in order to get them, one must forget them: the desire of the artist is always said to be concentrated and fixed upon the realization of his ideal of beauty.

The important case of the benevolent affections is at first sight somewhat more doubtful. On the one hand it is of course true, that when those whom we love are pleased or pained, we ourselves feel sympathetic pleasure and pain: and further, that the flow of love or kindly feeling is itself highly pleasurable. So that it is at least plausible to interpret the benevolent impulse as aiming ultimately at the attainment of one or both of these two kinds of pleasures, or at the averting of sympathetic pain. But we may observe, first, that the impulse to beneficent action produced in us by sympathy is often so much out of proportion to any actual consciousness of sympathetic pleasure and pain in ourselves, that it would be paradoxical to regard this latter as its object. Often indeed we cannot but feel that a tale of actual suffering arouses in us an excitement on the whole more pleasurable than painful, like the excitement of witnessing a tragedy; and yet at the same time stirs in us an impulse to relieve it, even when the process of relieving is painful and laborious and involves various sacrifices of our own pleasures. Again, we may often free ourselves from sympathetic pain most easily by merely turning our thoughts from the external suffering that causes it: and we sometimes feel an egoistic impulse to do this, which we can then distinguish clearly from the properly sympathetic impulse prompting us to relieve the original suffering. And finally, the much-commended pleasures of benevolence seem to require, in order to be felt in any considerable degree, the pre-existence of a desire to do good to others for their sake and not for our own. As Hutcheson explains, we may *cultivate* benevolent affection for the sake of the pleasures attending it (just as the gourmand cultivates appetite), but we cannot produce it at will, however strong may be our desire of these pleasures: and when it exists, even though it may owe its origin to a purely egoistic impulse, it is still essentially a desire to do good to others for their sake and not for our own.

It cannot perhaps be said that the self-abandonment and self-forgetfulness, which seemed an essential condition of the full development of the other elevated impulses before noticed, characterize benevolent affection normally and permanently; as love seems naturally to involve a desire for reciprocated love, strong in proportion to the intensity of the emotion; and thus the consciousness of self and of one's own pleasures and pains seems often heightened by the very intensity of the affection that binds one to others. Still we may at least say that this self-suppression and absorption of consciousness in the thought of other human beings and their happiness is observable as a frequent incident of all strong affections: and it is said that persons who love intensely sometimes feel a sense of antagonism between the egoistic and altruistic elements of their desire, and an impulse to suppress the former, which occasionally exhibits itself in acts of fantastic and extravagant self-sacrifice.

If then reflection on our moral consciousness seems to shew that "the pleasure of virtue is one which can only be obtained on the express condition of its not being the object sought[1]," we need not distrust this result of observation on account of the abnormal nature of the phenomenon. We have merely another illustration of a psychological law, which, as we have seen, is exemplified throughout the whole range of our desires. It is not (as Kant seems to hold) that the *natural* determination of the Will is by motives of pleasure and pain, but that when our action is truly *rational*, a higher law of causation comes into play. Rather (as Butler maintains) in the promptings of Sense no less than in those of Intellect or Reason we find the phenomenon of strictly disinterested impulse: base and trivial external ends may be sought without ulterior aim, as well as the sublime and ideal: and there are pleasures of the merely animal life which can only be obtained on condition of not being directly sought, no less than the satisfactions of a good conscience.

§ 3. So far I have been concerned to insist on the felt incompatibility of 'self-regarding' and 'extra-regarding' impulses only as a means of proving their essential distinctness. I do not wish to overstate this incompatibility: I believe that most commonly it is only momentary, and that our greatest happiness—if that be our deliberate aim—is generally attained by

[1] Lecky, *Hist. of European Morals*, Introduction.

means of a sort of alternating rhythm of the two impulses in consciousness. A man's predominant desire is, I think, most commonly not a conscious impulse towards pleasure; but where there is strong desire in any direction, there is commonly keen susceptibility to the corresponding pleasures; and the most devoted enthusiast is sustained in his work by the recurrent consciousness of such pleasures. But it is important to point out that the familiar and obvious instances of conflict between self-love and some extra-regarding impulse are not paradoxes and illusions to be explained away, but phenomena which the analysis of our consciousness in its normal state, when there is no such conflict, would lead us to expect. If we are continually acting from impulses whose immediate objects are something other than our own happiness, it is quite natural that we should occasionally yield to such impulses when they prompt us to an uncompensated sacrifice of pleasure. Thus a man of weak self-control, after fasting too long, may easily indulge his appetite for food to an extent which he knows to be unwholesome: and that not because the pleasure of eating appears to him, even in the moment of indulgence, at all worthy of consideration in comparison with the injury to health: but merely because he feels an impulse to eat food, too powerful to be resisted. Thus, again, men have sacrificed all the enjoyments of life, and even life itself, to obtain posthumous fame: not from any illusory belief that they would be somehow capable of deriving pleasure from it, but from a direct desire of the future admiration of others, and a preference of it to their own pleasure. And so, again, when the sacrifice is made for some ideal end, as Truth, or Freedom, or Religion: it is or may be a real sacrifice of the individual's happiness, and not merely the preference of one highly refined pleasure (or of the absence of one special pain) to all the other elements of happiness. No doubt this preference is possible: a man may feel that the high and severe delight of serving his ideal is a "pearl of great price" outweighing in value all other pleasures. But he may also feel that the sacrifice will not repay *him*, and yet determine that it shall be made.

So far, then, from our conscious active impulses being always directed towards the attainment of pleasure or avoidance of pain for ourselves, it would seem that we find everywhere in consciousness extra-regarding impulses, directed towards something that is not pleasure, nor relief from pain; and, in fact, that a most important part of our pleasure depends upon the existence of such impulses: while on the other hand they are in many cases so far incompatible with the desire of our own pleasure that the two kinds of impulse do not easily coexist in the same moment of consciousness; and more occasionally (but by no means rarely) the two come into irreconcileable conflict, and prompt to opposite courses of action. And this incompatibility (though it is important to notice it in other instances) is no doubt specially prominent in the case of the impulse towards the end which most markedly competes in ethical controversy with pleasure; the love of virtue for its own sake, or desire to do what is right as such.

§ 4. The psychological observations on which my argument is based will not perhaps be directly controverted, at least to such an extent as to involve my main conclusion: but there are two lines of reasoning by which it has been attempted to weaken the force of this conclusion without directly denying it. In the first place, it is urged that Pleasure, though not the only conscious aim of human action, is yet always the result to which it is unconsciously directed. The proposition would be difficult to disprove: since no one denies that pleasure in some degree normally accompanies the attainment of a desired end: and when once we go beyond the testimony of consciousness there seems to be no clear method of determining which among the consequences of any action is the end at which it is aimed. For the same reason, however, the proposition is at any rate equally difficult to prove. But I should go further, and maintain that if we seriously set ourselves to consider human action on its unconscious side, we can only conceive it as a combination of movements of the parts of a material organism: and that if we try to ascertain what the 'end' in any case of such movements is, it is reasonable to conclude that it is some material result, some organic condition conducive to the preservation either of the individual organism or of the race to which it belongs. In fact, the doctrine that pleasure (or the absence of pain) is the end of all human action can neither be supported by the results of introspection, nor by the results of external observation and inference: it rather seems to be reached by an arbitrary and illegitimate combination of the two.

But again, it is sometimes said that whatever be the case with our present adult consciousness, our original impulses were all directed towards pleasure[1] or from pain, and that any impulses otherwise directed are derived from these by "association of ideas." I have seen no evidence tending to prove this: so far as we can observe the consciousness of children, the two elements, extra-regarding impulse and desire for pleasure, seem to coexist in the same manner as they do in mature life. In so far as there is any difference, it seems to be in the opposite direction; as the actions of children being more instinctive and less reflective are more prompted by extra-regarding impulse, and less by conscious aim at pleasure. No doubt the two kinds of impulse, as we trace back the development of consciousness, gradually become indistinguishable: but this obviously does not justify us in identifying with either of the two the more indefinite impulse out of which both have been developed. But even supposing it were found that our earliest appetites were all merely appetites for pleasure, it would have little bearing on the present question. What I am concerned to maintain is that men do not *now* normally desire pleasure alone, but to an important extent other things also: some in particular having impulses towards virtue, which may and do conflict with their conscious desire for their own pleasure. To say in answer to this that all men *once* desired pleasure is, from an ethical point of view, irrelevant: except on the assumption that there is an original type of man's appetitive nature, to which, as such, it is right or best for him to conform. But probably no Hedonist would expressly maintain this; though such an assumption, no doubt, is frequently made by writers of the Intuitional school.

[1] I must ask the reader to distinguish carefully the question discussed in this chapter, which relates to the *objects* of desires and aversions, from the different question whether the *causes* of these impulses are always to be found in antecedent experiences of pleasure and pain. The bearing of this latter question on Ethics, though not unimportant, is manifestly more indirect than that of the question here dealt with: and it will be convenient to postpone it till a later stage of the discussion. Cf. *post* Book II. ch. vi. § 2 and Book IV. ch. iv. § 1.

NOTE.—An interesting criticism on the views maintained in this chapter has been appended by Prof. Bain to c. 8 of his treatise on the Will [*The Emotions and the Will*, Ed. III.]. He thinks it true that we are not "every moment occupied with the thought of the subjective pleasure or pain connected with our pursuits;" and further, that "it is an advantage to intermit our subjectivity...a merit and recommendation of certain exercises, that they take us out of ourselves for the time." But he thinks that there is nothing in this "to destroy our character as rational beings, which is to desire everything exactly according to its pleasure value." For though "our desires do fasten upon the indifferent objective accompaniments of our pleasures...they do not set up these indifferent accompaniments as ends of pursuit, even when divorced from the pleasures that brought them into notice;" *e.g.* "when a man loses his enjoyment in hunting, he does not continue to desire hunting," &c.

I do not think that Mr Bain has quite apprehended the point of my argument as regards the pleasures of successful pursuit (which I have tried to make more clear in this edition). Let me take as an illustration of the point at issue the pleasure of scientific curiosity. I quite admit that one is sustained in the pursuit of truth by a consciousness of the pleasure it affords: and that if it ceased to yield such pleasure it would probably be abandoned. But I urge that this specific enjoyment is strictly unattainable, so long as one desires knowledge *merely* as a means to it: until the desire of knowledge for its own sake is somehow aroused in us, we cannot experience either the agreeable ardour of investigation or the true delight of discovery. Then when this desire has become strong, it may possibly, though it does not ordinarily, conflict with our desire for our pleasure on the whole: so that the love of knowledge may be not only disinterested but even self-sacrificing. I ought to say that Mr Bain recognizes self-sacrifice as an actual fact, but only as prompted by sympathy with other human (or sentient) beings. I quite agree with him, that on no other supposition could "the dominion of Rome have ever been established, or England have attained her present power." But I think that this recognition is rather too restricted: and that we may similarly say that without other disinterested impulses, the fabric of science would not have been constructed, nor the treasures of art accumulated.

CHAPTER V.

FREE WILL.

§ 1. In the preceding chapters I have treated first of rational, and secondly of disinterested action, without introducing the vexed question of the Freedom of the Will. The metaphysical difficulties connected with this question have been proved by long dialectical experience to be so great, that I am anxious to confine them within as strict limits as I can, and keep as much of my subject as possible free from their perturbing influence. And it appears to me that the identification which Kant and others after him have sought to establish between (1) Disinterested and Rational and (2) Rational and Free action, is in the former case opposed to psychological experience, while in the latter case it is at least misleading, and tends to obscure the real issue raised in the Free Will controversy. In the last chapter I have tried to show that action strictly disinterested, that is, disregardful of foreseen balance of pleasure to ourselves, is found in the most instinctive as well as in the most deliberate and self-conscious region of our volitional experience: nay, it appears to have a place (as far as any phenomenon known to us only by introspective observation may reasonably be thought to have a place) in the life of the lower animals. We have at any rate just as much ground for saying that a faithful dog acts disinterestedly, as we have for saying that he acts interestedly. Again, the conception of acting rationally, as explained in the last chapter but one, is certainly not bound up with the notion of acting 'freely,' as maintained by Libertarians generally against Determinists: rational action, as I conceive it, remains rational, however complete may be the triumph of Determinism. I say "Libertarians generally," because in the statements made by disciples of Kant as to the connexion of Freedom and Rationality, there appears to me to be a confusion between two meanings of the term Freedom, which require to be carefully distinguished in any discussion of Free Will. When a disciple of Kant says that a man "is a free agent in so far as he acts under the guidance of reason," the statement easily wins assent from ordinary readers; since it is no doubt true, as Whewell says, that we ordinarily "consider our Reason as being ourselves rather than our desires and affections. We speak of Desire, Love, Anger, as mastering *us*, or of *ourselves* as controlling them. If we decide to prefer some remote and abstract good to immediate pleasures, or to conform to a rule which brings us present pain, (which decision implies exercise of Reason,) we more particularly consider such acts as our *own* acts[1]." I cannot, therefore, object on the score of usage to this application of the term "free" to denote voluntary actions in which the seductive solicitations of appetite or passion are successfully resisted: and I am sensible of the gain in effectiveness of moral persuasion which is obtained by thus enlisting the powerful sentiment of Liberty on the side of Reason and Morality. But it is clear that if we say that a man is "a free agent in so far as he acts rationally," we cannot also say—in the same sense—that it is by his own "free" choice that he acts irrationally, when he does so act; and it is this latter proposition which Libertarians generally have been concerned to maintain. They have thought it of fundamental importance to show the 'Freedom' of the moral agent, on account of the connexion that they have held to exist between Freedom and Moral Responsibility: and it is obvious that the Freedom thus connected with Responsibility is not the Freedom that is only manifested in rational action, but the Freedom to choose between right and wrong which is manifested equally in either choice. Now it is I suppose an undoubted fact—to which the Christian consciousness of "wilful sin" bears testimony—that men do deliberately and with complete self-consciousness choose to act irrationally. They do not merely prefer self-interest to duty (for here is rather a conflict of claims to rationality than

[1] *Elements of Morality*, Bk. I. c. ii.

clear irrationality): but (*e.g.*) sensual indulgence to health, revenge to reputation, &c., though they know that such preference is opposed to their true interests[1]. Hence it does not really correspond to our experience as a whole to represent the conflict between Reason and passion as a conflict between 'ourselves' on the one hand and a force of nature on the other. We may say, if we like, that when we yield to passion, we become 'the slaves of our desires and appetites': but we must at the same time admit that our slavery is self-chosen. Can we say, then, of the wilful wrongdoer that his wrong choice was 'free'; meaning that he might have chosen rightly, not merely if the antecedents of his volition, external and internal, had been different, but supposing these antecedents unchanged? This, I conceive, is the substantial issue raised in the Free Will controversy; which I now propose briefly to consider. As I shall presently explain, I do not think that a solution of this metaphysical problem is really important for the general regulation of human conduct, whatever method be adopted for framing such regulation: it will appear, however, that the question has a special connexion with one department of morality, according to the common sense view of it, which hereafter in examining the Intuitional Method we shall attempt to make as precise as possible.

§ 2. We may conveniently begin by defining more exactly the notion of Voluntary action, to which, according to all methods of Ethics alike, the predicates 'right' and 'what ought to be done'—in the strictest ethical sense—are exclusively applicable. In the first place, Voluntary action is distinguished as 'conscious' from actions or movements of the human organism which are 'unconscious' or 'mechanical.' The person whose

---

[1] The difficulty which Socrates and the Socratic schools had in conceiving a man to choose deliberately what he knows to be bad for him—a difficulty which drives Aristotle into real Determinism in his account of purposed action, even while he is expressly maintaining the "voluntariness" and "responsibility" of vice—seems hardly to exist for the modern mind. This is at least partly due to the fact that we have separated the notion of 'one's own good' into the two *primâ facie* distinct notions of 'interest' and 'duty': thus, being familiar with the conception of deliberate choice, consciously opposed *either* to interest *or* to duty, we can without difficulty conceive of such choice in conscious opposition to both.

organism performs such movements only becomes aware of them, if at all, after they have been performed; accordingly they are not imputed to him as a person, or judged to be morally wrong or imprudent; though they may sometimes be judged to be good or bad in respect of their consequences, with the implication that they ought to be encouraged or checked so far as this can be done indirectly by conscious effort.

So again, in the case of conscious actions, the agent is not regarded as morally responsible, except in an indirect way, for effects which he did not foresee at the moment of volition. No doubt when a man's action has caused some unforeseen harm, the popular moral judgment often blames him for carelessness; but it would be generally admitted by reflective persons that in such cases strictly moral blame only attaches to the agent in an indirect way, in so far as his carelessness is the result of some wilful neglect of duty. Thus the proper immediate objects of moral approval or disapproval would seem to be always the results of a man's volitions so far as they were intended—*i.e.* represented in thought as certain or probable[1] consequences of such volitions—: or, more strictly, the volitions themselves in which they were so intended, since we do not consider that a man is relieved from moral blame because his wrong intention remains unrealized owing to external causes.

This view seems at first sight to differ from the common opinion that the morality of acts depends on their 'motives'; if by motives are understood the desires that we feel for some of the foreseen consequences of our acts. But I do not think that those who hold this opinion would deny that we are blameworthy for any prohibited result included in our intention, whether it was the object of desire or not. And though it is certainly held that acts, similar as regards their foreseen results, may be 'better' or 'worse'[2] through the presence of certain desires or aversions; still probably all who hold this

[1] I need not here raise the question how far we are responsible for all the foreseen consequences of our actions, or only, in the case of definite unconditional moral rules, for their results within a certain range—a question which will have to be considered when we come to examine the Intuitional Method.

[2] In a subsequent chapter (c. ix.) I shall examine more fully the relation of the antithesis 'right' and 'wrong' to the vaguer and wider antithesis 'good' and 'bad,' in our practical reasonings.

would admit on reflection that so far as these feelings are not directly under the control of the will the judgment of 'right' and 'wrong' does not strictly apply to them: but rather to the exertion or omission of voluntary effort to check bad motives and encourage good ones, or to the conscious adoption of an object of desire as an end to be aimed at—which, as I have before said, is a species of volition.

We may conclude then that judgments of right and wrong relate properly to volitions accompanied with intention— whether the intended consequences be external, or some effects produced on the agent's own feelings or character. This excludes from the scope of such judgments those conscious actions which are not intentional, strictly speaking; as when sudden strong feelings of pleasure and pain cause movements which we are aware of making, but which are not anteceded by any representation in idea either of the movements themselves or of their effects. For such actions, which we may distinguish as 'instinctive,' we are only held to be responsible indirectly so far as any bad consequences of them might have been prevented by voluntary efforts to form habits of more complete self-control.

We have to observe further that our common moral judgments recognize an important distinction between *impulsive* and *deliberate* wrongdoing, condemning the latter more strongly than the former. The line between the two cannot be sharply drawn: but we may define 'impulsive' actions as those where the connexion between the feeling that prompts and the action prompted is so simple and immediate that, though intention is distinctly present, the consciousness of personal choice of the intended result is evanescent. In deliberate volitions there is always a conscious selection of the result as one of two or more practical alternatives.

In the case, then, of volitions which are preeminently the objects of moral condemnation and approbation, the psychical fact 'volition' seems to be a somewhat complex phenomenon; including besides what I may call the mere sensation of (psychical) action[1] intention or representation of the results of

---

[1] By this phrase I mean to denote the psychical fact of volition in its most elementary form, as it exists even in instinctive actions. It might perhaps

action and also the consciousness of self as choosing, resolving, determining these results. And the question which I understand to be at issue in the Free Will controversy may be stated thus: Is the self to which I refer my deliberate volitions a self of strictly determinate moral qualities, a definite character partly inherited, partly formed by my past actions and feelings, and by any physical influences that it may have unconsciously received; so that my voluntary action, for good or for evil, is at any moment completely caused by the determinate qualities of this character, together with my circumstances, or the external influences acting on me at the moment—including under this latter term my present bodily conditions? or is there always a possibility of my choosing to act in the manner that I now judge to be reasonable and right, whatever my previous actions and experiences may have been?

I have avoided using terms which imply materialistic assumptions, because, though a materialist—in modern times—is pretty sure to be a determinist, a determinist is not always a materialist. In the above questions a materialist would substitute 'brain and nervous system' for 'character,' and thereby obtain certainly a clearer notion; but I have taken the view of common sense, or Natural Dualism, which distinguishes the agent from his body. For the present purpose the difference is unimportant. The substantial dispute relates to the completeness of the causal dependence of any volition upon the state of things at the preceding instant, whether we specify these as 'character and circumstances,' or 'brain and environing forces[1].'

be described as feeling of the kind which when intense we call effort. This feeling accompanies the initiation of muscular actions in our organism, except where these are unconscious or mechanical; but it must be distinguished from the sense of expended muscular energy: for we experience it when by an effort of self-control we resist a strong impulse to muscular action of any kind and remain passive.

[1] It is not uncommon to conceive of each volition as connected by uniform laws with our past states of consciousness. But any uniformities we might trace among a man's past consciousnesses, even if we knew them all, would yet give us very imperfect guidance as to his future action: as there would be left out of account

(1) all inborn tendencies and susceptibilities, as yet latent or incompletely exhibited;

(2) all past physical influences, of which the effects had not been perfectly represented in consciousness.

On the Determinist side there is a cumulative argument so strong as almost to amount to complete proof. The belief that events are determinately related to the state of things immediately preceding them, is now held by all competent thinkers in respect of all kinds of occurrences except human volitions. It has steadily grown both intensively and extensively, both in clearness and certainty of conviction and in universality of application, as the human mind has developed and human experience has been systematized and enlarged. Step by step in successive departments of fact conflicting modes of thought have receded and faded, until at length they have vanished everywhere, except from this mysterious citadel of Will. Everywhere else the belief is so firmly established that some declare its opposite to be inconceivable: others even maintain that it always was so. Every scientific procedure assumes it: each success of science confirms it. And not only are we finding ever new proof that events are cognizably determined, but also that the different modes of determination of different kinds of events are fundamentally identical and mutually dependent: and naturally, with the increasing conviction of the essential unity of the cognizable universe, increases the indisposition to allow the exceptional character claimed by Libertarians for the department of human action.

Again, when we fix our attention on human action, we observe that the portion of it which is originated unconsciously is admittedly determined by physical causes: and we find that no clear line can be drawn between acts of this kind, and those which are conscious and voluntary. Not only are many acts of the former class entirely similar to those of the latter, except in being unconscious: but we remark further that actions which we habitually perform continually pass from the latter class into the former: and the further we investigate, the more the conclusion is forced upon us, that there is no kind of action originated by conscious volition which cannot also, under certain circumstances, be originated unconsciously. Again, when we look closely at our conscious acts, we find that in respect of such of them as I have characterized as 'impulsive,'—acts done suddenly under the stimulus of a momentary sensation or emotion—our consciousness can hardly be said to suggest that they are not completely determined by the strength of the stimulus and the state of our previously determined temperament and character at the time of its operation: and here again, as was before observed, it is difficult to draw a line clearly separating these from the actions in which the apparent consciousness of 'free choice' becomes distinct.

Further, we always explain[1] the voluntary action of all men except ourselves on the principle of causation by character and circumstances. Indeed otherwise social life would be impossible: for the life of man in society involves daily a mass of minute forecasts of the actions of other men, founded on experience of mankind generally or of particular classes of men, or of individuals; who are thus necessarily regarded as things having determinate properties, causes whose effects are calculable. We infer generally the future actions of those whom we know from their past actions; and if our forecast turns out in any case to be erroneous, we do not attribute the discrepancy to the disturbing influence of Free Will, but to our incomplete acquaintance with their character and motives. And passing from individuals to communities, whether we believe in a "social science" or not, we all admit and take part in discussions of social phenomena in which the same principle is assumed: and however we may differ as to particular theories, we never doubt the validity of the method: and if we find anything inexplicable in history, past or present, it never occurs to us to attribute it to an extensive exercise of free will in a particular direction. Nay even as regards our own actions, however 'free' we feel ourselves at any moment, however unconstrained by present motives and circumstances and unfettered by the result of what we have previously been and felt our volitional choice may appear: still when it is once well past, and we survey it in the series of our actions, its relations of causation and resemblance to other parts of our life appear, and we naturally explain it as an effect of our nature, education and circumstances. Nay we even apply the

---

[1] I do not mean that this is the only view that we take of the conduct of others: I hold (as will presently appear) that in judging of their conduct morally, we ordinarily apply the conception of Free Will. But we do not ordinarily regard it as one kind of causation, limiting and counteracting the other kind.

same conceptions to our future action, and the more, in proportion as our moral sentiments are developed: for with our sense of duty generally increases our sense of the duty of moral culture, and our desire of self-improvement: and the possibility of moral self-culture depends on the assumption that by a present volition we can determine to some extent our actions in the more or less remote future. No doubt we habitually take at the same time the opposite, Libertarian, view as to our future: we believe, for example, that we are perfectly able to resist henceforward temptations to which we have continually yielded in the past. But it should be observed that this belief is (as moralists of all schools admit and even urge) *at any rate to a great extent* illusory and misleading. Though Libertarians contend that it is *possible* for us at any moment to act in a manner opposed to our acquired tendencies and previous customs: still, they and Determinists alike teach that it is much less easy than men commonly imagine to break the subtle unfelt trammels of habit.

It is said, however, that the conception of the Freedom of the Will, alien as it may be to speculative science, both generally and in the special department of human action, is yet indispensable to Ethics and Jurisprudence: that, as Kant says, our recognition of the moral law is *ratio cognoscendi* of the Freedom of the Will; since in judging that I "ought" to do anything I imply that I "can" do it, and similarly in praising or blaming the actions of others I imply that they "could" have acted otherwise. If a man's actions are mere links in a chain of causation which, as we trace it back, ultimately carries us to events anterior to his personal existence, he cannot, it is said, really have either merit or demerit: and thus the reasonableness of the criminal law depends on the same assumption of Free Will; since if he has not merit or demerit, it is repugnant to the moral reason and sentiments of mankind to reward or punish him.

Now it seems to me clear that this is the natural and primary view of the matter: that, on the Determinist theory, "ought," "responsibility," "desert," and similar terms, have to be used, if at all, in new significations: and that the conception of Freedom is, so to say, the hidden pivot upon which our moral sentiments naturally play. On the other hand, it seems no less undeniable that the Determinist can give to the fundamental terms of Ethics perfectly clear and definite meanings: that the distinctions thus obtained give us a practically sufficient basis for criminal law: while the normal sentiments actually existing are seen to be appropriate and useful, as a part of the natural adaptation of social man to his conditions of life. The Determinist allows that, in a sense, "ought" implies "can," that a man is only morally bound to do what is "in his power," and that only acts from which a man "could have abstained" are proper subjects of punishment or moral condemnation. But he explains "can" and "in his power" to imply only the absence of all insuperable obstacles *except* want of sufficient motive. It is precisely in such cases, he maintains, that punishment and the expression of moral displeasure are required to supply the desiderated motive force. True, the meaning of punishment is altered: it can no longer be regarded as strictly retributory, but rather as reformatory and deterrent: but it may be fairly said that this is the more practical view, and the one towards which civilization—quite apart from the Free-will controversy—seems on the whole to tend. In fact so far as the preventive view of punishment diverges in practice from the retributive view, it may largely claim the support of the common sense of mankind, as exhibited in actual legislation and administration of justice. Thus (*e.g.*) we commonly think it right to punish negligence when it causes death, without requiring proof that the negligence was the result, directly or indirectly, of wilful disregard of duty; and we do not punish such pernicious acts as rebellion or assassination less, because we know that they were done from a sincere desire to serve God or to benefit mankind: although we certainly consider the illdesert of such acts to be less in this case. If, again, the Libertarian urges that our moral feelings and judgments involve the conception of 'free' agency, since it is unreasonable to resent voluntary harm any more than involuntary, if both are equally resultant effects of complex natural forces; the Determinist answers that the reasonableness depends on the effect of the resentment, which obviously tends to prevent the one kind of action and not the other: nay, he retorts, indignation is only reasonable on the assumption that men's actions are determined by motives, among which the fear of others' indignation may be reckoned. If, finally it be maintained, that however useful moral sentiments may be on this theory, its general adoption would practically prevent their development and effective operation; it may fairly be replied, first that such an assertion stands in need of much more empirical proof than has ever yet been offered; and secondly, that, even if it were proved, to conclude from the practical efficacy of the belief to its speculative truth is to use a doubtful and now generally discredited method of inference.

§ 3. We must conclude, then, that against the formidable array of cumulative evidence offered for Determinism there is but one opposing argument of real force; the immediate affirmation of consciousness in the moment of deliberate action. And certainly, in the case of actions in which I have a distinct consciousness of choosing between alternatives of conduct, one of which I conceive as right or reasonable, I find it impossible not to think that I can now choose to do what I so conceive, however strong may be my inclination to act unreasonably, and however uniformly I may have yielded to such inclinations in the past[1]. This belief seems to me bound up with the belief that I *ought*, in the strictest sense, to choose any course; when I have ascertained the former to be to any extent illusory, the latter is immediately restricted to a corresponding extent. I recognize that each concession to vicious desire makes the difficulty of resisting it greater when the desire recurs: but the difficulty always seems to remain separated by an impassable gulf from impossibility. Whether this amounts to an affirmation of what any Libertarian metaphysicians have maintained as 'Free Will,' is a difficult and subtle question. But at any rate it will be admitted that the absence of adequate motive to do what I judge to be reasonable cannot be regarded by me, in deliberation, as a rational ground for not doing it. And since it is with the grounds or reasons of rational action, and not with

---

[1] It should be observed that it is not the possibility of merely indeterminate choice, of an "arbitrary freak of unmotived willing," with which we are concerned from an ethical point of view; but the possibility of action in conformity with practical reason.

the causes of irrational action, that Ethics is primarily concerned; there seems to be so far no practical necessity for any reflective person considering what it is reasonable for him to do, to determine the metaphysical validity of his consciousness of freedom to choose what he may conclude to be reasonable.

It may however be urged that in considering how we ought to act in any case, though we cannot suppose the action that is the immediate object of consideration to be irrational, we are obliged to take into account the probable future actions of others, and also of ourselves; and that with regard to these it is necessary to decide the question of Free Will, in order that we may know whether the future is capable of being predicted from the past. But here, again, it seems to me that no definite practical consequences would logically follow from this decision. For however far we may go in admitting Free Will as a cause, the actual operation of which may falsify the most scientific forecasts of human action, still since it is *ex hypothesi* an absolutely unknown cause, our recognition of it cannot lead us to modify any such forecasts: at most, it can only affect our reliance on them.

We may illustrate this by an imaginary extreme case. Suppose we were somehow convinced that all the planets were endowed with Free Will, and that they only maintained their periodic motions by the continual exercise of free choice, in resistance to strong centrifugal or centripetal inclinations. Our general confidence in the future of the solar system might reasonably be impaired, though it is not easy to say how much[1]: but the details of our astronomical calculations would be clearly unaffected: the free wills could in no way be taken as an element in the reckoning. And the case would be similar, I suppose, in the forecast of human conduct, if psychology and sociology should ever become exact sciences. At present, however, they are so far from being such that this additional element of uncertainty can hardly have even any emotional effect.

To sum up, we may say that, in so far as we reason to any

[1] In order to determine this we should require first to settle another disputed question, as to the general reasonableness of our expectation that the future will resemble the past.

definite conclusions concerning the future actions of ourselves or others, we must consider them as determined by unvarying laws: if they are not completely so determined our reasoning is *pro tanto* liable to error: but no other is open to us. While on the other hand, when we are ascertaining (on any principles) what choice it is reasonable to make between two alternatives of present conduct, it is just as impossible to apply determinist assumptions as it was in the former case inevitable. And from neither point of view is it practically important, for the general regulation of conduct, to decide the metaphysical question at issue in the Free-will Controversy.

§ 4. It is, however, of obvious practical importance to ascertain precisely how far the power of the will (whether metaphysically free or not) actually extends: for this defines the range within which ethical judgments are in the strictest sense applicable. This inquiry is quite independent of the question of metaphysical freedom; we might state it in Determinist terms as an inquiry into the range of effects which it would be possible to cause by human volition, provided that adequate motive were not wanting. These effects seem to be of three kinds: first, changes in the external world consequent upon muscular contractions: secondly, changes in the train of ideas and feelings that constitutes our conscious life: and thirdly, changes in the tendencies to act hereafter in certain ways under certain circumstances.

I. The sphere of volitional causation is by some confined entirely to such events as can be produced by muscular contractions: and certainly these constitute the most obvious and prominent part of it. As regards these, it is sometimes said that it is properly the muscular contraction that we will, and not the more remote effects: for these require the concurrence of other causes, and therefore we can never be absolutely certain that they will follow. But no more is it certain, strictly speaking, that the muscular contraction will follow, since our limb may be paralysed, &c. And hence some say that the immediate object of the will is some molecular change in the motor nerves. And this is no doubt an inseparable concomitant of such volitions: but we are never thinking of our motor nerves and their changes, nor indeed commonly of the muscular contractions that follow them: and therefore it seems a misuse of terms to describe either as the 'object' of the mind in willing: since it is always some more remote effect, which we consciously will and intend. Still of all effects of our will on the external world, some contraction of our muscles is always an indispensable antecedent: and when that is over our part in the causation is completed.

II. We can control to some extent our thoughts and feelings. We cannot indeed directly summon or dismiss any thought or state of consciousness: and in the case of emotion an important part of what we commonly call 'control of feeling' comes under the head just discussed. Our control over our muscles enables us to keep down the expression of the feeling and to resist its promptings to action: and as the giving free vent to a feeling tends, generally speaking, to sustain and prolong it, this muscular control amounts to a certain power over the emotion. But there is not the same connexion between our muscular system and our thoughts: and yet experience shews that most men (though some, no doubt, much more than others) can voluntarily determine the direction of their thoughts, and pursue at will a given line of meditation. How then is this control exercised, and what is it precisely that the effort of will effects? It seems to be the concentration of our consciousness on a part of that which is present to it, so that this part grows more vivid and clear, while the rest tends to become obscure and ultimately to vanish. Frequently this voluntary exertion is only needed to initiate a train of ideas, which is afterwards continued without effort: as in recalling a series of past events or going through a familiar train of reasoning. By such concentration we can free ourselves of many thoughts and feelings upon which we do not wish to dwell: but our power to do this is very limited, and if the feeling be strong and its cause persistent, it requires a very unusual effort of will to banish it thus.

III. The effect of volition, however, to which I especially wish to direct the reader's attention is the alteration in men's tendencies to future action which must be assumed to be a consequence of general resolutions as to future conduct, so far as they are effective. Even a resolution to do a particular act—if it is worth while to make it, as experience shews it to be—must be supposed to produce a change of this kind in the person who makes it: it must somehow modify his present tendencies to act in a certain way on a foreseen future occasion. But it is in making general resolutions for future conduct that it is of most practical importance for us to know what is within the power of the will. Let us take an example. A man has been in the habit of drinking too much brandy nightly: one morning he resolves that he will do so no more. In making this resolve he acts under the belief that by a present volition he can so far alter his habitual tendency to indulgence in brandy, that some hours hence he will resist the full force of his habitual craving for the stimulant. Now whether this belief is well or ill-founded is not the question usually discussed between Determinists and Libertarians: they rather debate whether in taking the resolution one is free or entirely swayed by motives, &c. At the same time the two questions are liable to be confused. It is sometimes vaguely thought that a belief in Free Will requires us to maintain that at any moment we can alter our habits to any extent by a sufficiently strong exertion. And no doubt most commonly when we make such efforts, we believe at the moment that they will be completely effectual. We will to do something hours or days hence with the same confidence with which we will to do something next minute: and do not very clearly distinguish the two. But on reflection, no one, I think, will maintain that a future act is in his power in the same sense that a present one is: or that at the moment of making such a resolution he has an immediate cognition of its future effects. Not only does continual experience shew us that such resolves have a limited and too frequently an inadequate effect: but the common belief is really inconsistent with the very doctrine of Free Will that is thought to justify it: for if by a present volition I can finally determine a future act, when the time comes to do that act I shall find myself no longer free. We must therefore accept the conclusion that each such resolve has only a limited effect: and that we cannot know when making it whether this effect will exhibit itself in the performance of the act resolved upon. At the same time it can hardly be denied that such resolves sometimes succeed in breaking old habits: and even when they fail to do this, they often substitute a painful struggle for smooth and easy indulgence. Hence it is reasonable to suppose that they always produce some effect in this direction; whether they operate by causing new motives to present themselves on the side of reason, when the time of inner conflict arrives; or whether they directly weaken the impulsive force of habit in the same manner as an actual breach of custom does, though in an inferior degree [1].

If this account of the range of volition be accepted, it will, I trust, dispel any lingering doubts which the argument of the preceding section, as to the practical unimportance of the Free Will controversy, may have left in the reader's mind. For it may have been vaguely thought that while on the Determinist theory it would be wrong, in certain cases, to perform a single act of virtue if we had no ground for believing that we should hereafter duly follow it up; on the assumption of Freedom we should boldly do always what would be best if consistently followed up, being conscious that such consistency is in our power. But the supposed difference vanishes, if it be admitted that by any effort of resolution at the present moment we can only produce a certain limited effect upon our tendencies to action at some future time, and that immediate consciousness cannot tell us that this effect will be adequate to the occasion, nor indeed how great it will really prove to be. For the most extreme Libertarian must then allow that before pledging ourselves to any future course of action we ought to estimate carefully, from our experience of ourselves and general knowledge of human nature, what the probability is of our keeping present resolutions in the cir-

[1] It should be observed that the same kind of change is sometimes brought about, without volition, by a powerful emotional shock, due to extraneous causes: and hence it might be inferred that in all cases it is a powerful impression of an emotional kind that produces the effect: and that the will is only concerned in concentrating our attention on the benefits to be gained or evils to be avoided by the change of habit, and so intensifying the impression of these. But though this kind of voluntary contemplation is a useful auxiliary to good resolutions, it does not seem to be this effort of will that constitutes the resolution: we can clearly distinguish the two. Hence this third effect of volition cannot be resolved into the second, but must be stated separately.

cumstances in which we are likely to be placed. It is no doubt morally most important that we should not tranquilly acquiesce in any weakness or want of self-control: but the fact remains that such weakness is not curable by a single volition: and whatever we can do towards curing it by any effort of will at any moment, is as clearly enjoined by reason on the Determinist theory as it is on the Libertarian. On neither theory is it reasonable that we should deceive ourselves as to the extent of our weakness, or ignore it in the forecast of our conduct, or suppose it more easily remediable than it really is.

§ 5. But though I hold, on the grounds above argued, that it is of no practical importance for a man to decide, with a view to the general regulation of his conduct, whether he is or is not a 'free agent' (in the metaphysical sense); there is a special department of his behaviour to others, in dealing with which it appears to make some practical difference whether or not he is to regard those others as having been free agents—I mean in the determination of what Justice requires him to do to them. For Justice as commonly understood implies the due requital of good and ill Desert, and the common notion of Desert, when closely scrutinized, seems (as I have already said) to involve free choice of good or evil: so that the denial of such free choice, dissipating our primitive notion of Desert, leaves us the problem of determining Justice on some different principle. Thus as we saw, on the Determinist theory, punishment is regarded as preventive instead of retributive. And though roughly and generally the two views will coincide in practice, we have already noticed that they may diverge to a considerable extent. This divergence is, perhaps, especially marked as regards the *quantity* of punishment that ought to be inflicted in any case: for example, the fact that men are urged by strong natural impulses to commit a crime may be a reason for making its punishment more severe, if this be considered purely as preventive: but it certainly seems to render the ill-desert of the act less rather than greater. But the further consideration of this point had better be deferred till we have examined more closely the notion of Justice[1].

[1] Cf. *post*, Book III. c. 5.

CHAPTER VI.

ETHICAL PRINCIPLES AND METHODS.

§ 1. THE results of the three preceding chapters may be briefly stated as follows.

The aim of Ethics is to render scientific—*i.e.* true, and as far as possible systematic—the apparent cognitions that most men have of the rightness or reasonableness of conduct, whether the conduct be considered as right in itself, or as the means to some end conceived as ultimately reasonable[1]. These cognitions are normally accompanied by emotions of various kinds, known as "moral sentiments:" but an ethical judgment cannot be explained as affirming merely the existence of such a sentiment: indeed it is an essential characteristic of a moral feeling that it is bound up with an apparent cognition of something more than mere feeling. Such cognitions, again, I have called 'dictates,' or 'imperatives'; because, in so far as they relate to conduct on which one is deliberating, they are accompanied by a certain impulse to do the acts recognized as right. For ethical purposes it is not of primary importance to determine anything more about this impulse than the direction in which it prompts: if a man acts in accordance with his conceptions of duty, the main question is, whether these con-

[1] As I have before said, the applicability of a method for determining right conduct relatively to an ultimate end—whether Happiness or Perfection—does not necessarily depend on the acceptance of the end as prescribed by reason: it only requires that it should be in some way adopted as ultimate and paramount. I have, however, confined my attention in this treatise to ends which are widely accepted as reasonable: and I shall afterwards endeavour to exhibit the self-evident practical axioms which appear to me to be implied in this acceptance. Cf. *post*, Book III. c. 13.

ceptions are true or false: the exact characteristics of the emotional states that precede his volitions are a matter of only secondary concern. And this remains true even if the force actually operating on his will is mere desire for the pleasures that he foresees will attend right conduct, or aversion to the pains that will result from doing wrong: though we observe that in this case his action does not correspond to our common notion of strictly virtuous conduct: and though there seems to be no ground for regarding such desires and aversions as the sole, or even the normal motives of human volitions. Nor, again, is it necessary to determine whether we are always, metaphysically speaking, 'free' to do what we see to be right. What I 'ought' to do, in the strictest use of the word 'ought,' is always 'in my power,' in the sense that there is no obstacle to my doing it except absence of adequate motive; and it is impossible for me, in deliberation, to regard such absence of motive as a reason for not doing what I otherwise judge to be reasonable.

What then do we commonly regard as valid ultimate reasons for acting or abstaining? This, as was said, is the starting point for the discussions of the present treatise: which is not primarily concerned with proving or disproving the validity of any such reasons, but rather with the critical exposition of the different 'methods'—or rational procedures for determining right conduct in any particular case—which are logically connected with the different ultimate reasons widely accepted. In the first chapter we found that such reasons were supplied by the notions of Happiness, Perfection (including Virtue or Moral Perfection as a prominent element), regarded as ultimate ends, and Duty as prescribed by unconditional rules. It may seem, however, that these notions by no means exhaust the list of reasons which are widely accepted as ultimate grounds of action. Many religious persons think that the highest reason for doing anything is that it is God's Will: while to others 'Self-realization' or 'Self-development,' and to others, again, 'Life according to nature' appear the really ultimate ends. And it is not hard to understand why such principles as these are felt to supply deeper and more completely satisfying answers to the fundamental question of Ethics, than those before named. For the latter do not merely define 'what ought to be,' as such; they define it in an apparently simple and universal relation to what is. God, Nature, Self, are the fundamental facts of existence; the knowledge of what will accomplish God's Will, what is 'according to Nature,' what will realize the true Self in each of us, would seem to solve the deepest problems of Metaphysics as well as of Ethics. But just because these notions combine the ideal with the actual, the complete examination of them belongs in my view not to Ethics as I define it, but to Philosophy—or whatever we call the supreme architectonic study which is concerned with the relations of all objects of knowledge. When, on the other hand, we confine our attention to the strictly practical import of each notion, we find that, in so far as it is ascertainable by reasoning and reflection, it is always found to be identical with one or other of the principles previously distinguished.

To begin with the theological conception of 'God's Will.' Here the connexion between 'what is' and 'what ought to be' is perfectly clear and explicit. The content of God's Will we conceive as presently existing, in idea: its actualization is the end to be aimed at. There is indeed a difficulty in understanding how God's Will can fail to be realized, whether we do right or wrong: or how, if it cannot fail to be realized in either case, its realization can be the ultimate reason for doing right. But this difficulty it belongs to Theology rather than Ethics to solve. The practical question is, assuming that God wills in a special sense what we ought to do, how we are to ascertain this in any particular case. This must be either by Revelation or by Reason, or by both combined. If an external Revelation is proposed as the standard, we are obviously carried beyond the range of our science: on the other hand, when we try to ascertain by reason the Divine Will, the practical result seems always to lead us back, directly or indirectly, into one or other of the methods already marked out; since we cannot know anything to be the Divine Will, which we do not also, by the same exercise of thought, know to be reasonable. Thus either it is assumed that God desires the happiness of men, in which case our efforts should be concentrated on its production: or that He desires their perfection and that that should be our end: or that whatever His end may be (into which perhaps we have no right to inquire) His Laws are immediately cognizable, being in fact the first principles of Intuitional Morality. Or else it is explained that God's Will is to be learnt by examining our own constitution or that of the world we are in: so that 'Conformity to God's Will' would resolve itself into 'Self-realization,' or 'Life according to nature.' In any case, this notion, though it may supply a new motive for doing what we believe to be right, does not—apart from Revelation—suggest any special criterion of rightness. It rather presents itself as a common form under which a religious mind is disposed to regard whatever method of determining conduct it apprehends to be rational.

§ 2. The implication of 'what is' and 'what ought to be' in the notion of 'Conformity to Nature' and 'Self-realization' is somewhat more difficult to disentangle. The latter it will be convenient to consider in the following chapter: where I shall distinguish different interpretations of the term 'Egoism,' which I have taken to denote one of the three principal species of ethical method. As regards the former, in order to obtain a principle distinct from 'Self-realization,' we must suppose that the 'Nature' to which we are to conform is not each one's own individual nature, but human nature generally: that we are to find the standard in a certain type of human existence which we can somehow abstract from observation of actual human lives. And the belief that it is our duty to conform to such a type must depend on the Theism implicit in the notion of 'Nature'; that is, on the more or less definite recognition of Design exhibited in the empirically known world. Can we, then, by contemplating the actual constitution of human beings, and the *ensemble* of their impulses and dispositions, ascertain what kind of life they were designed to live? It is, perhaps, not difficult to describe, in a way that all would accept, the general outline of man's natural life; but I do not see how we can obtain from such a description a method for solving practical problems. For it does not help us to say with Butler "that the supremacy of Reason is Natural," as we start by assuming that we are to do what Reason prescribes, and that this is conformity to Nature, and so our line of thought would become circular: the Nature that we are to follow must be distinguished from our Practical Reason, if it is to become a guide to it. In a sense, as Butler observes, any impulse is natural: but it is manifestly idle to bid us follow Nature in this sense: for the question of duty is never raised except when we are conscious of a conflict of impulses, and wish to know which to follow. How then are we to distinguish 'natural impulses'—in the sense in which they are to guide rational choice—from the unnatural? Those who have occupied themselves with this distinction seem generally to have interpreted the Natural to mean either the *common* as opposed to the rare and exceptional, or the *original* as opposed to what is later in development; or, negatively, what is not the effect of human volition. But it can hardly be maintained explicitly that the frequency of an impulse or the priority of its appearance in time is clearly indicative that God designs us to follow it: especially since, when we take a retrospective view of the history of the human race, we find that some impulses which all admire, such as the love of knowledge and enthusiastic philanthropy, are both rarer and later in their appearance than others which all despise. Nor, again, can we eschew as unnatural and opposed to the Divine design all such impulses as have been produced in us by the institutions of society, or our use of human arrangements and contrivances, or that result in any way from the deliberate action of our fellow-men: for this were arbitrarily to exclude society and human action from the scope of the Divine purposes. And besides it is clear that many impulses so generated are auxiliary to morality and in other ways beneficial; and though others no doubt are pernicious and misleading, it seems that we can only distinguish these latter from the former by taking note of their effects, and not by any precision that reflection can give to the notion of 'natural.' If, again, we fall back upon a more physical view of our nature and endeavour to ascertain for what end our corporeal frame was constructed, we find that such contemplation determines very little. We can infer from our nutritive system that we are intended to take food, and similarly that we are to exercise our various muscles in some way or other, and our brain and organs of sense. But this carries us a very trifling way, for the practical question almost always is, not whether we are to use our organs or leave them unused, but to what extent or in what manner we are to use them: and it does not appear that a definite answer to this question can ever be elicited, by a logical process of inference, from observations of what actually exists.

Nor, again, does it help us to adopt the more modern view of Nature, which regards the organic world as exhibiting, not an aggregate of fixed types, but a continuous and gradual process of changing life. For granting that this 'evolution'—as the name implies—is not merely a process from old to new, but a progress from less to more of certain definite characteristics; no one, I think, will deliberately maintain that we ought *therefore* to take these characteristics as Ultimate Good, and make it our whole endeavour to accelerate the arrival of an inevitable future. That whatever is to be will be better than what is, we all hope; but there seems to be no more reason for summarily identifying 'what ought to be' with 'what certainly will be,' than for finding it in 'what commonly is,' or 'what originally was.'

On the whole, it appears to me that no definition that has ever been offered of the Natural exhibits this notion as really capable of furnishing an independent ethical first principle. And no one maintains that 'natural' like 'beautiful' is a notion that though indefinable is yet clear, being derived from a simple unanalysable impression. Hence I see no way of extracting from it a definite practical criterion of the rightness of actions.

§ 3. It thus appears that not all the different views that are taken of the ultimate reason for observing rules of conduct lead to different methods of determining what these rules shall be. Indeed we seem to find on closer examination that almost any method may be connected with almost any ultimate reason by means of some possible—or even plausible—assumption. Hence arises considerable perplexity and confusion in the classification and comparison of ethical systems: for these appear to have different affinities according as we consider Method or Ultimate Reason, and hence are not easy to classify even when both elements are made clear: which is often not the case, as some writers lay stress on Method, and are hesitating and uncertain in their enunciation of Ultimate Reason, while others chiefly confine themselves to the discussion of the latter and leave the former obscure.

These and other difficulties in our classification will be seen more clearly as our investigation proceeds. In the meantime the list of first principles already given seems to me to omit none that has a valid claim to independent consideration; and it corresponds to what seem the most fundamental distinctions that we apply to human existence; the distinction between the conscious being and the stream of conscious experience, and the distinction (within this latter) of Action and Feeling. For Perfection is thought to be the goal of the development of a human being, considered as a permanent entity; while by Duty, we mean the kind of Action that we think ought to be done; and similarly by Happiness or Pleasure we mean an ultimately desired or desirable kind of Feeling. At the same time I do not profess to prove *a priori* that there are these practical first principles and no more; nor, again, that my statement of methods gives an exhaustive analysis of all possible modes of determining right conduct. My results have been reached merely empirically, by reflection on the moral reasoning of myself and other men, whether professed moralists or not: and though it seems to me improbable that I have overlooked any important phase of method, it is always possible that I may have done so.

On the other hand my primary threefold division of methods may by some readers be blamed for excess rather than defect. Having been taught to believe that "the common sense of mankind has in every age led to *two* seemingly opposite schemes of morality, that which makes *Virtue* and that which makes *Pleasure* the guide of human action;" they may consider it a fault in my treatment of the subject that it somewhat obliterates this fundamental distinction. In my view, however, it is of the greatest importance to avoid any identification or blending of Egoistic and Universalistic Hedonism, and even any representation of their differences as secondary and subordinate; since the distinction between aiming at one's own and aiming at the general happiness appears to me one of the most fundamental that morality exhibits. No doubt it is a postulate of the practical Reason, that it must be consistent with itself: and hence we have a strong predisposition to reduce any two methods to unity. But it is just because this postulate has been the source of a large amount of bad reasoning in ethics, that it is a special object of the present work to avoid all hasty and premature reconciliations, and to exhibit fairly the divergence of the different methods without extenuation or exaggeration: and no divergence is *primâ facie* more obvious and glaring than that between the two systems not unfrequently confounded under the name of Utilitarianism.

At the same time it is not difficult to find reasons for this close union between Epicureanism and the Universalistic, or Benthamite[1] Hedonism, to which I propose to restrict the term Utilitarianism. In the first place, they are essentially similar in being both *dependent* systems; that is, in prescribing actions as means to an end distinct from, and lying outside the actions; and thus both consist of rules which are not absolute but relative, and only valid if they conduce to the end. Again, the ultimate end is in both systems the same in quality, *i.e.* pleasure; or, more strictly, the maximum of pleasure attainable, pains being subtracted. Besides, it is of course to a great extent true that the conduct recommended by the one principle coincides with that inculcated by the other. Though it would seem to be only in an ideal polity that 'self-interest well understood' leads to the perfect discharge of all social duties, still, in a tolerably well-ordered community it prompts to the fulfilment of most of them, unless under very exceptional circumstances. And, on the other hand, a sincere Benthamite may fairly hold that his own happiness is that portion of the universal good which it is most in his power to promote, and which therefore is most especially entrusted to his charge. And the practical blending of the two systems is sure to go beyond their theoretical coincidence. It is much easier for a man to move in a sort of diagonal between egoistic and universalistic hedonism, than to be practically a consistent adherent of either. Few men are so completely selfish, whatever their theory of morals may be, as not occasionally to seek the general good of some smaller or larger community from natural sympathetic impulse unsupported by Epicurean calculation. And probably still fewer are so resolutely unselfish as never to find "all men's good" in their own with rather too ready conviction.

[1] See note at the end of the chapter.

In spite of all this, the distinction between one's own happiness and that of people in general is so natural and obvious, and so continually forced upon our attention by the circumstances of life; that some other reason is required to explain the persistent confusion between the systems that respectively adopt either end as furnishing the right and reasonable standard for each individual's conduct. And such a reason is found in the theory of human action held by Bentham (and generally speaking by his disciples), which has been discussed in a previous chapter—the doctrine, I mean, that every human being always does aim at his own greatest apparent happiness: and that, consequently it is useless to point out to a man the conduct that would conduce to the general happiness, unless you convince him at the same time that it would conduce to his own. On this view, egoistic and universalistic considerations must necessarily be combined in any practical treatment of morality: and this being so, it was perhaps to be expected that Bentham[1] or his disciples would go further, and attempt to base on the Egoism which they accept as inevitable the Universalistic Hedonism which they approve and inculcate. And accordingly we find that the latest expositor of Utilitarianism, J. S. Mill, does try to establish a logical connexion between the psychological and ethical principles which he holds in common with Bentham, and to convince his readers that because each man naturally seeks his own happiness, therefore he ought to seek the happiness of other people[2].

Nevertheless, it can hardly be denied that the affinity between Utilitarianism and Intuitionism, if we consider not the principles of the methods but their practical results, is really much greater than that between the two forms of Hedonism. Many moralists who have maintained as practically valid the judgments of right and wrong which the Common Sense of mankind seems intuitively to enunciate, have yet regarded Happiness as an end to which the rules of morality were means. I do not mean merely that they believed happiness to

---

[1] See note at the end of the chapter.
[2] We shall have occasion to consider Mill's argument on this point in a subsequent chapter. Cf. *post*, Book III. c. 13.

be annexed as a Divine reward to the observance of these rules: but that they believed that such observance by any individual tended naturally to promote general happiness, and that the rules had been implanted by Nature or revealed by God to this end. Such a belief implies that, though I am bound to take, as *my* ultimate standard in acting, conformity to a rule which is for me absolute, still the Divine and (we may say) *intrinsic* reason for the rule laid down is Utilitarian. On this view, the *method* of Utilitarianism is certainly rejected: the connexion between right action and happiness is not ascertained by a process of reasoning. But we can hardly say that the Utilitarian principle is altogether rejected: rather the limitations of the human reason are supposed to prevent it from apprehending adequately the real connexion between the true principle and the right rules of conduct. This connexion, however, has always been to a large extent recognized by all reflective persons. Indeed so clear is it that in most cases the observance of the commonly received moral rules tends to render human life tranquil and happy, that even moralists (as Whewell) who are most strongly opposed to Utilitarianism have, in attempting to exhibit the "necessity" of moral rules, been led to dwell on utilitarian considerations.

And during the first period of ethical controversy in modern England, after the audacious enunciation of Egoism by Hobbes had roused in real earnest the search for a philosophical basis of morality, Utilitarianism appears in friendly alliance with Intuitionism. It was not to supersede but to support the morality of Common Sense, against the dangerous innovations of Hobbes, that Cumberland declared "the common good of all Rationals" to be the end to which moral rules were the means. We find him quoted with approval by Clarke, who is commonly taken to represent Intuitionism in an extreme form. Nor does Shaftesbury, in introducing the theory of a "moral sense," seem to have dreamt that it could ever impel us to actions not clearly conducive to the Good of the Whole: and his disciple Hutcheson expressly identified its promptings with those of Benevolence. Butler, I think, was the first writer who dwelt on the discrepancies between Virtue as commonly understood and "conduct likeliest to produce an overbalance of happiness[1]. When Hume presented Utilitarianism as a mode of explaining current morality, it was seen or suspected to have a partially destructive tendency. But it was not till the time of Paley and Bentham that it was offered as a method for determining conduct, which was to overrule all traditional precepts and supersede all existing moral sentiments. And even this complete and final antagonism relates rather to theory and method than to practical results: indeed the discrepancy in results between Utilitarianism and Common Sense has been rather extenuated than exaggerated by most utilitarians. The practical conflict, in ordinary human minds, is so palpably between Self-interest and Social Duty, however determined, that the sense of this continually tends to draw together Utilitarianism and Intuitionism into their old alliance. Indeed from a practical point of view Egoism and Utilitarianism may fairly be regarded as extremes between which the Common-Sense morality is a kind of *media via*. For this latter is commonly thought to leave a man free to pursue his own happiness under certain definite limits and conditions: whereas the "greatest happiness of the greatest number" seems to self-love a principle more oppressive from the comprehensive, indefinite, and unceasing character of its exactions. And thus, as Mill remarks, Utilitarianism is sometimes attacked from two precisely opposite sides: from a confusion with Egoistic Hedonism it is called base and grovelling: while at the same time it is more plausibly charged with setting up too high a standard of unselfishness and making exaggerated demands on human nature.

A good deal remains to be said, in order to make the principle and method of Utilitarianism perfectly clear and explicit: but it seems best to defer this till we come to the investigation of its details. It will be convenient to take this as the final stage of our examination of methods. For on the one hand it is simpler that the discussion of Egoistic should precede that

---

[1] See Dissertation II. *Of the Nature of Virtue* appended to the *Analogy*. It may be interesting to notice a gradual change in Butler's view on this important point. In the first of his Sermons on Human Nature published some years ago before the *Analogy* he does not notice, any more than Shaftesbury and Hutcheson, any possible want of harmony between Conscience and Benevolence. A note to Sermon XII., however, seems to indicate a stage of transition between the view of the first Sermon and the view of the Dissertation.

of Universalistic Hedonism: and on the other, it seems desirable that we should obtain in as exact a form as possible the enunciations of Intuitive Morality, before we compare these with the results of the more doubtful and difficult calculations of utilitarian consequences.

In the remaining chapters of this Book I shall endeavour to remove certain ambiguities as to the general nature and relations of the other two methods, as designated respectively by the terms Egoism and Intuitionism, before proceeding to the fuller examination of them in Books II. and III.

NOTE.—I have called the ethical doctrine that takes universal happiness as the ultimate end and standard of right conduct by the name of Bentham, because the thinkers who have chiefly taught this doctrine in England during the present century have referred it to Bentham as their master. And it certainly seems to me clear—though Mr Bain (cf. *Mind*, January, 1883, p. 48) appears to doubt it —that Bentham adopted this doctrine explicitly, in its most comprehensive scope, at the earliest stage in the formation of his opinions; nor do I think that he ever consciously abandoned or qualified it. We find him writing in his common-place book, in 1773—4 (cf. *Works*, Bowring's edition, vol. x. p. 70), that Helvetius had "established a standard of rectitude for actions";—the standard being that "a sort of action is a right one, when the tendency of it is to augment the mass of happiness in the community." And we find him writing fifty years later (cf. *Works*, vol. x. p. 79) the following account of his earliest view, in a passage which contains no hint of later dissent from it. "By an early pamphlet of Priestley's...light was added to the warmth. In the phrase 'the greatest happiness of the greatest number,' I then saw delineated, for the first time, a plain as well as a true standard for whatever is right or wrong...in human conduct *whether in the field of morals or of politics.*"

At the same time I must admit that in other passages Bentham seems no less explicitly to adopt Egoistic Hedonism as the method of 'private Ethics' as distinct from Legislation: and in his posthumous 'Deontology' the two principles appear to be reconciled by the doctrine, that it is always the individual's true interest, even from a purely mundane point of view, to act in the manner most conducive to the general happiness. This latter proposition—which I regard as erroneous—is not, I think, definitely put forward in any of the treatises published by Bentham in his life-time, or completely prepared by him for publication: but I must confess that after carefully studying these treatises—especially the "Principles of Morals and Legislation "—I am unable to elicit from them a clear and definite view as to the relations of Egoistic and Universalistic Hedonism, in the field of private morality.

CHAPTER VII.

EGOISM AND SELF-LOVE.

§ 1. In the preceding chapters I have used the term "Egoism," as is now commonly done, to denote a system which prescribes actions as means to the end of the individual's happiness or pleasure. The ruling motive in such a system is commonly said to be "self-love." But both terms admit of other interpretations, which it will be well to distinguish and set aside before proceeding further, as the ambiguous meaning of "egoism" and "self-love" has been a frequent source of confusion in ethical discussion.

I may illustrate this by a reference to the doctrines of Hobbes. His method is naturally and quite properly called egoistic, but it is not throughout, strictly speaking, hedonistic. In fact his deviations from pure Hedonism are considerable: and it is of some interest to notice them, as they are essential characteristics of his system, which in its original plan and purpose, (though not perhaps in its effect upon mankind,) was the reverse of destructive. His aim was to promulgate philosophical principles of conduct upon which the social order might firmly rest, and escape the storms and convulsions with which it seemed to be menaced from the vagaries of the unenlightened conscience. Now pure egoistic hedonism, as I shall presently shew, cannot furnish a solid basis for such social construction: and even such imperfect constructiveness as Hobbism attained is only managed by means of qualifications and assumptions alien to pure Hedonism. For example, it is not "self-love" in Butler's sense—the object of which is the individual's pleasure—but "self-preservation," which determines the first of those precepts of rational egoism which he calls "Laws of Nature." It is true that his psychological theory that "pleasure helpeth vital actions" made him to some extent blend the two notions: for so by aiming at pleasure a man would seek to increase if not strictly to preserve his vitality. Still in the development of his system we often find that it is Preservation rather than Pleasure that he has in view. I do not mean, merely that he considers social rules to be enjoined by prudence on the individual as "articles of peace:" for peace is a means to the end of Pleasure as well as of Preservation. But in determining the very important question, when the same prudence or egoistic reason will prompt the individual *not* to conform to his articles of peace, he decides that such non-conformity is justifiable at the point at which submission would tend to interfere not with his pleasure, but with his life and freedom of action; "when death or imprisonment are threatened" by society.

Again in Spinoza's view the principle of rational action is necessarily egoistic, and is (as with Hobbes) the impulse of self-preservation. The individual mind, says Spinoza, like everything else, strives so far as it is able to continue in its state of being: indeed this effort is its very essence. It is true that the object of this impulse cannot be separated from pleasure or joy: because pleasure or joy is "a passion in which the soul passes to higher perfection." Still it is not at Pleasure that the impulse primarily aims, but at the mind's Perfection or Reality: as we should now say, at Self-development. Of this, according to Spinoza, the highest form consists in a clear comprehension of all things in their necessary order as modifications of the one Divine Being, and that willing acceptance of all which springs from this comprehension. In this state the mind is purely active, without any admixture of passion or passivity: and thus its essential nature is realized or actualized to the greatest possible degree.

We perceive that this is the notion of self-realization as defined not only *by* but *for* a philosopher: and that it would mean something quite different in the case of a man of action

—such, for example, as the reflective dramatist of Germany introduces exclaiming:

> Ich kann mich nicht
> Wie so ein Wortheld, so ein Tugend-Schwätzer
> An meinem Willen warmen, und Gedanken.....
> Wenn ich nicht wirke mehr, bin ich vernichtet[1].

The artist again often contemplates his essentially different manner of life under the same notion: and moralists of a certain turn of mind, in all ages, have regarded the sacrifice of inclination to duty as the highest form of self-development; and held that true self-love prompts us always to obey the commands issued by the governing principle—Reason or Conscience—within us, as in such obedience, however painful, we shall be realizing our truest self.

We see, in short, that the term Egoism, as it merely implies that some reference to self is made in laying down first principles of conduct, does not really indicate in any way the substance of such principles. For all our impulses, high and low, sensual and moral alike, are so far similarly related to self, that—except when two or more impulses come into conscious conflict—we identify ourselves with each as it arises. Thus self-consciousness may be prominent in yielding to any impulse: and egoism, in so far as it merely implies such prominence, is a notion equally applicable to all varieties of external behaviour, and a common form into which any moral system may be thrown.

It may be said, however, that we do not, properly speaking, 'develope' or 'realize' self by yielding to the impulse which happens to be predominant in us; but by exercising, each in its due place and proper degree, all the different faculties, capacities, and propensities, of which our nature is made up. But here there is an important ambiguity. What do we mean by 'due proportion and proper degree'? These terms may imply an ideal, into conformity with which the individual mind has to be trained, by restraining some of its natural impulses and strengthening others, and developing its higher faculties rather than its lower: or they may merely refer to the original combination and proportion of tendencies in the character with

---

[1] Schiller's *Wallenstein*.

which each is born; to this, it may be meant, we ought to adapt as far as possible the circumstances in which we place ourselves and the functions which we choose to exercise, in order that we may "be ourselves," "live our own life," &c. According to the former interpretation rational Self-development is merely another term for the pursuit of Perfection for oneself: while in the latter sense it hardly appears that Self-development (when clearly distinguished) is really put forward as an absolute end, but rather as a means to happiness; for supposing a man to have inherited propensities clearly tending to his own unhappiness, no one would recommend him to develope these as fully as possible, instead of modifying or subduing them in some way. But it is sometimes thought that actually the best way of seeking happiness is to give free play to one's nature; a view which we shall hereafter consider more fully in the course of our examination of Hedonism.

The notion, then, of Self-realization is to be avoided in a treatise on ethical method, on account of its indefiniteness: and for a similar reason we must discard a common account of Egoism which describes its ultimate end as the 'good' of the individual: for the term 'good' really contains undeveloped (but therefore unreconciled) all possible views of the ultimate end of rational conduct. Indeed it may be said that Egoism in this sense was assumed in the whole ethical controversy of ancient Greece. For when men inquired, "What is the Supreme Good?" they meant the supreme good for each individual inquirer[1], and assumed that this was for him the right and proper end of action. But the question still remained open whether it was Pleasure or Virtue, or anything else, that was intrinsically Good or the Highest Good. Nor is the ambiguity removed if we follow Aristotle in confining our attention to the Good attainable in human life, and call this Εὐδαιμονία, Wellbeing. For we may still argue with the Stoics, that virtuous or excellent actions and not pleasures are the elements of which true human Well-being is composed. Indeed Aristotle himself

---

[1] I shall afterwards try to explain how it comes about that, in modern thought, the proposition 'My own Good is my only reasonable ultimate end' is not a mere tautology, even though we define 'Good' as that at which it is ultimately reasonable to aim. Cf. *post*, Book III. chaps. xiii. xiv.

adopts this view, and determines the details of εὐδαιμονία accordingly: though he does not, with the Stoics, regard the pursuit of Virtue and that of Pleasure as competing alternatives, holding rather that the "best pleasure" is an inseparable concomitant of the most excellent action. Even the English term Happiness is not free from a similar ambiguity[1]. It seems, indeed, to be commonly used in Bentham's way as convertible with Pleasure,—or rather as denoting that of which the elements are pleasures—; and it is in this sense that I think it most convenient to use it. Sometimes, however, in ordinary discourse, the term is rather employed to denote a particular kind of agreeable consciousness, which is distinguished from and even contrasted with definite specific pleasures—such as the gratifications of sensual appetite or other keen and vehement desires—as being at once calmer and more indefinite: we may characterize it as the feeling which accompanies the normal activity of a "healthy mind in a healthy body," and of which specific pleasures seem to be rather stimulants than elements. Sometimes, again—though, I think, with a more manifest divergence from common usage—"happiness" or "true happiness" is understood in a definitely non-hedonistic sense, as denoting results other than agreeable feelings of any kind[2].

[1] Aristotle's selection of εὐδαιμονία to denote what he elsewhere calls "Human" or "Practicable" good, and still more the fact that, after all, we have no better rendering for εὐδαιμονία than "Happiness" or "Felicity," has caused his whole system to be misunderstood: so that he is often erroneously thought to have taught a doctrine resembling modern Hedonism. We may conjecture that it was not without doing some violence to common usage that Aristotle could bring his readers to understand by εὐδαιμονία that kind of Well-being that consists of Well-doing, and of which pleasure is not the element but the inseparable concomitant: and if the term "happiness" is used, it is almost impossible for the English reader to seize Aristotle's exact view. Thus when Stewart (*Philosophy of the Active and Moral Powers*, Book II. ch. 2) says that "by many of the best of the ancient moralists...the whole of ethics was reduced to this question... What is most conducive on the whole to our happiness?" the remark, if not exactly false, is certain to mislead his readers, since by Stewart as by most English writers "Happiness" is definitely conceived as consisting of "Pleasures" or "Enjoyments."

[2] Thus Green (*Prolegomena to Ethics*, Book III. ch. iv. § 228) says, "it is the realisation of those objects in which we are mainly interested, *not the succession of enjoyments which we shall experience in realising them*, that forms the definite content of our idea of true happiness, so far as it has such content at all." Cf. also § 238.

§ 2. To be clear, then, we must particularize as the object of self-love, and End of the method which I have distinguished as Egoistic Hedonism, the kind of feeling which we call Pleasure[1], taken in its widest sense, as including every species of "delight," "enjoyment," or "satisfaction;" except so far as any particular species may be excluded by its incompatibility with some greater pleasures, or as necessarily involving concomitant or subsequent pains. It is obvious that Hedonism, strictly understood, should be a method that aims at pleasure as pleasure and nothing else; and so at pleasure generally, not any particular kind of pleasure. And Self-love, as understood by Butler and other English moralists after him, is similarly a desire of one's own pleasure generally, and of the greatest amount of it obtainable, from whatever source it may be obtained. In fact, it is upon this generality and comprehensiveness that the 'authority' 'and reasonableness' attributed to it in Butler's system are founded. For since satisfaction or pleasure of some kind results from gratifying any impulse; when antagonistic impulses compete for the determination of the Will, the desire for pleasure in general prompts us to compare the pleasures which we foresee will respectively attend their gratification, and when we have ascertained which set of pleasures is the greatest, reinforces the corresponding impulse. It is thus called into play whenever impulses conflict, and is therefore naturally regulative and directive (as Butler argues) of other springs of action. On this view, so far as Self-love operates, we merely consider the *amount* of pleasure or satisfaction: to use Bentham's illustration, "quantity of pleasure being equal, push-pin is as good as poetry."

This position, however, seems to many offensively paradoxical; and consequently an eminent disciple of Bentham[2] has thought it desirable to abandon it and to take into account differences in quality among pleasures as well as differences in degree. Now here we may observe, first, that it is quite consistent with the view quoted as Bentham's to describe some kinds of pleasure as inferior in quality to others, if by 'a pleasure' we mean (as is often meant) a whole state of consciousness which

---

[1] See the note at the end of the chapter.
[2] J. S. Mill.

is only partly pleasurable; and still more if we take into view subsequent states causally connected with this. For many pleasures are not free from pain even while enjoyed: and many more have painful consequences. These are, in Bentham's phrase, "impure:" and as the pain has to be set off against the pleasure, it is in accordance with strictly quantitative measurement of pleasure to call them inferior in kind. And again, we must be careful not to confound intensity of *pleasure* with intensity of *sensation*: as a pleasant feeling may be strong and absorbing, and yet not so pleasant as another that is more subtle and delicate. With these explanations, it seems to me that in order to develope consistently the method that takes pleasure as the sole ultimate end of rational conduct, Bentham's proposition must be accepted, and all *qualitative* comparison of pleasures must really resolve itself into quantitative. All pleasures are understood to be so called because they have a common property of pleasantness, and may therefore be compared in respect of this common property. If, then, what we are seeking is pleasure as such, and pleasure alone, we must evidently always prefer the more pleasant pleasure to the less pleasant: no other choice seems reasonable, unless we are aiming at something besides pleasure. And often when we say that one kind of pleasure is better than another—as (*e.g.*) that the pleasures of reciprocated affections are superior in quality to the pleasures of gratified appetite—we mean that they are more pleasant. No doubt we may mean something else: we may mean, for instance, that they are nobler and more elevated, although less pleasant. But thus we are clearly introducing a non-hedonistic ground of preference: and if this is held to be a valid reason for choosing the less pleasure rather than the greater, the method adopted may fairly be called Intuitionism in the garb of Hedonism.

To sum up, Egoism, if we merely understand by it a method that aims at Self-realization, seems to be a form into which almost any ethical system may be thrown, without modifying its essential characteristics. And even when further defined as Egoistic Hedonism, it becomes indistinguishable from some phase of Intuitionism if qualitative superiority of pleasures is admitted as distinct from and overruling quantitative. There remains then Pure or Quantitative Egoistic Hedonism, which, as a method essentially distinct from all others and widely maintained to be rational, seems to deserve a detailed examination. According to this the rational agent regards quantity of consequent pleasure and pain to himself as alone important in choosing between alternatives of action; and seeks always the greatest attainable surplus of pleasure over pain—which, without violation of usage, we may designate as his 'greatest happiness.' It seems to be this view and attitude of mind which is commonly intended by the vaguer terms 'egoism,' 'egoistic:' and therefore I shall allow myself to use these terms in this more precise signification.

NOTE.—The terms "Interest" and "Happiness" are generally used by Butler and his followers, no less than by Bentham and the utilitarians, to denote the total or aggregate of agreeable feeling at which "Self-love" or "Self-regard" is conceived to aim, and of which the elements are variously spoken of as "pleasures," "delights," "enjoyments," "satisfactions." Of these terms I have selected 'pleasure' as that best adapted to denote generally the kind of feeling which we desire to sustain or produce in our conscious experience; as "delight," and perhaps "enjoyment," seems only appropriate to designate such feelings when they reach a certain degree of intensity; and "satisfaction," again, is most properly applied to the pleasures that attend upon the attainment of a desired object. I observe, however, that in Green's *Prolegomena to Ethics* the term "satisfaction" is used in a peculiar sense in which it is expressly distinguished from pleasure; since the author, while holding as I do that pleasure is not the sole object of desire or conscious pursuit, still maintains that "in all willing" or "all enacted desire" there is "self-satisfaction sought" (pp. 163, 5). Green's statements do not appear to me to give explicitly any definite positive notion of this self-satisfaction; but since it is explained to be "a certain possible state" of the agent "which in the gratification of his desire he seeks to reach," and yet is not pleasure, I infer that it is the cognitive or intellectual element of the consciousness of attainment, as distinguished from the emotional or sensational element. To this view there appear to me to be two decisive objections: (1) many men often desire and aim at other objects besides their own conscious states—(*e. g.*) materialists aim at the welfare of remote posterity: and (2) the mere thought or cognition of fulfilled desire—as distinguished on the one hand from the fact of fulfilment or the existence of the desired object, and on the other hand from the agreeable feeling included in the consciousness of fulfilment—is not desired or judged desirable by me; nor, as I believe, by others.

CHAPTER VIII.

INTUITIONISM.

§ 1. I HAVE used the term 'Intuitional' to denote the view of ethics which regards as the practically ultimate end of moral actions their conformity to certain rules of Duty unconditionally prescribed. There is, however, considerable ambiguity as to the exact antithesis implied by the terms 'intuition,' 'intuitive,' and their congeners, as currently used in ethical discussion, which we must now endeavour to remove. Sometimes, as I before noticed, 'intuitive knowledge' of the rightness of actions is understood to imply that this rightness is ascertained by simply "looking at" the actions themselves, without considering their ulterior consequences. This view, indeed, can hardly be extended to the whole range of duty; since no morality ever existed which did not consider ulterior consequences to some extent. Prudence or Forethought has always been reckoned a virtue: and all modern lists of Virtues have included Rational Benevolence, which aims at the happiness of other human beings generally, and therefore necessarily takes into consideration even remote effects of actions. It must be observed, too, that it is difficult to draw the line between an act and its consequences: as the effects which follow each of our volitions form a continuous series stretching to infinity, and we seem to be conscious of causing all these effects, so far as at the moment of volition we foresee them to be probable. However, we find that in the common notions of different kinds of actions, a line is actually drawn between the results included in the notion and regarded as forming part of the act, and those considered as its consequences. For example, in speaking truth to a jury, I may foresee that my words, operating along with other statements and indications, will lead them to a wrong conclusion as to the guilt or innocence of the accused, nearly as certainly as I foresee that they will produce a right impression as to the particular matter of fact to which I am testifying: still, we commonly consider the latter foresight or intention to determine the nature of the act as an act of veracity, while the former merely relates to a consequence. We must understand then that the disregard of consequences, which the Intuitional view, according to this interpretation of it, is taken to imply, only relates to certain determinate classes of actions (such as Truth-speaking) where the general notions of the acts indicate clearly enough what events are to be included, and what excluded.

But again; we have to observe that the antithesis between Intuitionism and Hedonism is sometimes inadvertently stated in such a way as to imply that the only consequences of actions which can possibly be of ethical importance are pleasures and pains. It can hardly, however, be denied that men may and do judge remote as well as immediate results to be in themselves desirable, without considering them in relation to the feelings of sentient beings. I have already assumed this to be the view of those who adopt the general Perfection, as distinct from the Happiness, of human society as their ultimate end; and it would seem to be the view of many who concentrate their efforts on some more particular results, other than morality, such as the promotion of Art or Knowledge. Such a view, if expressly distinguished from Hedonism, would probably be classed by many as Intuitional; but if so the antithesis implied by the term would be a different one to that defined in the preceding paragraph: it would be meant that these ultimate ends are judged to be good immediately, and not by 'induction from experience' of the pleasures which they produce. And it would seem to be frequently this latter antithesis that is in the minds of those who contrast 'intuitive' or '*a priori*' with 'inductive' or '*a posteriori*' morality. But such a contrast seems to indicate a certain confusion of thought. For what the 'inductive' moralist professes to know *a posteriori*, by induction from experience, is commonly not the same thing as what the intuitive moralist professes to know by intuition. In the former case it is the conduciveness to pleasure of certain kinds of action that is methodically ascertained: in the latter case, their rightness: there is therefore no proper opposition. If Hedonism claims to give authoritative guidance, this can only be in virtue of the principle that pleasure is the only reasonable ultimate end of human action: and this principle cannot be known by induction from experience. Experience can at most tell us that all men always do seek pleasure as their ultimate end (that it does not support this conclusion I have already tried to show): it cannot tell us that any one ought so to seek it. If this latter proposition is legitimately affirmed in respect either of private or of general happiness, it must either be immediately known to be true,—and therefore, we may say, a moral intuition—or be inferred ultimately from premises which include at least one such moral intuition; hence either species of Hedonism, regarded from the point of view taken in this treatise, might be legitimately said to be in a certain sense 'intuitional.' It seems, however, to be the prevailing opinion of ordinary moral persons, and of most of the writers who have maintained the existence of moral intuitions, that certain kinds of actions are unconditionally prescribed without regard to ulterior consequences: and I have accordingly treated this doctrine as a distinguishing characteristic of the Intuitional method, during the main part of the detailed examination of that method which I attempt in Book III.

§ 2. But further; the common antithesis between 'intuitive' and 'inductive' morality is misleading in another way: since a moralist may hold the rightness of actions to be cognizable apart from the pleasure produced by them, while yet his method may be properly called Inductive. For he may hold that it is always this or that individual action, which is in the first place apprehended to be right: and that all valid general propositions in ethics are obtained by generalization from such particular judgments.

For example, when Socrates is said by Aristotle to have applied inductive reasoning to ethical questions, it is this kind of induction which is meant[1]. He discovered, as we are told, the latent ignorance of himself and other men: that is, that they used general terms confidently, without being able when called upon to explain the meaning of those terms. His plan for remedying this ignorance was to obtain, or work towards, the true definition of each term, by examining and comparing different instances of its application. Thus the definition of Justice would be sought by comparing different particular actions commonly judged to be just, and framing a general proposition that would harmonize with all these particular judgments.

Again the popular view of Conscience seems—at least *primâ facie*—to point to such a method. We most commonly think of the dictates of conscience as relating to particular actions: and when a man is bidden, in any particular case, to 'trust to his conscience,' it commonly seems to be meant that he should exercise a faculty of judging morally this particular case without reference to general rules, and even in opposition to conclusions obtained by systematic deduction from such rules. And it is by this view of Conscience that the contempt often expressed for 'Casuistry' may be most easily justified: for if the particular case can be satisfactorily settled by conscience without reference to general rules, 'Casuistry,' which consists in the application of general rules to particular cases, is at best superfluous. But then, on this view, we shall have no practical need of any such general rules, or of a science of Ethics at all. We may of course form general propositions by induction from these particular conscientious judgments, and arrange them systematically: but any interest which such a system may have will be purely speculative. And this accounts, perhaps, for the indifference or hostility to systematic morality shewn by some conscientious persons. For they feel that they can at any rate do without it: and they fear that the cultivation of it may place the mind in a wrong attitude in relation to practice, and prove rather unfavourable than otherwise to the proper development of the practically important faculty by which we pass particular moral judgments.

[1] It must however be remembered that Aristotle regarded the general proposition obtained by induction as really more certain (and in a higher sense knowledge), than the particulars through which the mind is led up to it.

The view above described may be called, in a sense, 'ultra-intuitional,' since, in its most extreme form, it recognizes simple immediate intuitions alone and discards as superfluous all modes of reasoning to moral conclusions: and we may find in it one phase or variety of the Intuitional method,—if we may extend the term 'method' to include a procedure that is completed in a single judgment.

§ 3. But though probably all moral agents have experience of such particular intuitions, and though they constitute a great part of the moral phenomena of most minds, comparatively few are so thoroughly satisfied with them, as not to demand some more certain moral knowledge, even for practical purposes. And I conceive that in the case, at least, of reflective persons, even when the decision of the moral faculty relates primarily to some particular action, there is commonly at least a latent belief that its rightness or wrongness must be dependent upon certain general characteristics of the action, agent, and circumstances: and accordingly that the moral truth apprehended must be intrinsically universal, though particular in our first apprehension of it[1]. Again, these particular intuitions do not, to reflective persons, present themselves as quite indubitable and irrefragable. Frequently when they have put the ethical question to themselves with all sincerity, they are not conscious of clear immediate insight in respect of it. Again, when we compare the utterances of our conscience at different times, we often find it difficult to make them altogether consistent: the same conduct will wear a different aspect at one time from that which it wore at another, although our view of its circumstances and conditions remains unchanged. Thirdly, we become aware that the intuitions of different minds, to all appearance equally competent to judge, frequently conflict: one condemns what another approves. In this way serious doubts are aroused as to the validity of each man's moral perceptions: and we are led to endeavour to set these doubts at rest by appealing to general rules, more immutable, and resting on a firmer basis of common consent, than such particular intuitions.

[1] This belief affords a kind of justification for the use of the term Moral Reason for the faculty of apprehending moral truth, even as exercised in particular cases.

And in fact, though the view of conscience before discussed is one which much popular language seems to suggest, it is not that which Christian and other moralists have usually given. They have rather represented the process of conscience as analogous to one of jural reasoning, such as is conducted in a Court of Law. Here we have always a system of universal rules given, and any particular action has to be brought under one of these rules before it can be pronounced lawful or unlawful. Now the rules of positive law are not discoverable by the individual's reason: this may teach him that law ought to be obeyed, but what law is must be communicated to him from some external authority. And this is not unfrequently the case with the conscientious reasoning of ordinary persons when any dispute or difficulty forces them to reason: they have a genuine impulse to conform to the right rules of conduct, but they are not conscious, in difficult or doubtful cases, of seeing for themselves what these are: they have to inquire that of their priest, or their sacred books, or perhaps the common opinion of the society to which they belong. In so far as this is the case we cannot strictly call their method Intuitional. They follow rules generally received, not intuitively apprehended. Other persons however (or perhaps all to some extent) do seem to see for themselves the truth[1] and bindingness of all or most of these current rules. They may still put forward 'common consent' as an argument for the validity of these rules: but only as supporting the individual's intuition, not as a substitute for it or as superseding it.

Here then we have a second Intuitional Method: of which the fundamental assumption is that we can discern certain general rules with really clear and finally valid intuition. It is held that such general rules are implicit in the moral reasoning of ordinary men, who apprehend them adequately for most practical purposes, and are able to enunciate them roughly; but that to state them with proper precision requires a power of contemplating clearly and steadily abstract moral notions, which is only obtained by special cultivation. The moralist's

---

[1] Strictly speaking, the attributes of truth and falsehood only belong to Rules when they are changed from the imperative mood ("Do X") into the indicative ("X ought to be done").

function then is to do this, and to arrange them as systematically as possible, and by proper definitions and explanations to remove vagueness and prevent conflict. It is such a system as this which seems to be generally intended when Intuitive or *à priori* morality is mentioned, and which will chiefly occupy us in Book III.

By philosophic minds, however, the 'Morality of Common Sense' (as we may call it), even when made as precise and orderly as possible, is often found unsatisfactory as a system, although they have no disposition to question its general authority. They find it difficult to accept as scientific first principles the moral generalities that they obtain by reflection on the ordinary thought of mankind. Even if these rules can be so defined as perfectly to fit together and cover the whole field of human conduct, without coming into conflict and without leaving any practical questions unanswered: still the resulting code seems an accidental aggregate of precepts, which stands in need of some rational synthesis. In short, without being disposed to deny that conduct commonly judged to be right is so, we may yet require some deeper explanation *why* it is so. From this demand springs a third species or phase of Intuitionism, which, while accepting the morality of common sense as in the main sound, still attempts to find for it a philosophic basis which it does not itself offer: to get one or more principles more absolutely and undeniably true and evident, from which the current rules might be deduced, either just as they are commonly received or with slight modifications and rectifications[1].

§ 4. The three phases of Intuitionism just described may be treated as three stages in the scientific development of Intuitive Morality: we may term them respectively Perceptional, Dogmatic, and Philosophical. The last-mentioned I have only defined in the vaguest way: in fact, as yet I have presented it only as a problem, of which it is impossible to foresee how many solutions may be attempted: but it does not seem desirable to investigate it further at present, as it

[1] It should be observed that such principles will not necessarily be "intuitional" in the narrower sense that excludes consequences; but only in the wider sense as being self-evident principles relating to 'what ought to be.'

will be more satisfactorily studied after examining in detail the Morality of Common Sense.

It must not be thought that these three phases are sharply distinguished in the moral reasoning of ordinary men: but then no more is Intuitionism of any sort sharply distinguished from either species of Hedonism. A loose combination or confusion of methods is the most common type of actual moral reasoning. Probably most moral men believe that their instinct in any case will guide them fairly right, but also that there are general rules for determining right action, those that prescribe the several virtues known as such: and that probably for these again a philosophical explanation may be found, deducing them from a smaller number of fundamental principles. Still for systematic direction of conduct, we require to know on what judgments we may rely as ultimately valid. Hence it would be desirable that professional moralists of the Intuitional school should take more care than they sometimes do to make this point clear in expounding their system. I observe, for example, that Dugald Stewart uses the term "perception" to denote the immediate operation of the moral faculty; which certainly suggests that it judges primarily of the individual action, as "perception" is by metaphysicians chiefly used to denote cognition of an individual thing or quality. At the same time, in describing what is thus perceived, he always seems to have in view general rules or notions.

Still we can tolerably well distinguish among English ethical writers those who have confined themselves mainly to the definition and arrangement of the morality of Common Sense, from those who have aimed at a more philosophical treatment of the content of Moral intuition. And we find that the distinction corresponds in the main to a difference of periods: and that—what perhaps we should hardly have expected—the more philosophical school is the earlier. The explanation of this may be partly found by referring to the doctrines in antagonism to which, in the respective periods, the Intuitional method asserted and developed itself. In the first period all orthodox moralists were occupied in refuting Hobbism. But this system, though based on Materialism and Egoism, was yet, as I have said, intended as ethically constructive. Accepting in the main the commonly received rules of social morality, it explained them as the conditions of peaceful existence which enlightened self-interest directed each individual to obey; provided only the social order to which they belonged was not merely ideal, but made actual by a strong government. Now no doubt this view renders the theoretical basis of duty seriously unstable, as depending upon the arbitrary commands of an actual government: still, assuming a decently good government, Hobbism may claim to at once explain and establish, instead of undermining, the morality of Common Sense. And therefore, though some of Hobbes' antagonists (as Cudworth) contented themselves with simply reaffirming the absoluteness of morality, the more thoughtful felt that system must be met by system and explanation by explanation, and that they must penetrate beyond the dogmas of common sense to some more irrefragable certainty. And so, while Cumberland found this deeper basis in the notion of "the common good of all Rationals" as an ultimate end, Clarke sought to exhibit the more fundamental of the received rules as axioms of perfect self-evidence, necessarily forced upon the mind in contemplating human beings and their relations. Clarke's results, however, were not satisfactory: the more *bizarre* attempt of Wollaston in the same direction was a more complete failure: the attempt to exhibit morality as a body of scientific truth fell into discredit, and the disposition to dwell on the emotional side of the moral consciousness became prevalent. But when ethical discussion thus passed over into psychological analysis and classification, the conception of the objectivity of duty, on which the authority of moral sentiment depends, fell gradually out of view, without its being perceived how serious the loss was: for example, we find Hutcheson asking why the moral sense should not vary in different human beings, as the palate does, without dreaming that there is any peril to morality in admitting such variations as legitimate. When, however, the new doctrine was endorsed by the dreaded name of Hume, its dangerous nature, and the need of bringing again into prominence the cognitive element of the moral consciousness, was clearly seen: and this work was undertaken as a part of the general philosophic protest of the Scotch school against the Empiricism that had culminated in Hume. But this school claimed as its characteristic merit that it met Empiricism on its own ground; and shewed among the facts of psychological experience which Empiricism professed to observe, the principles and assumptions which it repudiated. And thus in Ethics it was led rather to expound and reaffirm the morality of Common Sense, than to offer any profounder principles which could not be so easily supported by an appeal to common experience.

So far I have been mainly concerned with differences in intuitional method due to difference of generality in the intuitive beliefs recognized as ultimately valid. There is, however, another class of differences which arise from a variation of view as to the precise quality immediately apprehended in the moral intuition. These are peculiarly subtle and difficult to fix in clear and precise language, and I therefore reserve them for a separate chapter.

CHAPTER IX.

GOOD.

§ 1. WE have hitherto spoken of the quality of conduct discerned by our moral faculty as 'rightness,' which is the term commonly used by English moralists. We have regarded this term, and its equivalents in ordinary use, as implying the existence of a dictate or imperative of reason, which, according to the Intuitional view, prescribes certain actions unconditionally, without reference to ulterior consequences.

It is, however, possible to take a view of duty in which, though the validity of moral intuitions is not disputed, this notion of rule or dictate is at any rate only latent or implicit, the moral ideal being presented as attractive rather than imperative. That is, we may consider the action to which we are morally prompted as 'good' in itself—not merely as a means to some ulterior Good, but as a part[1] of what is conceived as the agent's Ultimate Good. This, as was before noticed, was the fundamental ethical conception in the Greek schools of Moral Philosophy generally; including even the Stoics, though their system is in this respect a transitional link between ancient and modern ethics. And this historical illustration may serve to exhibit one important result of substituting the idea of 'goodness' for that of 'rightness' of conduct, which at first sight might be thought a merely verbal change. For the chief characteristics of ancient ethical controversy as distinguished from modern may be traced to this, that a generic

[1] As I have before said, the doctrine that Right conduct is the *sole* Good of the agent does not commend itself to the common sense of a modern Christian community: it rather tends to be regarded as a Stoical paradox.

notion is used instead of a specific one in expressing the common moral judgments on actions. Virtue or Right action is commonly regarded as only a species of the Good: and so, on this view of the moral intuition, the first question that offers itself, when we endeavour to systematize conduct, is how to determine the relation of this species of good to the rest of the genus. It was on this question that the Greek thinkers argued, from first to last. Their speculations can scarcely be understood by us unless with a certain effort we throw the quasi-jural notions of modern ethics aside, and ask (as they did) not "What is Duty and what is its ground?" but "Which of the objects that men desire and think good is truly or most desirable, the Good or the Highest Good?" or, in the more specialized form of the question which the moral intuition introduces, "What is the relation of the kind of Good we call Virtue, the qualities of conduct and character which men commend and admire, to other good or desirable things?"

And we may perhaps observe as a fundamental characteristic of the process of ethical thought in Greece, that it continually brings into greater clearness and sharpness the antagonism between different elements included in the comprehensive denotation of 'good.' When the effort to make conduct rational was initiated, in the latter half of the fifth century B.C., by those remarkable public lecturers commonly known as the Sophists, this antagonism either was not seen or was treated as a mere illusion of the vulgar. The Sophists did not profess to teach a man his duty as distinct from his interest, or his interest as distinct from his duty, but Good Conduct conceived as duty and interest identified. And this same identification is implied in the notion of what Socrates, on his negative side, continually sought in vain to know: and this is what, as a positive teacher, he was always employed in demonstrating, with that singular mixture of solid common sense and fine-drawn argumentative ingenuity which characterized his discourses. And though Plato felt the conflict between Virtue and Pleasure far more intensely, so that in one phase of his mental development he repudiated the latter as an object of rational pursuit: still his general tendency—no less than that of Aristotle—is to regard the two as inseparable. The Good which he investigated persistently and profoundly we must conceive as something of which the manifestation in concrete human life involves the attainment of the greatest real pleasure of which human nature is capable, as well as the realization of Virtue. It is not until the post-Aristotelian period that the antithesis presents itself as an absolute antagonism; and that the main influence of philosophy upon mankind is divided between the two schools which present Virtue and Pleasure as competing interpretations of the problematical notion of Ultimate Good.

This, then, is the first difference to be noticed between the two forms of the intuitive judgment. In the recognition of conduct as 'right' is involved an authoritative prescription to do it: but when we have judged conduct to be good, it is not yet clear that we ought to prefer this kind of good to all other good things. In short, the notion of 'rightness' is essentially positive, and that of 'goodness' admits of degrees; so that some standard for estimating the relative values of different 'goods' has still to be sought: and, as a preliminary to such a search, we require to examine the import of the notion 'Good' in the whole range of its application.

§ 2. We may begin by observing that—as it is for the constituents of ultimate good that we require a standard of measurement—we are not primarily concerned with things that are only thought to be good as means to the attainment of ulterior ends. If, indeed, we had only this case to consider, we might perhaps interpret 'good' without reference to human desire or choice, as meaning merely 'fit' or 'adapted' for the production of certain effects—a good horse for riding, a good gun for shooting, &c. But having also the notion of things as good independently of ulterior ends, we must, as the word itself does not seem to have different significations in the two cases, find a meaning for it which will cover both applications.

There is, however, a simple interpretation of the term—which is widely maintained to be the true one—according to which everything which we judge to be good is implicitly conceived as a means to the end of pleasure, even when we do not make in our judgment any explicit reference to this or any other ulterior end. On this view, any comparison of things in respect of their 'goodness' is necessarily a more or less unconscious comparison of them as sources of pleasure; so that any attempt to systematize our intuitions of goodness, whether in conduct and character or in other things, must reasonably lead us straight to Hedonism. And no doubt, if we consider the application of the term, outside the sphere of character and conduct to things that are not definitely regarded as means to the attainment of some ulterior object of desire, we find a close correspondence between our apprehension of pleasure derived from an object, and our recognition that the object is in itself 'good.' The good things of life are things which give pleasure, whether sensual or emotional: as good wines, good landscapes, pictures, music: and this gives a *primâ facie* support to the interpretation of 'good' as equivalent to 'pleasant.' I think, however, that further reflection on the application of the term to the cases most analogous to that of conduct—i.e. to what we may call 'objects of taste'—will shew that this interpretation of it has not really the support of common sense. In the first place, allowing that the judgment that any object is good of its kind is closely connected with the apprehension of pleasure derived from it, we must observe that it is generally to a specific kind of pleasure that the affirmation of goodness corresponds: and that if the object happens to give us pleasure of a different kind, we do not therefore call it good—at least without qualification. For instance, we should not call a wine good solely because it was very wholesome; nor a poem on account of its moral lessons. And hence when we come to consider the meaning of the term 'good' as applied to conduct, there is no reason, so far, to suppose that it has any reference or correspondence to *all* the pleasures that may result from the conduct. Rather the perception of goodness or virtue in actions would seem to be analogous to the perception of beauty[1] in material things: which is normally

---

[1] It is, however, necessary to distinguish between the ideas of *Moral Goodness* and *Beauty* as applied to human actions: although there is much affinity between them, and they have frequently been identified, especially by the Greek thinkers. No doubt both the ideas themselves and the corresponding pleasurable emotions, arising on the contemplation of conduct, are often indistinguishable: a noble action affects us like a scene, a picture, or a strain of music: and the delineation of human virtue is an important part of the means which the artist has at his disposal for producing his peculiar effects. Still, on looking closer, we see not only that there is much good conduct which is not beautiful,

accompanied with a specific pleasure which we call 'æsthetic,' but has often no discoverable relation to the general usefulness or agreeableness of the thing discerned to be beautiful: indeed, we often recognize this kind of excellence in things hurtful and dangerous.

But further; as regards æsthetic pleasures, and the sources of such pleasures that we commonly judge to be good, it is the received opinion that some persons have more and others less 'good taste:' and it is only the judgment of persons of good taste that we recognize as valid in respect of the real goodness of the things enjoyed. We think that of his own pleasure each individual is the final judge, and there is no appeal from his decision; but the affirmation of goodness in any object involves the assumption of a universally valid standard, which, as we believe, the judgment of persons to whom we attribute good taste approximately represents. And it seems clear that the term 'good' as applied to 'taste' does not mean 'pleasant'; it merely imports the conformity of the æsthetic judgment so characterized to the supposed ideal, deviation from which implies error and defect. Nor does it appear to be always the person of best taste who derives the greatest enjoyment from any kind of good and pleasant things. We are familiar with the fact that connoisseurs of wines, pictures, &c., often retain their intellectual faculty of appraising the merits of the objects which they criticize, and deciding on their respective places in the scale of excellence, even when their susceptibilities to pleasure from these objects are comparatively blunted and exhausted. And more generally we see that freshness and fulness of feeling by no means go along with taste and judgment: and that a person who possesses the former may derive more pleasure from inferior objects than another may from the best.

or at least does not sensibly impress us as such; but even that certain kinds of crime and wickedness have a splendour and sublimity of their own. For example, such a career as Cæsar Borgia's, as a French critic of fine moral as well as æsthetic sensibility says, is "beau comme une tempête, comme un abime." It is true, I think, that in all such cases the beauty depends upon the exhibition in the criminal's conduct of striking gifts and excellences mingled with the wickedness: but it does not seem that we can abstract the latter without impairing the æsthetic effect. And hence, I conceive, we have to distinguish the sense of beauty in conduct from the sense of moral goodness.

In short: the general admission that things which are called 'good' are productive of pleasure, and that the former quality is inseparable in thought from the latter, does not involve the inference that the common estimates of the goodness of conduct may be fairly taken as estimates of the amount of pleasure resulting from it. For (1) analogy would lead us to conclude that the attribution of goodness, in the case of conduct as of objects of taste generally, may correspond not to all the pleasure that is caused by the conduct, but to a specific pleasure, in this case the contemplative satisfaction which the conduct causes to a disinterested spectator: and (2) it may not excite even this specific pleasure generally in proportion to its goodness, but only (at most) in persons of good moral taste: and even in their case we can distinguish the intellectual apprehension of goodness—which involves the conception of an ideal objective standard—from the pleasurable emotion which commonly accompanies it and may suppose the latter element of consciousness diminished almost indefinitely.

§ 3. When we pass from the *adjective* to the *substantive* 'good,' it is at once evident that this latter cannot be understood as equivalent to 'pleasure' or 'happiness' by any persons who affirm—as a significant proposition and not as a mere tautology—that the Pleasure or Happiness of human beings is their Good or Ultimate Good. Such affirmation, which would, I think, be ordinarily made by Hedonists, obviously implies that the *meaning* of the two terms is different however closely their denotation may coincide. And it does not seem that any fundamental difference of meaning is implied by the grammatical variation from adjective to substantive.

What then, it may be asked, can we state as the general meaning of the term 'good'? I should answer that the notion it represents does not admit—any more than that expressed by the words 'right,' 'ought,' &c.—of being analysed into more elementary notions. We can only make it clearer by determining its relations; we can (as above) distinguish Good from Pleasure and the Pleasant; and we can indicate its relation to desire and choice by giving as its equivalent the term 'desirable'. What I recognize as 'desirable' for me I conceive as something which I either do desire (if absent) or should desire if my impulses were in harmony with reason: we may say that I 'ought to desire it,' but—since irrational desires cannot always be dismissed at once by voluntary effort—we can only say this in the wider sense[1] of 'ought'; in which it merely connotes an ideal or standard, divergence from which it is our duty to avoid as far as possible, though, even when it is distinctly recognized, we may not always be able to avoid it at will.

The distinction, however, that is thus drawn between what is 'desirable' and what is actually *desired* would not be universally accepted. Some who would admit 'desirable' as an interpretation or equivalent of 'good,' would maintain that by either term no more is signified than the object of actual desire, whatever that may be. They would admit that we all recognize some desires to be bad, and directed to what is not really good for us: but they would explain this by saying that such desires prompt to actions for the consequences of which, when they arrive, we feel, on the whole, aversion more intense than the former desire. On this view, then, my 'good on the whole' may be taken to mean what I should actually desire and seek if all the future aversions and desires which would be roused in me by the consequences of seeking it could be fully realized by me at the time of making my choice.

There is much in this view that seems to me true and important. I hold myself that the satisfaction of any desire is *pro tanto* good; and that an equal regard for all the moments of our conscious experience—so far, at least, as the mere difference of their position in time is concerned—is an essential characteristic of rational conduct. I cannot, however, admit the fact, that a man does not afterwards feel for the consequences of an action aversion strong enough to cause him to regret it, to be a complete proof that he has acted for his 'good on the whole.' Nor do I think that this is in accordance with common sense: for we commonly reckon it among the worst consequences of some kinds of conduct that they alter men's tendencies to desire, and make them desire their lesser good more than their greater: and we think it all the worse for a man—even in this world—if he is never roused out of such a condition and lives

---

[1] Cf *ante*, ch. iii. § 3.

till death the life of a contented pig, when he might have been something better. To avoid this objection, it would have to be said that a man's "true good" is what he would desire on the whole if all the consequences of all the different lines of conduct open to him were actually exercising on him an impulsive force proportioned to the desires or aversions which they would excite if actually experienced. So far as I can conceive this hypothetical object of desire, I am not prepared to deny that it would be 'desirable' in the sense which I give to the term: but such a hypothetical composition of impulsive forces involves so elaborate and difficult a conception, that it is surely paradoxical to say that this is what we *mean* when we talk of a man's 'good on the whole.'

Different meanings, again, are given to the term 'good' by writers who speak of the object—not of Desire generally but—either (1) of the desire that prevails in an act of deliberate purpose, or (2) of any desire that takes effect in conscious action whether impulsive or deliberate, as the 'apparent good' of the agent[1]. The adoption, however, of either of these interpretations implies a denial of the psychological proposition maintained by me in previous chapters[2]; viz. that men not only impulsively but even deliberately yield to appetite or passion in conscious opposition to reason, and choose to act in a way which they believe while choosing will be 'worse' for them on the whole. And this statement seems to me to be borne out by the common experience of reflective moral persons, in modern Christian societies.

I cannot, then, define the ultimately good or desirable otherwise than by saying that it is that of which we should desire the existence if our desires were in harmony with reason, or (to put it otherwise) with an ideal standard from which our actual desires are found more or less to diverge. Let us turn now to the special application of the term to conduct in which, according to the Intuitional view, conduct is judged to be good, or desirable in itself independently of its consequences. This judgment differs, as I have said, from the judgment that

---

[1] The latter of these statements gives what I understand to be the view of Green (*Prolegomena to Ethics*, Book II. Ch. ii.).

[2] Cf. Ch. IV. § 1 and Ch. V. § 1.

such conduct is 'right,' in so far as it does not involve a definite precept to perform it; since it still leaves it an open question whether this good is the greatest good that we can under the circumstances obtain. It differs further, as we may now observe, in so far as good or excellent actions are not implied to be in our power in the same strict sense as 'right' actions—any more than any other good things: and in fact there are many excellences of behaviour which we cannot attain by any effort of will, at least directly and at the moment: hence we often feel that the recognition of goodness in the conduct of others does not carry with it a clear precept to do likewise, but rather

> the vague desire
> That stirs an imitative will.

In so far as this is the case, Goodness of Conduct becomes an ulterior end, the attainment of which lies outside and beyond the range of immediate volition.

§ 4. It remains to consider by what standard the value of conduct, thus intuitively judged to be good in itself, is to be coordinated and compared with that of other good things. I shall not now attempt to establish such a standard; but a little reflection may enable us to limit considerably the range of objects for which it is required. At first sight, indeed, it may seem that there are many other things regarded as intrinsically desirable; and even that the notion of Ultimate Good is more ordinarily applied to a variety of comparatively permanent results, material or otherwise, than it is to virtuous actions or pleasant feelings. If, however, we consider carefully such permanent results as are commonly judged to be good, other than qualities of human beings, mental or bodily, we find nothing that, on reflection, appears to possess this quality of goodness out of relation to human beings, or at least to some consciousness or feeling. No doubt there is a point of view, sometimes adopted with great earnestness, from which the whole universe and not merely a certain condition of rational or sentient beings is contemplated as 'very good': just as the Creator in Genesis is described as contemplating it. But such a view can scarcely be developed into a method of Ethics. For practical purposes, we require to conceive some parts of the universe as at least less good than they might be. And we do not seem to have any ground for drawing such a distinction between different portions of the non-sentient universe, considered in themselves and out of relation to conscious or sentient beings. An exception to this statement may be taken from the fact that we commonly judge some inanimate objects, scenes, &c. to be objectively beautiful, and others indifferent or even unsightly. Still no one would consider it rational to aim at the production of beauty in external nature, apart from any possible contemplation of it by human beings. In fact when beauty is maintained to be objective, it is not commonly meant that it exists as beauty out of relation to any mind whatsoever: but only that there is some standard of beauty valid for all minds.

This leads us however to observe that there are results commonly judged to be good, which, though we do not conceive them to exist out of relation to human beings (or at least minds of some kind), are yet so far separable as ends from the human beings on whom their existence depends, that their realization may conceivably come into competition with the perfection or happiness of these beings. Thus, though beautiful things cannot be thought worth producing except as possible objects of contemplation, still a man may devote himself to their production without any consideration of the persons who are to contemplate them. Similarly knowledge is a good which cannot exist except in minds: and yet one may be more interested in the development of knowledge than in its possession by any particular minds; and may take the former as an ultimate end without regarding the latter. And the same may be said of other elements of that complex of ideal good, with the realization of which the finest minds of our race have been concerned.

Still, as soon as this view is clearly stated, it will, I think, be generally rejected. It will be admitted that all objects of this kind, as well as all external material things, are only reasonably to be sought in so far as they conduce either to the Happiness (which we do not at present consider) or to the Perfection or Excellence of human existence. I say "human," for though most utilitarians consider the pleasure (and freedom from pain) of the inferior animals to be included in the Happiness which they take as the right and proper end of conduct, no one seems to contend that we ought to aim at perfecting them, except as a means to our ends, or at least as objects of scientific or æsthetic contemplation for us.

Nor, again, can we include, as a practical end, the existence of beings above the human. We certainly apply the idea of Good to the Divine Existence, just as we do to His work, and indeed in a preeminent manner: and when it is said that "we should do all things to the glory of God," it may seem to be implied that the existence of God is made better by our glorifying Him. Still this inference when explicitly drawn appears somewhat impious; and theologians generally recoil from it, and refrain from using the notion of a possible addition to the Goodness of the Divine existence as a ground of human duty. Nor can the influence of our actions on other extra-human intelligences besides the Divine be at present made matter of scientific discussion.

We may conclude then, that if there be any ultimate permanent Good to be sought by man it can only be the Goodness, Perfection, or Excellence of Human Existence. How far this notion includes more than Virtue, what its precise relation to Pleasure is, and to what method we shall be logically led if we accept it as fundamental, are questions which we shall more conveniently discuss after the detailed examination of these two other notions, in which we shall be engaged in the two following Books.

NOTE. In this chapter I have refrained from discussing the distinction and relation between 'Good' taken absolutely or universally, and the Good of this or that individual; since this discussion, in my view, is more conveniently placed in chap. xiii. of Book III. ('Philosophical Intuitionism').

BOOK II.
EGOISM.

BOOK II.

CHAPTER I.

THE PRINCIPLE AND METHOD OF EGOISM.

§ 1. THE object of the present Book is to examine the method of determining reasonable conduct which has been already defined in outline under the name of Egoism. It is, perhaps, a sufficient reason for considering this first of the three methods with which this treatise is principally concerned, that there seems to be more tendency to agreement among reflective persons as to the reasonableness of its fundamental principle, than exists in the case either of Intuitionism or of that Universalistic Hedonism to which I propose to restrict the name of Utilitarianism. For even Utilitarians of the school of Bentham (as has been already noticed), although they put forward the greatest happiness of the greatest number as the 'right and proper' end of conduct, yet regard it as natural and normal, and so reasonable or not unreasonable, that each individual should aim at his own greatest happiness. And similarly the most famous English moralist of the Intuitional school seems to grant "that our ideas of happiness and misery are of all our ideas the nearest and most important to us...that, though virtue or moral rectitude does indeed consist in affection to and pursuit of what is right and good as such: yet, when we sit down in a cool hour, we can neither justify to ourselves this or any other pursuit till we are convinced that it will be for our happiness, or at least not contrary to it[1]."

[1] Butler, Serm. XI.

And even Clarke[1]—notwithstanding the emphatic terms in which he has maintained that "Virtue truly deserves to be chosen for its own sake and Vice to be avoided "—yet admits that it is "not truly reasonable that men by adhering to Virtue should part with their lives, if thereby they eternally deprived themselves of all possibility of receiving any advantage from that adherence."

And, generally, in the ages of Christian faith, it has been obvious and natural to hold that the realization of Virtue is essentially an enlightened and far-seeing pursuit of Happiness for the agent. Nor has this doctrine been held only by persons of a cold and calculating turn of mind: we find it urged with emphasis by so chivalrous and highminded a preacher as Bishop Berkeley. No doubt this is only one side or element of the Christian view: the opposite doctrine, that an action done from motives of self-interest is not properly virtuous, has continually asserted itself as either openly conflicting or in some manner reconciled with the former. Still the former, though less refined and elevated, seems to have been the commoner view. And generally speaking, we may say that common sense assumes that 'interested' actions, tending to promote the agent's happiness, are *primâ facie* reasonable: and that the *onus probandi* lies with those who maintain that disinterested conduct, as such, is reasonable.

But, as has been before said, in the common notions of 'interest,' 'happiness,' and also of 'egoism,' 'egoistic,' &c., there is a certain amount of vagueness and ambiguity: so that in order to fit these terms for the purposes of scientific discussion, we must, while retaining the main part of their signification, endeavour to make it more precise. Accordingly, we must explain that by Egoism we mean Egoistic Hedonism, a system that fixes as the reasonable ultimate end of each individual's action his own greatest possible Happiness: and by 'greatest Happiness,' again, we must definitely understand the greatest possible amount of pleasure[2]; or more strictly, as pains have to be balanced against pleasures, the greatest

---

[1] *Boyle Lectures* (1705). Prop. I. p. 116.

[2] This is manifestly the interpretation implicitly given to the term by Butler and Clarke—and, I believe, by all English writers on Morals until very recently.

possible surplus of pleasure over pain—the two terms being used, with equally comprehensive meanings, to include respectively all kinds of agreeable and disagreeable feelings. And we must add that, if the method is to be clear and consistent, pleasures must be sought in proportion to their pleasantness; and therefore the less pleasant consciousness must not be preferred to the more pleasant, on the ground of any other qualities that it may possess. The distinctions of *quality* that Mill and others urge can only be admitted as grounds of preference, if and in so far as they can be resolved into distinctions of quantity. This, as has been said, is not the only method that may fairly be called Egoism: but it is the type to which the practical reasoning that is commonly called 'Egoistic' tends to conform, when we rigorously exclude all ambiguities and inconsistencies: and it is only in this more precise form that it seems worth while to subject such reasoning to a detailed examination. We must therefore understand by an Egoist a man who when two or more courses of action are open to him, represents to himself as accurately as he can the amounts of pleasure and pain that are likely to result from each, and chooses the one which he thinks will yield him the greatest surplus of pleasure over pain.

§ 2. It must however be pointed out that the adoption of the fundamental *principle* of Egoism, as just explained, by no means necessarily implies the ordinary empirical method of seeking one's own pleasure or happiness. A man may aim at the greatest happiness within his reach, and yet not attempt to ascertain empirically what amount of pleasure and pain is likely to attend any given course of action; believing that he has some surer, deductive, method for determining the species of conduct which will make him most happy in the long run. He may believe this on grounds of Positive Religion, because God has promised happiness as a reward for obedience to certain definite commands: or of Natural Religion, because God being just and benevolent must have so ordered the world that Happiness will in the long run be distributed in proportion to Virtue. It is (*e.g.*) by a combination of both these arguments that Paley connects the Universalistic Hedonism that he adopts as a method for determining duties, with the Egoism which seems to him self-evident as a fundamental principle of rational conduct. Or again, a man may connect virtue with happiness by a process of *a priori* reasoning, purely ethical; as Aristotle seems to do by the assumption that the 'best' activity will be always attended by the greatest pleasure as its inseparable concomitant; 'best' being determined by a reference to moral intuition, or to the common moral opinions of men generally, or of well-bred and well-educated men. Or the deduction by which Maximum Pleasure is inferred to be the result of a particular kind of action may be psychological or physiological: we may have some general theory as to the connection of pleasure with some other physical or psychical fact, according to which we can deduce the amount of pleasure that will attend any particular kind of behaviour: as (*e.g.*) we may believe ourselves to know that a perfectly healthy and harmonious exercise of our different bodily and mental functions will always produce the greatest pleasure in the long run. In this latter case, though accepting unreservedly the Hedonistic principle, we shall not be called upon to estimate and compare particular pleasures, but rather to define the notions of 'perfect health' and 'harmony of functions' and consider how these ends may be attained. Still those who advocate such deductive methods commonly appeal to consciousness, at least as supplying confirmation or verification. And since it is generally admitted that pleasures and pains are facts of ordinary experience, of which the quantity and quality are only directly known, by reflection or introspection, to the individual who experiences them; it would seem that—at any rate—the obvious method of Egoistic Hedonism is that which we may call Empirical-reflective: and it is this I conceive that is commonly used in egoistic deliberation. It will be well therefore to examine this method in the first instance; to ascertain clearly the assumptions which it involves, and estimate the exactness of its results.

CHAPTER II.

EMPIRICAL HEDONISM.

§ 1. THE first and most fundamental assumption, involved not only in the empirical method of Egoistic Hedonism, but in the very conception of 'Greatest Happiness' as an end of action, is the commensurability of Pleasures and Pains. By this I mean that we must assume the pleasures sought and the pains shunned to have determinate quantitative relations to each other; for otherwise they cannot be conceived as possible elements of a total of which we are to seek the maximum. It is not absolutely necessary to exclude the supposition that there are some kinds of pleasure so much more pleasant than others, that the smallest conceivable amount of the former would outweigh the greatest conceivable amount of the latter; since, if this were ascertained to be the case, the only result would be that any hedonistic calculation involving pleasures of the former class might be simplified by treating those of the latter class as practically non-existent. And we find it sometimes asserted by persons of enthusiastic and passionate temperament, that there are feelings so exquisitely delightful, that one moment of their rapture is preferable to an eternity of agreeable consciousness of an inferior kind. These assertions, however, are perhaps consciously hyperbolical, and not intended to be taken as scientific statements: but in the case of pain, it has been deliberately maintained by a thoughtful and subtle writer[1], with a view to important practical conclusions, that "torture" so extreme as to be "incommensurable with moderate pain" is an

---

[1] Mr E. Gurney, in the *Fortnightly Review* for December 1881.

actual fact of experience. This doctrine, however, does not correspond to my own experience; nor does it appear to me to be supported by the common sense of mankind :—at least I do not find, in the practical forethought of persons noted for caution, any recognition of the danger of agony such that, in order to avoid the smallest extra risk of it, the greatest conceivable amount of moderate pain should reasonably be incurred. I think that in all ordinary prudential reasoning, at any rate, the assumption is implicitly made that all the pleasures and pains that man can experience bear a finite ratio to each other in respect of pleasantness. From this it follows that (to use Bentham's terms) the Intensity of a pleasure (or pain) can be balanced against its Duration[1]: for if one pleasure (or pain), finite in duration, be intensively greater than another in some finite degree, the latter may be increased extensively until it just balances the former in amount.

If pleasures, then, can be arranged in a scale, as greater or less in some finite degree; we are naturally led to the assumption of a hedonistic zero, or perfectly neutral feeling, as a point from which the positive quantity of pleasures may be measured. And this latter assumption emerges still more clearly when we consider the comparison and balancing of pleasures with pains, which Hedonism necessarily involves. For pain must be reckoned as the negative quantity of pleasure, to be balanced against and subtracted from the positive in estimating happiness on the whole; we must therefore con-

---

[1] Bentham gives four qualities of any pleasure or pain (taken singly) as important for purposes of Hedonistic calculation: (1) Intensity, (2) Duration, (3) Certainty, (4) Proximity. If we assume (as above argued) that Intensity must be commensurable with Duration, the influence of the other qualities on the comparative value of pleasures and pains is not difficult to determine: for we are accustomed to estimate the value of chances numerically, and by this method we can tell exactly (in so far as the degree of uncertainty can be exactly determined) how much the doubtfulness of a pleasure detracts from its value: and *proximity* is a property which it is reasonable to disregard except in so far as it is a particular case of certainty. For my feelings a year hence should be just as important to me as my feelings next minute, if only I could make an equally sure forecast of them. Indeed this equal and impartial concern for all parts of one's conscious life is perhaps the most prominent element in the common notion of the *rational*—as opposed to the merely *impulsive*—pursuit of pleasure.

ceive, as at least ideally possible, a point of transition in consciousness at which we pass from the positive to the negative. It is not absolutely necessary to assume that this strictly indifferent or neutral feeling ever actually occurs. Still experience seems to shew that a state at any rate very nearly approximating to this is even common: and we certainly experience continual transitions from pleasure to pain and *vice versa*, and thus (unless we conceive all such transitions to be abrupt) we must exist at least momentarily in this neutral state.

Here we may notice the paradox of Epicurus[1] that the state of painlessness is equivalent to the highest possible pleasure; so that if we can obtain absolute freedom from pain, the goal of Hedonism is reached, after which we may vary, but cannot increase, our pleasure. This doctrine is opposed to common sense and common experience; but it is, I conceive, merely the exaggeration of an empirical truth that it is important to notice: namely, that this neutral feeling—hedonistic zero, as I have called it—is not (as might vaguely be thought) the normal condition of our consciousness, out of which we occasionally sink into pain, and occasionally rise into pleasure. Nature has not been so niggardly to man as this: so long as health is retained, and pain and irksome toil banished, the mere sense of living and performing the ordinary habitual functions of life is a continual source of moderate pleasures. Thus we may venture to say that the "apathy" which so large a proportion of Greek moralists in the post-Aristotelian period regarded as the ideal state of existence, was not really conceived by them as "without one pleasure and without one pain;" but rather as a state of placid intellectual contemplation, which in philosophic minds might easily reach a high degree of pleasure.

§ 2. This last observation will have shewn the desirability of getting a more precise notion of pleasure and pain than we have yet attained. To avoid prolixity, I shall for the future, in hedonistic discussions, speak usually of pleasure only, assuming that pain may be regarded as the negative quantity of pleasure, and that accordingly any statements made with respect to the former may be at once applied, *mutatis mutandis*, to the latter.

[1] Cf. Cic. de Fin. Bk. I.

The equivalent phrase for Pleasure, according to Mr Spencer[1], is "a feeling which we seek to bring into consciousness and retain there;" and I have already (ch. iv. § 2) accepted this definition as adequate for purposes of distinction. But it is not therefore clear that it is exactly appropriate for purposes of quantitative comparison of pleasures; and that we can say universally that pleasures are greater and less exactly in proportion as they exercise more or less influence in stimulating the will to actions tending to sustain or produce them. It would be admitted, indeed, by all that the *ideas* of absent pleasures do not stimulate us to aim at their realization in strict proportion to their intensity when actually felt: but it may still be thought that, as Mr Bain says, "pleasure and pain, *in the actual or real experience*, are to be held as identical with motive power." By this Mr Bain does not, of course, mean that all pleasures when actually felt actually stimulate to exertion of some kind; since this is obviously not true of the pleasures of repose, a warm bath, &c. The stimulus must in such cases be understood to be latent and potential; only becoming actual when action is required to prevent the cessation or diminution of the pleasure. But even when thus qualified, Mr Bain's statement does not appear to me to be altogether in accordance with experience. He himself contrasts the "disproportionate strain of active powers in one direction," to which "any sudden and great delight may give rise," with the "proper frame of mind under delight," which is "to inspire no endeavours except what the charm of the moment justifies[2]." And he elsewhere explains that "our pleasurable emotions are all liable to detain the mind unduly," through the "atmosphere of excitement" with which they are surrounded, carrying the mind "beyond the estimate of pleasure and pain, to the state named 'passion,'" in which a man is not "moved solely by the strict value of the pleasure," but also by "the engrossing power of the excitement[3]." It is true that in all such cases[4] Mr Bain seems to hold that the stimulus of the

[1] *Principles of Psychology*, ch. ix. § 125.
[2] *The Emotions and the Will*, 3rd Edition, p. 392.
[3] *Mental and Moral Science*, Book IV. ch. iv. § 4.
[4] It ought to be observed, however, that in another work (*The Senses and the*

"mere excitement"—which he identifies with the "tendency of a fixed idea to act itself out,"—does not operate[1] when the pleasure is actually felt, but only when it is represented in idea as an object to be aimed at. I do not, however, find in my own experience any support for this latter view: it seems to me that exciting pleasures are liable to exercise, even when actually felt, a volitional stimulus out of proportion to their intensity as pleasures[2]. If this be so, it is obviously to a certain extent inexact to define pleasure, *for purposes of measurement*, as the kind of feeling that we seek to retain in consciousness. Shall we then say that there is a measurable quality of feeling expressed by the word "pleasure", which is independent of its relation to volition, and strictly undefinable from its simplicity?—like the quality of feeling expressed by "sweet", of which also we are conscious in varying degrees of intensity. This seems to be the view of some writers: but, for my own part, when the term is used in the more extended sense which I have adopted, to include the most refined and subtle intellectual and emotional gratifications, no less than the coarser and more definite sensual enjoyments, I can find no common quality in the feelings so designated except some relation to desire or volition. Hence, if it be admitted that we cannot define Pleasure, when we are considering its "strict value" for purposes of quantitative comparison, as the kind of feeling which we actually desire and aim at, it only remains to define it as that which, when experienced by intelligent beings, is implicitly apprehended as desirable or preferable. We thus recognize that the exact equation which is often assumed to exist between volitional stimulus and intensity of pleasure is merely a normal or typical relation, from which the actual

Intellect, Book I. § 12) Mr Bain distinguishes certain kinds of pleasure as "unvolitional" or "serene" in contrast with those that he terms "volitional". But as this passage does not appear in subsequent editions, I am not sure that it represents his present view.

[1] He does not, however, say more than that "the disturbances and ano-"malies of the will *scarcely* begin to tell in the actual feeling." *Mental and Moral Science*, Book IV. ch. v. § 4.

[2] Mr Bain himself seems to recognize this in a passage where he says (*Mental and Moral Science*, Book III. ch. i. § 8) that "acute pleasures and pains stimulate the will perhaps more strongly than an equivalent stimulation of the massive kind."

relation between the two psychical facts is liable more or less to diverge.

Here, however, a new question comes into view. When I stated in the preceding chapter, as a fundamental assumption of Hedonism, that it is reasonable to prefer pleasures in proportion to their intensity, and not to allow this ground of preference to be outweighed by any merely qualitative difference, I implied that the preference of pleasures on grounds of quality as opposed to quantity—as 'higher' or 'nobler'—is actually possible: and, indeed such non-hedonistic preference is commonly thought to be of frequent occurrence. But if we take the definition of pleasure just given—that it is the feeling which we apprehend to be desirable or preferable—it seems to be a contradiction in terms to say that the less pleasant feeling can ever be thought preferable to the more pleasant.

This contradiction may, I think, be avoided as follows. As I have already said, it will be generally admitted that the pleasantness of a feeling is only directly cognizable by the individual who feels it at the time of feeling it. Thus, though others may know (on general grounds) that by preferring this gratification to some other which he might hereafter enjoy he will obtain less happiness on the whole, and so far may rightly pronounce his choice mistaken; and though (as I shall presently argue), in so far as any estimate of pleasantness involves comparison with feelings only represented in idea, it is liable to be erroneous through imperfections in the representation; still, no one is in a position to controvert the preference of the sentient individual, so far as the quality of the present feeling alone is concerned. When, however, we judge of the preferable quality (as 'elevation' or 'refinement') of a state of consciousness as distinct from its pleasantness[1], we seem to appeal to some common standard which others can apply as well as the sentient individual. Hence I should conclude that when one kind of consciousness is judged to be qualitatively superior to another, although less pleasant, it is not the feeling itself that

---

[1] It was before observed that by saying that one pleasure is superior in *quality* to another we may mean that it is preferable when considered merely as pleasant: in which case difference in kind resolves itself into difference in degree.

is preferred, but something in the circumstances under which it arises, in the active or passive relations of the sentient individual to other persons or things or permanent objects of thought. For certainly if we in thought distinguish any feeling from all its circumstances and conditions (and also from all its effects on the subsequent feelings of the same individual or of others) and contemplate it merely as the transient feeling of a single subject; it seems impossible to find in it any other preferable quality than that which we call its pleasantness, the degree of which is only cognizable directly by the sentient individual[1].

---

[1] It is sometimes said (as *e. g.* by Green, Introd. to Vol. II. of Hume's *Treatise on Human Nature*) that "pleasure as feeling, in distinction from its conditions which are not feelings, cannot be conceived." This is true, in a certain sense of the word 'conceive'; but not in any sense which would prevent us from taking Pleasure as an end of rational action. To adopt an old comparison, it is neither more nor less true than the statement that an angle cannot be 'conceived' apart from its sides. We certainly cannot form the notion of an angle without the notion of sides containing it; but this does not prevent us from apprehending with perfect definiteness the magnitude of any angle as greater or less than that of any other, without any comparison of the pairs of containing sides. Similarly, we cannot form a notion of any pleasure existing apart from some "conditions which are not feelings"; but this is no obstacle to our comparing a pleasure felt under any given conditions with any other, however otherwise conditioned, and pronouncing it equal or unequal: and we require no more than this to enable us to take 'amount of pleasure' as our standard in deciding between alternatives of conduct.

In his more recent *Prolegomena to Ethics*, Green again says that "pleasure (in distinction from the facts conditioning it) is not an object of the understanding." To which it seems sufficient to answer that in several parts of this very treatise, arguments respecting pleasure are carried on which are only intelligible if this distinction between pleasure and the facts conditioning it is thoroughly grasped and steadily contemplated by the understanding: and we may add that the distinction is carried by Green to a degree of subtlety far beyond that which ordinary Hedonism requires—as (*e.g.*) when 'pleasure' is distinguished from the 'satisfaction' involved in the consciousness of attainment (p. 166). Nor are these arguments merely critical and negative in respect of the possibility of measuring pleasure: we find for instance that Green has no doubt that certain measures "needed in order to supply conditions favourable to good character, tend also to make life *more pleasant on the whole*" (p. 365); and again that "it is easy to show that *an overbalance of pain would on the whole result* to those capable of being affected by it" from the neglect of certain duties. In these cases it would seem that pleasure and pain, in distinction from the facts conditioning them, being conceived capable—in whatever degree—of quantitative measurement, cannot but be "objects of the understanding."

It should be observed that if this definition of pleasure be accepted, the fundamental proposition of ethical Hedonism has chiefly a negative significance; for, it being assumed in the definition of pleasure that it is 'desirable,' the statement that 'Pleasure is the ultimate Good' is only important so far as it affirms that nothing is ultimately desirable except desirable feeling. For the same reason it may be made an objection to the definition that it could not be accepted by a moralist of stoical turn, who while recognizing pleasure as a fact refused to recognize it as in any degree ultimately desirable. I do not however think that such a moralist need deny that an implied judgment that a feeling is *per se* desirable is inseparably connected with its recognition as pleasure; though he might hold that sound philosophy shews the illusoriness of such judgments. This, in fact, seems to have been substantially the view of the Stoic school[1].

However this may be, I conceive that the preference which pure Hedonism regards as ultimately rational, should be defined as the preference of feeling valued merely as feeling, according to the estimate implicitly or explicitly made by the sentient individual at the time of feeling it; without any regard to the conditions and relations under which it arises. Accordingly we may state as the fundamental assumption of what I have called Quantitative Hedonism,—implied in the adoption of "greatest surplus of pleasure over pain" as the ultimate end —that all pleasure and pains, estimated merely as feelings,

---

[1] A further objection may perhaps be taken to the definition, on the score of its inconsistency with statements made in the preceding book. It may be said that since the term desirable was there explained to mean that which 'ought' to be desired or aimed at, a proposition affirming desirability must come within the class of ethical judgments which has before been said to be 'objective': yet how, it may be asked, can a judgment be objective when it relates to what is only directly cognizable by a single subject? I admit that the application of the term "objective" to such judgments would be somewhat confusing, and I have therefore avoided it; but in applying the term to ethical propositions in general I was careful to explain it as importing only that such propositions could not be contradicted without error on one side or the other: and this remains true of propositions respecting the desirability of feelings, even if the judgment of the sentient individual be taken as incontrovertible. Some further discussion of the terms 'subjective' and 'objective', in their ethical application will be found in the following book (ch. i. and ch. xiv.).

have definite degrees of desirability, positive or negative; observing further, that the empirical method of Hedonism can only be applied so far as we assume that these degrees of desirability are definitely given in our experience of pleasure and pain.

There is one more assumption of a fundamental kind, which is not perhaps involved in the acceptance of the Hedonistic calculus considered as purely theoretical, but is implied if it be put forward as a practical method for determining right conduct: the assumption, namely, that we can by foresight and calculation increase our pleasures and decrease our pains. It may be thought that this must be granted without discussion, and that it is even pedantic to state it formally. And in fact no one will deny that the conditions upon which our pleasures and pains depend are to some extent cognizable by us and within our own control. But, as we shall see, it has been maintained that the practice of Hedonistic observation and calculation has an inevitable tendency to decrease our pleasures generally, or the most important of them: so that it becomes a question whether we can gain our greatest happiness by seeking it, or at any rate by trying to seek it with scientific exactness.

NOTE.—It is sometimes thought to be a necessary assumption of Hedonists that a surplus of pleasure over pain is actually attainable by human beings: a proposition which an extreme pessimist would deny. But the conclusion that life is always on the whole painful would not prove it to be unreasonable for a man to aim ultimately at minimizing pain, if this is still admitted to be possible; though it would, no doubt, drive a rational egoist to immediate suicide.

CHAPTER III.

EMPIRICAL HEDONISM CONTINUED.

§ 1. LET, then, pleasure be defined as feeling that is preferable or desirable, considered merely as feeling, and therefore from a point of view from which the judgment of the sentient individual is final; and not considered in respect of its causes, or of the relations of the sentient individual to other persons or things, or of any other facts that come directly within the cognizance and judgment of others beside the sentient individual. And let it be assumed that feelings generally can be compared from this point of view, and empirically known to be more or less pleasant in some definite degree. Then the empirical-reflective method of Egoistic Hedonism will be, to represent beforehand the different series of feelings that our knowledge of physical and psychical causes leads us to expect from the different lines of conduct that lie open to us; judge which series, as thus represented, appears on the whole preferable, taking all probabilities into account; and adopt the corresponding line of conduct. It may be objected that the calculation is too complex for practice; since any complete forecast of the future would involve a vast number of contingencies of varying degrees of probability, and to calculate the Hedonistic value of each of these chances of feeling would be interminable. Still we may perhaps reduce the calculation within manageable limits, without serious loss of accuracy, by discarding all manifestly imprudent conduct, and neglecting the less probable and less important contingencies: as we do in some of the arts that have more definite ends, such as strategy and medicine. For if the general in ordering a march, or the physician in recommending a change of abode, took into consideration all the circumstances that were at all relevant to the end sought, their calculations would become impracticable; accordingly they confine themselves to the most important; and we may deal similarly with the Hedonistic art of life.

There are however objections urged against the Hedonistic method which go much deeper; and by some writers are pressed to the extreme of rejecting the method altogether. A careful examination of these objections seems to be the most convenient way of obtaining a clear view, both of the method itself and of the results that may reasonably be expected from it.

It should, however, be premised that the objections with which we are primarily concerned are only those that can be taken, so to say, from *within* the system; arguments, that is, against the possibility of attaining by it the results at which it aims. We are not now to consider whether the principle of Egoistic Hedonism, supposing it to afford a practicable basis for the systematization of men's reasoned activity, is to be accepted without reservation as the supreme maxim of conduct; or whether the rules deduced from it coincide with the current opinions as to what is right. The position here taken is that there are certain principles of conduct which, having a *primâ facie* claim to be accepted as rational, merit a detailed examination; one of these being that what ultimately concerns each agent is his own feeling, and that therefore his ultimate aim should be to get this as pleasant as possible. Whether the observance of the recognised rules of morality is for each individual the best means to this end, it will be important presently to inquire; but I shall do this impartially, without prejudging the question whether it is reasonable for the individual to conform to the dictates of Egoism or to the generally accepted rules of morality, if the two are found to conflict.

If then we confine our attention, for the present, to the objections tending to shew the intrinsic impracticability of Hedonism as a rational method, we find ourselves, in the first place, met by a criticism which, if valid at all, must be admitted to be decisive. It has been maintained, by one of the leading writers of a school which appears to have not a few adherents at the present time, that the phrase "greatest possible "sum of pleasures" is "intrinsically unmeaning" and "nonsense" because "pleasant feelings are not quantities to be added¹." By this assertion, however, it is not "intended to deny that there "may be in fact such a thing as a desire for a sum or contemplated "series of pleasures, or that a man may be so affected by it "as to judge that some particular desire should not be grati- "fied;" but merely, as I understand, that a sum of pleasures cannot be possessed or enjoyed *as a sum;* that is, all at once. Each pleasure, we are told, "is over before the other is en- "joyed:" a man "cannot accumulate pleasures; if he experi- "ences a pleasure every hour for the next 50 years, he will "have no more in possession, and will be in no better state, "than if he is pleased the next minute and then comes to an "end²." But unless the transiency of pleasure diminishes its pleasantness—which the writer from whom I am quoting does not expressly maintain—I cannot see that the possibility of realizing the hedonistic end is at all affected by the necessity of realizing it in successive parts. The argument seems to assume that by an "end" must be meant a goal or consummation, which, after gradually drawing nearer to it, we reach all at once: but this is not, I conceive, the sense in which the word is ordinarily understood by ethical writers: and certainly all that I mean by it is an object of rational aim—whether attained in successive parts or not—which is not sought as a means to the attainment of any ulterior object, but for itself. And so long as any one's prospective balance of pleasure over pain admits of being made greater or less by immediate action in one way or another, there seems no reason why 'Maximum Happiness' should not provide as serviceable a criterion of conduct as any 'chief good' capable of being possessed all at once, or in some way independently of the condition of time.

---

[1] The writer to whom I refer is the late Professor T. H. Green, from whose posthumous *Prolegomena to Ethics* I have already more than once quoted. The school which he represents has been on various occasions designated by different critics (including myself) as 'Hegelian', 'Transcendentalist', and 'Neokantian'; but no one of these terms appears to be altogether satisfactory to the persons to whom it is applied.

[2] Cf. *Prolegomena to Ethics*, Book IV. ch. iv. p. 401; and *Mind*, No. VI. pp. 267—9; also the Introduction to Hume's *Treatise on Human Nature*, § 7.

§ 2. If, however, it be maintained, that the consciousness of the transiency of pleasure either makes it less pleasant at the time or causes a subsequent pain, and that the deliberate and systematic pursuit of pleasure tends to intensify this consciousness; the proposition, if borne out by experience, would certainly constitute a relevant objection to the method of Egoistic Hedonism. And this view would seem to be in the mind of the writer above quoted (though it is nowhere clearly put forward): since he affirms that it is "impossible that self-satisfaction should be found in any "succession of pleasures[1]"; as self-satisfaction being "satisfaction "for a self that abides and contemplates itself as abiding" must be at least "relatively permanent[2]:" and it is, I suppose, implied that the disappointment of the Hedonist, who fails to find self-satisfaction where he seeks for it, is attended with pain or loss of pleasure[3]. If this be so, and if the self-satisfaction thus missed can be obtained by the resolute adoption of some other principle of action, it would certainly seem that the systematic pursuit of pleasure is in some danger of defeating itself: it is therefore important to consider carefully how far this is really the case.

So far as my own experience goes, it does not appear to me that the mere transiency of pleasures is a serious source of discontent, so long as one has a fair prospect of having as much pleasure in the future as in the past—or even so long as the life before one has any substantial amount of pleasure to offer. But I do not doubt that an important element of happiness, for all or most men, is derived from the consciousness of possessing "relatively permanent" sources of pleasure—whether external, as wealth, status, family, friends; or internal, as knowledge, culture, self-control, and lively interest in the wellbeing of fairly prosperous persons or institutions. This, however, does not, in my opinion, constitute an objection to Hedonism: it rather seems obvious, from the hedonistic point of view, that "as soon "as intelligence discovers that there are fixed objects, permanent "sources of pleasure, and large groups of enduring interests, "which yield a variety of recurring enjoyments, the rational

---

[1] *Prolegomena to Ethics*, p. 183.   [2] *l. c.* p. 248.

[3] I cannot state this positively, because Green expressly distinguishes self-satisfaction from pleasure, and does not expressly affirm that its absence is attended by pain.

"will, preferring the greater to the less, will unfailingly devote "its energies to the pursuit of these[1]." It may be replied that if these permanent sources of pleasure are sought merely as a means to the hedonistic end, they will not afford the happiness for which they are sought. With this I to a great extent agree; but I think that if the normal complexity of our impulses be duly taken into account, this statement will be found not to militate against the adoption of Hedonism, but merely to signalize a danger against which the Hedonist has to guard. In a previous chapter[2] I have, after Butler, laid stress on the difference between impulses that are, strictly speaking, directed towards pleasure, and 'extra-regarding' impulses which do not aim at pleasure, though much, perhaps most, of our pleasure consists in the gratification of these latter, and therefore depends upon their existence. I there argued that in many cases the two kinds of impulse are so far incompatible that they do not easily coexist in the same moment of consciousness. I added, however, that in the ordinary condition of our activity the incompatibility is only momentary, and does not prevent a real harmony from being attained by a sort of alternating rhythm of the two impulses in consciousness. Still it seems undeniable that this harmony is liable to be disturbed; and that while on the one hand individuals may and do sacrifice their greatest apparent happiness to the gratification of some imperious particular desire; so on the other hand, self-love is liable to engross the mind to a degree incompatible with a healthy and vigorous outflow of those "disinterested" impulses towards particular objects, the pre-existence of which is necessary to the attainment, in any high degree, of the happiness at which self-love aims. I should not, however, infer from this that the pursuit of pleasure is necessarily self-defeating and futile; but merely that the principle of Egoistic Hedonism when applied with a due knowledge of the laws of human nature, is practically self-limiting; *i. e.* that a rational method of attaining the end at which it aims requires that we should to some extent put it out of sight and not directly aim at it. I have before spoken of this

---

[1] Sully, *Pessimism*, ch. xi. p. 282.
[2] Book I. ch. iv.

conclusion as the 'Fundamental Paradox of Egoistic Hedonism'; but though it presents itself as a paradox, there does not seem to be any difficulty in its practical realization, when once the danger indicated is clearly seen. For it is an experience only too common among men, in whatever pursuit they may be engaged, that they let the original object and goal of their efforts pass out of view, and come to regard the means to this end as ends in themselves: so that they at last even sacrifice the original end to the attainment of what is only secondarily and derivatively desirable. And if it be thus easy and common to forget the end in the means overmuch, there seems no reason why it should be difficult to do it to the extent that Rational Egoism prescribes.

It is true that, as our desires cannot ordinarily be produced by an effort of will—though they can to some extent be repressed by it—if we started with no impulse except the desire of pleasure, it might seem difficult to execute the practical paradox of attaining pleasure by aiming at something else. Yet even in this hypothetical case the difficulty is less than it appears. For the reaction of our activities upon our emotional nature is such that we may commonly bring ourselves to take an interest in any end by concentrating our efforts upon its attainment. So that, even supposing a man to begin with absolute indifference to everything except his own pleasure, there is no reason to believe that if he were convinced that the possession of other desires and impulses were necessary to the attainment of the greatest possible pleasure, he could not succeed in producing these. But this supposition is never actually realized. Every man, when he commences the task of systematizing his conduct, whether on egoistic principles or any other, is conscious of a number of different impulses and tendencies within him, other than the mere desire for pleasure, which urge his will in particular directions, to the attainment of particular results: so that he has only to place himself under certain external influences, and these desires and impulses will begin to operate without any effort of will.

It is sometimes thought, however, that there is an important class of refined and elevated impulses with which the supremacy of self-love is in a peculiar way incompatible; such as the love of virtue, or personal affection, or the religious impulse to love and obey God. But at any rate in the common view of these impulses, this difficulty does not seem to be recognised. None of the school of moralists that followed Shaftesbury in contending that it is a man's true interest to foster in himself strictly disinterested social affections, has noted any inherent incompatibility between the existence of these affections and the supremacy of rational self-love. And similarly the Christian preachers before mentioned, who have commended the religious life as really the happiest, have not thought genuine religion irreconcileable with the conviction that each man's own happiness is his most near and intimate concern.

Other persons, however, seem to carry the religious consciousness and the feeling of human affection to a higher stage of refinement, at which a stricter disinterestedness is exacted. They maintain that the essence of either feeling, in its best form, is absolute self-devotion and self-sacrifice. And certainly these seem incompatible with self-love, however cautiously self-limiting. A man cannot both wish to secure his own happiness and be willing to lose it. And yet how if willingness to lose it is the true means of securing it? Can self-love not merely reduce indirectly its prominence in consciousness, but directly and unreservedly annihilate itself?

This emotional feat does not seem to me possible: and therefore I must admit that a man who embraces the principle of Rational Egoism cuts himself off from the special pleasure that attends this absolute sacrifice and suppression of self. But however exquisite this may be, the pitch of emotional exaltation and refinement necessary to attain it is so comparatively rare, that it is scarcely included in men's common estimate of happiness. I do not therefore think that an important objection to Rational Egoism can be based upon its incompatibility with this particular consciousness: nor that the common experience of mankind really sustains the view that the desire of one's own happiness, if accepted as supreme and regulative, inevitably defeats its own aim through the consequent diminution and desiccation of the impulses and emotional capacities necessary to the attainment of happiness in a high degree; though it certainly shews a serious and subtle danger in this direction.

§ 3. There is, however, another way in which the habit of mind necessarily resulting from the continual practice of hedonistic comparison is sometimes thought to be unfavourable to the attainment of the hedonistic end: from a supposed incompatibility between the habit of reflectively observing and examining pleasure, and the capacity for experiencing pleasure in normal fulness and intensity. And it certainly seems important to consider what effect the continual attention to our pleasures, in order to observe their different degrees, is likely to have on these feelings themselves. The inquiry is not an easy one, as it seems to lead us at once to an antinomy or irreconcileable contradiction in our view of pleasure. For if pleasure only exists as it is felt, the more conscious we are of it, the more pleasure we have: and it would seem that the more our attention is directed towards it, the more fully we shall be conscious of it. On the other hand Hamilton's statement that "knowledge and feeling" (cognition and pleasure or pain) are always "in a certain inverse proportion to each other," corresponds *primâ facie* to our common experience: for consciousness, in so far as it is purely cognitive, is neither pleasurable nor painful, and the more our consciousness is occupied with the one element, the less room there would seem to be for the other.

How then shall we deal with this apparent contradiction? In the first place, a closer inspection shews that Hamilton's doctrine rests on the assumption that the total intensity of our consciousness is a constant quantity; so that when one element of it positively increases, the rest must positively—as well as relatively—diminish. Now it does not appear to me that experience gives us any valid ground for making this general assumption: indeed it seems clear that at certain times in our life intellect and feeling are simultaneously feeble; so that it is at least possible that they may be intensified simultaneously by the same causes.

Still it seems to be a fact that any very powerful feeling, reaching to the full intensity of which our consciousness is normally capable, is commonly diminished by a contemporaneous stroke of cognitive effort: and indeed it has often been noticed as a difficulty in the way of exact observation of our emotions that the object cognized seems to shrink and dwindle in proportion as the cognitive regard grows keen and eager. How then are we to reconcile this with the proposition first laid down, that pleasure only exists as we are conscious of it? Perhaps we may conclude that so far as mere consciousness of a present feeling is concerned—apart from any distinct representative elements,—the cognition cannot diminish the feeling of which it is an indispensable and inseparable condition: but in what we call introspective cognition we go beyond the present feeling, comparing and classifying it with past feelings; and the effort of representing and comparing these other feelings tends to decrease the mere presentative consciousness of the actual pleasure.

I conclude, then, that there is a real danger of diminishing pleasure by the attempt to observe and estimate it. But the danger seems only to arise in the case of very intense pleasures, and only if the attempt is made at the moment of actual enjoyment; and since the most delightful periods of life have frequently recurring intervals of nearly neutral feeling, in which the pleasures immediately past may be compared and estimated without any such detriment, I do not regard the objection founded on this danger as particularly important.

§ 4. More serious, in my opinion, are the objections urged against the possibility of performing, with definite and trustworthy results, the comprehensive and methodical comparison of pleasures and pains which the adoption of the Hedonistic criterion involves. It is not, of course, denied that it is natural and habitual to all or most men to compare pleasures and pains in respect of their intensity: that (*e. g.*) when we pass from one state of consciousness to another, or when in any way we are led to recall a state long past, we often pronounce unhesitatingly that the present state is more or less pleasant than the past: that we declare some pleasant experiences to have been "worth," and others "not worth," the trouble it took to obtain them, or the pain that followed them; and so forth. But it is maintained (1) that this comparison as naturally made is both occasional and very rough, and that it can never be extended as scientific Hedonism seems to require, nor applied, with any accuracy, to all possible states however differing in quality: and (2) that as commonly practised it is liable to illusion, of which we can never measure the precise amount, while we are continually forced to recognize its existence. We may observe that this illusion has been urged by Plato and others as a ground for distrusting the apparent affirmation of consciousness in respect of *present* pleasure. Plato thought that the apparent intensity of the coarser bodily pleasures was illusory; because these states of consciousness, being preceded by pain, were really only states of relief from pain, and so properly neutral, neither pleasant nor painful—in fact the hedonistic zero, as I have called it: only appearing pleasant from contrast with the preceding pain.

To this, however, it has been answered, that in estimating pleasure there is no conceivable appeal from the immediate decision of consciousness: that here the Phenomenal is the Real—there is no other real that we can distinguish from it. And this seems to me true, in so far as we are concerned only with the present state. But then—apart from the difficulty just noticed of observing a pleasure while it is felt without thereby diminishing it—it is obvious that in any estimate of its intensity we are necessarily comparing it with some other state. And this latter must generally be an ideal, not an actual feeling: for though we can sometimes experience two or perhaps more pleasures at once, we are rarely thus enabled to compare them satisfactorily: for either the causes of the two mutually interfere, so that neither reaches its normal degree of intensity; or, more often, the two blend into one state of pleasant consciousness, the elements of which we cannot estimate separately. But if it is therefore inevitable that one term at least in our comparison should be an imagined pleasure, we see that there is a possibility of error in any such comparison; for the ideal state may not adequately represent the pleasantness of the corresponding actual state. And in the egoistic comparison, the validity of which we are now discussing, the objects primarily to be compared are all represented or ideal states: for we are desiring to choose between two or more possible courses of conduct, and therefore to forecast future feelings.

Let us then examine more closely the manner in which this comparison is ordinarily performed, that we may see what positive grounds we have for mistrusting it.

In estimating for practical purposes the value of different

pleasures open to us, we commonly trust most to our prospective imagination: we project ourselves into the future, and imagine what such and such a pleasure will amount to under hypothetical circumstances. This imagination, so far as it involves conscious inference, seems to be chiefly determined by our own experience of past pleasures, which are usually recalled generically, or in large aggregates, though sometimes particular instances of important single pleasures occur to us as definitely remembered: but partly, too, we are influenced by the experience of others sympathetically appropriated: and here again we sometimes definitely refer to particular experiences which have been communicated to us by individuals, and sometimes to the traditional generalizations which are thought to represent the common experience of mankind.

Now it does not seem that such a process as this is likely to be free from error: and indeed, no one pretends that it is. In fact there is scarcely any point upon which moralizers have dwelt with more emphasis than this, that man's forecast of pleasure is continually erroneous. Each of us frequently recognizes his own mistakes: and each still more often attributes to others errors unseen by themselves, arising either from misinterpretation of their own experience, or from ignorance or neglect of that of others.

How then are these errors to be eliminated? The obvious answer is that we must substitute for the instinctive, implicit, inference just described a more scientific process of reasoning: by deducing the probable degree of our future pleasure or pain under any circumstances from inductive generalizations based on a sufficient number of careful observations of our own and others' experience. We have then to consider whether a process of this kind can be satisfactorily developed; a question which seems to resolve itself into the three following; First, how far can each of us estimate accurately his own past experience of pleasures and pains? secondly, how far can this knowledge of the past enable him to forecast, with any certainty, the greatest happiness within his reach in the future? thirdly, how far can he appropriate, for the purposes of such forecasts, the past experience of others?

As regards the first of these questions, it seems at first

sight a simple thing to take note of our different pleasures and pains as they occur, and to generalize from a series of such observations. But it must be remembered that what we have to note is the positive or negative degree of each feeling; it is not sufficient to know generally that we derive pleasures and pains from such and such sources; unless we can estimate them quantitatively, it is absurd to try to aim at our *greatest possible* happiness. We have therefore to compare each pleasure as it occurs, or as recalled in imagination, with other imagined pleasures: and the question is, whether such comparisons can ever be altogether trustworthy, or take rank as scientific observations.

Now for my own part, when I reflect on my pleasures and pains, and endeavour to compare them in respect of intensity, it seems to me that the comparative judgments which I pass are by no means clear and definite, even taking each separately in its simplest form:—whether the comparison is made at the moment of experiencing one of the pleasures, or between two states of consciousness recalled in imagination. This is true even when I compare feelings of the same kind: and the vagueness and uncertainty increases, in proportion as the feelings differ in kind. Let us begin with sensual gratifications, which are thought to be especially definite and palpable. Suppose I am enjoying a good dinner: if I ask myself whether one kind of dish or wine gives me more pleasure than another, sometimes I can decide, but very often not. So if I reflect upon two modes of bodily exercise that I may have taken: if one has been in a marked degree agreeable or tedious, I take note of it naturally: but it is not natural to me to go further than this in judging of their pleasurableness or painfulness, and the attempt to do so does not seem to lead to any clear affirmation. And similarly of intellectual exercises and states of consciousness predominantly emotional: even when the causes and quality of the feelings compared are similar, it is only when the differences in pleasantness are great, that hedonistic comparison seems to yield any definite result. But when I try to arrange in a scale pleasures differing in kind; to compare (*e.g.*) labour with rest, excitement with tranquillity, intellectual exercise with emotional effusion, the pleasure of scientific apprehension with that of beneficent action, the delight of social expansion with the delight of æsthetic reception; my judgment wavers and fluctuates far more, and it is but rarely that I can give any confident decision. And if this is the case with what Bentham calls 'pure'—*i.e.* painless—pleasures, it is still more true of those even commoner states of consciousness, where a certain amount of pain or discomfort is mixed with pleasure, although the latter preponderates. If it is hard to say which of two different states of contentment was the greater pleasure, it seems still harder to compare a state of placid satisfaction with one of eager but hopeful suspense, or with triumphant conquest of painful obstacles. And perhaps it is still more difficult to compare pure pleasures with pure pains, and to say how much of the one kind of feeling we consider to be exactly balanced by a given amount of the other when they do not occur simultaneously: while an estimate of simultaneous feelings is, as we have seen, generally unsatisfactory from the mutual interference of their respective causes.

§ 5. But again if these judgments are not clear and definite, still less are they consistent. I do not now mean that one man's estimate of the value of any kind of pleasures differs from another's: for we have assumed each sentient individual to be the final judge of the pleasantness and painfulness of his own feelings, and therefore this kind of discrepancy does not affect the validity of the judgments, and creates no difficulty until any one tries to appropriate the experience of others. But I mean that each individual's judgment of the comparative value of his own pleasures is apt to be different at different times: and that this variation is a legitimate ground for distrusting the validity of any particular comparison.

The causes of this variation seem to belong partly to the state of the mind at the time of making the representation; and partly to the represented feeling, or rather to certain universal conditions of its being represented, independent of the particular state of the representing mind. To begin with the latter: common reflection has long ago anticipated the observation of the scientific psychologist, that different kinds of pleasures and pains are not equally recoverable in idea. For example, I find it at this moment much more easy to recall the discomfort of expectancy which preceded sea-sickness than the pain of the actual nausea: although I infer—from the recollection of judgments passed at the time—that the former pain was trifling compared with the latter. To this cause it seems due that past hardships, toils, and anxieties often appear pleasurable when we look back upon them, after some interval; for the excitement, the heightened sense of life that accompanied the painful struggle, would have been pleasurable if taken by itself; and it is this that we recall rather than the pain. In estimating pleasures the other cause of variation is more conspicuous; we are conscious of changes occasional or periodic in our estimate of them, depending upon changes in our mental or bodily condition. *E.g.* it is a matter of common remark with respect to the gratifications of appetite that we cannot estimate them adequately in the state of satiety, and that we are apt to exaggerate them in the state of desire. (I do not mean to deny that intensity of antecedent desire intensifies the pleasure of fruition when that comes—that this pleasure not only *appears*, as Plato thought, but actually *is* greater. Still it is also a matter of common experience that pleasures which have been intensely desired are found to disappoint expectation.)

There seem to be no special states of aversion, determined by bodily causes, and related to certain pains as our appetites to their correspondent pleasures; but most persons are liable to be thrown by the prospect of certain pains into the state of passionate aversion which we call fear; and thereby led to estimate such pains as worse than they would be judged to be in a calmer mood.

Further, when feeling any kind of pain or uneasiness we seem liable to underrate its opposite: as Horace observes, in danger we value repose, overlooking its *ennui*, while the tedium of security makes us long for the excitement of danger. And again when we are absorbed in any particular pleasure, pleasures of a different kind are apt to be contemned: they appear coarse or thin, as the case may be: and this constitutes a fundamental objection to any attempt to note the exact degree of a pleasure at the time of experiencing it. The state of eager desire is generally inseparable from a similar bias: indeed any strong excitement tends to make us contemptuous of alien pleasures and pains alike. And, speaking more generally, we cannot represent to ourselves as very intense a pleasure of a kind that at the time of representing it we are incapable of experiencing: as (*e.g.*) the pleasures of intellectual or bodily exercise at the close of a wearying day: or any emotional pleasure when our susceptibility to the special emotion is temporarily exhausted. On the other hand it is not easy to guard against error, as philosophers have often thought, by making our estimate in a cool and passionless state. For there are many pleasures which require precedent desire, and even enthusiasm and highly wrought excitement, in order to be experienced in their full intensity: and it is not likely that we should appreciate these adequately in a state of perfect tranquillity.

§ 6. These considerations place in a clearer light the extent of the fundamental assumption of Empirical Quantitative Hedonism as stated in the preceding chapter: viz. (1) that our pleasures and pains, considered merely as feelings, have each a definite degree of desirability or undesirability: and (2) that this degree is empirically cognizable. In the first place, if we admit, as was said, that pleasure only exists as it is felt, it is hard to see how the degree of any pleasure can be proved to have any real existence. For the pleasure only has the degree as compared with other feelings, of the same or some different kind; but, generally speaking, since this comparison can only be made in imagination, it can only yield the hypothetical result that if certain feelings could be felt together, precisely as they have been felt separately, one would be found more or less desirable than the other in some definite ratio. What adequate ground, then, have we for regarding this imaginary result as a valid representation of reality? We can only answer that the general belief in its validity seems to be irresistibly suggested in reflection on experience, and—though not, strictly speaking, proved—remains at any rate uncontradicted by experience.

But secondly, granting that each of our pleasures and pains has really a definite degree of pleasantness and painfulness; the question still remains whether we have actually any means of accurately knowing these degrees. Is there any reason to suppose that the mind is ever in such a state as to be a perfectly neutral and colourless medium for imagining all kinds of pleasures? Experience certainly shews us the frequent occurrence of moods in which we have an apparent bias for or against a particular kind of feeling. Is it not probable that there is always some bias of this kind? that we are always more in tune for some pleasures, more sensitive to some pains, than we are to others? Here again it must, I think, be admitted that the exact cognition of the place of each of our feelings in a scale of desirability, measured positively and negatively from a zero of perfect indifference, is at best an ideal to which we can never tell how closely we approximate. But in the variations of our judgment and the disappointment of our expectations we have experience of errors of which we can trace the causes, and allow for them, at least roughly; correcting in thought the defects of imagination. And since what we require for practical guidance is to estimate not individual past experiences, but the value of a kind of pleasure or pain, as obtained under certain circumstances or conditions; we can to some extent diminish the chance of error in this estimate by making a number of observations and imaginative comparisons, at different times and in different moods. In so far as these agree we may legitimately feel an increased confidence in the result: and in so far as they differ, we can at least reduce our possible error by striking an average between the different estimates. It will be evident, however, after all that has been said, that such a method as this cannot be expected to yield more than a rough approximation to the supposed truth.

§ 7. We must conclude then that our estimate of the hedonistic value of any past pleasure or pain, is liable to an amount of error which we cannot calculate exactly; because the represented pleasantness of different feelings fluctuates and varies indefinitely with changes in the actual condition of the representing mind. We have now to observe that, for similar reasons, even supposing we could adequately allow for, and so exclude, this source of error in our comparison of past pleasures, it is liable to intrude again in arguing from the past to the future. For our capacity for particular pleasures may be about to change, or may have actually changed since the experiences that form the data of our calculation. We may have reached the point of satiety in respect of some of our past pleasures, or otherwise lost our susceptibility to them, owing to latent changes in our constitution: or we may have increased our susceptibility to pains inevitably connected with them: or altered conditions of life may have generated in us new desires and aversions, and given relative importance to new sources of happiness. Or any or all of these changes may be expected to occur, before the completion of the course of conduct upon which we are now deciding. The most careful estimate of a girl's pleasures (supposing a girl gifted with the abnormal habit of reflection that would be necessary) would not much profit a young woman: and the hedonistic calculations of youth require modification as we advance in years.

It may be said, however, that no one, in making such a forecast, can or does rely entirely on his own experience: when endeavouring to estimate the probable effect upon his happiness of new circumstances and influences, untried rules of conduct and fashions of life, he inevitably argues from the experience of others. And it is no doubt true that the most important and anxious deliberations in a man's life, and those in which he most strongly feels the need of making the hedonistic calculation as complete and exact as possible, generally concern changes of conduct recommended solely or chiefly by an inference from the advantages that other men have derived from similar changes. But a new source of error is thus introduced; for this inference proceeds on the assumption of a similarity of nature among human beings, an assumption which is never exactly true, while we can never exactly know how much it falls short of the truth: though we have sufficient evidence of the striking differences between the feelings produced in different men by similar causes, to convince us that the assumption would in many cases be wholly misleading. Hence (*e.g.*) the short method that Plato and others have proposed for deciding the issue between the Philosopher and the Sensualist is palpably inadequate. The philosopher, it is said, has tried both kinds of pleasure, sensual as well as intellectual; and prefers the delights of philosophic life. The sensualist ought therefore to trust his decision and follow his example. But who can tell that the philosopher's constitution is not such as to render the enjoyments of the senses, in his case, comparatively feeble? while on the other hand the sensualist may not be able to attain more than a thin shadow of the philosopher's delight. And so, generally speaking, if we are to be guided by another's experience, we require to be convinced not only that he is generally accurate in observing, analysing, and comparing his sensations, but also that his relative susceptibility to the different kinds of pleasure and pain in question coincides with our own. If he is unpractised in introspective observation, it is possible that he may mistake even the external conditions of his own happiness; and so the communication of his experience may be altogether misleading. But however accurately he has analysed and determined the causes of his feelings, that similar causes would produce similar effects in us must always be uncertain. And the uncertainty is increased indefinitely if our adviser has to recall in memory out of a distant past some of the pleasures or pains to be compared. Thus in the ever-renewed controversy between Age and Youth, wisdom is not after all so clearly on the side of maturer counsels as it seems to be at first sight. When a youth is warned by his senior to abstain from some pleasure, on the ground of prudence, because it is not worth the possible pleasures that must be sacrificed for it and the future pains that it will entail; it is difficult for him to know how far the elder man can recall—even if he could once feel—the full rapture of the delight that he is asking him to renounce. No doubt we can reduce this liability to error, if we can ascertain how far we and the persons whose experience we wish to appropriate have been similarly influenced by similar circumstances in the past; for so we can infer in what respects our natures are similar to theirs, and in what different; but we can never make this inference complete, and often the requisite comparison is not in our power.

And further, this source of error besets us in a more extended and more subtle manner than has yet been noticed. For our sympathetic apprehension of alien experiences of pleasure and pain has been so continually exercised, in so many ways, during the whole of our life, both by actual observation and oral communication with other human beings, and through books and other modes of symbolic suggestion; that it is impossible to say how far it has unconsciously blended with our own experience, so as to colour and modify it when represented in memory. Thus we often overlook the discrepancy between our own experience and that of others, in respect of the importance of certain sources of pleasure and pain, if no sudden and striking disappointment of expectations has forced it on our notice. Only with considerable care and attention can sympathetic persons separate their individual likes and dislikes from those of their associates: and we can never tell whether this separation has been completely effected.

But again: the practical inference from the past to the future is further complicated by the fact that we can alter ourselves. For it may be that our past experience has been greatly affected by our being not properly attuned to certain pleasures, as (*e.g.*) those of art, or study, or muscular exercise, or society, or beneficent action: or not duly hardened against certain sources of pain, such as toil, or anxiety, or abstinence from luxuries: and there may be within our power some process of training or hardening ourselves which may profoundly modify our susceptibilities. And this consideration is especially important,—and at the same time especially difficult to deal with—when we attempt to appropriate the experience of others. For we may find that they estimate highly pleasures which we not only have never experienced at all, but which we cannot experience without a considerable alteration of our nature. For example, the pleasures of the religious life, the raptures of prayer and praise and the devotion of the soul to God, are commonly thought to require Conversion or complete change of nature before they can be experienced. And in the same way the sacrifice of sensual inclination to duty is disagreeable to the non-moral man when he at first attempts it, but affords to the truly virtuous man a deep and strong delight. And similarly almost all the more refined intellectual and emotional pleasures require training and culture in order to be enjoyed: and since this training does not always succeed in producing any considerable degree of susceptibility, it may always be a matter of doubt for one from whom it would require the sacrifice of other pleasures, whether such sacrifice is worth making.

The foregoing considerations must, I think, seriously reduce our confidence in what I have called the Empirical-reflective method of Egoistic Hedonism. I am far from implying that it should lead us to reject it altogether: indeed I am perfectly conscious that, in spite of all the difficulties that I have urged, I continue to make comparisons between pleasures and pains with complete practical reliance on their results. But I think we must admit that it would be highly desirable, with a view to the systematic direction of conduct, to control and supplement the results of such comparisons by the assistance of some other method: if we can find any on which we see reason to rely.

CHAPTER IV.

OBJECTIVE HEDONISM AND COMMON SENSE.

§ 1. BEFORE we examine those methods of seeking one's own happiness which are more remote from the empirical, inasmuch as they change fundamentally the direction of rational aim, and depend on assumptions which carry us into different lines of thought; it will be well to consider how far we can avoid the difficulties and uncertainties of the method of reflective comparison, by relying on the current opinions and accepted estimates of the value of different objects commonly sought as sources of pleasure. It certainly seems more natural to men, at least in the main plan and ordering of their lives, to seek and consciously estimate the objective conditions and sources of happiness, rather than happiness itself: and it may plausibly be said that by relying on such estimates of objects we avoid the difficulties that beset the introspective method of comparing feelings: and that the common opinions as to the value of different sources of pleasure express the net result of the combined experience of mankind from generation to generation; in which the divergences due to the limitations of each individual's experience, and to the differently tinged moods in which different estimates have been taken, have balanced and neutralized each other and so disappeared.

And no doubt many persons are guided more by such current opinions in the direction of their egoistic aims than by any hedonistic calculations of their own: and perhaps most of us would be rather puzzled if we were suddenly deprived of the guidance of common sense in our pursuit of happiness, and had to rely entirely on the experiences of individuals.

When, however, we consider these common opinions as premises for the deductions of systematic egoism, they appear open to the following grave objections.

In the first place Common Sense gives us only, at the best, an estimate true for an average or typical human being: and it is probable that any particular individual will be more or less divergent from this type. In any case, therefore, each person will have to correct the estimate of common opinion by the results of his own experience in order to obtain from it trustworthy guidance for his own conduct: and this process of correction, it would seem, must be involved in all the difficulties from which we are trying to escape. And, secondly, the experience of the mass of mankind is confined within limits too narrow for its results to be of much avail in the present inquiry. The majority of human beings spend most of their time in labouring to avert starvation and severe bodily discomfort: and the brief leisure that remains to them, after supplying the bodily needs of food, sleep, &c., is spent in ways determined rather by impulse, routine, and habit, than by a deliberate estimate of probable pleasure. It would seem, then, that the common sense to which we have here to refer can only be that of a minority of comparatively rich and leisured persons.

But again, we cannot tell that the mass of mankind, or any section of the mass, is not generally and normally under the influence of some of the causes of mal-observation previously noticed. We avoid the "idola specus" by trusting Common Sense, but what is to guard us against the "idola tribus"? Moreover, the common estimate of different sources of happiness seems to involve all the confusion of ideas and points of view, which in defining the empirical method of Hedonism we have taken some pains to eliminate. In the first place it does not distinguish between objects of natural desire and sources of experienced pleasure. Now we have seen (Bk. I. ch. 4) that these two are not exactly coincident. No doubt we all desire pleasure, and our desires of external objects are in close relation to our experiences of pleasure. But whether or not they have originally sprung altogether from experiences of pleasure, they are certainly not at any period of our life exactly in harmony with the results of such experiences—indeed we find numerous examples of men who continue not only to feel but to indulge desires, the gratification of which they know by ample experience to be attended with more pain than pleasure. And therefore the current estimate of the desirability of objects of pursuit cannot be taken to express simply men's experience of pleasure and pain: for men are apt to think desirable what they strongly desire, whether or not they have found it conducive to happiness on the whole: and so the common opinion will tend to represent a compromise between the average force of desires and the average experience of the consequences of gratifying them.

We must allow again for the intermingling of moral and æsthetic preferences with the purely hedonistic in the estimate of common sense. For even when men definitely expect greater happiness from the course of conduct which they choose than from any other, it is often because they think it the right, or more excellent, or more noble course; and make, more or less unconsciously, the assumption (which we shall presently have to consider) that the most excellent action will prove to be also the most pleasant.

Again, the introduction of the moral and æsthetic points of view suggests the following doubt. Are we to be guided by the preferences which men avow, or by those which their actions would lead us to infer? On the one hand, we cannot doubt that men often, from weakness of character, fail to seek what they sincerely believe will give them most pleasure in the long run: otherwise all who accept the Christian creed would conform to the Christian code. On the other hand, as a genuine preference for virtuous or refined pleasure is a mark of the man of genuine virtue or refined taste, men who do not really feel such preference are unconsciously or consciously influenced by a desire to gain credit for it, and their express estimate of pleasures is thus modified and coloured.

§ 2. But, even if we had no doubt on general grounds that Common Sense would prove our best guide in the pursuit of happiness, we should still be perplexed by finding its utterances on this topic very deficient in clearness and consistency. I do not merely mean that they are different in different ages and countries:—that we might explain as due to variations in the general conditions of human life—but that serious conflicts and ambiguities are found if we consider only the current common sense of our own age and country. We may perhaps make a list of sources of happiness apparently recommended by an overwhelming *consensus* of current opinion: as health, wealth, fame and social position, power, the enjoyment of society, especially family society, congenial occupation and amusement, including the gratification, in some form, of curiosity, and of those more refined, partly sensual, partly emotional, susceptibilities which we call æsthetic[1]. But if we inquire into the relative value of these objects of common pursuit, we seem to get no clear answer from Common Sense: unless, perhaps, it would be generally agreed that health ought to be paramount to all other secondary ends: though even on this point we could not infer general agreement from observation of the actual conduct of mankind. Nay, even as regards the positive estimate of these sources of happiness, we find on closer examination that the supposed *consensus* is much less clear than it seemed at first. Not only are there numerous and important bodies of dissidents from the current opinions: but the very same majority, the same Common Sense of Mankind that maintains these opinions, is found in a singular and unexpected manner to welcome and approve the paradoxes of these dissidents. Men shew a really startling readiness to admit that the estimates of happiness which guide them in their ordinary habits and pursuits are erroneous and illusory: and that from time to time the veil is, as it were, lifted, and the error and illusion made manifest.

For, first, men seem to attach great value to the ample gratification of bodily appetites and needs: the wealthier part of mankind spend a considerable amount of money and forethought upon the means of satisfying these in a luxurious manner: and though they do not often deliberately sacrifice health to this gratification—common sense condemns that as irrational—yet one may say that they are habitually courageous in pressing forward to the very verge of this imprudence.

And yet the same people are fond of saying that "hunger is the best sauce," and that "temperance and labour will make

[1] The consideration of the importance of Morality as a source of happiness is reserved for the next chapter.

plain food more delightful than the most exquisite products of the culinary art." And they often argue with perfect sincerity that the rich have really no advantage, or scarcely any advantage, over the comparatively poor, in respect of these pleasures; for habit soon renders the more luxurious provision for the satisfaction of their acquired needs no more pleasant to the former than the appeasing of his more primitive appetites is to the poor man. And the same argument is often extended to all the material comforts that wealth can purchase. It is often contended that habit at once renders us indifferent to these while they are enjoyed, and yet unable to dispense with them without annoyance: so that the pleasures of the merely animal life are no greater to the rich than to the poor, but only more insecure. And from this there is but a short step to the conclusion, that wealth, in the pursuit of which most men agree in concentrating their efforts, and on the attainment of which all congratulate each other;—wealth, for which so many risk their health, shorten their lives, reduce their enjoyments of domestic life, and sacrifice the more refined pleasures of curiosity and art,—is really a very doubtful gain; that the cares and anxieties which it entails balance, for most men, the slight advantage of the luxuries which it purchases[1].

And similarly, although social rank and status is, in England, an object of passionate pursuit, yet it is continually said, with general approval, that it is of no intrinsic value as a means of happiness; that though the process of ascending from a lower grade to a higher is perhaps generally agreeable, and the process of descending from a higher to a lower certainly painful, yet permanent existence on the loftier level is no more pleasant than on the humbler; that happiness is to be found as easily in a cottage as in a palace (if not, indeed, more easily in the former): and so forth.

[1] It is striking to find the author of the *Wealth of Nations*, the founder of that long line of plutologists who are commonly believed to exalt the material means of happiness above all other, declaring that "wealth and greatness are mere trinkets of frivolous utility," and that "in ease of body and peace of mind, all the different ranks of life are nearly upon a level, and the beggar who suns himself by the side of the highway possesses that security which kings are fighting for." Adam Smith, *Moral Sentiments*, Part IV. c. i.

Still more trite are the commonplaces as to the emptiness and vanity of the satisfaction to be derived from Fame and Reputation. The case of posthumous fame, indeed, is a striking instance of the general proposition before laid down, that the commonly accepted ends of action are determined partly by the average force of desires that are not directed towards pleasure, nor conformed to experiences of pleasure. For posthumous fame seems to rank pretty high among the objects that common opinion regards as good or desirable for the individual: and the pursuit of it is not ordinarily stigmatized as contrary to prudence, even if it leads a man to sacrifice other important sources of happiness to a result of which he never expects to be actually conscious. Yet the slightest reflection shews such a pursuit to be *primâ facie* irrational[1], from an egoistic point of view; and every moralizer has found this an obvious and popular topic. The actual consciousness of present fame is no doubt very delightful to most persons: still the moralizer does not find it difficult to maintain that even this is attended with such counterbalancing disadvantages as render its hedonistic value very doubtful.

Again, the current estimate of the desirability of Power is tolerably high, and perhaps the more closely and analytically we examine the actual motives of men, the more widespread and predominant its pursuit will appear: for many men seem to seek wealth, knowledge, even reputation, as a means to the attainment of power, rather than for their own sakes or with a view to other pleasures. And yet men assent willingly when they are told that the pursuit of power, as of fame, is prompted by a vain ambition, never satisfied, but only rendered more uneasy by such success as is possible for it: that the anxieties that attend not only the pursuit but the possession of power, and the jealousies and dangers inseparable from the latter, far outweigh its pleasures.

Society of some sort no one can deny to be necessary to

---

[1] No doubt such a pursuit may be justified to self-love by dwelling on the pleasures of hope and anticipation which attend it. But this is obviously an after-thought. It is not for the sake of those originally that posthumous fame is sought by him whom it spurs

"To scorn delights and live laborious days."

human happiness: but still the kind and degree of social intercourse which is actually sought by the more wealthy and leisured portion of the community, with no little expenditure of time, trouble and means, is often declared to yield a most thin and meagre result of pleasure.

We find, no doubt, great agreement among modern moralizers as to the importance of the exercise of the domestic affections as a means of happiness: and this certainly seems to have a prominent place in the plan of life of the majority of mankind. And yet it is difficult to prove that men in general do value doméstic life very highly, apart from the gratification of their sensual passions. Certainly whenever any part of civilized society is in such a state that men can freely indulge these passions and at the same time avoid the burden of a family, without any serious fear of social disapprobation, celibacy tends to become common: it has even become so common as to excite the grave anxiety of legislators. And though such conduct has always been disapproved by common sense, it seems to have been rather condemned as anti-social than as imprudent.

Thus our examination seems to shew great instability and uncertainty in the most decisive judgments of common sense; since these objects—bodily comfort and luxury, wealth, fame, power, society—are those which common opinion seems most confidently to recommend as sources of pleasure. For though the pleasures derived from Art and the contemplation of the beautiful in Nature, and those of curiosity and the exercise of the intellect generally, are highly prized, it will I think be admitted that they are usually postponed to those above enumerated. And in truth it seems almost impossible to formulate a "common opinion" in respect of these more refined delights. For the very high estimates often set upon them seem to express the real experience of only small minorities. And though these have persuaded the mass of mankind, or that portion of it which is possessed of leisure, to let Culture be regarded as an important source of happiness; they can scarcely be said to have produced any generally accepted opinion as to its importance in comparison with the other sources before mentioned, the pleasures of which are more genuinely appreciated by the majority; still less as to the relative value of different elements of this culture.

But even supposing the *consensus*, in respect of sources of happiness, were far more complete and clear than impartial reflection seems to shew, its value would still be considerably impaired by the dissent of important minorities, which we have not yet noticed. For example, many religious persons regard all the mundane pleasures of which we have been speaking, as not only relatively contemptible, in comparison with the lofty delights of the religious life, but positively mean and trifling; so full of vanity and emptiness that the pursuit of them is not only occasionally but normally illusory, and leads to bitter disappointment. And a somewhat similar judgment, though from a different point of view, has in all ages been passed by the majority of the class known as Philosophers. And when we consider, as Plato urges, that these latter have paid especial attention to the subject in debate, which the mass of mankind have not done, we shall hesitate to let our conclusion be determined by merely counting heads. On the other hand, as has been already observed, the philosopher's susceptibilities and capacities of feeling do not fairly represent those of humanity in general: and hence if he ventures to erect the results of his individual experience into a universal standard, he is likely to overrate some pleasures and underrate others. Perhaps the most convincing illustrations of this are furnished by thinkers not of the idealist or transcendental type, but professed Hedonists, such as Epicurus and Hobbes. We cannot accept as fair expressions of the average or common experience of the race either the former's identification of painlessness with the highest degree of pleasure, or the latter's asseveration that the gratifications of curiosity "far exceed in intensity all carnal delights." Thus we seem to be in this dilemma: the mass of mankind, to whose common opinion we are naturally referred for catholically authoritative beliefs respecting the conditions of happiness, are deficient in the faculty and the habit of observing and recording their experience: and usually, in proportion as a man is, by nature and practice, a better observer, the phenomena that he has to observe are more and more divergent from the ordinary type.

§ 3. On the whole it must, I think, be admitted that the Hedonistic method cannot be freed from inexactness and uncertainty by appealing to the judgments of common sense respecting the sources of happiness. At the same time I would not exaggerate the difficulty of combining these into a tolerably coherent body of probable doctrine, not useless for practical guidance. For first, it must be observed, that it is only occasionally and to a limited extent that these commonly commended sources of happiness come into competition with one another and are presented as alternatives. For example, the pursuit of wealth often leads also to power (besides the power that lies in wealth) and to reputation: and again, these objects of desire can usually be best attained—as far as it is in our power to attain them at all—by employment which in itself gives the pleasure that normally attends energetic exercise of one's best faculties: and this congenial employment is not incompatible with adequate exercise of the affections, social and domestic; nor with cultivated amusement (which must always be carefully limited in amount if it is to be really amusing). And no one doubts that to carry either employment or amusement to a degree that injures health involves generally a sacrifice of happiness, no less than over-indulgence in sensual gratifications.

And as for the quasi-philosophical paradoxes as to the illusoriness of sensual enjoyments, wealth, power, fame, &c. we may explain the general acceptance which these find by admitting a certain amount of inevitable exaggeration in the common estimates of such objects of desire, which from time to time causes a reaction and an equally excessive temporary depreciation of them. For as we saw (ch. 3) it is natural for men to value too highly the absent pleasures for which they hope and long. Power and Fame, for example, are certainly attended with anxieties and disgusts which are not foreseen when they are represented in longing imagination: yet it may still be true that they bring to most men a clear balance of happiness on the whole. It seems clear, again, that luxury adds *less* to the ordinary enjoyment of life than most men struggling with penury suppose: there are special delights attending the hard-earned meal, and the eagerly expected amusement, which must be weighed against the profuser pleasures that the rich can command: so that we may fairly conclude that increase of happiness is very far from keeping pace with increase of wealth. Though, on the other hand, when we take into account all the pleasures of Culture, Power, Fame, and Beneficence, and still more the security that wealth gives against the pains of privation and the anxieties of penury, we can hardly doubt that increase of wealth brings on the average *some* increase of happiness. So that it would be extravagant optimism to affirm that happiness is " equally distributed through all ranks and callings," while yet we may reasonably conclude that it is *more* equally distributed than the aspect of men's external circumstances would lead us to infer: especially if the pleasures that attend the exercise of the affections are to most persons really the most important of all. Again common sense is quite prepared to recognize that there are persons of peculiar temperament to whom the commoner pleasures of life are really quite trifling in comparison with more refined enjoyments: and also that men generally are liable to fall, for certain periods, under the sway of absorbing impulses, which take them out of the range within which the judgments of common sense are even broadly and generally valid. No one (*e.g.*) expects a lover to care much for anything except the enjoyments of love: nor considers that an enthusiast sacrifices happiness in making everything give way to his hobby.

In fact we may say that common sense scarcely claims to provide more than rather indefinite general rules, which no prudent man should neglect without giving himself a reason for doing so. Such reasons may either be drawn from one's knowledge of some peculiarities in one's nature, or from the experience of others whom one has ground for believing to be more like oneself than the average of mankind are. For though, as we saw, there is considerable risk of error in thus appropriating the special experience of other individuals—and in fact the expression of it will sometimes appear to be as hesitating and contradictory as the judgments of common sense—we may perhaps extract from it counsel sufficiently consistent and authoritative to supplement at least roughly the deficiencies of our own empirical generalizations. Still, it does not appear that by any process of this kind,—either by appealing to the common opinion of the many, or to that of cultivated persons, or to that of those whom we judge most to resemble ourselves,—we can hope to solve with precision or certainty the problems of egoistic conduct.

The question then remains, whether any general theory can be attained of the causes of pleasure and pain so certain and practically applicable that we may by its aid rise above the ambiguities and inconsistencies of common or sectarian opinion, no less than the shortcomings of the empirical-reflective method, and 'establish the Hedonistic art of life on a thoroughly scientific basis. To the consideration of this question I shall proceed in the next chapter but one: but before entering upon it, I wish to examine carefully a common belief as to the means of attaining happiness which—though it hardly claims to rest upon a scientific basis—is yet generally conceived by those who hold it to have a higher degree of certainty than ordinary current opinions. This is the belief that a man will attain the greatest happiness open to him by the performance of his Duty as commonly recognized and prescribed—except so far as he may deviate from this standard in obedience to a truer conception of the conduct by which universal good is to be realized or promoted[1]. The special importance of this opinion to a writer on Morals renders it desirable to reserve our discussion of it for a separate chapter.

[1] In the following chapter I have not entered into any particular consideration of the case in which the individual's conscience is definitely in conflict with the general moral consciousness of his age and country: because, though it is commonly held to be a man's duty always to obey the dictates of his own conscience, even at the risk of error, it can hardly be said to be a current opinion that he will always attain the greatest happiness open to him by conforming to the dictates of his conscience even when it conflicts with received morality.

CHAPTER V.

HAPPINESS AND DUTY.

§ 1. THE belief in the connexion of happiness with Duty is one to which we find a general tendency among civilized men, at least after a certain stage in civilisation has been reached. But it is doubtful whether it would be affirmed, among ourselves, as a generalization from experience, and not rather as a matter of direct Divine Revelation, or an immediate inference from the proposition that the world is governed by a perfectly Good and Omnipotent Being; which latter doctrine again is held to be proved either by miraculous Revelation, or the intuitions of Natural Religion, or both combined. To examine thoroughly the validity of the belief in the Moral Government of the World is one of the most important tasks that human reason can attempt: but involving as it does an exhaustive enquiry into the evidences of Natural and Revealed Religion, it could hardly be included within the scope of the present treatise[1]. Here, then, I shall only consider the coincidence of Duty and Happiness in so far as it is maintained by arguments drawn from experience and supposed to be realized in our present earthly life. Perhaps, as so restricted, the coincidence can hardly be said to be "currently believed:" indeed it may be plausibly urged that the reverse belief is implied in the general admission of the necessity of rewards and punishments in a future state,

[1] Such discussion of the question as seemed desirable in such a work as this will be found in the concluding chapter of the treatise.

in order to exhibit and realize completely the moral government of the world. Still, this implication is not strictly necessary; for it may be held that even here virtue is always rewarded and vice punished, so far as to make the virtuous course of action always the most prudent; only that the rewards and punishments are not sufficient to satisfy our sense of justice. Allowing that the virtuous man is often placed on earth in circumstances so adverse that his life is not as happy as that of many less virtuous; it may still be maintained that by virtue he will gain the maximum of happiness that can be gained under these circumstances, all appearances to the contrary notwithstanding. And this view has certainly been held by moralists of reputation on grounds drawn from actual experience of human life; and seems often to be emphatically, though not very definitely, put forward on similar grounds by popular preachers and moralizers. It appears therefore desirable to subject this opinion to a careful and impartial examination. In conducting this examination, at the present stage of our enquiry, we shall have to use the received notions of Duty without further definition or analysis: but it is commonly assumed by those whose view we are to examine that these conceptions—as they are found in the moral consciousness of ordinary well-meaning persons—are at least approximately valid and trustworthy; and the preceding chapters will have fully shewn that the generalizations of Hedonism must be established, if at all, by large considerations and decisive preponderances, and that it would be idle in considering a question of this kind to take account of slight differences, and to pretend to weigh in our mental scales comparatively small portions of happiness.

§ 2. Accepting, then, the common division[1] of duties into self-regarding and social, it may be conceded that as far as the first are concerned the view that we are examining is not likely to provoke any controversy: for by 'duties towards oneself' are commonly meant acts that tend directly or indirectly to promote one's happiness. We may therefore confine our atten-

[1] Whatever modifications of this division may afterwards appear to be necessary (cf. Bk. III. c. 2) will not, I think, tend to invalidate the conclusions of the present chapter.

tion to the social department of Duty, and consider whether by observing the moral rules that prescribe certain modes of behaviour towards others we shall always tend to secure the greatest balance of happiness to ourselves.

Here it will be convenient to adopt with some modification the point of view and terminology of Bentham. It has been already observed, that while stating General Happiness as the right and proper end of human action, Bentham still held that every human agent actually does aim at his own individual happiness. He therefore considered human pleasure (and pain as its negative quantity) from two quite distinct points of view: first as constituting the end and standard of right conduct, and so determining the rules which Bentham and other rational philanthropists would desire to be generally obeyed in any community: and secondly as constituting the motives (whether pleasures or pains) by which each member of the community is or may be induced to conform to these rules. These motives or 'sanctions' we may classify as External and Internal. The former class will include both 'Legal Sanctions,' or penalties inflicted by the authority, direct or indirect, of the sovereign; and 'Social Sanctions,' which are either the pleasures that may be expected from the approval and goodwill of our fellow-men generally, and the services that they will be prompted to render both by this goodwill and by their appreciation of the usefulness of good conduct, or the annoyance and losses that are to be feared from their distrust and dislike. In so far as the happiness earned by virtue comes from internal sources, it will lie in the pleasurable emotion attending virtuous action, or in the absence of remorse, or will result from some effect on the mental constitution of the agent produced by the maintenance of virtuous dispositions and habits. This classification is important, not merely from the intrinsic differences of the sanctions themselves but also because the systems of rules to which they are respectively attached may be mutually conflicting. The Positive Morality of any community—as no Intuitionist would deny—undergoes development, and is thus subject to changes which affect the consciences of the few before they are accepted by the many; so that the rules at any time sustained by the strongest social sanctions, may not only fall short of, but even clash with, the intuitions of those members of the community who have most moral insight. For similar reasons Law and Positive Morality may be at variance, in details. For though a law could not long exist, which it was universally thought wrong to obey; there may easily be laws commanding conduct that is considered immoral by some more or less enlightened minority of the community, some sect or party that has a public opinion of its own: and any individual may be so much more closely connected with this minority than with the rest, of the community, that the social sanction may in his case practically operate against the legal.

No doubt in a thoroughly well-ordered state there would be no such conflict of sanctions: Law would always be in harmony with current moral sentiments, and these latter would always be found supporting such rules of behaviour as an enlightened moralist would lay down. And such a state of things, of course, is that to which Benthamites (and other philanthropists) are continually trying to approximate: it is their object so to adjust legal penalties, and influence public opinion, and train and develope the moral habits and social sentiments of all individuals, that, as far as possible,

"Each may find his own in all men's good."

What they have therefore to consider is how the impulsive force of different sanctions on the minds of ordinary men may be increased or better directed. But the question that we are now investigating is fundamentally different: it is, namely, whether these sanctions as at present existing, or rather as capable of being foreseen, are sufficient in all cases to determine a rational egoist to the performance of social duty. And from this point of view the actual conflict of sanctions is of great importance: for the more stress we lay on either the legal or the social sanctions of moral conduct, the greater difficulty we shall have in proving the coincidence of duty and self-interest in the exceptional cases in which we find these sanctions arrayed against what we conceive to be duty.

But even if we put these cases out of sight, it still seems clear that the external sanctions of morality alone are not always sufficient to render immoral conduct also imprudent.

I hardly need occupy time in showing that this is the case with legal sanctions, considered by themselves. We must indeed admit that in an even tolerably well-ordered society, *i.e.* in an ordinary civilized community in its normal condition, all serious open violation of law is contrary to prudence, unless it is an incident in a successful process of violent revolution: and further, that violent revolutions would very rarely—perhaps never—be made by a combination of persons, perfectly under the control of enlightened self-love; on account of the general and widespread destruction of security and of other means of happiness which such disturbances inevitably involve. Still, so long as actual human beings are not all rational egoists, such times of disorder will be liable to occur: and we cannot say that *under existing circumstances* it is a clear universal precept of Rational Self-love that a man should "seek peace and ensue it:" since some men gain, by the disturbance of political order, wealth, fame, and power, to an extent to which in peaceful times they could not hope to approximate: and though there is always some risk involved in this mode of pursuing these goods, it may be reduced to a comparatively small amount by a cool and skilful person who has the art of fishing in troubled waters[1]. And even admitting that this road to success is clearly over-hazardous for prudent men in tolerably good circumstances; still, it is not clear that such men will find it their interest to make any great sacrifices in averting or resisting political disorder. In short, though we may admit that a society composed entirely of rational egoists would, when once organized, be in a stable and orderly condition, it does not follow that the adoption of rational egoism by a minority of thoughtful persons would tend to bring about this result in any existing community.

But at any rate, in the most orderly societies with which we are acquainted, the administration of law and justice is never in so perfect a state as to render *secret* crimes always acts of folly, on the score of the legal penalties attached to

[1] I do not here consider the case of revolutionists aiming sincerely at the general wellbeing; since the morality of such revolutions will generally be so dubious, that these cases cannot furnish any clear argument on either side of the question here discussed.

them. For however much these may outweigh the advantages of crime, cases must inevitably occur in which the risk of discovery is so small, that on a sober calculation the almost certain gain will more than compensate for the slight chance of the penalty. And finally, in no community is the law actually in so perfect a state that there are not certain kinds of flagrantly anti-social conduct, such as common sense regards as intrinsically criminal, which slip through its meshes and escape legal penalties altogether.

§ 3. Let us proceed, then, to consider how far the social sanction in such cases supplies the defects of the legal. No doubt the hope of praise and liking and services from one's fellow-men, and the fear of forfeiting these and incurring instead blame, aversion, refusal of aid, and social exclusion, are considerations often important enough to determine the rational egoist to law-observance, even in default of adequate legal penalties. Still these sanctions are liable to fail just where the legal penalties are defective; social no less than legal penalties are evaded by secret crimes; and even in cases of the most clearly criminal revolutionary violence, the efficacy of the social sanction is apt to be seriously impaired by the party spirit enlisted on the side of the criminal. For it has to be observed that the force of the social sanction diminishes very rapidly, in proportion to the number of dissidents from the common opinion that awards it. Disapprobation that is at once intense and quite universal, would be so severe a penalty as perhaps to outweigh any imaginable advantages: since it seems impossible for a human being to live happily, whatever other goods he may enjoy, without the kindly regards of some of his fellows: and so, in contemplating the common philosophic portrait of the tyrant of old time, who is represented as necessarily suspicious of those nearest him, even of the members of his own family, we feel prepared to admit that such a life must involve the extreme of unhappiness. But when we contemplate the modern tyrannical usurpers, wicked statesmen, successful leaders of unwarranted rebellion, and, speaking generally, the great criminals whose position raises them out of the reach of legal penalties, though the moral odium under which they lie is in most cases a source of some pain, it does not appear that it must necessarily count for much in an egoistic calculation of the gain and loss resulting from their conduct. For this disesteem is only expressed by a portion of the community: and its utterance is often drowned in the loud-voiced applause of the multitude whose admiration is largely independent of moral considerations.

It seems, then, impossible to affirm, without admitting important exceptions, that the external sanctions of men's legal duties will always be sufficient to identify them with their interests. And a corresponding assertion would be still more unwarranted in respect of that part of Positive Morality which extends beyond the sphere of Law. In saying this, I am fully sensible of the force of what may be called the Principle of Reciprocity, by which certain utilitarians have endeavoured to prove the coincidence of the individual's interests with his social duties. Virtues (they say) are qualities either useful or directly agreeable to others: thus they either increase the market value of the virtuous man's services, and cause others to purchase them at a higher rate and to allot to him more dignified and interesting functions: or they dispose men to please him, both out of gratitude and in order to enjoy the pleasure of his society in return: and again—since man is an imitative animal—the exhibition of these qualities is naturally rewarded by a reciprocal manifestation of them on the part of others, through the mere influence of example. I do not doubt that the hope of these advantages is an adequate motive for cultivating many virtues and avoiding much vice. Thus on such grounds a rational egoist will generally be strict and punctual in the fulfilment of all his engagements, and truthful in his assertions, in order to win the confidence of other men; and he will be zealous and industrious in his work, in order to obtain gradually more important and therefore more honourable and lucrative employment; and he will control such of his passions and appetites as are likely to interfere with his efficiency; and will not exhibit violent anger or use unnecessary harshness even towards servants and subordinates; and towards his equals and superiors in rank he will be generally polite and complaisant and good-humoured, and prompt to shew them all such kindness as costs but little in proportion to the pleasure it gives. Still, reflection seems to shew that the conduct recommended by this line of reasoning does not really coincide with moral duty. For, first, what one requires for social success is that one should *appear*, rather than *be*, useful to others: and hence this motive will not restrain one from doing secret harm to others, or even from acting openly in a way that is really harmful, though not perceived to be so. And again, a man is not useful to others by his virtue only, but sometimes rather by his vice: or more often by a certain admixture of unscrupulousness with his good and useful qualities. And further, morality prescribes the performance of duties equally towards all, and that we should abstain as far as possible from harming any: but on the principle of Reciprocity we should exhibit our useful qualities chiefly towards the rich and powerful, and abstain from injuring those who can retaliate; while we may reasonably omit our duties to the poor and feeble, if we find a material advantage in so doing, unless they are able to excite the sympathy of persons who can harm us. Moreover, some vices, (as for example, many kinds of sensuality and extravagant luxury) do not inflict any immediate or obvious injury on any individual, though they tend in the long run to impair the general happiness: hence few persons find themselves strongly moved to check or punish this kind of mischief.

It may perhaps be said that in the last-mentioned cases the mere disrepute inevitably attaching to open immorality is sufficient to render it always really imprudent. But I do not think that this will be seriously maintained by any one who has duly considered the variety of coexisting codes, which we everywhere find when we examine the actual condition of those bodies—or rather streams—of social opinion upon which the good or ill repute of individuals mainly depends. Many moralists have noticed the discrepancy in modern Europe between the Law of Honour (or the rules maintained by the social sanction of polite persons) and the morality professed in society at large. This discrepancy generally lies in the greater laxity of the former rules: but in a few instances conflicting duties are prescribed by the two codes, as in the case of duelling. The Law of Honour, however, is by no means the only instance of a special code, divergent in certain points from the moral rules generally accepted in the community where it exists. Most religious sects and parties, and probably the majority of trades and professions, exhibit this phenomenon in some degree. I do not mean merely that special rules of behaviour are imposed upon members of each profession, corresponding to their special social functions and relations: I mean that a peculiar moral opinion is apt to grow up, conflicting to a certain extent with the opinion of the general public. The most striking part of this divergence consists generally in the approval or excusal of practices disapproved by the current morality: as (*e. g.*) license among soldiers, bribery among politicians in certain ages and countries, unveracity of various degrees among priests and advocates, fraud in different forms among tradesmen. In such cases there are generally strong natural inducements to disobey the stricter rule (in fact it would seem to be to the continual pressure of these inducements that the relaxation of the rule has been due): while at the same time the social sanction is weakened to such an extent that it is sometimes hard to say whether it outweighs a similar force on the other side. For a man who, under these circumstances, conforms to the general code, if he does not actually meet with contempt and aversion from those of his calling, is at least liable to be called eccentric and fantastic. And this is still more the case, if by conformity to the generally received rule he foregoes advantages not only to himself but to his relatives or friends or party. Very often this professional or sectarian excusal of immorality of which we are speaking is not so clear and explicit as to amount to the establishment of a rule, conflicting with the generally received rule: but is still sufficient to weaken indefinitely the social sanction in favour of the latter. More generally, we may almost say that in most civilized societies there are two different degrees of positive morality, both maintained in some sort by common consent; a stricter code being publicly taught and avowed, while a laxer set of rules is privately admitted as the only code which can be supported by social sanctions of any great force. By refusing to conform to the stricter code a man is often not liable to incur exclusion from social intercourse, or any material hindrance to professional advancement, or even serious dislike on the part of any of the persons whose society he will most naturally seek; and under such circumstances the mere loss of a certain amount of reputation is not likely to be felt as a very grave evil, except by persons peculiarly sensitive to the pleasures and pains of reputations. I admit the difficulty of giving a general estimate of the relative hedonistic value of this class of feelings, which no doubt varies very much with different individuals: but at any rate we may say that there are many men whose happiness does not appear to depend on the approbation or disapprobation of the moralist—and of mankind in general in so far as they support the moralist—to such an extent as to make it prudent for them to purchase this praise by any great sacrifice of other goods.

§ 4. We must conclude, then, that if the conduct prescribed to the individual by the highest morality of the community of which he is a member can be shewn to coincide with that to which Rational Self-love would prompt, it must be, in many cases, on the score of the internal sanctions only. In considering the force of these sanctions, we have first to distinguish and eliminate those pleasures and pains which lie in the anticipation of rewards and punishments in a future life: for as we are now supposing the calculations of Rational Egoism to be performed without taking into account any feelings that are beyond the range of experience, it will be more consistent to exclude also the pleasurable or painful anticipations of such feelings.

If, then, we contemplate by itself the satisfaction that attends the performance of duty as such (without taking into consideration any ulterior consequences), and the pain that follows on its violation, we cannot doubt that they are sufficiently intense to constitute very powerful motives with some minds. At the same time, though the discussions of the two preceding chapters will have shewn the great difficulty of weighing exactly these pleasures and pains against others, there are very strong grounds for believing that <u>they are not sufficiently intense to turn</u> the balance of prospective happiness always in favour of <u>duty</u>. This will hardly be denied if the question is raised in respect of isolated acts of duty. Let us take an extreme case, which is yet quite within the limits of experience. The call of duty has often impelled a soldier or other public servant, or the adherent of a persecuted religion, to face certain and painful death, under circumstances where it might be avoided with little or no loss even of reputation. To prove such conduct always reasonable from an egoistic point of view, we have to assume that, in all cases where such a duty could exist and be recognized, the mere pain[1] that would follow on evasion of duty would be so great as to render the whole remainder of life hedonistically worthless. Surely such an assumption would be paradoxical and extravagant. It rather appears that while the majority of persons in any society are generally able to discern their duty (according to the code and standard currently accepted in their society), the number of those in whom the moral feelings taken alone form a preponderant or even important element of happiness is by no means large. A striking evidence of this is furnished by those Christian writers of the last century who treat the *moral* unbeliever as a fool who sacrifices his happiness both here and hereafter. These men were, for the most part, earnestly engaged in the practice of virtue, and yet this practice had not made them love virtue so much as to prefer it, even under ordinary circumstances, to the sensual and other enjoyments that it excludes. It seems then absurd to suppose that, in the case of persons who have not developed and strengthened by habit their virtuous impulses, the pain that might afterwards result from resisting the call of duty would always be sufficient to neutralize all other sources of pleasure. And even if we take more ordinary cases, where a man is called on to give up, for virtue's sake, not life, but a considerable share of the ordinary sources of human happiness;

[1] Under the notion of 'moral pain' (or pleasure) I intend to include, in this argument, all pain (or pleasure) that is due to sympathy with the feelings of others. It is not convenient to enter, at this stage of the discussion, into a full discussion of the relation of Sympathy to Moral Sensibility: but I may say that it seems to me certain, on the one hand, that these two emotional susceptibilities are actually distinct in most minds, whatever they may have been originally; and on the other hand that sympathetic and strictly moral feelings are almost inextricably blended in the ordinary moral consciousness: so that, for the purposes of the present argument it is not of fundamental importance to draw a distinction between them. I have, however, thought it desirable to undertake a further examination of sympathy—as the internal sanction on which Utilitarians specially lay stress—in the concluding chapter of this treatise: to which, accordingly, the reader may refer.

can we say that all, or even most, men are so constituted that the satisfactions of a good conscience are certain to repay them for such sacrifices, or that the pain and loss involved in them would certainly be outweighed by the remorse that would follow the refusal to make them?

Perhaps, however, so much as this has scarcely ever been expressly maintained. What Plato in his most famous treatise, and others since Plato, have rather tried to prove, is not that at any particular moment duty will be, to every one on whom it may devolve, productive of more happiness than any other course of conduct: but rather that it is every one's interest on the whole to choose the life of the virtuous man. But even this it is very difficult even to render probable: as will appear, I think, if we examine the lines of reasoning by which it is commonly supported.

To begin with Plato's argument, which seems to have found no little acceptance, even in modern times. He represents the soul of the virtuous man as a well-ordered polity of impulses, in which every passion and appetite is duly obedient to the rightful sovereignty of reason, and operates only within the limits laid down by the latter. He then contrasts the tranquil peace of such a mind with the disorder of one where a succession of baser impulses, or some ruling passion, lords it over reason: and asks which is the happiest, even apart from external rewards and punishments. But we may grant all that Plato claims, and yet be no further advanced towards the solution of the question before us. For here the issue does not lie between Reason and Passion, but rather—in Butler's language—between Rational Self-love and Conscience. We are supposing the Egoist to have all his impulses under control, and are only asking how this control is to be exercised. Now we have seen that the regulation and organization of life best calculated to attain the end of self-interest appears *primâ facie* divergent at certain points from that to which men in general are prompted by a sense of duty. In order to maintain Plato's position it has to be shewn that this appearance is false; and that a system of self-government, which under certain circumstances leads us to pain, loss, and death, is still that which self-interest requires. It can scarcely be said that our nature is such that only this latter kind of regulation is possible; that the choice lies between this and none at all. It is easy to imagine a rational egoist, strictly controlling each of his passions and impulses—including his social sentiments—within such limits that its indulgence should not involve the sacrifice of some greater gratification: and experience seems to shew us many examples of persons who at least approximate as closely to this type, as any one else does to the ideal of the ordinary moralist. Hence it would seem that if the regulation according to the notions of duty be really the best means to the individual's happiness, it must be on account of the specific emotional pleasure that attends the indulgence of the moral sentiments, and the specific pain consequent on their repression and violation.

Before, however, we proceed further, a fundamental difficulty must be removed which has probably some time since suggested itself to the reader. If a man thinks it reasonable to seek his own interest, it is clear that he cannot himself disapprove of any conduct that comes under this principle or approve of the opposite. And hence it may appear that the pleasures and pains of conscience cannot enter into the calculation whether a certain course of conduct is or is not in accordance with Rational Egoism, because they cannot attach themselves in the egoist's mind to any modes of action, which have not been already decided, on other grounds, to be reasonable or the reverse. And this is to a certain extent true; but we must here recur to the distinction (indicated in Book I. ch. 3, § 1) between the general impulse to do what we believe to be reasonable, and special sentiments of liking or aversion for special kinds of conduct, independent of their reasonableness. In the moral sentiments as they exist in ordinary men, these two kinds of feeling are indistinguishably blended: because it is commonly believed that the rules of conduct to which the common moral sentiments are attached are in some way or other reasonable. We can however conceive the two separated: and in fact, as was before said, we have experience of such separation whenever a man is led by a process of thought to adopt a different view of morality from that in which he has been trained: for in such a case there will always remain in his mind some quasi-moral likings and aversions, no longer sustained by his deliberate judgment of right and wrong. And thus there is every reason to believe that most men, however firmly they might adopt the principles of Egoistic Hedonism, would still feel sentiments prompting to the performance of social duty, as commonly recognized in their society, independently of any conclusion that the actions prompted by such sentiments were reasonable and right. For such sentiments would always be powerfully supported by the sympathy of others, and their expressions of praise and blame, liking and aversion: and since it is agreed that the conduct commonly recognized as virtuous is *generally* coincident with that which enlightened self-love would dictate, a rational egoist's habits of conduct will be such as naturally to foster these 'quasi-moral' feelings. The question therefore before us is not whether the egoist should cherish and indulge these sentiments up to a certain point—which all would admit—but whether he should allow them to grow to such a pitch that they will always prevail over the strongest opposing considerations; whether, in fact, he should give them the rein and let them carry him whither they will. We have already seen ground for believing that Rational Self-love will best attain its end by limiting its conscious operation and allowing free play to disinterested impulses: but we are now asked to accept the further paradox that it is reasonable for it to abdicate its supremacy altogether over some of these impulses.

On a careful consideration of the matter, it will appear, I think, that this abdication of self-love is not really a possible occurrence in the mind of a sane person, who still regards his own interest as the reasonable ultimate end of his actions. Such a man may, no doubt, resolve that he will devote himself unreservedly to the practice of virtue, without any particular consideration of what appears to him to be his interest: he may perform a series of acts in accordance with this resolution, and these may gradually form in him strong habitual tendencies to acts of a similar kind. But it does not seem that these habits of virtue can ever become so strong as to gain irresistible control over a sane and reasonable will. When the occasion comes on which virtue demands from such a man an extreme sacrifice —the imprudence of which must force itself upon his notice, however little he may be in the habit of weighing his own pleasures and pains—he must always be able to deliberate afresh, and to act (as far as the control of his will extends) without reference to his past actions. It may, however, be said that though an egoist retaining his belief in rational egoism cannot thus abandon his will to the sway of moral enthusiasm: still, supposing it possible for him to change his conviction and prefer duty to interest, or supposing we compare him with another man who makes this choice, we shall find that a gain in happiness on the whole results from this preference. It may be held that there is so great a difference in respect of pleasure between the emotions attendant upon such virtuous or quasi-virtuous habits as are compatible with adhesion to egoistic principles, and the raptures that attend the unreserved and passionate surrender of the soul to virtue; that it is really a man's interest—even with a view to the present life only—to obtain, if he can, the convictions that render this surrender possible, although under certain circumstances it must necessarily lead him to act in a manner which, considered by itself, would be undoubtedly imprudent. This is certainly a tenable proposition and I am quite disposed to think it true of persons with specially refined moral sensibilities. But—though from the imperfections of the hedonistic calculus the proposition cannot in any case be conclusively disproved—it seems to me opposed to the broad results of experience, so far as the great majority of mankind are concerned. As I have before said experience would lead us to suppose that most men are so constituted as to feel far more keenly pleasures (and pains) arising from some other source than the conscience; either from the gratifications of sense, or from the possession of power and fame, or from strong human affections, or from the pursuit of science, art, &c.; so that in many cases perhaps not even early training could have succeeded in giving to the moral feelings the requisite predominance: and certainly where this training has been wanting, it seems highly improbable that a mere change of ethical conviction could develope their moral susceptibilities so far as to make it clearly their earthly interest to resolve on facing all sacrifices for the fulfilment of duty.

To sum up. Although the performance of duties towards others and the exercise of social virtue seem to be *generally* the best means to the attainment of the individual's happiness, and it is easy to exhibit this coincidence between Virtue and Happiness rhetorically and popularly; still, when we carefully analyse and estimate the consequences of Virtue to the virtuous agent, it appears improbable that this coincidence is complete and universal. We may conceive the coincidence becoming perfect in a Utopia where men were as much in accord on moral as they are now on mathematical questions, where Law was in perfect harmony with Moral Opinion, and all offences were discovered and duly punished: or we may conceive the same result attained by intensifying the moral sentiments of all members of the community, without any external changes (which indeed would then be unnecessary). But just in proportion as existing societies and existing men fall short of this ideal, rules of conduct based on the principles of Egoistic Hedonism must diverge from those which most men are accustomed to recognize as prescribed by Duty and Virtue.

CHAPTER VI.

OTHER METHODS OF EGOISTIC HEDONISM.

§ 1. IN the preceding chapter we have seen reason to conclude that, while the habit of obeying recognized rules of duty is, under ordinary circumstances, an important source of happiness to the agent, there are yet no adequate empirical grounds for regarding the performance of duty as a universal or infallible means to the attainment of this end. Even, however, if it were otherwise, even if it were demonstrably reasonable for the egoist to choose duty at all costs under all circumstances, the systematic endeavour to realize this principle would not—according to common notions of morality—solve or supersede the problem of determining the right method for seeking happiness. For the received moral code allows within limits the pursuit of our own happiness, and even seems to regard it as morally prescribed[1]; and still more emphatically inculcates the promotion of the happiness of other individuals, with whom we are in various ways specially connected: so that, under either head, the questions that we have been considering as to the determination and measurement of the elements of happiness would still have to be answered in some way or other.

It remains to ask how far a scientific investigation of the causes of pleasure and pain can assist us in dealing with this practical problem.

Here, in the first place, a distinction has to be made of

---

[1] "It should seem that a due concern about our own interest or happiness, "and a reasonable endeavour to secure and promote it,...is virtue, and the con-"trary behaviour faulty and blamable." Butler (in the dissertation 'of the 'nature of Virtue' appended to the *Analogy*).

fundamental importance. It is obvious that for deciding which of two courses of action is preferable on hedonistic grounds, we require not only to measure pains and pleasures of different kinds, but also to ascertain how they may be produced or averted. In most important prudential decisions, a complex chain of consequences, often very long, is foreseen as intervening between the volition we are immediately to initiate and the states of consciousness which constitute the ultimate end of our efforts; and the degree of accuracy with which we forecast each link of this chain—and of other chains compared with it—obviously depends upon our knowledge, implicit or explicit, of the relations of cause and effect among various natural phenomena. But if we suppose the different elements and immediate sources of happiness to have been duly ascertained and valued, the investigation of the conditions of production of each does not, I conceive, belong to a general treatise on the method of ethics; but rather to some one or other of the special arts subordinate to the general art of conduct. Of these subordinate arts some have a more or less scientific basis; while others are in a merely empirical stage and can only be to a very slight extent communicated in a general form. Thus, if we have decided how far health is to be sought, it belongs to the systematic art of medicine, based on physiological science, to furnish a detailed plan of seeking it; so far, on the other hand, as we aim at power or wealth or domestic happiness, such instruction as the experience of others can give will be chiefly obtained in an unsystematic form, either from advice relative to our own special circumstances, or from biographical or other accounts of success and failure in analogous situations. In either case the exposition of such special arts does not appear to come within the scope of the present treatise; and it is obvious that it could not help us to avoid the difficulties of measuring pleasures and pains, which we have considered in the previous chapters.

It seems, however, to be thought by some persons that a knowledge of the causes of pleasure and pain may carry us beyond the determination of the means of gaining particular kinds of pleasure and avoiding particular kinds of pain; may enable us, in fact, to substitute some deductive method of evaluing the elements of happiness generally for the empirical-reflective method of which we have seen the defects. This view may perhaps have been suggested to some readers by Mr Herbert Spencer's statement[1] that "it is the business of moral science to deduce, from the laws of life and the conditions of existence, what kind of actions necessarily tend to produce happiness, and what kinds to produce unhappiness," and that when it has done this, "its deductions are to be recognized as laws of conduct; and are to be conformed to irrespective of a direct estimate of happiness or misery." Mr Spencer, however, has made clear in his latest treatise that the only cogent deductions of this kind which he conceives to be possible relate to the behaviour not of men here and now, but of ideal men living in an ideal society, and living under conditions so unlike those of actual humanity that all their actions produce "pleasure unalloyed by pain anywhere[2]." The laws—or uniformities—of conduct in this Utopia constitute, in Mr Spencer's view, the subject-matter of "Absolute Ethics;" which he distinguishes from the "Relative Ethics" that concerns itself with the conduct of the imperfect men who live under the present imperfect social conditions, and of which the method is, as he admits, to a great extent "necessarily empirical[3]." How far such a system as Mr Spencer calls Absolute Ethics can be rationally constructed, and how far its construction would be practically useful, I shall consider further in a later part of this treatise, when I come to deal with the method of Universalistic Hedonism[4]: these questions do not concern us at present[5], since I do not understand even Mr Spencer to maintain that his Absolute Ethics is capable of furnishing important practical guidance to an individual seeking his own greatest happiness here and now.

Mr Spencer's authority, therefore, cannot properly be quoted in favour of any method of seeking one's own happiness which claims to dispense with direct estimates of the pleasurable and painful consequences of actions. Indeed a hedonistic method that would dispense with such estimates altogether is almost as

---

[1] In a letter to J. S. Mill, published in Mr Bain's *Mental and Moral Science;* and partially reprinted in Mr Spencer's *Data of Ethics*, ch. iv. § 21.
[2] *Data of Ethics*, ch. xv. § 101.   [3] *Id.* § 108.
[4] Book IV. ch. iv.
[5] They have been already considered to some extent in Book I. ch. ii, § 2.

inconceivable as a method of astronomy that would dispense with observations of the stars. It is, however, conceivable that by induction from cases in which empirical measurement is easy we may obtain generalizations that will give us more trustworthy guidance than such measurement can do in complicated cases; we may be able to ascertain some general psychical or physical concomitant or antecedent of pleasure and pain, more easy to recognize, foresee, measure, and produce or avert in such cases, than pleasure and pain themselves. I am quite disposed to hope that this refuge from the difficulties of Empirical Hedonism may some time or other be open to us: but I cannot perceive that it is at present possible. There is at present, so far as I can judge, no satisfactorily established general theory of the causes of pleasure and pain; and such theories as have most currency are not adapted for the practical application that we require.

§ 2. To shew this, I will briefly examine some of the current theories on this subject. We may begin by noticing the doctrine of Sir William Hamilton[1], which refers pleasure and pain to certain immediate psychical antecedents; defining pleasure as the "reflex"—*i.e.* immediate consequent—of "spontaneous and unimpeded energy of a power of whose energy we are conscious," and pain as the "reflex of overstrained or repressed exertion." The phrases seem to me misleading; since all the terms suggest *active* as ordinarily distinguished from *passive* states, whereas Hamilton explains that "energy" and similar terms "are to be understood to denote indifferently all the processes of our higher and lower life of which we are conscious," on the ground that consciousness itself implies more than a mere passivity of the subject. And I think that Hamilton has been misled by his own terms; and that he does not always keep this wider meaning clearly in view. Thus he says that every energy has "an object about which it is conversant;" and distinguishes "spontaneous" and "unimpeded" as referring respectively to the absence of effort and constraint on the part

---

[1] It seems that Hamilton's theory still finds at least a modified acceptance in some quarters—in France, if not in England. Cf. Bouillier, *Du Plaisir et de la Douleur*, ch. iii.; and L. Dumont, *Théorie Scientifique de la Sensibilité*, ch. iii.

of the subject, and the absence of obstacles on the part of the object. But what meaning has this distinction in relation to organic feelings of the kind ordinarily called passive—*i.e.* only active in the sense that we are conscious of them? The consciousness accompanying a toothache is as much without effort or constraint on the part of the subject[1] as the consciousness of a warm bath—except so far as "constraint" is implied in the very definition of pain, since it is a feeling that we have, though we desire not to have it; but since this constraint is an essential characteristic of the effect to be explained, no step towards explanation is gained by attributing the same characteristic to its cause. And even if we confine the theory to pleasures that depend on voluntary action, it cannot be regarded as satisfactory. It is not true that the exercise of our powers is always made less pleasant by the presence of obstacles; since some obstacles increase pleasure by drawing out force and skill to overcome them, as in the case of games and sports: and even if we understand "unimpeded" to imply the absence of such obstacles as repress and diminish action, I do not think that the criterion is supported by experience, except so far as the repression causes the specific discomfort of unsatisfied desire. I do not find that the mere weakening or shortening of a pleasure through unfavourable external conditions, has any tendency to turn it into a pain unless it carries with it the sense of a disappointed craving for more pleasure; which is by no means always the case, to any appreciable extent.

The theory becomes more plausible if we drop the antithesis of "spontaneous" and "unimpeded," and, passing to a physical point of view, mean by "activity" the activity of an *organ*. We thus reach what is substantially Mr Spencer's doctrine, that pains are the psychical concomitants of excessive or deficient actions of organs, while pleasures are the concomitants of medium activities[2]; where "excessive" and "deficient" are to be understood in a merely quantitative sense, as meaning action above or below a certain degree of intensity. In considering

---

[1] It must be remembered that the 'subject' in Hamilton's philosophic terminology is the mind as distinguished from the body. Cf. *Lectures on Metaphysics*, ch. ix. "Explication of Terms."

[2] *Psychology*, ch. ix. § 128.

this theory it will be convenient to take pleasures and pains separately. As applied to pains, the formula no doubt corresponds to a good deal of our sensible experience; any one can easily recall a number of cases in which the mere intensification of the action of an organ turns the accompanying feeling from pleasant or indifferent into painful. Thus when we gradually increase the intensity of sensible heat, pressure, muscular effort, we encounter pain at a certain point of the increase; "deafening" sounds are highly disagreeable: and to confront a tropical sun with unprotected eye-balls would soon become torture. And it is noteworthy that, as Spencer points out, some pains arise from the excessive actions of organs whose normal actions yield no feelings: as when the digestive apparatus is overtaxed. On the other hand I cannot but regard as unwarranted the general conclusion which Wundt[1] founds on these instances; that there is no quality of sensation absolutely pleasant or unpleasant, but that every kind of sensation as it grows in intensity begins at a certain point to be pleasurable and continues such up to a certain further point at which it passes rapidly through indifference into pain. I cannot agree with Wundt that all disagreeable odours and flavours may be made positively agreeable by diminution; I find that some are disagreeable till they become indifferent and then vanish; hence I should refer the discomfort they cause to some kind of discordant, jarring, inharmonious action of the respective nerves, rather than to mere excess of action. A similar explanation suggests itself for the digestive discomforts which arise, as many do, from an improper kind rather than an improper quantity of food: and even more obviously for the important class of pains which are clearly connected with destruction or disease of organs and tissues, whether due to external or to internal causes. So again, among pleasurable sensations some certainly might be named which shew no capacity of being further intensified into pains—at least in healthy persons. While in the case of emotional pains and pleasures, the notion of quantitative difference seems altogether inapplicable: the pains of shame, disappointed ambition, wounded love, do not appear to be distinguishable from the pleasures of fame, success, reciprocated affection, by

---

[1] *Grundzüge der physiologischen Psychologie*, ch. x.

any difference of intensity in the impressions or ideas accompanied by the pleasures and pains respectively. On the other hand, if the explanation above suggested be adopted, we are enabled to regard the pains that, according to Mr Spencer, arise from "deficient" action as fundamentally similar in respect of physical causation with those which he attributes to excessive action. As I have before observed[1], we have to distinguish from pains mere "cravings" which may be powerful as impulses to action, without being painful in any appreciable degree: and, so far as my experience goes, it is not the mere inaction of an organ that causes pain, but only such degree of inaction as is beginning to produce some kind of derangement in the organ. Thus hunger, in my experience, may be extremely keen without being at all painful; and when it becomes really painful, a temporarily reduced power of assimilation is apt to follow, shewing that the digestive apparatus has been somewhat disorganized.

However this may be, whether we conceive the nervous action of which pain is an immediate consequent or concomitant as merely excessive in quantity, or in some way discordant or disorganized in quality, it is obvious that neither explanation can furnish us with any important practical guidance: since we have no general means of ascertaining, independently of our experience of pain itself, what nervous actions are excessive or disorganized: and the cases where we have such means do not present any practical problems which the theory enables us to solve. No one doubts that wounds and diseases are to be avoided under all ordinary circumstances: and in the exceptional circumstances in which we may be moved to choose them as the least of several evils, the exactest knowledge of their precise operation in causing pain is not likely to assist our choice.

Still less useful, if possible, is the theory above discussed in its relation to pleasure. In the first place, even if we consent to attribute all pains to "excessive action," the broad statement that pleasures are the concomitants of moderate or normal activities of organs or tissues remains *primâ facie* opposed to common experience: in the *routine* of ordinary daily life

[1] Book I. ch. iv.

pleasure, in any recognizable degree, appears as an occasional phenomenon, the majority of states in which consciousness is of moderate intensity being nearly or quite indifferent. And I know no grounds—except the exigencies of theoretical symmetry —for adopting Mr Grant Allen's suggestion that "doubtless every activity when not excessive or of a sort destructive to the tissues is in itself faintly pleasurable; but owing to the commonness and faintness of the feeling we habitually disregard it[1]." Certainly, so far as my own experience goes, the most careful introspection would leave indifference at least a frequently recurring characteristic of the normal processes of commonplace, everyday, life.

At any rate, all admit that the intensity of pleasure bears no proportion to the intensity of the "medium activity" of which the pleasure is a concomitant. How are we to explain this? One part of the explanation, I have no doubt, is to be found in the preponderant objectivity of our everyday consciousness, the absorption of our attention in contemplation of, or action upon, the objective world: this absorption certainly seems to prevent small pleasures from being felt, and therefore, in my view, from existing as pleasures. The experience of pleasure and pain involves an intensification of the consciousness of self that is faint or evanescent in a great part of our ordinary life: hence Wundt, speaking of pleasures of sense, is inclined to see in the pleasure (or pain) the "symptom of a more central process" than that psychically manifested in the quality or strength of the sense-impression itself. But this seems to me erroneous; as I apprehend my own experience, intensity of pleasure or pain is rather antecedent and cause of the intensification of self-consciousness which attends it; while on the other hand this intensification of selfconsciousness often occurs without the presence of pleasure or pain in an appreciable degree.

Some quite different explanation must therefore be sought for the varying degrees in which pleasure accompanies normal activities. Can we find this in a suggestion of Mr Spencer's, developed by Mr Grant Allen, that the pleasurableness of normal activities depends on their *intermittence*, and that "the amount of pleasure is probably...in the inverse ratio of the natural

---

[1] *Physiological Aesthetics*, ch. ii.

frequency of excitation" of the nerve-fibres involved. This theory certainly finds some support in the fact that the sensual pleasures generally recognized as greatest are those attending the activities of organs which are normally left unexercised for considerable intervals. On the other hand it does not explain the great differences in the pleasures obtainable at any given time by different stimulations of the same sense: and there are certain facts in my own experience that appear to conflict with it—*e.g.* that the exercise of the visual organs after apparently dreamless sleep does not give appreciably keener pleasure than it does at ordinary times. But accepting the theory as partially true, we may still ask how the intermittence operates. The effect can hardly be attributed—as Mr Spencer and Mr Grant Allen seem rather inclined to attribute it—to the greater intensity of the nervous action that takes place when long unexercised and well nourished nerve-centres begin to act: for why, if that were the explanation, should the normal consciousness of full nervous activity, gradually attained—as when we are in the full swing of energetic unwearied work of a routine kind—be nearly or quite indifferent? It would seem rather that the pleasure of intermittent activities must depend on the *freshness* of the activities; *i.e.* on their relation to the states of inaction that precede them.

This leads us to the doctrine of Mr Bain[1] that "states of pleasure are concomitant with an increase, and states of pain with an abatement of some or all of the vital functions:" which Mr Spencer seems to identify with his own broader but vaguer proposition, that "every pleasure increases vitality, every pain decreases vitality[2]." This doctrine, Mr Spencer says, "is put beyond dispute by general experience as well as by the more special experience of medical men." If this be so, I certainly think that the indisputable conclusion should be more precisely defined. Let us take pain first; it clearly cannot be meant that pain is normally accompanied by abatement in the action of the organ primarily concerned; since we have just heard

---

[1] A doctrine to a great extent similar to this has been maintained by earlier writers—e.g. Hobbes—but it appears to me more profitable to criticize it in the form in which Mr Bain has stated it.

[2] *Data of Ethics*, ch. v. § 36 and note.

Mr Spencer say that pain accompanies excessive actions. Is it then meant that excessive action of a special organ, when it reaches the degree of pain, is accompanied by a decrease in the activity of the system generally? This is obviously not true of pains that can be repelled by muscular action; the immediate effect of these is to stir and brace the nervous system for the requisite activities: and I think we may go further and say that even where no such repellent action would be useful, the total effect of moderate and transient pains appears to be often tonic and stimulating rather than depressing. Intense pain, if at all prolonged, no doubt tends to be followed by nervous exhaustion: but this is also true of prolonged pleasurable excitement—as *e.g.* of gambling or novel reading at night. Again, while I do not deny that the immediate effect of specific pleasures on the vital functions generally is stimulating; I should hold that mere stimulation, mere increase of activity, may be produced, in an equal degree, not only—as I have said—by pains, but also by the neutral excitements of desire, aversion, suspense, surprise. And even if we limit the assertion, as regards pleasure, to the activities of the special organ or tissue primarily concerned, I do not see how we can attribute the pleasure of intermitted activities to the mere *amount* of change that occurs when they begin to be exercised; for great and sudden nervous changes often produce only the neutral excitement which we call surprise, and not pleasure at all.

It does not therefore seem to me that mere increase of functioning, mere quantity of change within normal limits, can be properly regarded as the physical concomitant or immediate antecedent of pleasure. So far as the cause of pleasure is rightly held to lie in a relation of transition between the nervous state of which pleasure is the psychical concomitant and the antecedent state of the nervous system, it must be in some more special kind or kinds of such relation. We find that the sudden transition from the state of pain causes the pleasure of "relief," the transition from the tension of desire causes the pleasure of satisfaction, the transition from muscular or intellectual exertion not perceptibly painful causes a pleasurable sensation of rest; and perhaps we may some day bring these cases—and others in which we cannot now discern any affinity with these—under a clearer common conception than we are at present able to do. But for our present purpose it would hardly be worth while to pursue this psychophysical speculation any further; since it must evidently have reached a much more advanced stage before it can furnish us with any practical criterion for the attainment of the greatest pleasure possible.

I may suggest, however, that in certain cases of apparently simple pleasures, where we have no ground for explaining the character of the consciousness by reference to any kind of transition or contrast, it may probably be due to some latent harmony between different elements of feeling, or of the nervous action which immediately precedes or accompanies it: *i.e.* to a cause similar in kind to that which is manifestly operative in the case of the complex pleasures which we distinguish as "æsthetic." These latter undoubtedly constitute an important element in the total happiness of cultivated persons: but the difficult task of explaining them is one which, I conceive, we are not here called upon to attempt; since the impossibility of giving any such explanation of them as would at all enable us to predict their intensity in any particular case would be almost universally admitted. All would agree that æsthetic gratification, when at all high, depends on a subtle harmony of different elements in a complex state of consciousness; and that the pleasure resulting from such harmonious combination is indefinitely greater than the sum of the simpler pleasures which the uncombined elements would yield[1]. But even those who estimate most highly the success that has so far been attained in discovering the conditions of this harmony, in the case of any particular art, would admit that mere conformity to the conditions thus ascertained cannot secure the production of æsthetic pleasure in any considerable degree. However subtly we state in general terms the objective relations of elements in a de-

[1] Writers who would agree in this general statement would differ considerably as to the more or less intellectual interpretation to be given to the æsthetic sensibility. Some would attribute the æsthetic result merely to the mutual strengthening of feelings having some degree of similarity or affinity; others would suppose an, at least, semi-conscious perception of ordered differences, "unity and variety." Both these views appear to me to be partially true: but the question is one which it would here be unduly discursive to discuss at all adequately.

lightful work of art, on which its delight seems to depend, we must always feel that it would be possible to produce out of similar elements a work corresponding to our general description which would give no delight at all; the touch that gives delight depends upon an instinct for which no deductive reasoning can supply a substitute. This is true, even without taking into account the wide divergences that we actually find in the æsthetic sensibilities of individuals: still less, therefore, is it needful to argue that, from the point of view of an individual seeking his own greatest happiness, none but a mainly inductive and empirical method of estimating æsthetic pleasures can be made available.

§ 3. I now pass to consider a theory which may be distinguished from those discussed in the preceding section as being biological rather than psychophysical: since it directs attention not to the actual present characteristics of the organic states or changes of which pleasures and pains are the concomitants or immediate consequents, but to their relations to the life of the organism as a whole. I mean the theory that "pains are the correlatives of actions injurious to the organism, while pleasures are the correlatives of acts conducive to its welfare." Mr Spencer, from whom the above propositions are quoted[1], subsequently explains "injurious" and "conducive to welfare" to mean respectively "tending to decrease or loss of life," and "tending to continuance or increase of life": but in the deductive argument by which the above conclusion is summarily established "injurious" and "beneficial" are used as equivalent simply to "destructive" and "preservative" of organic life: and it will be more convenient to take them first in this simpler signification.

Mr Spencer's argument is as follows:

"If we substitute for the word Pleasure the equivalent phrase—a feeling which we seek to bring into consciousness and retain there, and if we substitute for the word Pain the equivalent phrase—a feeling which we seek to get out of consciousness and to keep out; we see at once that, if the states of consciousness which a creature endeavours to maintain are the correlatives of injurious actions, and if the states of consciousness which it endeavours to expel are the correlatives of beneficial actions, it must quickly disappear through

[1] *Principles of Psychology*, § 125, and *Data of Ethics*, § 33.

persistence in the injurious and avoidance of the beneficial. In other words, those races of beings only can have survived in which, on the average, agreeable or desired feelings went along with activities conducive to the maintenance of life, while disagreeable and habitually-avoided feelings went along with activities directly or indirectly destructive of life; and there must ever have been, other things equal, the most numerous and long-continued survivals among races in which these adjustments of feelings to actions were the best, tending ever to bring about perfect adjustment."

Now I am not concerned to deny the value of this summary deduction for certain purposes. But if we consider it from the special point of view with which alone we are here concerned—in respect, namely, of the possibility of basing on it a deductive method of seeking maximum happiness for the individual, by substituting Preservation for Pleasure as the end directly aimed at—its inadequacy to afford such a basis is manifest on several grounds. To begin: Mr Spencer only affirms the conclusion to be true, as he rather vaguely says, "on the average": and it is obvious that though the tendency to find injurious acts pleasant or preservative acts painful must be a disadvantage to any species of animal in the struggle for existence, it may—if existing only to a limited extent—be outweighed by other advantages, so that the organism in which it exists may survive in spite of it. This, I say, is obvious *a priori*: and common experience, as Mr Spencer admits, shews "in many conspicuous ways" that this has been actually the case with civilized man during the whole period of history that we know: owing to the changes caused by the course of civilization, "there has arisen and must long continue a deep and involved derangement of the natural connexions between pleasures and beneficial actions and between pains and detrimental actions." This seems to give a sufficiently strong presumption against the possibility of founding a deductive method of Hedonism on Mr Spencer's general conclusion. But, from our present point of view, we are perhaps less concerned with the notorious tendency of civilized men to take pleasure in various forms of unhealthy conduct and to find conformity to the rules of health irksome; it is more important to note that they may be, and actually are, susceptible of keen pleasure from acts and processes that have no material tendency to preserve life. It need hardly be said that the "evolution hypothesis" affords us no general solution of the psychophysical question as to the relation of nervous action to feeling: hence we cannot argue from it *a priori* that the development of the nervous system in human beings may not bring with it intense susceptibilities to pleasures from non-preservative processes, if only the preservation of the individuals in whom such susceptibilities are developed is otherwise adequately provided. Now this latter supposition is obviously realized in the case of persons of leisure in civilized society; whose needs of food, clothing, shelter, &c., are abundantly supplied through the complex social habit which we call the institution of private property: and I know no empirical ground for supposing that a cultivated man tends, in consequence of the keen and varied pleasures which he seeks and enjoys, to live longer than a man who goes through a comparatively dull round of monotonous routine activity, interspersed by slightly pleasurable intervals of repose and play.

§ 4. If, however, the individual is not likely to obtain a maximum of Pleasure by aiming merely at Preservation, it remains to consider whether "increase of life" will serve any better. Now it is of course true that so far as nervous action is attended by consciousness pleasurable in quality, the more there is of it, the happier we shall be. And we recognize great variations in the fullness or intensity of the stream of consciousness: indeed we seem able to trace the heightening of life or consciousness—subjectively estimated—from a point not much above zero up to the state when powerful and complex emotional excitement is sustaining the most energetic action of which our system is capable. But even if we do not question the optimistic proposition that the more complex and full life is "on the average" the happier; it still by no means follows that we shall gain *maximum* pleasure by aiming merely at intensity of consciousness. For we experience intense pains even more indubitably than intense pleasures, and in those "full tides of soul," in which we seem to be most alive painful consciousness may be mixed in almost any proportion. And we have observed that pain (including that distress of mind which results from the prescience of worse pains to come) stimulates to energetic action no less than pleasure actual or prospective:

and though the action to which it prompts operates somewhat as an anodyne, this does not prevent the total consciousness from being intensely painful.

And even if we exclude distinctly painful consciousness (which is surely arbitrary), we still cannot say that consciousness tends to be pleasurable in proportion to its intensity. For we often experience excitement nearly or quite neutral in quality (*i.e.* not distinctly pleasurable or painful), which reaches a great pitch of intensity, as in the case of strong desire or vigorous action for an end of which the attainment remains quite uncertain. Indeed a large portion of reflective mankind have placed their ideal of happiness at the opposite pole to this excited or agitated consciousness: in 'apathy,' 'unperturbedness,'

> "Divine Tranquillity
> Without one pleasure and without one pain;"

which sometimes, as in the Buddhist Nirwâna, becomes scarcely distinguishable from absolute insensibility. If, however, in making "increase of life" our aim, we implicitly or explicitly add the qualification that the increment must be pleasurable; we are obviously brought round again to the old method of Empirical Hedonism, for which we have been trying to find a substitute.

Perhaps, however, "increase of life" may be taken to imply not merely intensity of consciousness, but a duly varied and harmonious development of all our different faculties or capacities; the cultivation, as it is said, of all sides of our nature. For a man may live a very intense life if he be passionately devoted to field-sports or beetles, or the service of his country or of his religion: but—it may be said—he would be happier if he exercised other faculties and capacities, if he added intellectual to physical activity, artistic to scientific interests, domestic affections to patriotism, &c. &c. And experience certainly seems to support the view that men lose happiness by allowing some of their faculties or capacities to be withered and dwarfed for want of exercise, and thus not leaving themselves sufficient variety of feelings or activities. As regards the bodily organs, it will be agreed that the due exercise of most, if not all, is indispensable to the health of the organism; and further, that the health maintained by this balance of functions is a more important source of the individual's happiness than the unhealthy over-exercise of any one organ can be; both from the absence of organic pain which it secures, and the positive though indefinite pleasure by which corporeal wellbeing is continually represented in consciousness. Still, it would appear that the harmony of functions necessary to health is a very elastic one, and admits of a very wide margin of variation, as far as the organs under voluntary control are concerned. A man (*e.g.*) who exercises his brain alone will probably be ill in consequence: but he may exercise his brain much and his legs little, or *vice versâ*, without any morbid results: and he may even repeat monotonously one short series of movements for the greater part of his waking life (as some workers in factories do) without any apparent injury to health. And, in the same way, we cannot lay down the proposition, that a varied and many-sided life is the happiest, with so much breadth and precision as would justify us in accepting it as a practical first principle. For it is also true, on the other side, that the more we come to exercise any faculty with sustained and prolonged concentration, the more fully we live in such exercise, up to the point at which it becomes wearisome, or turns into a semi-mechanical routine which renders consciousness dull and languid. It is no doubt, important for our happiness that we should keep within this limit: but we cannot fix it precisely in any particular case without specific experience: especially as there seems always to be a certain amount of weariness and tedium which must be resisted and overcome, if we would bring our faculties into full swing and obtain the full enjoyment of our labour. And similarly in respect of passive emotional consciousness: if too much sameness of feeling results in languor, too much variety inevitably involves shallowness: and here again the right mean between the two is hard to find, because we are liable to ebbs and pauses of feeling, intervals of unsusceptibility which do not really indicate that we are overstraining our capacity for the emotion in question. The point where concentration ought to stop, and where dissipation begins, varies from man to man, and must, it would seem, be decided by the specific experience of individuals.

What has just been said is perhaps sufficient to dispose of the suggestion (noticed in a previous chapter[1]) that the most effectual method of seeking one's own happiness may consist in aiming at the freest and fullest development of one's natural self; since I have no means of ascertaining with any precision the quality or strength of the tendencies to action or feeling which constitute my notion of my present self or mind, in so far as it is something definitely charactered and cognizable as like or unlike other minds, except by observing the manifestation of these tendencies in my conscious experience. But it may be worth while to point out further that there is an important amount of error in the implication—which the conception of self-development sometimes seems to carry with it—that we are beings with perfectly definite potentialities which we have only the alternative of developing or not developing. We are not born such beings, nor does it seem that we ever become such. Indeed it is obvious that as regards many of the faculties and dispositions which belong to any individual at any time, the notion of *acquisition* is to a considerable extent more appropriate than that of development: and, having been largely caused by my own previous actions and feelings, they are still capable of being modified by my own efforts co-operating with external circumstances. Thus the rule 'choose the life in which your faculties will be most developed' will always present us with alternatives, in deciding between which we shall be inevitably led back to the criterion already discussed of 'fullness' or 'intensity' of consciousness[2].

[1] Book I. Ch. vii. p. 84.

[2] Perhaps it may be said that the course of conduct which produces most effect on the whole must be that by which the agent is most developed. And probably most results of importance in human affairs are produced by sustained effort, in which the agent's energies are fully called out. Still (even if we had a satisfactory criterion for comparing the different magnitudes of different effects), we cannot strictly infer from greatness in the effect greatness, or fullness of development, in one of its causes; and the human agent is in every case only one cause among many. There are some circumstances under which a slight action in one direction may produce more effect than a great effort in another: as in a quarry, when a mine is laid, one may move more stone by momentarily pulling a trigger than one could by hacking and dragging rocks all day long. Hence there is no *a priori* reason to suppose that the line of most effective action will always be that which conduces most to self-development: nor does common experience appear to support this supposition.

There is, however, another and simpler way in which the maxim of 'giving free development to one's nature' may be—and often has been—understood: *i.e.* in the sense of yielding to spontaneous impulses, instead of endeavouring to govern these by elaborate forecasts of consequences. This course is doubtless frequently taken by persons who do not find it necessary to provide themselves with a scientific justification for it: but such a justification has been found in the theory that spontaneous or instinctive impulses really represent the effects on the organism in which they appear—or its ancestors—of previous experiences of pleasure and pain. Hence, it has been maintained that in complicated problems of conduct, experience will "enable the constitution to estimate the respective amounts of pleasure and pain consequent upon each alternative," where it is "impossible for the intellect" to do this: and "will further cause the organism instinctively to shun that course which produces on the whole most suffering[1]." That there is an important element of truth in this contention I would not deny. No doubt the consciousness of a strong 'instinctive' impulse ought always to be counted as an important element in deciding what course of conduct is likely to promote our happiness. And in estimating its importance we have not only to consider the pleasure to be gained by satisfying it, and the pain of ungratified desire; but also the *general* adaptation of our impulsive or appetitive nature to the circumstances of our life, and the consequent probability that the impulse is prompting us to an act which will be productive of happiness in other ways than by its own gratification. If our prudential comparison, apart from this latter consideration, gives an uncertain result, this may reasonably turn the scale in favour of the impulse.

But any broad conclusion that non-rational inclination is a better guide than reason to the individual's happiness would be quite unwarranted by anything that we know or can plausibly

[1] The quotations are from Mr Spencer's *Social Statics*, ch. iv: but I should infer from the manner in which Mr Spencer has referred to this earlier work in his more recent *Data of Ethics* that no doctrine in *Social Statics* can now with certainty be attributed to the author. I ought to add further that in the passage quoted Mr Spencer is not writing from the point of view of Egoistic Hedonism.

conjecture respecting biological evolution. In the first place, as we have before observed, the general effect of natural selection must be primarily to foster impulses tending to the preservation of the race rather than the pleasure of the individual: and the divergence between the two ends, especially in a social animal, may be very considerable. And even if we overlook this divergence and admit generally that every sentient organism tends to adapt itself to its environment, in such a manner as to acquire instincts of some value in guiding it to pleasure and away from pain: it is quite another thing to affirm that in the human organism one particular kind of adaptation, that which proceeds by unconscious modification of instinct, is to be preferred to that other kind of adaptation which is brought about by conscious comparison and inference. It is clear, that this proposition can only be justified by a comparison of the consequences of yielding to instinctive impulses with the consequences of controlling them by calculations of resulting pleasure and pain: that is, by the very method of which the comparative untrustworthiness is sought to be proved. We require then, at least, a very wide induction from those clear and simple cases in which the intellect is allowed to be capable of deciding between the amounts of happiness consequent respectively on two alternatives of conduct. But it will hardly be maintained that in the majority of clear instances where non-rational impulse conflicts with rational forecast, a subsequent calculation of consequences appears to justify the former; the assertion would be in too flagrant conflict with the common sense and common experience of mankind. Nor is it relevant to urge that, in other animals, the organism is continually adapted to its environment through the unconscious modification of instinct by experience. For the extent of the analogy between such animals and man is just the point at issue. It may fairly be argued on the other side that even in brutes, requiring as they do a far less complex adaptation to circumstances, the results of the unconscious process are imperfect: that conscious comparison and prudential forecast may be regarded as the natural substitute for and development of this unconscious adaptation in the more highly organized brain of man, related to far more complicated conditions of existence: that these comparisons and forecasts, again, become in their final form and most complete development the calculations of systematic hedonism which we have been examining: and that in proportion as Reason is developed the instincts that remain naturally sink into a subordinate place, and become more and more feeble and fallible guides. Indeed in many cases a man who took the resolution to rely on Instinct would simply surrender his will to a complicated conflict of wavering and alternating impulses, leading to the most ineffective fitfulness and fluctuation in external conduct. Experience, carefully examined, may perhaps lead us to the conclusion that there are certain special departments of life in which instinct is on the whole a safer guide than prudential calculation. The intrusion of Prudence into these regions will thus appear to be suicidal: and we are led by a different road to the conclusion previously stated, that Rational Egoism is properly self-limiting. Still, this would not in itself involve the substitution of any other method for that of Empirical Hedonism: as we have found so far no satisfactory mode of determining the limits to which prudential calculation may prudently be carried, except by this very calculation itself.

We seem, then, forced to conclude that there is no scientific short-cut to the ascertainment of the right means to the individual's happiness: every attempt to find a 'high priori road' to this goal brings us back inevitably to the empirical method. For instead of a clear principle universally valid, we only get at best a vague and general rule, based on considerations which it is important not to overlook, but the relative value of which we can only estimate by careful observation and comparison of individual experiences. Whatever uncertainty besets these processes must necessarily extend to all our reasonings about happiness. I have no wish to exaggerate these uncertainties, feeling that we must all continue to seek happiness for ourselves and for others, in whatever obscurity we may have to grope after it: but there is nothing gained by underrating them, and it is idle to argue as if they did not exist.

BOOK III.

INTUITIONISM.

BOOK III.

CHAPTER I.

INTUITIONISM.

§ 1. IN the effort to examine, closely but quite neutrally, the system of Egoistic Hedonism, with which we have been engaged in the last book, one effect that will probably have been produced on the reader's mind is a strong aversion to the principle and method examined. Certainly such an aversion is very commonly announced as the result of contemplating Egoism: I believe that it is felt by many even of those who (like myself) find it impossible not to admit the 'authority' of self-love, or the 'rationality' of seeking one's own individual happiness. In considering 'enlightened self-interest' as supplying a *primâ facie* tenable principle for the systematization of conduct, I have thought it well to give no expression to this sentiment of aversion. I have been anxious to ascertain with scientific impartiality the results to which this principle logically leads: and especially to know how far it can be reconciled with conscience, or common moral judgments and sentiments, and serve as a foundation of duty. When, however, we seem to find on careful examination that Egoism cannot fairly be represented as socially constructive, and that the common precepts of duty, which we are trained to regard as sacred, must be to the egoist rules to which it is only generally speaking and for the most part reasonable to conform, but which under special circumstances must be decisively ignored and broken; the sense of the ignobility[1] of Egoism adds force to that recoil from it which this perception of the conflict with common notions of duty naturally causes. We find it hard to believe that these are the results which practical Reason really prescribes: and so are disposed to fall back on whatever other principles for determining right conduct may present themselves as *primâ facie* reasonable. But further, we are accustomed to expect from Morality something like clearness and precision of precepts or counsels: and such rules as can be laid down for seeking the individual's greatest happiness cannot but appear wanting in these qualities. A dubious guidance to a despicable end appears to be all that the Hedonistic calculus has to offer. And it is by appealing to the superior clearness and certainty, with which the dictates of Conscience or the Moral Faculty are issued, that Butler maintains the practical supremacy of Conscience over Self-love, in spite of his admission (in the passage before quoted) of theoretical priority in the claims of the latter. We can see clearly, he says, what we ought to do: but we cannot see clearly what will lead to our happiness.

In saying this, Butler appears to me fairly to represent the common moral sense of ordinary mankind, in our own age no less than in his. The moral judgments that men habitually pass on one another in ordinary discourse imply for the most part that duty is usually not a difficult thing for an ordinary man to *know*, though various seductive impulses may make it difficult for him to do it. And in such maxims as that duty should be performed 'advienne qui pourra,' that truth should be spoken without regard to consequences, that justice should be done 'though the sky should fall,' it is implied that we have the power of seeing clearly, within a certain range, what actions are right and reasonable in themselves, apart from their consequences;—or rather with a merely partial consideration of consequences, from which other consequences admitted to be possibly good or bad are definitely excluded[2]. And such a

[1] I do not give this as a reason for rejecting the principle of Egoism, the rationality of which (as I have said on the preceding page) I find it impossible not to admit. But this 'sense of ignobility' is, in any case, a psychological fact worthy of notice. How this sentiment is to be explained, and how far it is capable of rational justification, are questions which I reserve for subsequent discussion.

[2] I have before observed (Book I. ch. viii. § 1) that in the common notion of

power is claimed for the human mind by most of the writers who have maintained the existence of moral intuitions; I have therefore thought myself justified in treating this claim as characteristic of the method which I distinguish as Intuitional. At the same time, as I have before observed, there is a wider sense in which the term 'intuitional' might be legitimately applied to either Egoistic or Universalistic Hedonism; so far as either system lays down as a first principle—which if known at all must be intuitively known—that happiness is the only rational ultimate end of action. To this meaning I shall recur in the concluding chapters (XIII. and XIV.) of this book; in which I shall discuss more fully the intuitive character of these hedonistic principles. But since the adoption of this wider meaning would not lead us to a distinct ethical method, I have thought it best, in the detailed discussion of Intuitionism which occupies the first eleven chapters of this book, to confine myself as far as possible to Moral Intuition understood in the narrower sense above defined.

§ 2. Here, perhaps, it may be said that in thus defining Intuitionism I have omitted its most fundamental characteristic; that the Intuitionist properly speaking—in contrast with the Utilitarian—does not judge actions by an external standard at all; that true morality, in his view, is not concerned with outward actions as such, but with the state of mind in which acts are done—in short with "intentions" and "motives." I think, however, that this objection is partly due to a misunderstanding. Moralists of all schools, I conceive, would agree that the moral judgments which we pass on actions relate primarily to intentional actions regarded as intentional. In other words, what we judge to be 'wrong'—in the strictest Ethical sense—is not any part of the actual effects, as such, of the muscular movements immediately caused by the agent's volition, but the effects which he foresaw in willing the act; or, more strictly, his volition or choice of realising the effects as foreseen[1]. When I speak therefore of acts, I must be under-

an act we include a certain portion of the whole series of changes partly caused by the volition which initiated the so-called act.

[1] No doubt we hold a man responsible for unintended bad consequences of his acts or omissions, when they are such as he might with ordinary care have

stood to mean—unless the contrary is stated—acts presumed to be intentional and judged as such: on this point I do not think that any dispute need arise.

The case of motives is different and requires careful discussion. In the first place the distinction between "motive" and "intention" in ordinary language is not very precise: since we apply the term "motive" to foreseen consequences of an act, so far as they are conceived to be objects of desire to the agent, or to the desire of such consequences: and when we speak of the intention of an act it is usually, no doubt, desired consequences that we have in view. I think, however, that for purposes of exact moral or jural discussion, it is best to include under the term 'intention' all the consequences of an act that are foreseen as certain or probable; since it will be admitted that we cannot evade responsibility for any foreseen bad consequences of our acts by the plea that we felt no desire for them, either for their own sake or as means to ulterior ends[1]. Thus the intention of an act may be judged to be wrong, while the motive is recognized as good; as when a man commits perjury to save a parent's or a benefactor's life. Such judgments are, in fact, continually passed in common moral discourse. It may, however, be said that an act cannot be right, even when the intention is such as duty would prescribe, if it be done from a bad motive: that, to take a case suggested by Bentham, a man who prosecutes from malice a person whom he believes to be guilty, does not really act rightly; for, though it may be his duty to prosecute, he ought not to do it from malice. It is doubtless true that it is our duty to get rid of bad motives if we can; and it is important to observe that morality prescribes internal acts—i.e. volitions in

foreseen; still, as I have before said (p. 57), we admit on reflection that moral blame only attaches to such careless acts or omissions indirectly, in so far as the carelessness is the result of some previous wilful neglect of duty.

[1] I think that common usage, when carefully considered, will be found to admit this definition. Suppose a nihilist blows up a railway train containing an emperor and other persons: it will no doubt be held correct to say simply that his intention was to kill the emperor; but it would be thought absurd to say that he 'did not intend' to kill the other persons, though he may have had no desire to kill them and may have regarded their death as a lamentable incident in the execution of his revolutionary plans.

which the foreseen consequences are conceived as solely effects on the agent's own feelings and character—no less than external acts. But no one, I think, will contend that we can always at will get rid of a strong emotion; so that, in the case supposed, what is prescribed strictly as duty can only be the internal act of suppressing as far as possible the feeling of personal malevolence; and such suppression will be especially difficult if one is to do the act to which the malevolent impulse prompts; while yet, if the prosecution be clearly a duty which no one else can so properly perform, it would be absurd to say that we ought to omit it because we cannot altogether exclude an objectionable motive. Hence, while I quite admit that many actions are commonly judged to be made better or worse by the presence or absence of certain motives, it still seems to me clear (1) that our judgments of right and wrong strictly speaking relate to intentions; and (2) that intentions to produce certain external effects form the primary content of the main prescriptions of duty, as commonly affirmed and understood[1].

It has, no doubt, been maintained by moralists of influence in different ages that the moral value of our conduct depends upon the degree to which we are actuated by the one motive which, as they hold, is truly moral: viz. the desire or free choice[2] to do what is right as such, to realize duty or virtue for duty or virtue's sake[3]. In the next and subsequent chapters I shall try to show that this doctrine—which we may conveniently distinguish as Stoical—is not on the whole sustained by a comprehensive survey and comparison of common moral judgments: that there are important classes of duties, in determining which we do not usually take account of motives as distinct from intentions: while in other cases acts appear to

[1] The view that moral judgments relate primarily or most properly to motives will be more fully discussed in ch. xii. of this Book.

[2] I use these alternative terms in order to avoid the Free Will Controversy.

[3] Many religious persons would probably say that the motive of obedience or love to God was the highest. But those who take this view would generally say that obedience and love are due to God as a Moral Being, possessing the attributes of Infinite Wisdom and Goodness, and not otherwise: and if so these religious motives would seem to be substantially identical with regard for duty and love of virtue, though modified and complicated by the addition of emotions belonging to relations between persons.

have the quality of virtue even more strikingly when performed from some motive other than the love of virtue as such. For the present I am more concerned to point out that the Stoical doctrine above stated is diametrically opposed to what I have called Psychological Hedonism—the view that the universal or normal motives of human action are either particular desires of pleasure or aversions to pain for the agent himself, or the more general regard to his happiness on the whole which I term Self-love; that it also excludes the less extreme doctrine that duties may be to some extent properly done from such self-regarding motives; and that one or other of these positions has frequently been held by writers who have expressly adopted an Intuitional method of Ethics. As an example of a thinker who held the hedonistic view in its extremest form we may refer to Locke. We find that Locke lays down, without reserve or qualification, that "good and evil are nothing but pleasure and pain, or that which occasions or procures pleasure or pain to us[1]:" so that "it would be utterly in vain to suppose a rule set to the free actions of man, without annexing it to some reward or punishment to determine his will." On the other hand, he expresses, with no less emphasis, the conviction that "from self-evident propositions, by necessary consequences, as incontestable as those in mathematics, the measures of right and wrong might be made out[2]," so that "morality might be placed among the sciences capable of demonstration." The combination of these two doctrines gives us the view that moral rules are essentially laws of God, which men are impelled to obey, solely or mainly, from fear or hope of what God may do to them in the future; and some such view as this seems to be widely accepted, by plain men without very refined moral sensibilities, though its heterogeneous elements are rarely presented with as much clearness and sharpness as in Locke's essay.

As an example, again, of thinkers who, while recognizing in human nature a disinterested regard for duty or virtue as such, still consider that self-love is a proper and legitimate motive to right conduct, we may refer to Butler and his disciples. Butler regards "reasonable self-love" as not merely a normal motive to

---

[1] Locke's *Essay*, II. c. 28, §§ 5, 6.   [2] *Ib.* IV. c. 3, § 18.

human action, but as being—no less than conscience—a "chief or superior principle in the nature of man;" so that an action "becomes unsuitable" to this nature, if the principle of self-love be violated. Accordingly the aim of his teaching is not to induce men to choose duty rather than interest, but to convince them that there is no inconsistency between the two; that self-love and conscience lead "to one and the same course of life."

This intermediate doctrine appears to me to be more in harmony with the common sense of mankind on the whole than either the Stoical or the Lockian. But, though I have thought it important to bring the three positions into clear contrast, I do not conceive that we are here called upon to exclude any of them as inconsistent with fundamental assumptions of the present method. The Intuitionism which tends to the exclusion, so far as possible, of non-moral motives, the Intuitionism which aims merely at the regulation of such motives, and the Intuitionism which rests ultimately on an egoistic basis, may all agree as to the particular kinds of intended outward effects, to the realisation of which the different motives ought to prompt. Even those who hold that human beings cannot reasonably be expected to conform to moral rules disinterestedly, or from any other motive than that supplied by the sanctions divinely attached to them, still commonly conceive God as Supreme Reason, whose laws must be essentially reasonable: and so far as such laws are held to be cognizable by the 'light of nature' —so that morality, as Locke says, may be placed among demonstrative sciences—the method of determining them will be none the less intuitional because it is combined with the belief that God will reward their observance and punish their violation. On the other hand those who hold that regard for duty as duty is an indispensable condition of acting rightly, would generally admit that it is not the only cognizable condition; that acting rightly is not adequately defined as acting from a pure desire to act rightly. In a certain sense, no doubt, a man who sincerely desires and intends to act rightly does all he can, and completely fulfils duty: but it will hardly be denied that such a man may have a wrong judgment as to his outward duty, and therefore, in another sense, may act wrongly. If this be admitted, it is evident that even on the view that the desire or determination to fulfil duty as such is essential to right action, a distinction between two kinds of rightness is required; which we may express by saying that an act is "formally"[1] right, if the agent in willing is moved by pure desire to fulfil duty or chooses duty for duty's sake; "materially" right, if he intends the right particular effects. This distinction being taken, it becomes plain that there is no reason why the same principles and method for determining material rightness, or rightness of particular effects, should not be adopted by thinkers who differ most widely on the question of formal rightness; and it is, obviously, with material rightness that the work of the systematic moralist is mainly concerned.

§ 3. Here, however, it should be observed, that the term formal rightness' may be also used, as implying not a *desire* or choice of the act as right, but merely a *belief* that it is so[2]. Now it is obvious that I cannot perform an act from pure love of duty without believing it to be right: but I can believe it to be right and yet do it from some other motive. Accordingly there is more agreement among moralists who adopt the Intuitional Method as to the moral indispensability of such a belief, than there is with respect to the question of motive: at least, it would, I conceive, be universally held that no act can be absolutely right, whatever its external aspect and relations, which is believed by the agent to be wrong. It may still be asked whether it is better in any particular case that a man should do what he mistakenly believes to be his duty, or what really is the right thing for him to do—when considered apart from his mistaken belief—and would be completely right if he could only think so. The question is rather subtle and perplexing to Common Sense: it is therefore worth while to point out that it can have only a limited and subordinate practical application.

---

[1] The words Form and Formal, as J. S. Mill has remarked, are used in several more or less analogous significations, which it is somewhat difficult to comprehend under one definition. In the present case we may understand them as denoting at once a *universal and essential*, and a *subjective* or *internal* condition of the rightness of actions.

[2] It is not, I conceive, commonly held to be indispensable, in order to constitute an act right, that a belief that it is right should be actually present in the agent's mind: it may be right, although the agent never actually raised the question of its rightness or wrongness.

For no one, in considering what he ought himself to do in any particular case, can distinguish what he believes to be right from what really is so: the necessity for such a choice between what we may call 'subjective' and 'objective' rightness can only present itself when we are considering the conduct of another person whom it is in our power to influence. If another is about to do what he thinks right while we believe it to be wrong, and we are able to bring other motives to bear on him that may overbalance his sense of duty, we have to decide whether we ought thus to tempt him to realize what we believe to be objectively right against his own convictions[1]. The moral sense of mankind would, under ordinary circumstances, pronounce against such temptation; thus regarding the Subjective rightness of an action as generally more important than the Objective, either for itself or for its ulterior consequences[2]. But however essential it may be that a moral agent should do what he believes to be right, this condition of right conduct is too simple to admit of systematic development: it is, therefore, clear that the details of our investigation must relate mainly to 'objective' rightness.

There is, however, one practical rule of some value, to be obtained by merely reflecting on the general notion of rightness[3], as commonly conceived. In a previous chapter[4] I endeavoured to make this notion clearer by saying that 'what is objectively right must be judged to be so by all rational beings who judge truly of the matter.' This statement does

---

[1] It is of course clear that it is right for us to alter his convictions if we can: the difficulty only occurs when we find ourselves unable to do this.

[2] The decision would, I think, usually be reached by weighing bad consequences to the agent's character against bad consequences of a different kind. In extreme cases the latter consideration would certainly prevail. Thus we should generally approve a statesman who crushed a dangerous rebellion by working on the fear or cupidity of a leading rebel who was rebelling on conscientious grounds. Cf. *post*, Book IV. ch. iii. § 2.

[3] The antithesis of 'subjective' and 'objective' cannot be applied to the condition of right conduct considered in this paragraph: for this formal condition is at once subjective and objective; being, as I argue, involved in our common notion of right conduct, it is, therefore, necessarily judged by us to be of really universal application: and, though it does not secure complete objective rightness, it is an important protection against objective wrongness.

[4] Cf. B. I. c. iii. § 2.

not imply that what is judged to be right for one man must necessarily be judged so for another: 'objective' duty may vary from A to B no less than the 'objective' facts of their nature and circumstances vary. There seems, however, to be this difference between our conceptions of ethical and physical objectivity respectively; that we commonly refuse to admit in the case of the former—what experience compels us to admit as regards the latter—variations for which we can discover no rational explanation. In the variety of coexistent physical facts we find an accidental or arbitrary element in which we have to acquiesce, as we cannot conceive it to be excluded by any extension of our knowledge of physical causation. If we ask, for example, why any portion of space empirically known to us contains more matter than any similar adjacent portion, physical science can only answer by stating (along with certain laws of change) some antecedent position of the parts of matter which needs explanation no less than the present; and however far back we carry our ascertainment of such antecedent positions, the one with which we leave off seems as arbitrary as that with which we started. But within the range of our cognitions of right and wrong, it will be generally agreed that we cannot admit a similar unexplained variation. We cannot judge an action to be right for A and wrong for B, unless we can find in the natures or circumstances of the two some difference which we see to be a reasonable ground for difference in their duties. If therefore I judge any action to be right for myself, I implicitly judge it to be right for any other person whose nature and circumstances do not differ from my own in some important respects. Now by making this latter judgment explicit, we may protect ourselves against the danger which besets the conscience, of being warped and perverted by strong desire, so that we too easily think that we ought to do what we very much wish to do. For if we ask ourselves whether we believe that any similar person in similar circumstances ought to perform the contemplated action, the question will often disperse the false appearance of rightness which our strong inclination has given to it. We see that we should not think it right for another, and therefore that it cannot be right for us. Indeed this test of the rightness of our volitions is so generally effective, that Kant seems to have regarded it as supplying a complete criterion of Duty[1]. But this appears to me an error analogous to that of supposing that Formal Logic supplies a complete criterion of truth. I should agree that a volition which does not stand this test is to be condemned; but I hold that volition which does stand it may after all be wrong. For as I have said, all (or almost all) persons who act conscientiously conform implicitly to Kant's precept of acting on maxims which they could sincerely will to become universal laws: while at the same time we continually find such persons in thoroughly conscientious disagreement as to what each ought to do, and in fact prepared to lay down a number of conflicting maxims, all equally possessing the potential universality which Kant requires. Under these circumstances, we cannot say that all such persons act rightly—in the objective sense—by acting on the potentially universal maxims; unless we refuse altogether to distinguish subjective and objective rightness and affirm that whatever any one thinks right is so. But such a doctrine is in flagrant conflict with common sense; and would seem to

[1] Mr Abbott (Kant's *Theory of Ethics*, Memoir, p. l) has denied the statement in the text, affirming that Kant "never attempted to deduce a complete code of duty from a purely formal principle." Mr Abbott refers to the *Tugendlehre*, which appeared in 1796 when Kant was 72, and in which, no doubt, the deduction of duties is worked out in a way which renders my criticism not obviously applicable. But I am surprised that Mr Abbott should deny its applicability to the *Grundlegung zur Metaphysik der Sitten*, published ten years earlier; in the face of Kant's unmistakeable statements in the second chapter of this treatise (pp. 269—273, Hart: pp. 54—63 of Abbott's translation). Here Kant first says "There is therefore but one categorical imperative, namely, this: *Act only on that maxim whereby thou canst at the same time will that it should become a universal law*. Now, if all imperatives of duty can be deduced from this one imperative as from their principle......we shall at least be able to show what we understand by [duty] and what this notion means." He then demonstrates the application of the principle to four cases, selected as representative of "the many actual duties"; and continues: "if now we attend to ourselves on occasion of *any* transgression of duty, we shall find that we in fact do not will that our maxim should be a universal law, for that is impossible for us"......: then, summing up the conclusion of this part of his argument, he says, "we have exhibited clearly and definitely for *every practical application* the content of the categorical imperative which must contain the principle of all duty, if there is such a thing at all." I can hardly conceive how the view attributed by me to Kant could be more clearly enunciated than it is in these passages.

render the construction of a scientific code of morality futile: as the very object of such a code is to supply a standard for rectifying men's divergent opinions.

We may conclude then that the moral judgments which the present method attempts to systematize are primarily and for the most part intuitions of the rightness or goodness (or the reverse) of particular kinds of external effects of human volition, presumed to be intended by the agent, but considered independently of the agent's own view as to the rightness or wrongness of his intention; though the quality of motives, as distinct from intentions, has also to be taken into account.

§ 4. But the question may be raised, whether it is legitimate to take for granted (as I have hitherto been doing) the existence of such intuitions? For this, no doubt, is frequently disputed: there are not a few persons who deliberately deny that reflection enables them to discover any such phenomenon in their conscious experience as the judgment or apparent perception that an act is in itself right or good in any absolute sense —i.e. in any other sense than that of being the right or fit means to the attainment of some ulterior end. I think, however, that such denials are—at any rate to a great extent—due to some confusion between three questions which ought to be carefully distinguished: viz. the psychological question as to *existence* of such moral judgments or apparent perceptions of moral qualities, what we may call the 'psychogonical' question as to their *origin*, and the ethical question as to their *validity*. This confusion has been partly, perhaps, caused by the use of the term "intuition," which has sometimes been understood to imply that the judgment or apparent perception so designated is *true*. I wish therefore to say expressly, that by calling any proposition as to the rightness or wrongness of actions "intuitive," I mean no more than it is affirmed unhesitatingly, and not as the result of reasoning, in ordinary thought and discourse: I do not mean to prejudge the question as to its ultimate validity, when philosophically considered. Any such "intuition" may turn out to have an element of error, which subsequent reflection and comparison enables us to correct—just as many apparent perceptions through the organ of vision are found to be partially illusory and misleading—indeed the sequel will shew that I hold this to be to an important extent the case with moral intuitions commonly so-called.

The question as to the validity of such intuitions being thus left open, it becomes obvious that the simple question 'whether they actually exist' is one which can only be settled for each person by direct introspection, supplemented by observation of the present phenomena of other minds as made known to us by means of language or other signs: and is altogether distinct from any question as to the origin of such phenomena, which has obviously to be investigated by quite different methods. Indeed it seems clear that the former question ought to be settled before an answer is sought for the latter: since it is premature to inquire into the origin of anything before we have ascertained that it actually exists. How then does it happen that the two inquiries are so often completely blended? so much so that the term "intuitive," in its application to moral judgments, is used as convertible with "innate," even by writers of deserved repute. The explanation seems to lie in an assumption, for the most part tacitly and implicitly made, that if it can be shown how certain mental phenomena, thoughts or feelings, have grown up—if we can point to the antecedent phenomena, of which they are the natural consequents—it is a legitimate inference that the phenomena which we began by investigating have vanished: that they are no longer there, but something else which we have mistaken for them, i.e. the "elements" of which they are said to be "composed." I have never seen any serious attempt to justify this inference: and I altogether deny its legitimacy. It has been encouraged perhaps by an infelicitous transference of the language and conceptions of Chemistry to Psychology. In Chemistry we regard the antecedents (elements) as still existing in and constituting the consequent (compound) because the latter is exactly similar to the former in some of its properties (weight, &c.), and because we can generally cause the compound to disappear and obtain the elements in its place. But we find nothing at all like this in the growth of new mental phenomena, so far as we can examine them; the psychical consequent is in no respect exactly similar to its antecedents, nor can it be resolved into them: and I know no established laws of psychical causation, which should lead us to regard the antecedents as really constituting the consequent.

It remains to ask whether there is more to be said on behalf of the connexion that has been held to exist between the Origin of the psychical facts which we call moral intuitions, and what I have called their Validity: that is, their truth when expressed as judgments or propositions. It has been very commonly assumed, both by Intuitionists and their opponents, that if our moral faculty can be shown to be 'derived' or 'developed' out of other preexistent elements of mind or consciousness, suspicion is thereby thrown upon its trustworthiness; while if, on the other hand, it can be shown to have existed in the human mind from its origin, its trustworthiness is thereby established. The two assumptions appear to me equally devoid of foundation. On the one hand, I can see no ground for supposing that a faculty thus derived, as such, is more liable to error than if its existence in the individual possessing it had been differently caused[1]: to put it otherwise, I cannot see how the mere ascertainment that a certain class of apparently self-evident judgments has been caused in certain known and determinate ways, can be in itself a valid ground for distrusting such cognitions. I cannot even admit that those who affirm the truth of such judgments are bound to show in their causes a tendency to make them true: indeed the acceptance of any such *onus probandi* would seem to me to render the attainment of philosophical certitude impossible; since the premises of the required demonstration must, I conceive, consist of caused beliefs, which as having been caused will equally stand in need of being proved true; and so on *ad infinitum*.

[1] It is now widely believed that every one of our cognitive faculties,—in short the human mind as a whole,—has been derived and developed, through a gradual process of physical change, out of some lower life in which cognition, properly speaking, had no place. On this view, the distinction between 'original' and 'derived' reduces itself to that between 'prior' and 'posterior' in development: and the fact that the moral faculty appears somewhat later in the process of evolution than other faculties can hardly be regarded as an argument against the validity of moral intuition; especially since this process is commonly conceived to be homogeneous throughout. Indeed such a line of reasoning would be suicidal; as the cognition that the moral faculty is developed is certainly later in development than moral cognition, and would therefore, by this reasoning, be less trustworthy.

Unless, indeed, it is held that we can find among the premises of our reasonings certain apparently self-evident judgments which have had no causes, and that these may on this ground be accepted as valid without proof!—paradoxes which are certainly not expressly maintained by the thinkers with whom I am now arguing. Otherwise, if all beliefs are equally in the position of having had invariable antecedents, it seems evident that this characteristic alone cannot serve to invalidate any of them.

I hold, therefore, that the *onus probandi* must be thrown the other way: those who dispute the validity of moral or other intuitions on the ground of their derivation must be required to show, not merely that they are the effects of certain causes, but that these causes are of a kind that tend to produce invalid beliefs. Now it is not, I conceive, possible to prove by any theory of the derivation of the moral faculty that the fundamental ethical conceptions 'right' or 'what ought to be done', 'good' or 'what it is reasonable to desire', are invalid, and that consequently *all* propositions of the form 'X is right' or 'good' are untrustworthy: for such ethical propositions, relating as they do to matter fundamentally different from that with which physical science or psychology deals, cannot be inconsistent with any physical or psychological conclusions. They can only be shown to involve error by being shown to contradict each other: and such a demonstration cannot lead us cogently to the sweeping conclusion that all are false. It may, however, be possible to prove that particular ethical beliefs have been caused in such a way as to make it probable that they are wholly or partially erroneous: and it will hereafter be important to consider how far any Ethical intuitions, which we find ourselves disposed to accept as valid, are open to attack on such psychogonical grounds. At present I am only concerned to maintain that no general demonstration of the derivedness or developedness of our moral faculty is an adequate ground for distrusting it.

On the other hand, if we have been once led to distrust our moral faculty on other grounds—as (*e.g.*) from the want of clearness and consistency in the moral judgments of each individual taken by themselves, and the discrepancies between the judgments of different individuals—it seems to me equally clear that our confidence in such judgments cannot properly be re-established by a demonstration of their 'originality.' I see no reason to believe that the 'original' element of our moral cognition can be ascertained; but if it could, I see no reason to hold that it would be especially free from error.

§ 5. How then can we hope to eliminate error from our moral intuitions? The common answer to this question was briefly suggested in a previous chapter where the different phases of the Intuitional Method were discussed. It was there said that in order to settle the doubts arising from the uncertainties and discrepancies that are found when we compare our judgments on particular cases, reflective persons naturally appeal to general rules or formulæ: and it is to such general formulæ that Intuitional Moralists commonly attribute ultimate certainty and validity. And certainly there are obvious sources of error in our judgments respecting concrete duty which seem to be absent when we consider the abstract notions of different kinds of conduct: since in any concrete case the complexity of circumstances necessarily increases the difficulty of judging, and our personal interests or habitual sympathies are liable to disturb the clearness of our moral discernment. Further, we must observe that most of us feel the need of such formulæ not only to correct, but also to supplement, our intuitions respecting particular concrete duties. Only exceptionally confident persons find that they always seem to see clearly what ought to be done in any case that comes before them. Most of us, however unhesitatingly we may affirm rightness and wrongness within the range of our ordinary experience, yet frequently meet with cases where our unreasoned judgment fails us; and where we could no more decide the moral issue raised without appealing to some general formulæ, than we could decide a disputed legal claim without reference to the positive law that deals with the matter.

And such formulæ are not difficult to find: it only requires a little reflection and observation of men's moral discourse to make a collection of such general rules, as to the validity of which there would be apparent agreement at least among moral persons of our own age and civilization, and which would cover with approximate completeness the whole of human conduct. Such a collection, regarded as a code imposed on an individual by the public opinion of the community to which he belongs, we have called the Positive Morality of the community: but when regarded as a body of moral truth, warranted to be such by the *consensus* of mankind,—or at least of that portion of mankind which combines adequate intellectual enlightenment with a serious concern for morality—it is more significantly termed the Morality of Common Sense.

When, however, we try to apply these currently accepted principles, we find that the notions composing them are generally deficient in clearness and precision. For instance, we should all agree in recognizing Justice and Veracity as important virtues; and we shall probably all accept the general maxims, that 'we ought to give every man his own' and that 'we ought to speak the truth': but when we ask (1) whether primogeniture is just, or the disendowment of corporations, or the determination of the value of services by competition, or (2) whether and how far false statements may be allowed in speeches of advocates, or in religious ceremonials, or to enemies or robbers, or in defence of lawful secrets, we do not find that these or any other current maxims enable us to give clear and unhesitating decisions. And yet such questions as these are, after all, those to which we naturally expect answers from the moralist. For we study Ethics, as Aristotle says, for the sake of Practice: and in practice we are concerned with particulars.

Hence it seems that if the formulæ of Intuitive Morality are really to serve as scientific axioms, and to be available in clear and cogent demonstrations; they must first be raised, by an effort of reflection which ordinary persons will not make, to a higher degree of precision than attaches to them in the common thought and discourse of mankind in general. We have, in fact, to take up the attempt that Socrates initiated, and endeavour to define satisfactorily the general notions of virtue which we all in common use for awarding approbation or disapprobation to conduct. This is the task upon which we shall be engaged in the nine chapters that follow. I must beg the reader to bear in mind that throughout these chapters I am not trying to prove or disprove Intuitionism, but merely by reflection on the Common Sense which I and my reader share, and to which appeal is so often made in moral disputes, to obtain as explicit, exact, and coherent a statement as possible of its fundamental principles.

CHAPTER II.

VIRTUE AND DUTY.

§ 1. BEFORE, however, we attempt to define the principles of particular virtues or departments of duty, it will be well to examine further the notions of Duty and Virtue in general, and of the relations between the two, as we find them implicitly conceived by the common sense of mankind, which we are endeavouring to express. Hitherto I have taken Duty to be broadly convertible with Right conduct: I have noticed, however, that the former term—like "ought" and "moral obligation"—implies at least the *potential* presence of motives prompting to wrong conduct; and is therefore not applicable to beings to whom no such conflict of motives can be attributed. Thus God is not conceived as performing duties, though he is conceived as realizing Justice and other kinds of Rightness in action. I have now to observe that, for a similar reason, we do not commonly apply the term 'duty' to right actions—however necessary and important—when we are so strongly impelled to them by non-moral inclinations that no moral impulse is conceived to be necessary for their performance. Thus we do not say generally that it is a duty to eat and drink enough: though we do often say this to invalids who have lost their appetites. So again, there are certain wanton injuries and gross breaches of decorum from which we do not ordinarily say that it is a man's duty to abstain, since we expect that he will abstain naturally. We should therefore keep most close to usage if we defined Duties as 'those Right actions or abstinences, for the adequate accomplishment of which a moral impulse is conceived to be at least occasionally necessary;' but as this line of distinction is vague, and continually varying, I shall not think it necessary to draw attention to it in the detailed discussion of duties.

It may be said, however, that there is another implication in the term duty which I have so far overlooked, but which its derivation—and that of the equivalent term 'obligation'—plainly indicates: viz. that it is "due" or owed *to* some one. But I think that here the derivation does not govern the established usage: rather, it is commonly recognized that duties *to* persons, or "relative" duties, are only one species, and that some duties—as (*e.g.*) Truth-speaking—have no such relativity. No doubt it is possible to view any duty as relative to the person or persons immediately affected by its performance; but it is not usual to do this where the immediate effects are harmful—as where truth-speaking causes a physically injurious shock to the person addressed—: and though it may still be thought to be ultimately good for society, and so "due" to the community or to humanity at large, that truth should even in this case be spoken, it rather belongs to the utilitarian than to the intuitional view to lay stress on this relation. But again, it may be thought by religious persons that the performance of duties is owed not to the human or other living beings affected by them, but to God as the author of the moral law. And I certainly am not prepared to deny that the conception of duty, in ordinary minds, carries with it this implied relation of an individual will to a universal will conceived as perfectly rational: but neither am I prepared to affirm that this implication is necessary, and an adequate discussion of the difficulties involved in it would lead to metaphysical controversies which I am desirous of avoiding. I propose, therefore, in this exposition of the Intuitional method, to abstract from this relation of Duty generally to a Divine Will: and, for reasons partly similar, to leave out of consideration the particular "duties to God" which Intuitionists have often distinguished and classified. Our view of the general rules of "duty to man" (or to other animals)—so far as such rules are held to be cognizable by moral intuition—will, I conceive, remain the same, whether or not we regard such rules as imposed by a Supreme Reasonable Will: since in any case they will be such as we hold it reasonable for all men to obey, and therefore such as a Supreme Reason would impose. I shall not therefore treat the term Duty as implying necessarily a relation either to a universal Imponent or to the individuals primarily affected by the performance of duties: but shall use it as equivalent generally to Right conduct, while admitting that it is commonly restricted to acts for which a moral impulse is thought to be more or less required.

The notion of Virtue presents more complexity and difficulty, and requires to be discussed from different points of view. We may perhaps conveniently begin this discussion by inquiring how far the sphere of Virtue coincides with that of Duty as above defined. Here the first point to notice is that there seem to be some virtues (such as Generosity) which may be realized in acts objectively wrong, from want of insight into their consequences: and even some (such as Courage) which may be exhibited in wrong acts that are known by the agent to be such. But it is doubtful whether in such cases we should deliberately regard the quality thus manifested as a Virtue, though it certainly excites in us a quasi-moral admiration: and we should not at any rate call such conduct virtuous. It will therefore involve no material deviation from usage if, in treating of the particular Virtues, we confine ourselves to qualities exhibited in actions judged to be right: accordingly for convenience of exposition I shall adopt this limitation in the present Book[1]. Shall we say then that the spheres of Duty and Virtue (as thus defined) are completely coincident? Some I think, would accept this statement without hesitation: still in its common use each term seems to include something excluded from the other. We should scarcely say that it was virtuous —under ordinary circumstances—to pay one's debts, or give one's children a decent education, or keep one's aged parents from starving; because these are duties which most men perform, and only bad men neglect. Again, there are excellent actions which we do not commonly call duties, though

[1] It is more convenient, for the purpose of expounding the morality of common sense, to understand by Virtue a quality exhibited in right conduct; for then we can use the common notions of the particular virtues as heads for the classification of the most important kinds or aspects of right conduct as generally recognized. And I think that this employment of the term is as much in accordance with ordinary usage as any other equally precise use would be.

we praise men for doing them; as for a rich man to live very plainly and devote his income to works of public beneficence. At the same time the lines of distinction are very doubtfully drawn on either side; for we certainly call men virtuous for doing what is strictly their duty when they are under strong temptations to omit it; and we can hardly deny that it is, in some sense, a man's strict duty to do whatever action he judges most excellent, so far as it is in his power.

I think we shall best interpret common sense by distinguishing between the questions 'what a man ought to do or forbear' and 'what other men ought to blame him for not doing or forbearing:' and recognizing that the standard normally applied in dealing with the latter question is laxer than would be right in dealing with the former. We should agree that a truly moral man cannot say to himself, "This is the best thing on the whole for me to do but yet it is not my duty to do it though it is in my power": this would certainly seem to common sense an immoral paradox[1]. How comes it then that in judging of the acts of others we commonly recognize that virtuous conduct may go beyond the limit of what we regard as a person's duty: and that even when there seems no doubt that the virtue beyond duty was within the power of the individual in question? One explanation of this may be found in the different degrees of our knowledge in our own case and in that of others: there are certain acts 'and forbearances' of which we can lay down definitely that they ought to be done or forborne under all circumstances, but with regard to other acts we can only decide when we have the complete knowledge of circumstances which a man commonly possesses only in his own case, and not in that of other men. Thus I may easily assure myself that I ought to subscribe to a given hospital: but I cannot judge whether my neighbour ought to subscribe, as I do not know the details

---

[1] If the phrase in the text were used by a moral person, with a sincere and predominant desire to do duty, it must, I conceive, be used in one of two senses: either (1) half-ironically, in recognition of a customary standard of virtuous conduct which the speaker is not prepared expressly to dispute, but which he does not really adopt as valid—as when we say that it would be virtuous to read a new book, hear a sermon, pay a visit, &c.; or (2) it might be used loosely to mean that such and such conduct *would* be best if the speaker were differently constituted. Cf. *ante*, pp. 69, 70.

of his income and the claims which he is bound to satisfy. I do not, however, think that this explanation is always applicable: I think that there are not a few cases in which we refrain from blaming others for the omission of acts which we do not doubt that we in their place should have thought it our duty to perform. In such cases the line seems drawn by a more or less conscious consideration of what men ordinarily do, and by a social instinct as to the practical effects of expressed moral approbation and disapprobation: we think that moral progress will on the whole be best promoted by our praising acts that are above the level of ordinary practice, and confining our censure—at least if precise and particular—to acts that fall clearly below this standard. But a standard so determined must be inevitably vague and tending to vary as the average level of morality varies in any community, or section of a community: indeed it ought to be the aim of moral persons to raise it continually. Hence it is not convenient to use it in drawing a theoretical line between Virtue and Duty: and I have therefore thought it best to employ the terms so that virtuous conduct may include the performance of duty as well as whatever good actions may be commonly thought to go beyond duty; though recognizing that Virtue in its ordinary use is most conspicuously manifested in the latter.

§ 2. So far I have been considering the term 'Virtuous' as applied to conduct. But both this general term, and the names connoting particular virtues—"just," "liberal," "brave" &c.—are applied to persons as well as to their acts: and the question may be raised which application is most appropriate or primary. Here reflection, I think, shows that these attributes are not thought by us to belong to acts considered apart from their agents: so that Virtue seems to be primarily a quality of the soul or mind, conceived as permanent in comparison with the transient acts and feelings in which it is manifested. As so conceived it is widely held to be a possession worth aiming at for its own sake; to be, in fact, a part of that Perfection of man which is by some regarded as the sole Ultimate Good. This view I shall consider in a subsequent chapter. Meanwhile it may be observed that Virtues, like other habits and dispositions, though conceived as comparatively permanent attributes of the mind, are yet attributes of which we can only form definite notions by conceiving the particular transient phenomena in which they are manifested. If then we ask in what phenomena Virtuous character is manifested, the obvious answer is that it is manifested in voluntary actions, so far as intentional; or, more briefly, in volitions. And many, perhaps most, moralists would give this as a complete answer. If they are not prepared to affirm with Kant that a good will is the only absolute and unconditional Good, they will at any rate agree with Butler that "the object of the moral faculty is actions, comprehending under that name active or practical principles: those principles from which men would act if occasions and circumstances gave them power." And if it be urged that more than this is included (*e.g.*) in the Christian conception of the Virtue of Charity, the "love of our neighbour," they will explain with Kant that by this love we must not understand the emotion of affection, but merely the resolution to benefit, which alone has "true moral worth."

I do not, however, think that this doctrine is really in harmony with the common sense of mankind. I think in our common judgments certain kinds of virtuous actions are held to be at any rate adorned and made better by the presence of certain emotions in the virtuous agent. No doubt the element of volition is the more important: beneficent dispositions unattended by the emotion of love are undoubtedly better than benevolent emotions that do not take effect in action: but we commonly think that a due combination of volition and emotion is more excellent than either. We recognize that benefits which spring from affection and are lovingly bestowed are more acceptable to the recipients than those conferred without affection, in the taste of which there is admittedly something harsh and dry: hence, in a certain way, the affection, if practical and steady, seems a higher excellence than the mere beneficent disposition of the will, as resulting in more excellent acts. In the case of Gratitude even the rigidity of Kant[1] seems to relax, and to admit an emotional element as indispensable to the virtue: and there are various other af-

---

[1] Cf. *Tugendlehre*, § 33: "diese Tugend welche mit Innigkeit der wohlwollenden Gesinnung zugleich Zärtlichkeit des Wohlwollens verbindet."

fections, such as Loyalty and Patriotism, which it is difficult—without paradox—either to exclude from a list of virtues or to introduce stripped bare of all emotional elements. Nor is it only benevolent feeling that is thus thought to enhance virtue: the same may in some cases be said of emotional aversion: thus the Virtue of Chastity or Purity, in its highest form, seems to include more than a mere settled resolution to abstain from unlawful lust, it includes some sentiment of repugnance to impurity. If it be objected that such emotions cannot be commanded at will, I can only answer that it does not seem to be characteristic of virtues as commonly conceived —any more than of other human excellences—that it is in the power of any one by a sufficient effort of will to exhibit them at any time in the form or degree which we judge to be the best possible. I admit, indeed, that no quality of conduct is ever called a virtue unless it is thought to be *to some extent* immediately attainable at will by all ordinary persons, when circumstances give opportunity for its manifestation: in fact it appears to me that the line between virtues and other excellences of behaviour is commonly drawn by this characteristic of voluntariness;—an excellence which we think no effort of will could at once enable us to exhibit in any appreciable degree is called a gift, grace, or talent, but not properly a virtue. Writers like Hume[1], who obliterate this line, seem to me to diverge manifestly from common sense. Still I regard it as at least an equal divergence on the other side to maintain that virtue in all degrees is completely voluntary: there are several other cases, besides those above discussed, in which it would be manifestly paradoxical to affirm this: thus (*e.g.*) no one would deny that courage is a Virtue, and yet no one would affirm that any ordinary man can at will exhibit the highest degree of courage, when occasion arises.

If the view above given of the relation of virtue to natural affection be accepted, the question (raised in the preceding chapter), whether an act is virtuous in proportion as it was done from regard for duty or virtue, is implicitly answered, so far as the morality of Common Sense is concerned: for it is admitted

[1] Cf. *Inquiry concerning the Principles of Morals*, Appendix IV.

that common sense does not hold this to be true of acts to which affection normally prompts. But I should even say that in some cases we commonly attribute virtue to conduct where regard for duty or virtue is not consciously present at all: as in the case of a heroic act of courage—let us say, in saving a fellow-creature from death—under an impulse of spontaneous sympathy: so again, what we call a "genuinely humble" man is a man who is not conscious that he is fulfilling a duty—still less that he is exhibiting a virtue—by being humble.

It further appears to me that in the case of many important virtues we do not commonly regard the ultimate spring of action at all—whether it be some emotional impulse or the rational choice of duty as duty—in attributing the virtue to particular persons: what we regard as indispensable is merely a settled resolve to intend or will a certain kind of external effects. Thus we call a man veracious if he has a settled habit of endeavouring in his speech to produce in the minds of others impressions exactly correspondent to the facts, whatever his motive may be for so doing: whether he is moved, solely or mainly, by a regard for duty or virtue generally, or by a love of truth in particular, or a sense of the degradation of falsehood, or a conviction that truth-speaking is in the long run the best policy in this world, or a belief that it will be rewarded hereafter, or a sympathetic aversion to the inconveniences which misleading statements cause to other people. Similarly we attribute Justice, if a man has a settled habit of weighing diverse claims and fulfilling them in the ratio of their importance; Good Faith if he has a settled habit of strictly keeping express or tacit engagements: and so forth.

And even when we take motives into account, it is often rather the force of seductive motives resisted than the particular nature of the prevailing springs of action which we consider; thus we certainly think virtue has been manifested in a higher degree in just or veracious conduct, when the agent had strong temptations to be unjust or unveracious; and in the same way there are certain tendencies to good conduct which are called virtues when there are powerful seductive motives operating and not otherwise; *e.g.* when a man eats and drinks a proper amount with no desire to exceed we do not attribute to him the virtue of temperance. We must note, however, that Common Sense seems to be involved in a kind of perplexity and even contradiction as to the relation of virtue to the moral effort required for resisting unvirtuous impulses. On the one hand a general assent would be given to the proposition that virtue is especially drawn out and exhibited in a successful conflict with natural inclination. On the other hand we should surely agree with Aristotle that Virtue is imperfect so long as the agent cannot do the virtuous action without a conflict of impulses; since it is from a wrong bent of natural impulse that we find it hard to do what is best, and it seems absurd to say that the more we cure ourselves of this wrong bent, the less virtuous we grow. Perhaps we may solve the difficulty by recognizing that there are two fundamentally different kinds of Virtue, the one constituting the most perfect ideal of moral excellence that we are able to conceive for human beings, while the other is manifested in the effort of imperfect men to attain this ideal: thus in proportion as a man comes to like any particular kind of good conduct and to do it without moral effort, we shall not say that his conduct becomes less virtuous but rather more in conformity with a true moral ideal; while at the same time we shall recognize that in this department of his life he has less room to exhibit that other kind of virtue which is manifested in resistance to seductive impulses and in the energetic striving of the will to get nearer to ideal perfection.

So far I have been considering the manifestation of virtue in emotions and volitions, and have not expressly adverted to the intellectual conditions of virtuous acts: though in speaking of such acts it is of course implied that the volition is accompanied with an intellectual representation of the particular effects willed. It is not, however, necessarily implied that such effects must be thought in willing them to be right or good: and I do not myself think that, in the view of common sense, this is an indispensable condition of the virtuousness of an act; for it seems that some kinds of virtuous acts may be done so entirely without deliberation that no moral judgment was passed on them by the agent. This might be the case for instance, with an act of heroic courage, prompted by an *élan* of sympathy with a fellow-creature in sudden peril. But it is, I conceive, necessary that such an act should not be even vaguely thought to be bad. It is perhaps more difficult to say how far an act which is conceived by the agent to be good but which is really bad can ever be judged to be virtuous: I do not, however, think that the term would ever be applied to an act that is judged bad on the whole (though no doubt conduct in some respects defective through ignorance is often regarded as highly virtuous[1]). If this be so, it is again obvious that the realization of virtue may not be in the power of any given person at any given time, through lack of the requisite intellectual conditions. This, I think, is a conclusion which common sense must accept: though I note a considerable reluctance to accept it; which, however, is not shown in the attribution of virtue to persons who do clearly wrong acts, but rather in an effort to explain their ignorance as caused by some previous wilful wrongdoing. We try to persuade ourselves that if (*e.g.*) Torquemada did not know that it was wrong to torture heretics, he might have known if he had not wilfully neglected means of enlightenment: but there are many cases in which this kind of explanation is unsupported by facts, and I see no ground for accepting it as generally true.

To sum up the results of a rather complicated discussion: I consider that Virtue is primarily attributed to the mind or character of the agent, and conceived to be only manifested in feelings and acts; but that as we only know it through such manifestations, in endeavouring to make precise our conceptions of the particular virtues, we are necessarily concerned mainly with the emotions and volitions in which they are manifested. Examining these, we find that the element of volition is primarily important, and in some cases almost of sole importance, but yet that the element of emotion cannot be altogether discarded without palpable divergence from common sense. Again, concentrating our attention on the volitional element, we find that it is primarily the volitions to produce certain particular

---

[1] I have before said that decidedly wrong acts are frequently considered to exhibit in a high degree the tendencies which, when exhibited in right acts, we call particular virtues—generosity, courage, patriotism, &c.: and this is especially true of acts bad through ignorance.

effects which we regard as grounds for attributing virtue; the general determination to do right as right, duty for duty's sake, is indeed thought to be of fundamental importance to a man's moral life; but rather as a generally necessary spring of virtuous action than as an indispensable condition of our attributing virtue in any particular case. Similarly in considering the emotional element, though an ardent love of virtue or aversion to vice generally is a valuable stimulus to virtuous conduct, it is not a universally necessary condition of it: and in the case of some acts the presence of other emotions—such as kind affection—makes the acts better than if they were done from a purely moral motive. Such emotions, however, cannot be commanded at will: and this is also true of the knowledge of what ought to be done—or rather of the absence of more than a certain amount of error through ignorance—which, in the view of common sense, seems required to render conduct virtuous. For these and other reasons I consider that though Virtue is distinguished by us from other excellences by the characteristic of voluntariness—it must be *to some extent* capable of being realized at will when occasion arises—this voluntariness attaches to it only in a certain degree; and that virtue in the highest degree is not always capable of being so realized. And thus we have a further explanation, besides those discussed in the previous section, of the common conception of Virtue exceeding strict Duty; since Duty is something that we can always do if we will. Or perhaps we should rather say that virtue in some cases only comes indirectly within the range of duty, so far as we recognize a duty of cultivating it. This duty of cultivation extends, of course, to all virtuous habits or dispositions in which we are found to be deficient, in so far as we can thus increase our tendency to do the corresponding acts in future; however completely such acts may on each occasion be within the control of the will. It is true that for acts of this latter kind, so far as they are perfectly deliberate, we do not seem to need any special virtuous habits; if only we have knowledge of what is right and best to be done, together with a sufficiently strong wish to do it[1]. But, in order to fulfil our duties thoroughly, we

[1] Hence the Socratic doctrine that 'all virtue is knowledge'; on the assumption that a rational being must necessarily wish for what is good.

are obliged to act during part of our lives suddenly and without deliberation, and (as we say) "instinctively:" on such occasions there is no room for moral reasoning, and sometimes not even for explicit moral judgment; so that in order to act virtuously, we require such particular habits and dispositions as are denoted by the names of the special virtues: and it is a duty to foster and develope these in whatever way experience shews this to be possible.

The complicated relation of virtue to duty, as above determined, must be borne in mind throughout the discussion of the particular virtues, to which I shall proceed in the following chapters. But, as we have seen, the main part of the manifestation of virtue in conduct consists in voluntary actions, which it is within the power of any individual to do—at least if they are recognized as right,—and which therefore come within our definition of Duty, as above laid down; it will not therefore be necessary, during the greater part of the ensuing discussion, to distinguish between principles of virtuous conduct and principles of duty; since the definitions of the two will coincide.

§ 3. Here, however, a remark is necessary, which to some extent qualifies what was said in the preceding chapter, where I characterized the common notions of particular virtues—justice, &c.—as too vague to furnish exact determinations of the actions enjoined under them. I there assumed that rules of duty ought to admit of precise definition in a universal form: and this assumption naturally belongs to the ordinary or jural view of Ethics as concerned with a moral code: since we should agree that if obligations are imposed on any one he ought at at least to know what they are, and that a law indefinitely drawn must be a bad law. But so far as we contemplate virtue as something that goes beyond strict duty and is not always capable of being realized at will, this assumption is not so clearly appropriate: since from this point of view we naturally compare excellence of conduct with beauty or excellence in the products of the Fine Arts: of which we commonly say, that though rules and definite prescriptions may do much, they can never do all; that the highest excellence is always due to an instinct or tact that cannot be reduced to definite formulæ. We can describe the beautiful products when they are produced, and to some extent classify their beauties, giving names to each; but we cannot prescribe any certain method for producing each kind of beauty. So, it may be said, stands the case with virtues: and hence the attempt to state an explicit maxim, by applying which we may be sure of producing virtuous acts of any kind, must fail: we can only give a general account of the virtue—a description, not a definition—and leave it to trained insight to find in any particular circumstances the act that will best realize it. This view, which I may distinguish as Æsthetic Intuitionism, I propose to consider more fully after I have thoroughly discussed what I have called the "jural" view; since the vaguer method to which the former would lead is one on which we shall naturally be disposed to fall back, if the effort to obtain exact definitions of the principles of duty is not found to yield satisfactory results. Our primary business is to examine the larger claims of those whom I may distinguish as Rational or Jural Intuitionists; who maintain that Ethics is—or ought to be—as much a science as Geometry; having therefore for its first principles the general rules of which we have spoken, or the most fundamental of them. In fact, it would seem to be only on some such view as this, which justifies the attempt to give Ethics a scientific treatment, that we can hope to get rid of the fluctuations and discrepancies of opinion, in which we acquiesce in æsthetic discussions, but which tend to endanger seriously the authority of ethical beliefs. And we cannot, I think, decide on the validity of such claims without examining in detail the propositions which have been put forward as ethical axioms, and seeing how far they prove to be clear and explicit, or how far others may be suggested presenting these qualities. For it would not be maintained, at least by the more judicious thinkers of this school, that such axioms are always to be found with proper exactness of form by mere observation of the common moral reasonings of men; but rather that they are at least latent in these reasonings and may be evolved from them, and that when evolved their truth is self-evident, and must be accepted at once by an intelligent and unbiassed mind. Just as some mathematical axioms are not known to the multitude, and cannot be known, as their certainty cannot be seen except by minds carefully prepared,—but yet, when their terms are properly understood, the perception of their absolute truth is immediate and irresistible. Similarly, if we are not able to claim for our moral axiom, in its precise form, an explicit and actual assent of "*orbis terrarum,*" we may still obtain one implicit and potential: though the formula educed be new, it may still be what men before vaguely intended, and what they will now unhesitatingly admit.

In this inquiry it is not of great importance in what order we take the virtues, nor even that our list should be perfectly complete and symmetrical. We are not to examine the system of any particular moralist, but the Morality (as it was called) of Common Sense; and the discussion of the general notions of Duty and Virtue, in which we have been engaged in the present chapter, will have shewn incidentally the great difficulty of eliciting from Common Sense any clear principle of classification of the particular duties and virtues. Hence I have thought it best to reserve what I have to say on the subject of classification till a later period of the discussion; and in the first place to take the matter to be investigated quite empirically, as we find it in the common thought expressed in the common language of mankind. The systems of moralists commonly attempt to give some definite arrangement to this crude material: but in so far as they are systematic they generally seem forced to transcend Common Sense, and define what it has left doubtful; as I shall hereafter try to shew.

For the present, then, it seems best, in this empirical investigation, to take the virtues rather in the order of their importance; and, as there are some that seem to have a special comprehensiveness of range, and to include under them, in a manner, all or most of the others, it will be convenient to begin with these. Of these Wisdom is perhaps the most obvious: in the next chapter, therefore, I propose to examine what we mean by Wisdom, and to consider at the same time some of the other terms which we use to denote cognate or connected virtues or excellences.

CHAPTER III.

WISDOM AND SELF-CONTROL.

§ 1. WISDOM was always placed by the Greek philosophers first in the list of virtues, and regarded as in a manner comprehending all the others: in fact in the post-Aristotelian schools the notion of the Sage or ideally Wise man ($\sigma o \phi \grave{o} s$) was regularly employed to exhibit in a concrete form the rules of life laid down by each system. In common Greek usage, however, the term just mentioned would signify excellence in purely speculative science, no less than practical wisdom[1]: and the English term Wisdom has, to some extent, the same ambiguity. It is, however, chiefly used in reference to practice: and even when applied to the region of pure speculation suggests especially such intellectual gifts and habits as lead to sound practical conclusions: namely, comprehensiveness of view, the habit of attending impartially to a number of diverse considerations difficult to estimate exactly, and skill in determining the relative importance of each. At any rate, it is only Practical Wisdom which we commonly class among Virtues, as distinguished from purely intellectual excellences. How then shall we define Practical Wisdom? Some would say that we mean by it merely the tendency to discern the best means, in the conduct of life generally, to the attainment of any ends that the natural play of human motives may lead us to seek. But if so, it is not easy to see how it has the characteristic of voluntariness—by which, as has been said, we distinguish virtues from other excel-

---

[1] Indeed Aristotle, who stood alone among the schools sprung from Socrates in distinguishing sharply 'theoretic' from 'practical' wisdom, restricts the term $\sigma o \phi \acute{\iota} a$ to the former, and uses another word ($\phi \rho \acute{o} \nu \eta \sigma \iota s$) to denote the latter.

lences—any more than any species of technical skill, or faculty of selecting the best means to given ends in a certain limited and special department of human action. Such skill in the special arts is partly communicable by means of definite rules, and partly a matter of tact or instinct, depending somewhat on natural gifts and predispositions, but to a great extent acquired by exercise and imitation: and similarly practical Wisdom, if understood to be Skill in the Art of Life, would involve a certain amount of scientific knowledge, the portions of different sciences bearing directly on human action, together with empirical rules relating to the same subject-matter; and also the tact or trained instinct just mentioned, which would even be more prominent here, on account of the extreme complexity of the subject-matter. But it does not appear from this analysis why this skill should be regarded as a virtue: nor in fact, does it seem to be merely this that we mean by wisdom; which certainly in its ordinary use appears to include more than a faculty of finding the best means to any ends. Thus we should not call the most accomplished swindler wise; whereas we should not hesitate to attribute to him cleverness, ingenuity, and other purely intellectual excellences. Again we apply the term "worldly-wise" to a man who skilfully chooses the best means to the end of ambition; but we should not call such a man 'wise' without qualification. Wisdom in short, appears to imply right judgment in respect of ends as well as means.

Here, however, a subtle question arises. For the assumption on which this treatise proceeds is that there are several ultimate ends of action, which all claim to be rational ends, such as all men ought to adopt. Hence, if Wisdom implies right judgment as to ends, it is clear that a person who regards some one end as the right or rational ultimate end will not consider a man wise who adopts any other ultimate end. Can we say then that in the common use of the word Wisdom any one ultimate end is distinctly implied? It may be thought, perhaps, that in the moral view of Common Sense which we are now trying to make clear, since Wisdom itself is prescribed or commended as a quality of conduct intuitively discerned to be right or excellent, the ultimate end which the wise man prefers must be just this attainment of rightness or excellence in conduct generally;

rather than pleasure for himself or others, or any other ulterior end. I think, however, that in the case of this notion it is impossible to carry out that analysis of ordinary practical reasoning into several distinct methods, each admitting and needing separate development, upon which the plan of this treatise is founded. For, as we saw, it is characteristic of Common Sense to assume coincidence or harmony among these different competing methods. And hence, while as regards most particular virtues and duties, the exercise of the moral faculty in ordinary men is *primâ facie* independent of hedonistic calculations, and occasionally in apparent conflict with their results, so that the reconciliation of the different procedures presents itself as a problem to be solved; in the comprehensive notion of Wisdom the antagonism is latent. Common Sense seems to mean by Wise a man who attains at once all the different rational ends: who by conduct in perfect conformity with the true moral code attains the greatest happiness possible both for himself and for mankind (or that portion of mankind to which his efforts are necessarily restricted). But if we find this synthesis unattainable; if, for example, Rational Egoism seems to lead to conduct opposed to the true interests of mankind in general, and we ask whether we are to call the man Wise who seeks, or him who sacrifices, his individual interests, Common Sense gives no clear reply.

§ 2. We are unable, then, to determine by reflecting on Common Sense the principles of conduct which Wisdom will lay down. But leaving this question on one side, we may still perhaps ask how far Wisdom, as exhibited in right judgment as to ends, is attainable at will, and so, according to our definition, a Virtue. At first sight, the perception of the right end may seem not to be voluntary any more than the cognition of any other kind of truth; and though most cognition is attained partly by voluntary effort, still it is not possible for any man, by this alone, to secure the attainment of truth, and the avoidance of error in intellectual processes. It is thought however that the cognition of Moral truth depends largely upon the 'heart', that is, upon a certain condition of our desires and other feelings, rather than the intellect: it is probably on this view that Wisdom is regarded as a Virtue;

and we may admit it as such, according to the definition before given, in so far as this condition is directly attainable by volition. Still, on closer scrutiny, there hardly seems to be more agreement as to the emotional conditions of the cognition of ends than there is as to the ends themselves: as some would say that prayer to God or ardent aspiration produced the most favourable state, while others would urge that emotional excitement is likely to perturb the judgment, and would say that we need for right apprehension rather tranquillity of feeling: and some would contend that a complete suppression of selfish impulses was the essential condition, while others would regard this as chimerical and impossible, or, if possible, a plain misdirection of effort. On these points we cannot decide in the name of Common Sense: but meanwhile most would agree that there are certain violent passions and sensual appetites which are liable to pervert moral apprehensions; and that these are to some extent under the control of the Will, and that a man who uses his moral efforts to control them, when he wishes to decide on ends of action, may be said to be so far voluntarily wise.

And this applies to some extent even to that other function of Wisdom, first discussed, which consists in the selection of the best means to the attainment of given ends. For experience seems to shew that our insight in practical matters is liable to be perverted by desire and fear, and that this perversion may be prevented by an effort of self-control: so that unwisdom, even here, is at least not altogether involuntary. And we may notice that volition has a more important part to play in developing or protecting our insight into the right conduct of life, than it has in respect of the technical skill to which we compared Practical Wisdom; in proportion as the reasonings in which the Practical Wisdom is exhibited are less clear and exact, and the conclusions inevitably more uncertain. For desire and fear could hardly make one go wrong in an arithmetical calculation; but in estimating a balance of complicated probabilities it is more difficult to resist the influence of strong inclination: and it would seem to be a more or less definite consciousness of the continual need of such resistance, which leads us to regard Wisdom as a Virtue.

So much for the influence of the Will on the decisions of the Reason. But when a man has decided what course of conduct is under any given circumstances rational, the question still remains whether he will certainly adopt it. Now I hardly think that Common Sense considers the *choice*, as distinct from the *cognition*, of right ends to belong to Wisdom; and yet we should scarcely call a man wise who deliberately chose to do what he knew to be contrary to reason. We may perhaps explain this by pointing out that, though the modern mind seems to have no serious difficulty in admitting the conception of deliberate irrationality of conduct[1], still such a notion is unfamiliar in comparison with those of (1) impulsive irrationality, and (2) mistaken choice of bad for good. The latter of these, as we commonly think, is to be averted by Wisdom; the former, by Self-control. If however we admit that "video meliora proboque, deteriora sequor" is often true of conduct planned with perfect deliberation, we must expressly recognize the duty of adopting, after deliberation, the decisions of the Practical Reason; whether we regard this as an exercise of Wisdom or of Self-control, or of both combined. We should distinguish from this the more difficult excellence of adhering to resolutions in spite of all gusts of impulse that the varying occasions of life may arouse. It is clearly our duty so to adhere, in so far as it is within the power of the will: as a resolution made after deliberation, in accordance with our view of what is right, should not be abandoned or modified except deliberately—at least if time for fresh deliberation be allowed—: and the tendency to resist impulses prompting to such abandonment or modification is commonly recognized as an indispensable auxiliary to Wisdom. But this species of Self-control, which we may perhaps call Firmness, can hardly be said to be altogether attainable at will, at least when it is most wanted: for the impulses against which we are especially required to be firm are often too rapid to leave room for a fully conscious act of volition. We can, however, cultivate this excellence more directly and certainly than others, by graving our resolves deeper in the moments of de-

---

[1] I have already adverted to the difference between the ancient and the modern mind in this respect. Cf. *ante*, B. I. c. v, § 1, p. 56 note.

liberation that continually intervene among the moments of impulsive action.

§ 3. In examining the functions of Wisdom, other subordinate excellences come into view, which are partly included in our ideal conception of Wisdom, and partly auxiliary or supplementary. Some of these however no one would exactly call virtues: such as Sagacity in selecting the really important points amid a crowd of others, Acuteness in seeing aids or obstacles that lie somewhat hidden, Ingenuity in devising subtle or complicated means to our ends, and other cognate qualities more or less vaguely defined and named. We cannot be acute, or ingenious, or sagacious when we please, though we may become more so by practice. The same may be said of Caution, so far as Caution implies taking into due account *material* circumstances unfavourable to our wishes and aims: for by no effort of will can we certainly see what circumstances are material; we can only look steadily and comprehensively. The term 'Caution,' however, may also be legitimately applied to a species of Self-control which we shall properly regard as a Virtue: viz. the tendency to deliberate whenever and so long as deliberation is judged to be required, even though powerful impulses urge us to immediate action[1].

And, in antithesis to Caution, we may notice as another minor virtue the quality called Decision, so far as we mean by Decision the habit of resisting an irrational impulse to which men are liable, of continuing to some extent in the deliberative attitude when they know that deliberation is no longer expedient, and that they ought to be acting. 'Decision,' however, is often applied (like 'Caution') to denote solely or chiefly a

---

[1] It may be observed that there is another meaning again in which the term 'Caution' is sometimes used. Since of the various means which we may use to gain any end, some are more and some less certain; and some are dangerous, that is, involve a chance of consequences either antagonistic to our pursuit, or on other grounds to be avoided, while others are free from such danger: 'Caution' is often used to denote the temper of mind which inclines to the more certain and less dangerous means. In this sense, in so far as the chance in each case of winning the end, and the value of the end as compared with other ends, and as weighed against the detriment which its pursuit may entail, can be precisely estimated, the limits of the duty of Caution may obviously be determined with exactness.

merely intellectual excellence; viz. the tendency to judge rightly as to the time for closing deliberation.

I conclude then that so far as such qualities as those which I have distinguished as Firmness, Caution, and Decision, are recognized as Virtues and not merely as intellectual excellences, it is as being, in fact, species of Self-control; i.e. as involving voluntary adoption of and adhesion to rational judgments as to conduct, in spite of certain irrational motives prompting in an opposite direction. Now it may seem at first sight that if we suppose perfect correctness of judgment combined with perfect self-control, the result will be a perfect performance of duty in all departments; and the realization of perfect Virtue, except so far as this involves the presence of certain special emotions not to be commanded at will. And no doubt a perfectly wise and self-controlled man cannot be conceived as breaking or neglecting any moral rule. But it is important to observe that even sincere and single-minded efforts to realize what we see to be right may vary in intensity; and that therefore the tendency to manifest a high degree of intensity in such efforts is properly praised as Energy, if the quality be purely volitional; or under some such name as Zeal or Moral Ardour, if the volitional energy be referred to intensity of emotion, and yet not connected with any emotion more special than the general love of what is Right or Good.

CHAPTER IV.

BENEVOLENCE.

§ 1. We have seen that the virtue of Practical Wisdom comprehends all others, so far as virtuous conduct in each department necessarily results from a clear knowledge and choice of the true ultimate end or ends of action, and of the best means to the attainment of such end or ends[1]. From this point of view, we may consider the names of the special virtues as denoting special departments of this knowledge; which it is now our business to examine more closely.

When, however, we contemplate these, we discern that there are other virtues, which, in different ways, may be regarded as no less comprehensive than Wisdom. Especially in modern times, since the revival of independent ethical speculation, there have always been thinkers who have maintained, in some form, the view that Benevolence is a supreme and architectonic virtue, comprehending and summing up all the others, and fitted to regulate them and determine their proper limits and mutual relations. The phase of this view most current at present would seem to be Utilitarianism, the principles and method of which will be more fully discussed hereafter: but in some form or other it has been held by many whose affinities are rather with the Intuitional school. This widely supported claim to supremacy seems an adequate reason for giving to Benevolence the first place after Wisdom, in our examination of the commonly received maxims of Duty and Virtue.

The general maxim of Benevolence would be commonly said to be, "that we ought to love all our fellow-men," or "all

[1] The qualifications which this proposition requires have been already noticed, and will be further illustrated as we proceed.

our fellow-creatures": but, as we have already seen, there is some doubt among moralists as to the precise meaning of the term "love" in this connexion: since, according to Kant and others, what is morally prescribed as the Duty of Benevolence is not strictly the affection of love or kindness, so far as this contains an emotional element, but only the determination of the will to seek the good or happiness of others. And I agree that it cannot be a strict duty to feel an emotion, so far as it is not directly within the power of the Will to produce it at any given time. Still (as I have said) it seems to me paradoxical to deny that this emotional element is included in our common notion of Charity or Philanthropy, regarded as a Virtue: or that it adds a higher excellence to the mere beneficent disposition of the will, as resulting in more excellent actions. If this be so, it will be a duty to cultivate the affection so far as it is possible to do so: and indeed this would seem (no less than the permanent disposition to do good) to be a normal effect of repeated beneficent resolves and actions. Even the poets and popular moralizers have observed that a benefit tends to excite love in the agent towards the person benefited, no less than in the latter towards the agent. It must be admitted, however, that this effect is less certain than the production of the disposition; and that some men are naturally so unattractive to others that these can feel no affection towards them, though they may entertain benevolent dispositions of will. At any rate, it would seem to be a duty generally, and till we find the effort fruitless, to cultivate kind affections towards those whom we ought to benefit; not only by doing kind actions (which are immediately a duty, and therefore need not be prescribed as a means to an end), but by placing ourselves under any natural influences which experience shews to have a tendency to produce affection.

But we have still to ascertain more particularly the nature of the actions in which this affection or disposition of will is shewn. They are described popularly as 'doing good.' Now we have before[1] noticed that the notion 'good,' in ordinary thought, includes, undistinguished and therefore unharmonized, the different conceptions that men form of the ultimate end of

[1] Cf. I. c. vii, ix.

rational action. It follows that there is a corresponding ambiguity in the phrase 'doing good:' since, though many would unhesitatingly take it to mean the promotion of Happiness, there are others who, holding that Perfection and not happiness is the true ultimate Good, consistently maintain that the real way to 'do good' to people is to increase their virtue or aid their progress towards Perfection. There are, however, even among anti-Epicurean moralists, some—such as Kant—who take an opposite view, and argue that my neighbour's Virtue or Perfection cannot be an end to me, because it depends upon the free exercise of his own volition, which I cannot help or hinder. But this seems to involve a too purely and one-sidedly Libertarian conception of human action: and it might equally be argued that I cannot *cultivate* Virtue in myself, but only practise it from moment to moment. But even Kant does not deny that we can cultivate virtuous dispositions in ourselves, and that in other ways than by the performance of virtuous acts: and Common Sense always assumes this to be possible and prescribes it as a duty. And surely it is equally undeniable that we can cultivate virtue in others: and indeed such cultivation is clearly the object not only of education, but of a large part of social action, and partly at least of all our expression of praise and blame, and even to some extent of Law. And if Virtue is an ultimate end for ourselves, to be sought for its own sake, benevolence must lead us to do what is possible to obtain it for our neighbour. And indeed we see that in the case of intense individual affection, the friend or lover generally longs that the beloved should be excellent and admirable as well as happy: perhaps, however, this is because love involves preference, and the lover desires that the beloved should be really worthy of preference as well as actually preferred by him, as otherwise there is a conflict between Love and Reason.

On the whole then, I do not find, in the common view of what Benevolence bids us promote for others, any clear selection indicated between the different and possibly conflicting elements of Good as commonly conceived. But we may say, I think, that the promotion of Happiness is practically the chief part of what Common Sense considers to be prescribed as the external duty of Benevolence: and for clearness' sake we will confine our attention to this in the remainder of the discussion[1]. It should be observed that by happiness we are not to understand the gratification of the actual desires of others, for men too often desire what would tend to their unhappiness in the long run: but the greatest possible amount of pleasure or satisfaction for them on the whole—in short, such happiness as was taken to be the rational end of each individual in the system of Egoistic Hedonism. It is this that Rational Benevolence bids us provide for others; and if one who loves is led from affectionate sympathy with the longings of the beloved to gratify those longings when the gratification is attended with an overplus of painful consequences, we commonly say that such affection is weak and foolish.

§ 2. It remains to ask towards whom this disposition or affection is to be maintained, and to what extent. And, firstly, it is not quite clear whether we owe benevolence to men alone, or to other animals also. That is, there is a general agreement that we ought to treat all animals with kindness; but it is questioned whether this is directly due to sentient beings as such, or merely prescribed as a means of cultivating kindly dispositions towards men. Intuitional moralists of repute have certainly maintained this latter view: I think, however, that Common Sense is disposed to regard this as a hard-hearted paradox and to hold with Bentham that the pain of animals is *per se* to be avoided; but the point is one which I am not prepared dogmatically to determine. It is of more importance to consider how our benevolence ought to be distributed among our fellow-men. Here we may conveniently make clear the Intuitional view by contrasting it with that of Utilitarianism. For Utilitarianism is sometimes said to resolve all virtue into Universal Benevolence: it does not, however, prescribe that we should love all men equally, but that we should aim at Happiness generally as our ultimate end, and so consider the happiness of any one individual as equally important with the equal happiness of any other, as an element

---

[1] A further reason for so doing will appear in the sequel; when we come to survey the general relation of Virtue to Happiness, as the result of that detailed examination of the particular virtues which forms the main subject of the present Book. Cf. *post*, c. xiv.

of this total; and should distribute our kindness so as to make this total as great as possible, in whatever way this result may be attained. Practically of course the distribution of any individual's services will, even on this view, be unequal: as each man will obviously promote the general happiness best by rendering services to a limited number, and to some more than others: but the inequality, on the Utilitarian theory, is secondary and derivative. Common Sense, however, seems rather to regard it as immediately certain without any such deduction that we owe special dues of kindness to those who stand in special relations to us. The question then is, on what principles, when any case of doubt or apparent conflict of duties arises, we are to determine the nature and extent of the special claims to affection and kind services which arise out of these particular relations of human beings. Are problems of this kind to be solved by considering which course of conduct is on the whole most conducive to the general happiness? or can we find independent and self-evident principles sufficiently clear and precise to furnish practical guidance in such cases. The different answers given to this fundamental question will obviously constitute the main difference between the Intuitional and Utilitarian methods; so far as the 'good' which the benevolent man desires and seeks to confer on others is understood to be Happiness.

When, however, we come to investigate this question we are met with a difficulty in the arrangement of the subject, which, like most difficulties of classification, deserves attentive consideration, as it depends upon important characteristics of the matter that has to be arranged. We are accustomed to distinguish and even contrast Benevolence and Justice; and though we may of course exercise both towards the same persons, still we commonly treat the spheres of external duty corresponding respectively to each as mutually exclusive, assuming that at any rate the special function of Benevolence begins where Justice ends. At the same time, if we consider the services that spring from affection as a debt that ought to be paid to persons in certain relations, the moral notion under which these duties are presented to us is hardly distinguishable from that of Justice; while yet these duties can hardly be withdrawn from the sphere of Benevolence. It is sometimes given as a distinction between Justice and Benevolence, that the services which Justice prescribes can be claimed as a right by their recipient, while Benevolence is essentially unconstrained: but we certainly think (*e.g.*) that parents have a right to filial affection and to the services that naturally spring from it. It is further said that the duties of Affection are essentially indefinite, while those we classify under the head of Justice are precisely defined: and no doubt this is partly true. We not only find it hard to say exactly how much a son owes his parents, but we are even reluctant[1] to investigate this: we do not think that he ought to ask for a precise measure of his duty, in order that he may do just so much and no more; while a great part of Justice consists in the observance of stated agreements and precise rules. At the same time it is difficult to maintain this distinction as a ground of classification; for the duties of Affection are admittedly liable to come into competition with each other, and with other duties; and when this apparent conflict of duties occurs, we manifestly need as precise a definition as possible of the conflicting obligations, in order to make a reasonable choice among the alternatives of conduct presented to us. In the following chapter (on Justice) I shall give what appears to me the best solution attainable of this difficulty of classification: meanwhile, it seems proper to treat in the present place of all duties that arise out of relations where affection naturally and normally exists, and where it ought to be cultivated, and where its absence is deplored if not blamed. For all are agreed that there are such duties, the non-performance of which is a ground for censure; over and above the obligations imposed by law, or arising out of specific contract, which will come under a different head.

Beyond these duties, however, there seems to be a region of performance where the services rendered cannot properly be claimed as of debt, and blame is not felt to be due for non-performance: and with regard to this region, too,—which clearly belongs to Benevolence as contrasted with Jus-

[1] This reluctance, however, seems largely due to the fact that this precise measure of duty is most frequently demanded when the issue lies between Duty and Self interest.

tice—there is some difficulty in stating the view of Common Sense morality. There are two questions to be considered. We have to ask, firstly, whether services rendered from affection, over and above what strict Duty is thought to require, are to be deemed Virtuous; and secondly, whether the affection itself is to be regarded as a moral excellence and worthy of admiration, and a mental condition that we should seek to attain. Now certainly the disposition to render substantial positive services to mankind generally, and promote their well-being, is thought to be virtuous, being indeed what is commonly known as the Virtue of Benevolence; and if such a disposition springs out of natural warmth and kindliness of feeling towards human beings generally, it is in some respects more attractive and admirable than if it is the result of moral effort and resolve, and—supposing it accompanied by equal intellectual enlightenment—seems to attain its end more perfectly: although we should also praise and call virtuous those who devote themselves to the service of mankind without general affection, because such service is right and noble; and some would find more manifest *merit* or good desert in this latter service[1]. On the other hand, it will be admitted that the more the benevolent impulse is combined with the habit of considering the complex consequences of different courses of action that may be presented as alternatives, and comparing the amounts of happiness to others respectively resulting from them, the more good, *ceteris paribus*, is likely to be caused by it on the whole. And so far as there seems to be a certain natural incompatibility between this habit of calculation and comparison and the spontaneous fervour of kindly impulse, Common Sense is somewhat puzzled which to prefer; and takes refuge in an ideal that transcends this incompatibility and includes the two.

Still we may say that Common Sense clearly regards kind affection as an excellence, when it is thus universal in its scope: and at the same time praises as virtuous the resolve to render services to mankind, without any emotional prompting. And the same may be said of the less comprehensive affection that impels men to promote the well-being of the community of

[1] Cf. *post* ch. v. § 6.

which they are members; and again of the affection that normally tends to accompany the recognition of rightful rule or leadership in others. In some ages and countries Patriotism and Loyalty have been regarded as almost supreme among the virtues; and even now Common Sense gives them a high place.

But when we pass to more restricted, and, ordinarily more intense, affections, such as those which we feel for relations and friends, it becomes more difficult to determine whether they are to be considered as moral excellences and cultivated as such.

First, to avoid confusion, we must remark that Love is not merely a desire to do good to the object beloved, although it always involves such a desire. It is primarily a pleasurable emotion, which seems to depend upon a certain sense of union with another person, and is aroused most strongly by his presence. It hence includes, besides the benevolent impulse, a desire of the society of the beloved: and this element may predominate over the former, and even conflict with it, so that the true interests of the beloved may be sacrificed. In this case we call the affection selfish, and do not praise it at all, but rather blame. If now we ask whether intense Love for an individual, considered merely as a benevolent impulse, is in itself a moral excellence, it is difficult to extract a very definite answer from Common Sense: but it perhaps inclines on the whole to the negative. We are no doubt generally inclined to admire any kind of conspicuously 'altruistic' conduct and any form of intense love, however restricted in its scope; yet it hardly seems that the susceptibility to such individualized benevolent emotions is exactly regarded as an essential element of moral Perfection, which we ought to strive after and cultivate like other moral excellences; we seem, in fact to doubt whether such effort is desirable in this case, at least beyond the point up to which such affection is thought to be required for the performance of recognized duties. And though we think it natural and desirable that in general each person should feel strong affection for a few individuals, and that his efforts to promote directly the well-being of others should, to a great extent, follow the promptings of such impulses; we are hardly prepared to recommend that he should render services to special individuals beyond what he is bound to render, and such as are the natural expression of an eager and overflowing affection, without having any such affection to express: although, as was before said, in certain intimate relations we do not approve of the limits of duty being too exactly measured.

On the whole, then, I conclude, that while we praise and admire enthusiastic Benevolence and Patriotism, and are touched and charmed by the spontaneous lavish outflow of Gratitude, Friendship, and the domestic affections; still what chiefly concerns us as moralists, under the present head, is the ascertainment of the right rules of distribution of services and kind acts, in so far as we consider the rendering of these to be morally obligatory. For provided a man fulfils these duties (and observes the other recognized rules of morality) Common Sense is not prepared to say how far it is right or good that he should sacrifice any other noble and worthy aim—such as the cultivation of knowledge or any of the fine arts—to the claims of philanthropy or personal affection: there seem to be no generally accepted "intuitional" principles for determining such a choice of alternatives[1].

§ 3. What then are the duties that we owe to our fellow-men? Perhaps the mere enumeration of them is not difficult. All would agree that we are bound to shew kindness to parents and children and spouse, and to other kinsmen to a certain extent: and to those who have rendered services to us and any others whom we may have admitted to our intimacy and called friends: and to neighbours and to our fellow-countrymen more than others: and perhaps we may say to those of our own race more than to black or yellow men, and generally to human beings in proportion to their affinity to ourselves. And to our country as a corporate whole we believe ourselves to owe the greatest sacrifices when occasion calls (but in a lower stage of civilization this debt is thought to be due rather to one's king or chief): and a similar obligation seems to be recognized, though less definitely and in a less degree, as regards minor corporations of which we are members. And to all men with whom we may be brought into relation we are held to owe slight services, and such as may be rendered without inconve-

[1] This question will be further discussed in the concluding chapter of this Book (ch. xiv.).

nience: but those who are in distress or urgent need have a claim on us for special kindness. These are generally recognised claims: but we find considerable difficulty and divergence, when we attempt to determine more precisely their extent and relative obligation: and the divergence becomes indefinitely greater when we compare the customs and common opinions now existing among ourselves in respect of such claims, with those of other ages and countries. For example, in earlier ages of society a peculiar sacredness was attached to the tie of hospitality, and claims arising out of it were considered peculiarly stringent: but this has changed as hospitality in the progress of civilization has become a luxury rather than a necessary, and we do not think that we owe much to a man because we have asked him to dinner. Or again we may take an instance where the alteration is perhaps actually going on—the claims of kindred in respect of bequest. We should now commonly think that a man ought usually to leave his property to his children: but, that if he has no children we think he may do what he likes with it, unless any of his brothers or sisters are in poverty, in which case compassion seems to blend with and invigorate the evanescent claim of consanguinity. But in an age not long past a childless man was held to be morally bound to leave his money to his collateral relatives: and thus we are naturally led to conjecture that in the not distant future, any similar obligation to children—unless in want—may have vanished out of men's minds. A similar change might be traced in the commonly recognised duty of children to parents.

It may however be urged that this variation of custom is no obstacle to the definition of duty, because we may lay down that the customs of any society ought to be obeyed so long as they are established, just as the laws ought, although both customs and laws may be changed from time to time. And no doubt it is generally expedient to conform to established customs: still, on reflection, we see that it cannot be laid down as an absolute duty. For the cases of Custom and Law are not similar: as in every progressive community there is a regular and settled mode of abrogating laws that are found bad: but customs cannot be thus formally abolished, and we only get rid of them by private individuals refusing to obey them: and therefore it must be sometimes right to do this, if some customs are vexatious and pernicious, as we frequently judge those of antique and alien communities to be. And if we say that customs should generally be obeyed, but that they may be disobeyed when they reach a certain degree of inexpediency, our method seems to resolve itself into Utilitarianism: for we cannot reasonably rest the general obligation upon one principle, and determine its limits and exceptions by another. If the duties above enumerated can be referred to independent and self-evident principles, the limits of each must be implicitly given in the intuition that reveals the principle.

§ 4. In order then to ascertain how far we possess such principles, let us examine in more detail what Common Sense seems to affirm in respect of these duties.

They seem to range themselves under four heads. There are (1) duties arising out of comparatively permanent relationships not voluntarily chosen, such as Kindred and in most cases Citizenship and Neighbourhood: (2) those of similar relationships voluntarily contracted, such as Friendship: (3) those that spring from special services received, or Duties of Gratitude: and (4) those that seem due to special need, or Duties of Pity. This classification is, I think, convenient for discussion; but I cannot profess that it clearly and completely avoids cross divisions; since, for example, the principle of Gratitude is often appealed to as supplying the rationale for duties of the first class; such as those owed by children to parents. Here, however, we come upon a material disagreement and difficulty in determining the maxim of this species of duty. It would be agreed that children owe to their parents respect and kindness generally, and assistance in case of infirmity or any special need: but it seems doubtful how far this is held by Common Sense to be due on account of the relationship alone, or of services rendered during infancy, and how far it be due to cruel or neglectful parents. Most perhaps would say, here and in other cases, that mere nearness of blood constituted a certain claim: but they would find it hard to agree upon its exact force[1].

---

[1] It may be said that a child owes gratitude to the authors of its existence. But life alone, apart from any provision for making life happy, seems a boon of

But, apart from this, there seems great difference of opinion as to what is due from children to parents who have performed their duty; as, for example, how far obedience is due from a child who is no longer in its parents' guardianship or dependent on them for support:—whether (*e.g.*) a son or a daughter is bound not to oppose a parent's wishes in marrying or choosing a profession. Practically we find that parental control is greater in the case of persons who can enrich their children by testament: still we can hardly take this into consideration in determining the ideal of filial duty: for to this, whatever it may be, the child is thought to be absolutely bound, and not as a *quidproquo* in anticipation of future benefits: and many would hold that a parent had no moral right to disinherit a child, except as a penalty for a transgression of duty.

And this leads to what we may conveniently examine next, the duty of parents to children. This too we might partly classify under a different head, viz. that of duties arising out of special needs: for no doubt children are naturally objects of compassion, on account of their helplessness, to others besides their parents. But on the latter they have a claim of a different kind, springing from the universally recognised duty of not causing pain or any harm to other human beings, directly or indirectly, except in the way of deserved punishment: for the parent, being the cause of the child's existing in a helpless condition, would be indirectly the cause of the suffering and death that would result to it if neglected. Still this does not seem an adequate explanation of parental duty, as recognised by Common Sense. For we commonly blame a parent who leaves his children entirely to the care of others, even if he pays for their being nourished and trained up to the time at which they can support themselves by their own labour. We think that he owes them affection (as far as this can be said to be a duty) and the tender and watchful care that naturally springs from affection: and, if he can afford it, somewhat more than the necessary minimum of food, clothing, and education. Still it does not seem clear how far beyond this he is bound to go. It is easy to say broadly that he ought to promote his children's

doubtful value, and one that scarcely excites gratitude when it was not conferred from any regard for the recipient.

happiness by all means in his power: and no doubt it is natural for a good parent to find his own best happiness in his children's; and we are disposed to blame any one who prefers his own interest to theirs. And yet it seems unreasonable that he should purchase a small increase of their happiness by a great sacrifice of his own: and moreover there are other worthy and noble ends which may (and do) come into competition with this. To take instances of actual occurrence: one parent is led to give up some important and valuable work, which perhaps no one else can or will do, in order to leave his children a little more wealth: another brings them to the verge of starvation in order to perfect an invention or prosecute scientific researches. We seem to condemn either extreme: yet what clear and accepted principle can be stated for determining the true mean?

Again, as we have seen, some think that a parent has no right to bequeath his inheritance away from his children, unless they have been undutiful: and there are countries in which this is even forbidden by law. Others, however, hold that children as such have no claims to their parents' wealth: but only if there is a tacit understanding that they will succeed to it, or, at any rate, if they have been reared in such habits of life and social relations as will render it difficult and painful for them to live without inherited wealth.

It would be tedious to go in detail through all the degrees of consanguinity, as it is perhaps clear that our conception of the mutual duties of kinsmen becomes vaguer as the kinship becomes more remote. Among children of the same parents, brought up together, affection of more or less strength grows up so naturally and commonly, that we regard those who do not love their brothers and sisters with a certain aversion and moral contempt, as somewhat inhuman: and we think that in any case the services and kind acts which naturally spring from affection ought to be rendered to some extent; but the extent seems quite undefined. And even towards remoter kinsmen we think that a certain flow of kindly feeling will attend the representation of consanguinity in men of good dispositions. Some indeed still think that cousins have a moral right to a man's inheritance in default of nearer heirs, and to assistance in any need: but it seems equally common to hold that they can at most claim to be selected *ceteris paribus* as the recipients of bounty, and that an unpromising cousin should not be preferred to a promising stranger.

§ 5. I have placed Neighbourhood along with Kindred among the relations out of which a certain claim for mutual services is thought to spring. However, no one perhaps would say that mere local juxtaposition is in itself a ground of duties: it seems rather that neighbours naturally feel more sympathy with one another than with strangers, as the tie of common humanity is strengthened even by such conjunction and mutual association as mere neighbourhood (without cooperation or friendship) may involve, and a man in whom this effect is not produced is thought somewhat inhuman. And so in large towns where this mutual sympathy does not so naturally grow up (for all the townsmen are in a sense neighbours, and one cannot easily sympathise with each individual in a multitude), the tie of neighbourhood is felt to be relaxed, and neighbour only claims from neighbour, as the nearest man, what one man may claim from another. For there are some services, slight in ordinary times but greater in the case of exceptional need, which any man is thought to have a right to ask from any other: and thus, the claim being so general, a trifling circumstance may make it natural that the service should be asked from one person rather than another: such as any degree of kinship (since the representation of this tends to produce a feeling of union and consequent sympathy), and so even the fact of belonging to the same province, as creating a slight probability of community of origin—thus Scotchmen are said to assist Scotchmen rather than others—and again similarities of various kinds, as one sympathises more easily with one's like, and so persons naturally seek aid in distress from those of the same age, or sex, or rank, or profession. The duty of neighbourhood seems therefore only a particular application of the duty of general benevolence or humanity. And the claim of Fellow-countrymen is of the same kind: that is, if they are taken as individuals; for one's relation to one's country as a whole is thought to be of a different kind, and to involve much more stringent obligations.

Still the duties of Patriotism are difficult to formulate. For the mere obedience to the laws of a country which morality requires from all its inhabitants seems to come under another head: and aliens are equally bound to this. And in the case of most social functions which men undertake, patriotism is at least not a prominent nor indispensable motive: for they undertake them primarily for the sake of payment; and having undertaken them, are bound by Justice and Good Faith to perform them adequately. However, if any of the functions of government are unpaid, we consider that men exhibit patriotism in performing them: for though it is plausible to say that they get their payment in social distinction, still on reflection this view does not appear to be quite appropriate; since social distinction is intended to express feelings of honour and respect, and we cannot properly render these as part of a bargain, but only as a tribute paid to virtue or excellence of some kind. But how far any individual is bound to undertake such functions is not quite clear: and the question seems generally decided by considerations of expediency, except in so far as duties of this kind devolve, legally or constitutionally, upon all the citizens in a free country, as is the case to some extent. Among these the duty of fighting the national enemies is prominent in many countries: and even where this function has become a salaried and voluntarily adopted profession, we call it in a peculiar sense the 'service of one's country,' and think it at least desirable and best that it should be performed with feelings of patriotism: as we find it somewhat degrading and repulsive that a man should slaughter his fellow-men for hire. And in great crises of national existence the affection of Patriotism is naturally intensified: and even in ordinary times we praise a man who renders services to his country over and above the common duties of citizenship. But whether a citizen is at any time morally bound to more than certain legally or constitutionally determined duties, does not seem to be clear: nor, again, whether he can rightfully relieve himself of all moral obligations to the community in which he was born by voluntary expatriation[1].

Nor, finally, does there seem to be any *consensus* as to

[1] On the question of the right of the individual to renounce citizenship the laws of different modern civilised communities appear to take different views.

what each man owes to his fellow-men, as such. The Utilitarian doctrine, as we have seen, is that each man ought to consider the happiness of any other as *theoretically* of equal importance with his own, and only of less importance *practically*, in so far as he is better able to realise the latter. And it seems to me difficult to say decidedly that this is *not* the principle of general Benevolence, as recognised by the common sense of mankind. But it must be admitted that there is also current a lower and narrower estimate of the services that we are held to be strictly bound to render to our fellow-men generally. This lower view seems to recognise (1)—as was before noticed—a negative duty to abstain from causing pain or harm to any of our fellow-men, except in the way of deserved punishment; to which we may add, as an immediate corollary, the duty of making reparation for any harm that we may have done them[1]: and (2) a positive duty to render, when occasion offers, such services as require either no sacrifice on our part, or at least one very much less in importance than the service rendered. Further, a general obligation of being 'useful to society' by some kind of systematic work is vaguely recognised; rich persons who are manifest drones incur some degree of censure from thoughtful persons. Beyond this somewhat indefinite limit of Duty extends the Virtue of Benevolence without limit: for excess is not thought to be possible in doing good to others, nor in the disposition to do it, unless it leads us to neglect definite duties.

Under the notion of Benevolence as just defined, the minor rules of Gentleness, Politeness, Courtesy, &c. may be brought, in so far as they prescribe the expression of general goodwill and abstinence from anything that may cause pain to others in conversation and social demeanour. There is, however, an important part of Politeness which it may be well to notice and discuss separately; the duty, namely, of shewing marks of Reverence to those to whom they are properly due.

[1] How far we are bound to make reparation when the harm is involuntary, and such as could not have been prevented by ordinary care on our part, is not clear: but it will be convenient to defer the consideration of this till the next chapter (§ 5): as the whole of this department of duty is commonly placed under the head of Justice.

Reverence we may define as the feeling which accompanies the recognition of Superiority or Worth in others. It does not seem to be necessarily in itself benevolent, though often accompanied by some degree of love. But its ethical characteristics seem analogous to those of benevolent affection, in so far as, while it is not a feeling directly under the control of the will, we yet expect it under certain circumstances and morally dislike its absence, and perhaps commonly consider the expression of it to be sometimes a duty, even when the feeling itself is absent.

Still, as to this latter duty of expressing reverence, there seems very great divergence of opinion. For the feeling seems to be naturally excited by all kinds of superiority: not merely moral and intellectual excellences, but also superiorities of rank and position: and indeed in the common behaviour of men it is to the latter that it is more regularly and formally rendered. And yet, again, it is commonly said that Reverence is more properly due to the former, as being more real and intrinsic superiorities: and many think that to shew any reverence to men of rank and position rather than to others is servile and degrading: and some even dislike the marks of respect which in most countries are exacted by official superiors from their subordinates, saying that obedience legally defined is all that is properly owed in this relation.

A more serious difficulty of a somewhat similar kind arises when we consider how far it is a duty to cultivate the affection of Loyalty: meaning by this term—which is used in various senses—the affection that is normally felt by a well-disposed servant or official subordinate towards a good master or official superior. On the one hand it is widely thought that the duties of obedience which belong to these relations will be better performed if affection enters into the motive, no less than the duties of the family relations: but in the former case it would seem that the habits of orderliness and Good Faith—ungrudging obedience to law and ungrudging fulfilment of contract—will ordinarily suffice, without personal affection: and it is urged, on the other hand, that a disposition to obey superiors beyond the limits of their legal or contracted rights to issue commands may easily be mischievous in its effects, if the superiors are ill-disposed. In a well-ordered modern state every individual's right to originate commands is strictly limited by law or custom: and though in the case of a wise and good superior it is obviously advantageous that inferiors should be disposed to obey beyond these limits, it is not clear that this disposition is one which it should be made a duty to cultivate beyond the degree in which it results spontaneously from a sense of the superior's goodness and wisdom. Nor do I think that any decided enunciation of duty on this point can be extracted from Common Sense.

§ 6. We have next to consider the duties of Affection that arise out of relationships voluntarily assumed. Of these the most important is the Conjugal Relation. And here it is important to know whether it be the duty of human beings generally to enter into this relation. It is no doubt normal to do so, and most persons are prompted to it by strong desires: but in so far as it can be said to be prescribed by Common Sense, it does not seem an independent duty, but derivative from and subordinate to the general maxims of Prudence and Benevolence[1]. And in all modern civilized societies, law and custom leave the conjugal union perfectly optional: but the conditions under which it may be formed, and to a certain extent the mutual rights and duties arising out of it, are carefully laid down by law; and it is widely thought that this department of law more than others ought to be governed by independent moral principles, and to protect, as it were, by an outer barrier, the kind of relation which morality prescribes. So far as the moral aim of the law of marriage is to prevent Incest or Impurity, it will come to be considered under another head: but apart from this, it seems to be commonly taken as unquestionable in modern European communities that the marriage union ought to be exclusively monogamic, and at least designed to be permanent. I do not, however, think that either proposition is ordinarily put forward as an independent intuition. Granting that Monogamy is the most natural arrangement, it is not therefore self-evident that

[1] We may observe that if the rule of 'living according to Nature' were really adopted as a first principle, in any obvious or ordinary meaning of the term 'nature', marriage would certainly seem to be a universal duty: but just this instance seems to shew that the principle is not accepted by Common Sense.

all but monogamic unions ought to be prohibited; and in fact it is generally recognized that such a prohibition can only be rationally maintained on utilitarian grounds[1]. Again, as regards the permanence of the marriage-contract all would no doubt agree that fidelity is admirable in all affections, and especially in so close and intimate a relation as the conjugal: but we cannot tell *à priori* how far it is possible to prevent decay of love in all cases: and we certainly do not discern intuitively that the conjugal relation ought to be maintained when love has ceased; nor that if the parties have separated by mutual consent they ought to be prohibited from forming fresh unions. In so far as we are convinced of the rightness of this regulation, it is always, I think, from a consideration of the generally mischievous consequences that would ensue if it were relaxed.

And it may be observed in considering the evils on the opposite side we are led to see that there is no little difference of opinion among moral persons as to the kind of feeling which is morally indispensable to this relation. For some would say that marriage without intense and exclusive affection is degrading even though sanctioned by law: while others would consider this a mere matter of taste, or at least of prudence, provided there was no mutual deception: and between these two views we might insert several different shades of opinion.

Nor, again, is there agreement as to the external duties arising out of the relationship. For all would lay down conjugal fidelity, and mutual assistance (according to the customary division of labour between men and women—unless this should be modified by mutual agreement). But beyond this we find divergence: for some state that "the marriage contract binds each party, whenever individual gratification is concerned, to prefer the happiness of the other party to its

---

[1] The moral necessity of prohibiting polygamy is sometimes put forward as an immediate inference from the equality of the numbers of the two sexes. This argument, however, seems to require the assumption that all men and women ought to marry: but this scarcely any one will expressly affirm: and actually considerable numbers remain unmarried, and there is no reason to believe that in countries where polygamy is allowed, paucity of supply has ever made it practically difficult for any one to find a mate.

own[1]:" while others would say that this degree of unselfishness is certainly admirable, but as a mere matter of duty it is enough if each considers the other's happiness equally with his (or her) own. And as to the powers and liberties that ought to be allowed to the wife, and the obedience due from her to the husband—I need scarcely at the present time (1874) waste space in proving that there is no *consensus* among moral persons.

§ 7. The conjugal relation is, in its origin, of free choice, but when it has once been formed, the duties of affection that arise out of it are commonly thought to be analogous to those arising out of relations of consanguinity. It therefore holds an intermediate position between these latter, and ordinary friendships, partnerships, and associations, which men are equally free to make and to dissolve. Now most associations that men form are for certain definite ends, determined by express contract or tacit understanding: and the duty arising out of them is merely that of fidelity to such contract or understanding. But this does not seem to be the case with what in a strict sense of the term are called Friendships[2]: for although Friendship frequently arises among persons associated for other ends, still the relation is always conceived to have its end in itself, and to be formed primarily for the development of mutual affection between the friends, and the pleasure which attends this. Still, it is thought that when such an affection has once been formed it creates mutual duties which did not previously exist: we have therefore to inquire how far this is the case, and on what principles these can be determined.

Now here a new kind of difficulty has to be added to those which we have already found in attempting to formulate Common Sense. For we find some who say that, as it is essential to Friendship that the mutual kindly feeling, and the services springing from it, should be spontaneous and unforced, neither the one nor the other should be imposed as a duty; and, in short, that this department of life should be fenced from the intrusion

---

[1] Cf. Wayland, *Elements of Moral Science*, Bk. II. P. 2, class 2, § 2.

[2] I use the term here to imply a mutual affection more intense than the kindly feeling which a moral man desires to feel towards all persons with whom he is brought into continual social relations, through business or otherwise.

of moral precepts, and left to the free play of natural instinct. And this doctrine all would perhaps admit to a certain extent: as, indeed, we have accepted it with regard to all the deeper flow and finer expression of feeling even in the domestic relations: for it seemed pedantic and futile to prescribe rules for this, or even (though we naturally admire and praise any not ungraceful exhibition of intense and genuine affection) to delineate an ideal of excellence for all to aim at. Still, there seemed to be an important sphere of strict duty—however hard to define—in the relations of children to parents, &c., and even in the case of friendship it seems contrary to common sense to recognise no such sphere; as it not unfrequently occurs to us to judge that one friend has behaved wrongly to another, and to speak as if there were a clearly cognizable code of behaviour in such relations.

Perhaps, however, we may say that all clear cases of wrong conduct towards friends come under the general formula of breach of understanding. Friends not unfrequently make definite promises of service, but we need not consider these, as their violation is prohibited by a different and clearer moral rule. But further, as all love is understood to include[1] a desire for the happiness of its object, the profession of friendship seems to bind one to seek this happiness to an extent proportionate to such profession. Now common benevolence (cf. *ante*, § 5) prescribes at least that we should render to other men such services as we can render without any sacrifice, or with a sacrifice so trifling as to be quite out of proportion to the service rendered. And since the profession of friendship (though the term is used to include affections of various degree) must imply a greater interest in one's friend's happiness than in that of men in general, it must announce a willingness to make more or less considerable sacrifices for him, if occasion offers. If then we decline to make such sacrifices, we do wrong by failing to fulfil natural and legitimate expectations. So far there seems no difficulty except the indefiniteness inevitably arising from the wide range of meanings covered by the term Friendship. But further questions arise in conse-

---

[1] It was before observed that this is only one—and not always the most prominent—element of the whole emotional state which we call love.

quence of the changes of feeling to which human nature is liable: first, whether it is our duty to resist such changes as much as we can; and secondly, whether if this effort fails, and love diminishes or departs, we ought still to maintain a disposition to render services corresponding to our past affection. And on these points there does not seem to be agreement among moral and refined persons. For, on the one hand, it is natural to us to admire fidelity in friendship and stability of affections, and we commonly regard these as most important excellences of character: and so it seems strange if we are not to aim at these as at all other excellences, as none more naturally stir us to imitation. And hence many would be prepared to lay down that we ought not to withdraw affection once given, unless the friend behaves ill: while some would say that even in this case we ought not to break the friendship unless the crime is very great. Yet, on the other hand, we feel that such affection as is produced by deliberate effort of will is but a poor substitute for that which springs spontaneously, and most refined persons would reject such a boon: while, again, to conceal the change of feeling seems insincere and hypocritical.

But as for services, a refined person would not accept such from a former friend who no longer loves him: unless in extreme need, when any kind of tie is, as it were, invigorated by the already strong claim which common humanity gives each man upon all others. Perhaps, therefore, there cannot be a duty to offer such services in any case, when the need is not extreme. Though this inference is not quite clear: for in relations of affection we often praise one party for offering what we rather blame the other for accepting. But it seems that delicate questions of this kind are more naturally referred to canons of good taste and refined feeling than of morality proper: or at least only included in the scope of morality in so far as we have a general duty to cultivate good taste and refinement of feeling, like other excellences.

On the whole, then, we may say that the chief difficulties in determining the moral obligations of friendship arise (1) from the indefiniteness of the tacit understanding implied in the relation, and (2) from the disagreement which we find as to the extent to which Fidelity is a positive duty. It may be observed that the latter difficulty is especially prominent in respect of those intimacies between persons of different sex which precede and prepare the way for marriage.

§ 8. I pass now to the third head, Gratitude. It has been already observed that the obligation of children to parents is sometimes based upon this: and in other affectionate relationships it commonly blends with and much strengthens the claims that are thought to arise out of the relations themselves; though none of the duties that we have discussed seem referable entirely to gratitude. But where gratitude is due, the obligation is especially clear and simple. Indeed the duty of requiting benefits seems to be recognized wherever morality extends; and Intuitionists have justly pointed to this recognition as an instance of a truly universal intuition. Still, though the general force of the obligation is not open to doubt (except of the sweeping and abstract kind with which we have not here to deal), its nature and extent are by no means equally clear.

In the first place, it may be asked whether we are only bound to repay services, or whether we owe the special affection called Gratitude; which seems generally to combine kindly feeling and eagerness to requite with some sort of emotional recognition of superiority, as the giver of benefits is in a position of superiority to the receiver. On the one hand we seem to think that, in so far as any affection can possibly be a duty, kindly feeling towards benefactors must be such: and yet to persons of a certain temperament this feeling is often peculiarly hard to attain, owing to their dislike of the position of inferiority; and this again we consider a right feeling to a certain extent, and call it 'independence' or 'proper pride;' but this feeling and the effusion of gratitude do not easily mix, and the moralist finds it difficult to recommend a proper combination of the two. Perhaps it makes a great difference whether the service be lovingly done: as in this case it seems inhuman that there should be no response of affection: whereas if the benefit be coldly given, the mere recognition of the obligation and settled disposition to repay it seem to suffice. And 'independence' alone would prompt a man to repay the benefit in order to escape from the burden of obligation. Still, it is doubtful whether in any case we are morally satisfied with this as the sole motive.

It is partly this impatience of obligation which makes a man desirous of giving as requital more than he has received; for otherwise his benefactor has still the superiority of having taken the initiative. But also the worthier motive of affection urges us in the same direction: and here, as in other affectionate services, we do not like too exact a measure of duty; a certain excess falling short of extravagance seems to be what we admire and praise. Still, in so far as conflict of claims makes it needful to be exact, we think perhaps that an equal return is what the duty of gratitude requires, or rather willingness to make such a return, if it be required, and if it is in our power to make it without neglecting prior claims. For we do not think it obligatory to requite services in all cases, even if it be in our power to do so, if the benefactor appear to be sufficiently supplied with the means of happiness: but if he either demand it or obviously stand in need of it, we think it ungrateful not to make an equal return. But when we try to define this notion of 'equal return,' obscurity and divergence begin. For (apart from the difficulty of comparing different kinds of services where we cannot make repayment in kind) Equality has two distinct meanings, according as we consider the effort made by the benefactor, or the service rendered to the benefited. Now perhaps if either of these be great, the gratitude is naturally strong: for the apprehension of great earnestness in another to serve us tends to draw from us a proportionate response of affection: and any great pleasure or relief from pain naturally produces a corresponding emotion of thankfulness to the man who has voluntarily caused this, even though his effort may have been slight. And hence it has been thought, that in proportioning the dues of gratitude we ought to take whichever of the two considerations will give the highest estimate. But this does not seem in accordance with Common Sense: for the benefit may be altogether unacceptable, and it is hard to bind us to repay in full every well-meant blundering effort to serve us: though we feel vaguely that some return should be made even for this. And though it is more plausible to say that we ought to requite an accepted service without weighing the amount of our benefactor's sacrifice, still when we take extreme cases the rule seems not to be true: (*e.g.*) if a poor man sees a rich one drowning and pulls him out of the water, we do not think that the latter is bound to give as a reward what he would have been willing to give for his life. Still, we should think him niggardly if he only gave his preserver half-a-crown: which, however, would be profuse repayment for the cost of the exertion. Something between the two seems to suit our moral taste: but I find no self-evident principle upon which the amount can be decided.

The last claim to be considered is that of Special Need. This has been substantially stated already, in investigating the obligation of General Benevolence or Common Humanity. For it was said that we owe to all men such services as we can render by a sacrifice or effort small in comparison with the service: and hence, in proportion as the needs of other men present themselves as urgent, we recognize the duty of relieving them out of our superfluity. But I have thought it right to notice the duty separately, because we are commonly prompted to fulfil it by the specific emotion of Pity or Compassion. Here, again, there seems a doubt how far this feeling ought to be fostered and encouraged: for, on the one hand, it tends to make the action of relieving need not only easier to the agent, but more graceful and pleasing: on the other hand, this feeling is perhaps more likely to lead us astray than the affections previously discussed; as suffering is sometimes wholesome for our fellow-creatures, and ought not to be relieved at all; while even where this is not the case it is often difficult to relieve it without doing more harm than good.

If, passing from this, we consider how we may define the external duty of relieving want, we do not seem to discern a clear rule. Indeed we find ourselves face to face with what is no mere problem of the closet, but a serious practical perplexity to most moral persons at the present day. For many ask whether it is not our duty to refrain from all superfluous indulgences, until we have removed the misery and want that exists around us, as far as it is removable by money. And it is hard to state a principle upon which this question can be clearly answered in the negative: and yet it does not seem that Common Sense answers it in the affirmative.

In conclusion, then, we must admit that while we find a number of broad and more or less indefinite rules unhesitatingly laid down by Common Sense in this department of duty, it is difficult or impossible to extract from them, so far as they are commonly accepted, any clear and precise principles for determining the extent of the duty in any case. And yet, as we saw, such particular principles of distribution of the services to which good will prompts seem to be required for the perfection of practice no less than for theoretical completeness; in so far as the duties which we have been considering are liable to come into apparent conflict with each other and with other prescriptions of the moral code.

In reply it may perhaps be contended that if we are seeking exactness in the determination of duty, we have begun by examining the wrong notion: that, in short, we ought to have examined Justice rather than Benevolence. It may be admitted that we cannot find as much exactness as is sometimes practically needed by considering the common conceptions of the duties to which men are prompted with natural affections; but it may still be maintained that we shall at any rate find such exactness adequately provided for under the head of Justice. This contention I will proceed to examine in the next chapter.

CHAPTER V.

JUSTICE.

§ 1. WE have seen that in delineating the outline of duty, as intuitively recognized, we have to attempt to give to common terms a definite and precise meaning. This process of definition always requires some reflection and care, and is sometimes one of considerable difficulty. But there is no case where the difficulty is greater, or the result more disputed, than when we try to define Justice.

Before making the attempt, it may be as well to remind the reader what it is that we have to do. We have not to inquire into the derivation of the notion of Justice, as we are not now studying the history of our ethical thought, but its actual condition. Nor can we profess to furnish a definition which will correspond to every part of the common usage of the term; for many persons are undoubtedly vague and loose in their application of current moral notions. But it is an assumption of the Intuitional method[1] that the term 'justice' denotes a quality which it is ultimately desirable to realize in the conduct and social relations of men; and that a definition may be given of this which will be accepted by all competent judges as presenting, in a clear and explicit form, what they have always meant by the term, though perhaps implicitly and vaguely. In seeking such a definition we may, so to speak, clip the ragged edge of common usage, but we must not make excision of any considerable portion[2].

---

[1] How far an independent principle of Justice is required for the Utilitarian method will be hereafter considered. (Book IV. ch. i.)

[2] Aristotle, in expounding the virtue of Δικαιοσύνη, which corresponds to our Justice, notices that the word has two meanings; in the wider of which

Perhaps the first point that strikes us when we reflect upon our notion of Justice is its connexion with Law. There is no doubt that just conduct is to a great extent determined by Law, and in certain applications the two terms seem interchangeable. Thus we speak indifferently of 'Law Courts' and 'Courts of Justice,' and when a man demands Justice, or his just rights, he means generally to demand that Law should be carried into effect. Still reflection shews that we do not mean by Justice merely conformity to Law. For, first, we do not always call the violators of law unjust, but only of some laws: not, for example, duellists or gamblers. And secondly, we often judge that Law as it exists does not completely realize Justice; our notion of Justice furnishes a standard with which we compare actual laws, and pronounce them just or unjust. And, thirdly, there is a part of just conduct which lies outside the sphere even of Law as it ought to be; for example, we think that a father may be just or unjust to his children in matters where the law leaves (and ought to leave) him free.

We must then distinguish Justice from what has been called the virtue or duty of Order, or Law-observance: and perhaps, if we examine the points of divergence just given, we shall be led to the true definition of Justice.

Let us therefore first ask, What kind of laws are they of which the observance is generally thought to be a realization of Justice? We might answer, Laws which define and secure the interests of assignable individuals. But this is scarcely complete, as Justice is admittedly concerned in the apportionment of taxation and public burdens generally as well as privileges, and, again, we demand that punishment should be justly awarded to each offender; though we should not say that a man had an interest in his share of taxation or punishment. Let us say, then, that the laws in which Justice is or ought to be realized, are laws which

---

it includes in a manner all Virtue, or at any rate the social side or aspect of Virtue generally. The word 'Justice' does not appear to be used in English in this comprehensive manner (except occasionally in religious writings, from the influence of the Greek word as used in the New Testament): although the verb "to justify" seems to have this width of meaning; for when I say that one is "justified" in doing so and so, I mean no more than that such conduct is right for him. In the present discussion, at any rate, I have confined myself to the more precise signification of the term.

distribute and allot to individuals either objects of desire, liberties and privileges, or burdens and restraints, or even pains as such. These latter, however, are only allotted by law to persons who have broken other laws. And as all law is enforced by penalties, we see how the administration of law generally may be viewed as the administration of Justice, in accordance with this definition: not because all laws are primarily and in their first intention distributive, but because the execution of law generally involves the due allotment of pains and losses and restraints to the persons who violate it. Or, more precisely, we should say that this legal distribution *ought* to realize Justice, for we have seen that it may fail to do so. We have next to ask, therefore, What conditions must be fulfilled in order that laws may be just?

Here, however, it may seem that we are transgressing the limit which divides Ethics, as defined in the present treatise, from Politics. For Ethics was said to be concerned with the rules which ought to govern the private conduct of individuals; and it is commonly thought that private persons ought to obey all laws, whether just or unjust, if established by lawful authority. Still, this is doubted in the case of laws that seem extremely unjust: as (*e.g.*) the Fugitive Slave-law in the United States before the rebellion. At any rate it seems desirable that we should here digress somewhat into political discussion; partly in order to elucidate the notion of Justice, which seems to be essentially the same in both regions, and partly because it is of great practical importance to individuals in directing private conduct beyond the range of Law-observance to know whether the laws and established order of the society in which they live are just or unjust.

Now perhaps the most obvious and commonly stated characteristic of just laws is that they are Equal: and in some departments of legislation, at least, the notion of Justice seems to be exhaustively expressed by that of Equality. We think, for example, that a system of taxation would be perfectly just if it were perfectly equal—if it imposed exactly equal sacrifices upon all[1]. No doubt this notion of 'equal sacrifice' is

[1] I ought to say that, in my view, this only applies to taxes in the narrower sense in which they are distinguished from payments for services received by

itself not altogether easy to define in theory, and yet harder to realize in practice: still we may say that Justice here is thought to resolve itself into a kind of equality. However, we cannot affirm generally that all laws ought to affect all persons equally, for this would leave no place for any laws allotting special privileges and burdens to special classes of the community; but we do not think all such laws necessarily unjust: (*e.g.*) we think it just that only persons appointed in a certain way should enact and execute laws, and that men should be forced to fight for their country but not women. Hence some have said that the only sense in which justice requires a law to be equal is that its execution must affect equally all the individuals belonging to any of the classes specified in the law. And no doubt this rule excludes a very real kind of injustice: it is of the highest importance that judges and administrators should never be persuaded by money or otherwise to shew 'respect of persons.' So much equality, however, is involved in the very notion of a law, if it be couched in general terms: and it is plain that laws may be equally executed and yet unjust: for example, we should consider a law unjust which compelled only red-haired men to serve in the army, even though it were applied with the strictest impartiality to all red-haired men. We may conclude, in short, that, in laying down the law no less than in carrying it out, all inequality[1] affecting the interest of individuals which

individuals from government. In the case of these latter, I conceive that Justice is rather held to lie in duly proportioning payment to amount of service received. Some persons have held that all payments made to government ought to be determined on this principle: and this view seems to me to be consistent with the individualistic ideal of political order, which I shall presently examine: but, as I have elsewhere tried to show (Princ. of Pol. Econ. v. ch. viii.) there is an important department of governmental expenditure to which this principle is not applicable.

[1] It may be well to notice a case in which the very equality of application, which is, as has been said, implied in the mere idea of a law couched in general terms, is felt to be unjust. This is the case where the words of a statute, either from being carelessly drawn, or on account of the inevitable defects of even the most precise terminology, include (or exclude) persons and circumstances which are clearly not included in (or excluded from) the real intent and purpose of the law. In this case a particular decision, strictly in accordance with a law which generally considered is just, may cause extreme injustice: and so the difference between actual Law and Justice is sharply brought out. Still we cannot in this way obtain principles for judging generally of the justice of laws.

appears arbitrary, and for which no sufficient reason can be given, is held to be unjust. We have to ask then, What kind of reasons for inequality does Justice admit? what is the general principle (or principles) from which all such reasons may be deduced?

§ 2. Perhaps we shall find it easier to answer this question, if we examine the notion of Justice as applied to that part of private conduct which lies beyond the sphere of law. Here, again, we may observe that the notion of Justice always involves allotment of something considered as advantageous or disadvantageous: whether it be money or other material means of happiness; or praise, or affection, or other immaterial good, or some merited pain or loss. And thus perhaps we may settle the question raised in the previous chapter (§ 3) as to the classification of the duties there discussed under the heads of Justice and Benevolence respectively. For the fulfilment of any duty of the affections, considered by itself, does not seem to exemplify Justice: but when we come to compare the obligations arising out of different affectionate relations, and to consider the right allotment of love and kind services, the notion of Justice becomes applicable. In order to arrange this allotment properly we have to inquire what is Just. What then do we mean by a just man in matters where law-observance does not enter? It is natural to reply that we mean an impartial man, one who satisfies all claims which he recognizes and does not let himself be unduly influenced by personal preferences. And this seems an adequate account of the disposition of justice so far as we consider it merely subjectively, and as a strictly moral quality, independently of the intellectual insight required for the realization of objective justice in action: if we neglect to give due consideration to any claim which we regard as reasonable, our action cannot be just in intention. This definition suffices to exclude wilful injustice: but it is obvious that it does not give us a sufficient criterion of just acts, any more than the absence of arbitrary inequality is a completely distinctive characteristic of just laws[1]. We want to know what are reasonable claims.

---

[1] It should be observed that we cannot even say, in hearing of the private conduct of individuals, that *all* arbitrary inequality is recognized as unjust: it

Well, of these the most obvious seems to be that resulting from contract. This is to a certain extent enforced by law: but we see it to be just to keep engagements generally, even when there may be no legal penalty attached to their violation. It is true that this duty is not always placed under the head of Justice: some have preferred to class it with Veracity, and it therefore seems convenient to consider it in detail separately.

Further, we include under the idea of binding engagements not merely verbal promises, but also what are called 'implied contracts,' or 'tacit understandings.' But this latter term is a difficult one to keep precise: and, in fact, is often used to include not only the case where A has in some way positively implied a pledge to B, but also the case where B has certain expectations of which A is aware. Here, however, the obligation is not so clear: for it would hardly be said that a man is bound to dispel all erroneous expectations that he may know to be formed respecting his conduct, at the risk of being required to fulfil them. Still, if the expectation was such as most persons would form under the circumstances, there seems to be some sort of moral obligation to fulfil it, if it does not conflict with other duties, though the obligation seems less definite and stringent than that arising out of contract. Indeed, we may go further and say more generally that Justice is, at least vaguely, held to prescribe the fulfilment of all such expectations (of services, &c.) as arise naturally and normally out of the relations, voluntary or involuntary, in which we stand towards other human beings. But the discussions in the preceding chapter have shewn the difficulty of defining even those duties of this kind which, in an indefinite form, appear certain and indisputable: while there were others which are only imposed by apparently arbitrary customs. And though while these customs persist, the expectations springing from them are in a sense natural and normal, so that a just man seems to be under a kind of obligation to fulfil them, this obligation cannot be regarded as clear or complete, for two reasons that were given in the last chapter; first, because customs are continually

would not be commonly thought unjust in a rich bachelor with no near relatives to leave the bulk of his property in providing pensions exclusively for indigent red-haired men, however unreasonable and capricious the choice might appear.

varying, and as long as any one is in a state of variation, growing or decaying, the validity of the customary claim is obviously doubtful; and secondly, because it does not seem right that an unreasonable custom should last for ever, and yet it can only be abolished by being "more honoured in the breach than in the observance."

This line of reflection therefore has landed us in a real perplexity respecting the department of duty which we are at present examining. Justice is something that we conceive to be intrinsically capable of perfectly definite determination. A scrupulously just man, we think, must be very exact and precise in his conduct: and indeed in some connexions the word 'just' is used as almost synonymous with 'exact' and 'precise.' But when we consider that part of Justice which consists in satisfying such natural and customary claims as arise independently of contract, it seems impossible to estimate these claims with any exactness. The attempt to map out the region of Justice reveals to us a sort of margin or dim borderland, tenanted by expectations which are not quite claims and with regard to which we do not feel sure whether Justice does or does not require us to satisfy them. For it is in human nature to expect that what has been will be; and so people expect that any man will do as others do in similar circumstances, and, still more, that he will continue to do whatever he has hitherto been in the habit of doing; and they tend to think themselves wronged by his suddenly omitting the act, if the omission causes them loss or inconvenience[1]. While on the other hand, if a man has given no pledge to maintain a custom or habit, it seems hard that he should be bound by the unwarranted expectations of others. In this perplexity, common sense often appears to decide differently cases similar in all respects, except in the quantity of disappointment caused by the change. For instance, if a poor man were to leave one tradesman and deal with another because the first had turned Quaker, we should hardly call it an act of injustice, though we might think it unreasonable. But if a rich landed proprietor in a country

---

[1] It may be observed that sometimes claims generated in this way have legal validity; as when a right of way is established without express permission of the landowner, merely by his continued indulgence.

place were to act similarly, many persons would say that it was unjust persecution.

The difficulty just pointed out extends equally to the stringent and sacred duties of the domestic and other affections, discussed in the previous chapter: and it now seems clear that we cannot get any new principle for settling any conflict that may present itself among such duties, by asking 'what Justice requires of us:' the application of the notion of Justice only leads us to view the problem in a new aspect—as a question of the right *distribution* of kind services—it does not help us to solve it. Having no clear and precise intuitive principles for determining the claims (*e. g.*) of parents on children, children on parents, benefactors on the recipients of their benefits, we cannot say generally at what point or to what extent the satisfaction of one of these claims ought in justice to be postponed to the satisfaction of another, or to any worthy aim of a different kind.

§ 3. If now we turn again to the political question, from which we diverged, we see that we have obtained from the preceding discussion one of the criteria of the justice of laws of which we were seeking—viz. that they must avoid running counter to natural and normal expectations—: but we see at the same time that the criterion cannot be made definite in its application to private conduct, and it is easy to show that there is the same indefiniteness and consequent difficulty in applying it to legislation. For Law itself is a main source of such expectations; and, since in ordinary times the alterations in law are very small in proportion to the amount unaltered, there is always a natural expectation that the existing laws will be maintained: and although this is, of course, an indefinite and uncertain expectation in a society like ours, where laws are continually being altered by lawful authority, it is sufficient for people in general to rely upon in arranging their concerns, investing their money, choosing their place of abode, their trade and profession, &c. Hence when such expectations are disappointed by a change in the law, the disappointed persons complain of injustice, and it is to some extent admitted that justice requires that they should be compensated for the loss thus incurred. But since these expectations are of all degrees of definiteness and importance, and generally extend more widely as they decrease in value, like the ripples made by throwing a stone into a pond, it is impossible to compensate them all: at the same time, I know no intuitive principle by which we could separate valid claims from invalid, and distinguish injustice from simple hardship.

But even if this difficulty were overcome further reflection must, I think, shew that the criterion above given is incomplete or imperfectly stated: otherwise it would appear that no old law could be unjust, since laws that have existed for a long time must create corresponding expectations. But this is contrary to Common Sense: as we are continually becoming convinced that old laws are unjust (*e.g.* laws establishing slavery): indeed, this continually recurring conviction seems to be one of the great sources of change in the laws of a progressive society.

Perhaps we may say that there are natural expectations which grow up from other elements of the social order, independent of and so possibly conflicting with laws: and that we call rules unjust which go counter to these. Thus *e.g.*, primogeniture appears to many unjust, because all the land-owner's children are brought up in equally luxurious habits, and share equally the paternal care and expenditure, and so the inequality of inheritance seems paradoxical and harsh. Still, we cannot explain every case in this way: for example, the conviction that slavery is unjust cannot be referred to anything in the established order of the slave-holding society, but seems to arise in a different way.

The truth is, this notion of 'natural expectations' is worse than indefinite: the ambiguity of the term conceals a fundamental conflict of ideas, which appears more profound and far-reaching in its consequences the more we examine it. For the word 'natural,' as used in this connexion, covers and conceals the whole chasm between the actual and the ideal—what is, and what ought to be. As we before noticed[1], it commonly blends the quite distinct ideas of (1) 'that which universally exists, or almost universally, and is *normal* as opposed to exceptional,' and (2) 'that which existed originally, in the primitive state of man, and would exist now, if it had not been

[1] Book I. c. vi, § 2.

changed by later conventions and institutions.' But it also used to signify, in more or less indefinite combination with these other meanings, 'what would exist in an ideal state of society.' And it is easy to see how these different meanings have been blended and confounded. For since by 'Nature' men have really meant God, or God viewed in a particular aspect—God, we may say, as known to us in experience—when they have come to conceive a better state of things than that which actually exists, they have not only regarded this ideal state as really exhibiting the Divine purposes more than the actual, and as being so far more 'natural:' but they have gone further, and supposed more or less definitely that this ideal state of things must be what God originally created, and that the defects recognizable in what now exists must be due to the deteriorating action of men. But if we dismiss this latter view, as unsupported by historical evidence, we recognize more plainly the contrast and conflict between the other two meanings of 'natural,' and the corresponding discrepancy between the two elements of the common notion of Justice. For, from one point of view, we are disposed to think that the *customary* distribution of rights, goods, and privileges, as well as burdens and pains, is natural and just, and that this ought to be maintained by law, as it usually is: while, from another point of view, we seem to recognize an ideal system of rules of distribution which ought to exist, but perhaps have never yet existed, and we consider laws to be just in proportion as they conform to this ideal. It is the reconciliation between these two views which is the chief problem of political Justice[1].

On what principles, then, is the ideal to be determined? This is, in fact, the question which has been chiefly in view from the outset of the chapter; but we could not satisfactorily discuss it until we had distinguished the two elements of Justice, as commonly conceived, one conservative of law and custom, and the other tending to reform them. It is on this latter that we shall now concentrate our attention.

[1] It is characteristic of an unprogressive society that in it these two points of view are indistinguishable: the Jural Ideal absolutely coincides with the Customary, and social perfection is imagined to consist in the perfect observance of a traditional system of rules.

When, however, we examine this Ideal, as it seems to shew itself in the minds of different men in different ages and countries, we observe various forms of it, which it is important to distinguish.

In the first place, it must be noticed that an ideal constitution of society may be conceived and sought with many other ends in view besides the right distribution of happiness among the individuals that compose it: as (*e.g.*) with a view to conquest and success in war, or to the development of industry and commerce, or to the highest possible cultivation of the arts and sciences. But any such political ideal as this is beyond the range of our present consideration, as it is not constructed on the basis of our common notion of Justice. Our present question is, Are there any clear principles from which we may work out an ideally just distribution of rights and privileges, burdens and pains, among human beings as such?

But again: when we examine the demands for, and delineations of, such a distribution which men have actually put forward, we find that they have been made from very different points of view, and involve very different degrees of divergence from the existing modes of distribution. According to one view, the main thing needed to make society just is that certain Natural Rights should be conceded to all members of the community, and that positive law should at least embody and protect these, whatever other regulations it may contain.

Such are the Right to Personal Security: the Right to hold Property, including the right to dispose of it freely by contract: and the Right to the enforcement of free contracts generally: in particular the Right to enter into the Marriage-contract, and to satisfy the desire for Family Society. And further—since by giving a man the right to acquire Property we do not necessarily give him any property, or the means of supporting a family, or even himself: and yet this is what he naturally desires—some have added a right to food and sustenance in exchange for labour, or (more broadly) a Right to Live: and also a Right to Education: and some, again, add Political Rights, as a Right to share in Legislation, personally or through representatives, or in Government generally. These seem to be the chief natural rights demanded in the name of Justice: and many political idealists would be content with a constitution of society in which every individual might count upon so much as this. But when we try to elicit from Common Sense some clear principles upon which these Natural Rights are to be demanded and no others, we find much difficulty and dispute; nor do we even meet with any definite agreement in the enumeration of them: for example, there is much difference of opinion as to the Right to Education, and Political Rights generally.

§ 4. There is, however, one mode of systematizing these Rights and bringing them under one principle, which has been maintained by influential thinkers; and which, though now perhaps somewhat antiquated, is still sufficiently current to deserve careful examination. It has been held that Freedom from interference is really the whole of what human beings, originally and apart from contracts, can be strictly said to *owe* to each other: at any rate, that the protection of this Freedom (including the enforcement of Free Contract) is the sole proper aim of Law, *i.e.* of those rules of mutual behaviour which are maintained by penalties inflicted under the authority of Government. All natural Rights, on this view, may be summed up in the Right to Freedom: so that the complete attainment of this is the complete realization of Justice; the Equality at which Justice is thought to aim being interpreted in this special sense of Equality of Freedom.

Now when I contemplate this as an abstract formula, though I cannot say that it is self-evident to me as the true fundamental principle of Ideal Law, I admit that it commends itself much to my mind, and I might perhaps persuade myself that it is owing to the defect of my faculty of moral (or jural) intuition that I fail to see its self-evidence. But when I endeavour to bring it into closer relation to the actual circumstances of human society, it soon comes to wear a different aspect.

In the first place, it seems obviously needful to limit the extent of its application. For it involves the negative principle that no one should be coerced for his own good alone: but no one would gravely argue that this ought to be applied to the case of children, or of idiots, or insane persons. But if so, can we know *à priori* that it ought to be applied to all sane adults?

since the above-mentioned exceptions are commonly justified on the ground that children, &c. will manifestly be better off if they are forced to do and abstain as others think best for them; and it is, at least, not intuitively certain that the same argument does not apply to the majority of mankind in the present state of their intellectual progress. Indeed, it is often conceded by the advocates of this principle that it does not hold even in respect of adults in a low stage of civilization. But if so, what criterion can be given for its application, except that it must be applied wherever human beings are sufficiently intelligent to provide for themselves better than others would provide for them? and thus the principle would present itself not as absolute and recognized by an independent intuition, but as a subordinate application of the principle of aiming at the general good.

But, again, the term Freedom is ambiguous. If we interpret it strictly, as meaning Freedom of Action alone, the principle seems to allow any amount of mutual annoyance except constraint. But obviously no one would be satisfied with such Freedom as this. If, however, we include in the idea absence from pain and annoyance inflicted by others, it becomes at once evident that we cannot prohibit all such annoyances without restraining freedom of action to a degree that would be intolerable; since there is scarcely any gratification of a man's natural impulses which may not cause some annoyance to others. Hence in distinguishing the mutual annoyances that ought to be allowed from those that must be prohibited we seem forced to balance, in the Utilitarian manner, the evils of constraint against pain and loss of a different kind: while if we admit the Utilitarian criterion so far, it is difficult to maintain that annoyance to individuals is never to be permitted in order to attain any positive good result.

Thirdly, in order to render a social construction possible on this basis, we must assume that the right to Freedom includes the right to limit one's freedom by contract; and that such contracts, if they are really voluntary and not obtained by fraud or force, and if they do not violate the freedom of others, are to be enforced by legal penalties. But, in the first place, it does not seem clear that enforcement of Contracts is strictly included in the notion of realizing Freedom; for a man seems to be most completely free when no one of his volitions is allowed to have any effect in causing the external coercion of any other. And, again, it may be asked whether this right of limiting Freedom is itself unlimited, and whether a man may thus freely contract himself out of freedom into slavery. For in this case the principle of freedom seems in a manner suicidal; and yet it is hard to see how from this principle any limitation of the right of contract can be deduced.

This question, how far the conception of Freedom involves unlimited right to limit Freedom by free contract, becomes important again in a rather subtle manner, when we consider the relation of ideal Justice and positive law. For those who take the view of abstract Justice which we are now discussing, commonly think that the obligation to obey law (except in so far as it protects Freedom) is not absolute and independent, but depends upon a 'social compact' which the individual members of each community are supposed to have made with each other. It remains to ascertain what this compact is: which, as it is admitted to be—either altogether or to a great extent—only tacit or implied, is somewhat difficult. The simplest view is that we are under an implied contract to obey the positive law of our society, at least in so far as it has been established by the authority customarily recognized as lawful. But then, in a country where despotic government was established and traditional, the principle of abstract Freedom would lead to the justification of the most unqualified concrete tyranny; nor need we stop here, for even slavery might be justified in the same way; and thus our theory would end by riveting men's chains under pretence of exalting their freedom. To avoid this conclusion, it is necessary to suppose this tacit social compact to be made with still more tacit reservations; which destroys the simplicity, and therefore the plausibility, of this whole theory of political obligation[1].

But if it be difficult to define Freedom as an ideal to be realized in the merely personal relations of human beings, the difficulty is increased when we consider the relation of men to the material means of life and happiness.

[1] The doctrine of the Social Compact will be discussed at more length in the next chapter.

For it is commonly thought that the individual's right to Freedom includes the right of appropriating material things. But, if Freedom be understood strictly, I do not see that it implies more than the right to non-interference while actually using such things as can only be used by one person at once: the right to prevent others from using at any future time anything that an individual has once seized seems an interference with the free action of others beyond what is needed to secure the freedom, strictly speaking, of the appropriator. It may perhaps be said that a man, in appropriating a particular thing, does not interfere with the freedom of others, because the rest of the world is still open to them. But others may want just this object: and they may not be able to find anything so good at all, or at least without much labour and search; for many of the instruments and materials of comfortable living are limited in quantity. This argument applies especially to property in land: and it is to be observed that, in this case there is a further difficulty in determining how much a man is to be allowed to appropriate by 'first occupation.' If it be said that a man is to be understood to occupy what he is able to use, the answer is obvious that the use of land by any individual may vary almost indefinitely in extent of surface required, while diminishing proportionally in intensity. For instance, it would surely be a paradoxical deduction from the principle of Freedom to maintain that an individual had a right to exclude others from pasturing sheep on any part of the land over which his hunting expeditions could extend[1]. But if so can it be clear that a shepherd has such a right against one who wishes to till the land, or that one who is using the surface has a right to exclude a would-be miner? I do not see how the deduction is to be made out. Again, it may be disputed whether the right of Property, as thus derived, is to include the right of controlling the disposal of one's possessions after death. For this to most persons seems naturally bound up with ownership: yet it is paradoxical to say that we interfere with a man's freedom of action by anything that we may do after his death to what he

---

[1] It has often been urged as a justification for expropriating savages from the land of new colonies that tribes of hunters have really no moral right to property in the soil over which they hunt.

owned during his life: and jurists have often treated this right as purely conventional and not therefore included in 'natural law.'

Other difficulties might be raised: but we need not pursue them, for if Freedom be taken simply to mean that one man's actions are to be as little as possible restrained by others, it is obviously more fully realized without appropriation. And if it be said that it includes, besides this, facility and security in the gratification of desires, and that it is Freedom in this sense that we think should be equally distributed, and that this cannot be realized without appropriation; then it may be replied, that in a society where nearly all material things are already appropriated, this kind of Freedom is not and cannot be equally distributed. A man born into such a society, without inheritance, is not only far less free than those who possess property, but he is less free than if there had been no appropriation. He is free to walk along the roads, to pluck heather on some of the mountain sides, and to drink of the rivers, when they do not run through private grounds: but what is this worth? It may be said that, having freedom of contract, he will give his services in exchange for the means of satisfying his wants. And a brilliant essayist[1] has attempted to shew that this exchange must necessarily give him more than he could have got if he had been placed in the world by himself; that, in fact, society by existing makes the earth more capable of affording gratification of desires to each and all of the after-born individuals than it would otherwise be. But, at the most, this does not prove that society, by appropriation, has not interfered with the natural freedom of its poorer members: but only that it compensates them for such interference, and that the compensation is adequate. However, even this, though it may be true as a general rule, is obviously not so in all cases: as men are sometimes unable to sell their services at all, and often can only obtain in exchange for them an insufficient subsistence. It is surely undeniable that any *equality* in the distribution of Freedom (in the sense of liberty to gratify desires) is prevented by the institution of property.

§ 5. It seems, then, that though Freedom is an object of

[1] Bastiat.

keen and general desire, and an important source of happiness, both in itself and indirectly from the satisfaction of natural impulses which it allows, the attempt to make it the fundamental notion of theoretical Jurisprudence is attended with insuperable difficulties: and that even the Natural Rights which it claims to cover cannot be brought under it except in a very forced and arbitrary manner[1]. But further, even if this were otherwise, an equal distribution of Freedom does not seem to exhaust our notion of Justice. Ideal Justice, as we commonly conceive it, seems to demand that not only Freedom but all other benefits and burdens should be distributed if not equally, at any rate justly,—Justice in distribution being regarded as not identical with Equality, but merely exclusive of arbitrary inequality.

How, then, shall we find the principle of this highest and most comprehensive ideal?

We shall be led to it, I think, by referring again to one of the grounds of obligation to render services, which was noticed in the last chapter: the claim of Gratitude. It there appeared that we have not only a natural impulse to requite benefits, but also a conviction that such requital is a duty, and its omission blameworthy, to some extent at least; though we find it difficult to define the extent. Now it seems that when we, so to say, *universalize* this impulse and conviction, we get the element in the common view of Justice, which we are now trying to define. For if we take the proposition 'that good done to any individual ought to be requited by him,' and leave out the relation to the individual in either term of the proposition, we seem to have an equally strong conviction of the truth of the more general statement 'that good deeds ought to be requited[2].' And if we take into consideration

---

[1] The further consideration of Political Freedom, with which we shall be occupied in the next chapter, will afford additional illustrations of the difficulties involved in the notion.

[2] If the view given in the text be sound, it illustrates very strikingly the difference between natural instincts and moral intuitions. For the impulse to requite a service is, on its emotional side, quite different from that which prompts us to claim the fruits of our labour, or "a fair day's wages for a fair day's work." Still, our apprehension of the *duty* of Gratitude seems capable of being subsumed under the more general intuition 'that desert ought to be requited.'

all the different kinds and degrees of services, upon the mutual exchange of which society is based, we get the proposition 'that men ought to be rewarded in proportion to their deserts.' And this would be commonly held to be the true and simple principle of distribution in any case where there are no claims arising from Contract or Custom to modify its operation.

For example, this seems obviously to be the principle on which the profits of any work or enterprise should be divided among those who have contributed to its success: if there has been no previous arrangement as to their division. And it may be observed, that some thinkers maintain the proposition discussed in the previous section—that Law ought to aim at securing the greatest possible Freedom for each individual—not as absolute and axiomatic, but as derivative from the principle that we are now examining; on the ground that the best way of providing that Desert shall be Requited is to leave men as free as possible to exert themselves for the satisfaction of their own desires, and so to win each his own requital. And this seems to be really the principle upon which the Right of Property is rested, when it is justified by the proposition that 'every one has an exclusive right to the produce of his labour.' For on reflection it is seen that no labour really 'produces' any material thing, but only adds to its value: and we do not think that a man can acquire a right to a material thing belonging to another, by spending his labour on it—even if he does so in the *bonâ fide* belief that it is his own property—but only to adequate *compensation* for his labour; this, therefore, is what the proposition just quoted must mean. The principle is, indeed, sometimes stretched to explain the original right of property in materials, as being in a sense 'produced' (*i.e.* found) by their first discoverer[1]; but here again, reflection shews that Common Sense does not grant this (as a *moral* right) absolutely, but only

---

[1] It certainly requires a considerable strain to bring the 'right of First Discovery' under the notion of 'right to the produce of one's labour.' Hence Locke and others have found it necessary to suppose, as the ultimate justification of the former right, 'a tacit consent' of mankind in general that all things previously unappropriated shall belong to the first appropriator. But this, as we have seen, is a rather desperate device of ethico-political construction: on account of the fatal facility with which it may be used to justify almost any arbitrariness in positive law.

in so far as it appears to be not more than adequate compensation for the discoverer's trouble. For example, we should not consider that the first finder of a large uninhabited region had a moral right to appropriate the whole of it. Hence this justification of the right of property refers us ultimately to the principle 'that every man ought to receive adequate requital for his labour.' So, again, when we speak of the world as justly governed by God, we seem to mean that, if we could know the whole of human existence, we should find that happiness is distributed among men according to their deserts. And Divine Justice is thought to be a pattern which Human Justice is to imitate as far as the conditions of human society allow.

This kind of Justice, as has been said, seems like Gratitude universalized: and the same principle applied to punishment may similarly be regarded as Resentment universalized; though the parallel is incomplete, if we are considering the present state of our moral conceptions. History shews us a time in which it was thought not only as natural, but as clearly right and incumbent on a man, to requite injuries as to repay benefits: but in the outset of moral reflection in Europe this notion was repudiated, and Socrates and Plato taught that it could never be right really to harm any one, however he may have harmed us. And this is the accepted doctrine in Christian societies, as regards individual Resentment. But in its universalized form the old conviction seems still to remain in the more ordinary view of Criminal Justice. For the principle that punishment should be merely deterrent and reformatory is, I think, too purely utilitarian for Common Sense; which seems still to incline to the view that a man who has done wrong ought to suffer pain in return (even if no benefit result either to him or to others from the pain), and that Justice requires this; although the individual wronged ought not to seek or desire to inflict the pain.

This, then, is one element of what Aristotle calls Corrective Justice, which is embodied in criminal law. It must not be confounded with the principle of Reparation, on which legal awards of damages are based. We have already noticed this as a simple deduction from the maxim of general Benevolence, which forbids us to do harm to our fellow-creatures: for if we have harmed them, we can yet approximately obey the maxim by giving compensation for the harm. Though here the question arises whether we ought to make reparation for harm that has been quite involuntarily caused: and it is not easy to answer it decisively. For to some it seems that one ought only to pay damages when one has been in fault: but others think that we ought, if possible, to allow no one to suffer through our agency; and hence that we ought to endeavour to make compensation for all harm, voluntary or involuntary, of which we have been the physical cause—at least unless it has been caused with the free consent of the person harmed. Common Sense does not seem clear on this point: and even if we could settle it without hesitation, there would still remain some difficulty, as we shall see presently, in drawing the line between 'voluntary' and 'involuntary' harm[1].

Between the principle of Reparative and that of Retributive Justice there is now[2] no danger of confusion or collision, as the one is manifestly concerned with the injured party, and the other with the wrongdoer. In the actual administration of Law they may sometimes present themselves as alternatives: but so far as this is the case actual Law is seen to fall short of ideal Justice, and therefore does not come under our consideration here. When however we turn again to the other branch of Retributive

---

[1] Cf. *post*, p. 292. The reader will find an interesting illustration of the perplexity of Common Sense on this point in Mr O. W. Holmes jun^r's book on *The Common Law*, chap. iii.; where the author gives a penetrating discussion of the struggle, in the development of the doctrine of torts in English Law, between two opposing views: (1) that "the risk of a man's conduct is thrown upon him as the result of some moral short-coming", and (2) that "a man acts at his peril always, and wholly irrespective of the state of his consciousness upon the matter". The former is the view that has prevailed in English Law; and this seems to me certainly in harmony with the Common Sense of mankind, so far as legal liability is concerned; but I do not think that the case is equally clear as regards moral obligation.

It may be added that there is often a further difficulty in ascertaining the amount of compensation due: for this frequently involves a comparison of things essentially disparate, and there are some kinds of harm which it seems impossible to compensate.

[2] In the earlier stage of moral development, referred to in the preceding paragraph, retribution inflicted on the wrongdoer was regarded as the normal mode of reparation to the person injured. But this view is contrary to the moral Common Sense of Christian Societies.

Justice, which is concerned with the reward of services, we find another notion, which I will call Fitness, often blended indistinguishably with the notion of Desert proper, and so needing to be carefully separated from it; and when the distinction has been made, we see that the two are liable to come into collision. I do not feel sure that the principle of 'distribution according to Fitness' is found, strictly speaking, in the analysis of the ordinary notion of Justice: but it certainly enters into our common conception of the ideal or perfectly rational order of society, as regards the distribution both of instruments and functions, and (to some extent at least) of other sources of happiness. We certainly think it reasonable that instruments should be given to those who can use them best, and functions allotted to those who are most competent to perform them: but these may not be those who have rendered most services in the past: and yet, if the functions are interesting and delightful in themselves, or such as are normally and properly attended with dignity and splendour of life, fame, material comfort and freedom from sordid cares, &c., it is natural to regard them as prizes to be given to those whose good deeds have deserved them most. And again, we think it reasonable that particular material means of enjoyment should fall to the lot of those who are susceptible of the respective kinds of pleasure; as no one would think of allotting pictures to a blind man, or rare wines to one who had no taste. Thus the notions of Desert and Fitness appear at least occasionally conflicting: but perhaps, as I have suggested, Fitness should rather be regarded as a utilitarian principle of distribution, inevitably limiting the realization of what is abstractly just, than as a part of the interpretation of Justice proper: and it is with the latter that we are at present concerned. At any rate it is the Requital of Desert that constitutes the chief element of Ideal Justice, in so far as this imports something more than mere Equality and Impartiality. Let us then examine more closely wherein Desert consists; and we will begin with Good Desert, as being of the most fundamental and permanent importance; for we may hope that crime and its punishment will decrease and gradually disappear as the world improves, but the right or best distribution of the means of wellbeing is an object that we must always be striving to realize.

§ 6. And first, the question which we had to consider in defining Gratitude again recurs: whether, namely, we are to apportion the reward to the effort made, or to the results attained. For it may be said that the actual utility of any service must depend much upon favourable circumstances and fortunate accidents, not due to any desert of the agent: or again, may be due to powers and skills which were connate, or have been developed by favourable conditions of life, or by good education, and why should we reward him for these? (for the latter we ought rather to reward those who have educated him). And certainly it is only in so far as *moral* excellences are exhibited in human achievements that they are commonly thought to be such as God will reward. But by drawing this line we do not yet get rid of the difficulty. For it may still be said that good actions are due entirely, or to a great extent, to good dispositions and habits, and that these are partly inherited and partly due to the care of parents and teachers; so that in rewarding these we are rewarding the results of natural and accidental advantages, and it is unreasonable to distinguish these from others, such as skill and knowledge, and to say that it is even ideally just to reward the former and not the latter. Shall we say, then, that the reward should be proportionate to the amount of voluntary effort for a good end? But Necessarians will say that even this is ultimately the effect of causes extraneous to the man's self. On the necessarian view, then, it would seem to be ideally just (if anything is so) that all men should enjoy equal amounts of happiness: for there seems to be no justice in making A happier than B, merely because circumstances beyond his own control have first made him better. But why should we not, instead of 'all men,' say 'all sentient beings'? for why should man have more happiness than any other animal? But thus the pursuit of ideal justice seems to conduct us to such a precipice of paradox that Common Sense is likely to abandon it. At any rate the ordinary idea of Desert has thus altogether vanished[1]. And thus we seem to be led to the

[1] The only possible necessarian interpretation of Desert is, I think, the Utilitarian: according to which, when a man is said to deserve reward for any services to society, the meaning is that it is expedient to reward him, in order

conclusion which I anticipated in Bk. I. ch. v.: that in this one department of our moral consciousness the idea of Free Will seems involved in a peculiar way in the moral ideas of Common Sense since if it is eliminated the important notions of Desert and Justice require essential modification. However, perhaps it would be superfluous to discuss this further[1]. For in any case it does not seem possible to separate in practice that part of a man's achievement which is due strictly to his free choice from that part which is due to the original gift of nature and to favouring circumstances[2]: so that we must necessarily leave to Providence the realization of what we conceive as the theoretical ideal of Justice, and content ourselves with trying to reward voluntary actions in proportion to the services actually rendered (that is, if *intentionally* rendered; for otherwise no one would think it deserving of reward).

If, then, we take as the principle of ideal justice so far as this can be practically aimed at in human society, the requital of voluntary services in proportion to their worth, it remains to consider on what principle or principles the comparative worth

that he and others may be induced to render similar services by the expectation of similar rewards. Cf. *post*, Book IV. ch. iii. § 4.

[1] Perhaps we may partly attribute to the difficulties above discussed, that the notion of Desert has sometimes dropped out of the ideal of Utopian reconstructors of society, and 'Equality of Happiness' has seemed to be the only end. Justice, it has been thought, prescribes simply that each should have an equal share of happiness, as far as happiness depends on the action of others. But there seems to be much difficulty in working this out: for (apart from the considerations of Fitness above mentioned) equal happiness is not to be attained by equal distribution of objects of desire. For some require more and some less to be equally happy. Hence, it seems, we must take differences of *needs* into consideration. But if merely mental needs are included (as seems reasonable) we should have to give less to cheerful, contented, self-sacrificing people than to those who are naturally moody and *exigeant*, as the former can be made happy with less. And this is too paradoxical to recommend itself to Common Sense.

[2] No doubt, it would be possible to remove, to some extent, the inequalities that are attributable to circumstances, by bringing the best education within the reach of all classes, so that all children might have an equal opportunity of being selected and trained for any functions for which they seemed to be fit: and this seems to be prescribed by ideal justice, in so far as it removes or mitigates arbitrary inequality. Accordingly in those ideal reconstructions of society, in which we may expect to find men's notions of abstract justice exhibited, such an institution as this has generally found a place. Still, there will be much natural inequality which we cannot remove or even estimate.

of different services is to be rationally estimated. There is no doubt that we commonly assume such an estimate to be possible; for we continually speak of the 'fair' or 'proper' price of any kind of services as something generally known, and condemn the demand for more than this as extortionate. It may be said that the notion of Fairness or Equity which we ordinarily apply in such judgments is to be distinguished from that of Justice; Equity being in fact often contrasted with strict Justice, which is held to be either realized in the fulfilment of contracts when made, and of definite legal prescriptions; and which is even capable of coming into collision with Equity. And this is partly true: but I think the wider and no less usual sense of the term Justice, in which it includes Equity or Fairness is the only one that can be conveniently adopted in an ethical treatise: for in any case where Equity comes into conflict with strict justice, its dictates are held to be in a higher sense just, and what ought to be ultimately carried into effect in the case considered—though, not, perhaps, by the administrators of law. I treat Equity, therefore, as a species of Justice; though noting that the former term is more ordinarily used in cases where the definiteness attainable is recognized as somewhat less than in ordinary cases of rightful claims arising out of law or contract. On what principle, then, can we determine the "fair" or "equitable" price of services? When we examine the common judgments of practical persons in which this judgment occurs, we find, I think that the 'fair' in such cases is ascertained by a reference to analogy and custom, and that any service is considered to be 'fairly worth' what is usually given for services of the kind. Hence this element of the notion of Justice may seem, after all, to resolve itself into that discussed in § 2. But probably no one would now maintain in its full breadth this identification of the Just with the Usual price of services: and indeed such judgments as those I have mentioned seem to be often superficial or merely inadvertent, and to ignore the mode in which prices are actually determined,— at least in the more civilized communities; for in some states of society it certainly appears that the payment to be given for services is as completely fixed by usage as any other customary duty, so that it would be a clear disappointment of normal expectation to deviate from this usage. But in more progressive countries it is determined more and more by free competition; and so the market value rises and falls, and is different at different places and times; and no properly instructed person can expect any fixity in it, or complain of injustice on account of any variation in it.

Can we then say that 'market value' (as determined by free competition) corresponds to our notion of what is ideally just?

This is a question of much interest, because this is obviously the mode of determining the remuneration of services that would be universal in a society constructed on the principle previously discussed, of securing the greatest possible Freedom of Action (only limited by Free Contract) to all members of the community. It should be observed that this, which we may call the Individualistic Ideal, is the type to which modern civilized communities have long been tending to approximate: and it is therefore very important to know whether it is one which completely satisfies the demands of morality; and whether Freedom, if not an absolute end or First Principle of abstract Justice, is still to be sought as the best means to the realization of a just social order by the general requital of Desert.

At first sight it seems plausible to urge that the 'market value' represents the estimate set upon anything by mankind generally, and therefore gives us exactly that 'commonsense' judgment respecting value which we are now trying to find. But on examination it seems likely that the majority of men are not properly qualified to decide on the value of many important kinds of services, from imperfect knowledge of their nature and effects; so that, as far as these are concerned, the true judgment will not be represented in the market-place. Even in the case of things which a man is generally able to estimate, it may be manifest in a particular case that he is ignorant of the real utility of what he exchanges; and in this case the 'free' contract hardly seems to be fair: though if the ignorance was not caused by the other party to the exchange, Common Sense is hardly prepared to condemn the latter as unjust for taking advantage of it. For instance, if a man has discovered by a legitimate use of geological knowledge and skill that there is probably a valuable mine on land owned by a stranger, reasonable persons would not blame him for concealing his discovery until he had bought the mine at its market value: yet it could not be said that the seller got what it was really worth. In fact Common Sense is rather perplexed on this point: and the *rationale* of the conclusion at which it arrives must, I conceive, be sought in economic considerations, which take us quite beyond the analysis of the common notion of Justice[1].

Again, there are social services recognized as highly important which generally speaking have no price in any market, on account of the indirectness and uncertainty of their practical utility: as, for instance, scientific discoveries. The extent to which any given discovery will aid industrial invention is so uncertain, that even if the secret of it could be conveniently kept, it would not be profitable to buy it.

But even if we confine our attention to products and services generally marketable, and to bargains thoroughly understood on both sides, there are still serious difficulties in the way of identifying the notions of 'free' and 'fair' exchange. Thus, where an individual, or combination of individuals, has the monopoly of a certain kind of services, the market-price of the aggregate of such services can under certain conditions be increased by diminishing their total amount; but it would seem absurd to say that the social Desert of those rendering the services is thereby increased, and a plain man has grave doubts whether the price thus attained is fair. Still less is it thought fair to take advantage of the transient monopoly produced by emergency: thus, if I saw Crœsus drowning with no one near, it would not be held fair in me to refuse to save him except at the price of half his wealth. But if so, can it be fair for any class of persons to gain competitively by the unfavourable economic situation of another class with which they deal? And if we admit that it would be unfair, where are we to draw the line? For any increase of the numbers of a class renders its situation for bargaining less favourable: since the market price of different

---

[1] Cf. *post*, Book IV. ch. iii. § 4.

services depends partly upon the ease or difficulty of procuring them—as Political Economists say, 'on the relation between the supply of services and the demand for them'—and it does not seem that any individual's social Desert can properly be lessened merely by the increased number or willingness of others rendering the same services. Nor, indeed, does it seem that it can be decreased by his own willingness, for it is strange to reward a man less because he is zealous and eager in the performance of his function: yet in bargaining the less willing always has the advantage. And, finally, it hardly appears that the social worth of a man's service is necessarily increased by the fact that his service is rendered to those who can pay lavishly; but his reward is certainly likely to be greater from this cause.

Such considerations as these have led some political thinkers to hold that Justice requires an entirely different mode of distributing payment for services from that at present effected by free competition: and that all labourers ought to be paid according to the intrinsic value of their labour as estimated by enlightened and competent judges. If this Socialistic Ideal —as we may perhaps call it—could be realized without counterbalancing evils, it would certainly seem to give a nearer approximation to what we conceive as Divine Justice than the present state of society affords. But this supposes that we have found the rational method of determining value: which, however, is still to seek. Shall we say that these judges are to take the value of a service as proportionate to the amount of happiness produced by it? If so, the calculation is, of course, exposed to all the difficulties of the hedonistic method discussed in Book II.: but supposing these can be overcome, it is still hard to say how we are to compare the value of different services that must necessarily be combined to produce happy life. For example, how shall we compare the respective values of necessaries and luxuries? for we may be more sensible of the enjoyment derived from the latter, but we could not have this at all without the former. And, again, when different kinds of labour cooperate in the same production, how are we to estimate their relative values? for even if all mere unskilled labour may be brought to a common standard, this seems almost impossible in the case of different kinds of skill. For how shall we compare the labour of design with that of achievement? or the supervision of the whole with the execution of details? or the labour of actually producing with that of educating producers? or the service of the *savant* who discovers a new principle, with that of the inventor who applies it?

I do not see how these questions, or the difficulties noticed in the preceding paragraph, can be met by any analysis of our common notion of Justice. To deal with such points at all satisfactorily we have, I conceive, to adopt quite a different line of reasoning: we have to ask, not what services of a certain kind are intrinsically worth, but what reward can procure them and whether the rest of society gain by the services more than the equivalent reward. We have, in short, to give up as impracticable the construction of an ideally just social order[1], in which all services are rewarded in exact proportion to their intrinsic value. And, for similar reasons, we seem forced to conclude, more generally, that it is impossible to obtain clear premises for a reasoned method of determining exactly different amounts of Good Desert. Indeed, perhaps, Common Sense scarcely holds such a method to be possible: for though it considers Ideal Justice to consist in rewarding Desert, it regards any attempt to realize this ideal in the general distribution of the means of happiness as Utopian. In the actual state of society it is only within a very limited range that any endeavour is made to reward Good Desert. Parents attempt this to some extent in dealing with their children, and the State in rewarding remarkable public services rendered by statesmen, soldiers, &c.: but reflection on these cases will shew how very rough and imperfect a standard is used in deciding the amount due. And ordinarily the only kind of Justice which we try to realize is that which consists in the fulfilment of contracts and definite expectations; leaving the general fairness of Distribution by Bargaining to take care of itself.

§ 7. When we pass to consider the case of Criminal Justice, we find, in the first place, difficulties corresponding to those which we have already noticed, although somewhat less in degree. We find, to begin, a similar implication and partial con-

[1] It is not perhaps necessary that I should here enlarge on the *practical* obstacles in the way of any attempt to realize such an ideal system.

fusion of the ideas of Law and Justice. For, as was said, by 'bringing a man to Justice' we commonly mean 'inflicting legal punishment' on him: and we think it right that neither more nor less than the penalty inflicted by law should be executed, although we often condemn the legal scale of punishment as unjust. At the same time, we have no such perplexity in respect of changes in the law as occurs in the case of Civil Justice; for we do not think that a man can acquire, by custom, prescriptive rights to over-lenient punishment, as he is thought to do to an unequal distribution of liberties and privileges. If, again, we investigate the ideal of Criminal Justice, as intuitively determined, we find the principle of Desert more thoroughly accepted by Common Sense than in the former case; for certainly in so far as punishment is not merely regarded as preventive (as it is on the Utilitarian view), it is commonly thought that it ought to be proportioned to the gravity of crime[1]. Still, when we endeavour to make the method of apportionment perfectly rational and precise, the difficulties seem at least as great as in the case of Good Desert. For, first, the assumption of Free Will seems necessarily to come in here also; since if a man's bad deeds are entirely caused by nature and circumstances, it certainly appears, as Robert Owen urged, that he does not properly deserve to be punished for them; we should rather devote our efforts to altering the conditions under which he acts (of course the prospect of punishment is one of these conditions, and it will not do to remove that, in so far as it prevents him from doing harm; but then it is retained on different grounds). And we certainly think that offences committed by persons who have had no moral training, or a perverted training, are really less criminal, and in a sense deserve less punishment—at any rate at God's hands; for it is commonly agreed that men cannot take this into account, and must punish a man for any evil which he has intended to do, and from which nothing prevented him from abstaining except absence

[1] Of course those who hold that the essence of Justice consists in securing external Freedom among the members of a community, and that punishment is only justified as a means to this end, naturally think that in awarding punishment we ought to consider merely its efficacy as such means. But this can scarcely be put forward as an interpretation of the common notion of Just Punishment.

of sufficient motive. Still the consciousness of this seems to render the penal arrangements of society imperfectly satisfying to our sense of Justice. And we actually do punish deliberate offences more than impulsive, perhaps as implying a more free choice of evil. And the presence of any very powerful motive, in itself natural and innocent, seems to us to lessen the essential criminality of an act, as when a man steals food to escape starvation. And, still more, if the motive be even laudable, as when a man kills a villain whose crimes elude legal punishment, or heads a hopeless rebellion for the good of his country. In such cases there is a widespread feeling that punishment ought to be mitigated: and so far as this sentiment is held in check, it is rather by a consideration of the mischievous consequences likely to result from leniency, than from any insight into a supposed principle of Justice as distinct from expediency.

But even if we neglect the motive, and take the intention only into account, it is not easy to state clear principles for determining the gravity of crimes. If it be said that punishment ought to be in proportion to the 'harm' intended, we require further to know what is meant by harm. If we say 'unhappiness' we seem to be in conflict with Common Sense; for in many cases the criminal, though he knows that he is doing wrong, does not intend to produce any unhappiness at all; as when a thief takes what he thinks will not be missed. Indeed, in such cases as those of the starving man, or the patriotic rebel, the intention of the criminal is clearly to produce happiness. Again, we do not commonly think that a crime is rendered less grave, by being kept perfectly secret; and yet a great part of the harm done by a crime is the 'secondary evil' (as Bentham calls it) of the alarm and insecurity which it causes; and this part is cut off by complete secrecy. It may be replied that this latter difficulty is not a practical one; because we are not called upon to punish a crime until it has been discovered, and then the secondary evil has been caused, and is all the greater because of the previous secrecy. But it remains true that it was not designed for discovery; and therefore that this part of the evil caused by the crime was not intended by the criminal. And if we say that the heinousness of the crime depends on the loss of happiness that would generally be caused by such acts if they were allowed to go unpunished, and that we must suppose the criminal to be aware of this; we seem to be endeavouring to force a utilitarian theory into an intuitional form by means of a legal fiction.

We have hitherto spoken of intentional wrong-doing: but positive Law awards punishment also for harm that is due to rashness or negligence; and the justification of this involves us in further difficulties. Some jurists seem to regard rashness and negligence as positive states of mind, in which the agent consciously refuses the attention or reflection which he knows he ought to give; and no doubt this sort of wilful recklessness does sometimes occur and seems as properly punishable as if the resulting harm had been positively intended. But the law as actually administered does not require evidence that this was the agent's state of mind (which indeed in most cases it would be impossible to give): but is content with proof that the harm might have been prevented by such care as an average man would have shewn under the circumstances. And most commonly by 'carelessness' we simply mean a purely negative psychological fact, *i.e.* that the agent did not perform certain processes of observation or reflection; it is therefore at the time strictly involuntary, and so scarcely seems to be justly punishable. It may be said perhaps that though the present carelessness is not blameworthy, the past neglect to cultivate habits of care is so. But in many individual instances we cannot reasonably infer even this past neglect; and in such cases the utilitarian theory of punishment, which regards it as a means of preventing similar harmful acts in the future, seems alone applicable[1].

The results of this examination of Justice may be summed up as follows. The prominent element in Justice as ordinarily conceived is a kind of Equality: that is, Impartiality in the observance or enforcement of certain general rules allotting good or evil to individuals. But when we have clearly dis-

---

[1] Similar difficulties arise, as was before hinted (p. 281), in determining the limits within which Reparation is due; that is, on the view that it is not incumbent on us to make compensation for any harm caused by our muscular actions, but only for harm which—if not intentional—was due to our rashness or negligence.

tinguished this element, we see that the definition of the virtue required for practical guidance is left obviously incomplete. Inquiring further for the right general principles of distribution, we find that our common notion of Justice includes—besides the principle of Reparation for injury—two quite distinct and divergent elements. The one, which we may call Conservative Justice, is realized (1) in the observance of Law and Contracts and definite understandings, and in the enforcement of such penalties for the violation of these as have been properly announced and generally accepted; and (2) in the fulfilment of natural and normal expectations. This latter obligation, however, is of a somewhat indefinite kind. But the other element, which we have called Ideal Justice, is still more difficult to define; for there seem to be two quite distinct conceptions of it, embodied respectively in what we have called the Individualistic and the Socialistic Ideals of a political community. The first of these takes the realization of Freedom as the ultimate end and standard of right social relations: but on examining it closer we find that the notion of Freedom will not give a practicable basis for social construction without certain arbitrary[1] definitions and limitations: and even if we admit these, still a society in which Freedom is realized as far as is feasible does not completely suit our sense of Justice. *Primâ facie*, this is more satisfied by the Socialistic Ideal of Distribution, founded on the principle of requiting Desert: but when we try to make this principle precise, we find ourselves again involved in grave difficulties; and similar perplexities beset the development of Criminal Justice on the same principle.

[1] By 'arbitrary' I mean such definitions and limitations as destroy the self-evidence of the principle; and, when closely examined, lead us to regard it as subordinate.

CHAPTER VI.

LAWS AND PROMISES.

§ 1. IN the discussion of Justice the moral obligations of obedience to Law and observance of Contract have been included, and have, indeed, appeared to be the most definite part of the complex system of private duties commonly included under that term. At the same time, as we have seen, there are some laws, the violation of which does not interfere with the rights of others, and therefore has not the characteristics of an act of Injustice. While again, the duty of Fidelity to promises is also commonly conceived as independent of any injury that might be done to the promisee by breaking it: for (*e.g.*) men ordinarily judge that a promise to the dead, though they are beyond the reach of injury, ought to be kept: indeed, some would regard it as even more sacred than a promise made to the living. It seems therefore desirable to examine the propositions 'that Law ought to be obeyed' and 'that promises ought to be kept,' considered as independent principles.

To begin with the former: how are we to ascertain what the Law is which, as is commonly thought, we are morally bound to obey, as such. It is plain that we cannot here distinguish Legal from other rules by considering the sanctions actually attached to them, as we had occasion to do in a previous chapter[1]. For commands may be issued by rebels and usurpers which we are morally bound to resist, though we may have to dread judicial penalties for disobedience. Shall we say then, as was proposed in Book I. c. 2, that Laws are those rules which *ought* to be enforced by a definitely

[1] Cf. *ante*, Bk. II. c. v. § 2.

organized infliction of punishments? This seems to be the definition most suitable for distinguishing theoretical Jurisprudence from Ethics proper: but it fails to indicate the special object and scope of the moral duty which we are now examining as commonly recognized: for Common Sense certainly holds, that, generally speaking, positive laws ought to be observed, even when they are such as a theoretical jurist would condemn. Hence it seems that for our present purpose we must define Laws to be Rules of Conduct which we are morally bound to obey, not solely on account of their intrinsic rightness, but on account of the Rightful Authority from which they are derived[1]. Of course it may be sometimes not only our interest but our duty to obey rules imposed by persons who have usurped authority to which they have no right: but it would be generally agreed that this is solely in order to avoid the greater evils which might result to ourselves and others from our disobedience; and that the extent of such a duty must be determined by considerations of expediency.

This rightful authority is commonly conceived to reside in some living men. No doubt in some societies, at some stages of their development, the whole or a part of the code of laws habitually observed, or at least recognized as binding, has been believed to be of divine or semi-divine institution; or perhaps from mere antiquity to possess a sanctity superior to that of any living authority, so as to be not legitimately alterable. But we hardly find this view in the Common Sense of civilized Europe, upon which we are now reflecting: at any rate in our societies there is not thought to be any portion of the definite prescriptions of positive law which, in virtue of its origin, is beyond the reach of alteration by any living authority.

What kind of authority, then, does Common Sense regard as legitimate?

It can hardly be said that there is any clear answer to be found to this question. For here the conflict between the Ideal and the Traditional or Customary, which has perplexed us in seeking the definition of Justice, meets us again in an even more complicated form. For not only do some say

[1] The distinction between Laws proper and special ordinances is not here important.

that obedience is always due to the established authority in any country, while others maintain that an authority constituted in accordance with certain abstract principles is essentially legitimate, and that a nation has a right to claim that such an authority shall be established, even at the risk of civil strife and bloodshed: but often, too, the authority actually established is not even traditionally legitimate. So that we have sometimes to distinguish *three* claims to authority: (1) that of the Government held to be ideally or abstractly right, and such as ought to be established: (2) that of the Government *de jure*, according to the constitutional traditions in any given country: and (3) that of the *de facto* Government. And, again, the attempt to define each of these claims, taken alone, involves us in considerable perplexity and disagreement, as a closer examination will shew.

§ 2. It will be convenient to begin by considering the Ideal. Here I do not propose to consider all views as to the right constitution of supreme authority which speculative thinkers have put forward; but only such as have a *primâ facie* claim to express the Common Sense of mankind on the subject. Of these the most important, and the most widely urged and admitted, is the principle that the Sovereign in any community can only be rightly constituted by the Consent of the Subjects. This, as was noticed in the preceding chapter, is involved in the adoption of Freedom as the ultimate end of political order: if no one originally owes anything to another except non-interference, he clearly can only be placed in the relation of Subject to Sovereign by his own consent. And thus, in order to reconcile the original right of Freedom with the actual duty of Law-observance, some supposition of a social contract appears necessary; by means of which Obedience to Law becomes merely a special application of the duty of keeping contracts.

In what way, then, are the terms of this fundamental compact to be known? No one now maintains the old view that the transition from the 'natural' to the 'political' state actually took place by means of an "original Contract," which conferred indelible legitimacy on some particular form of social organization. Shall we say, then, that a man by remaining a member of a community enters into a 'tacit undertaking' to obey the laws laid down by the authority generally recognized as lawful in that community. In this way however the most unlimited despotism, if established and traditional, might claim to rest on free consent as well as any other form of government: so that the theoretical freedom of the individual would become a useless fiction. To avoid this result, we must suppose that certain 'Natural Rights' are inalienable, and that laws are not strictly legitimate which deprive a man of these. But as to the exact definition of these inalienable rights there are several different opinions, leading to different views of the essential legitimacy of positive laws and constitutions. For (1) of those who would agree that all such rights may be summed up in the notion of Freedom, some would mean only civil Freedom: *i.e.* that no one was bound to submit to slavery, however much it might be established by law. But (2) it is easy to pass from civil to constitutional freedom: for, as we saw in the last chapter, the Right to one's own property is commonly included in the former notion: but all taxation is a forcible interference with property: hence it has been held that a man has a natural right to refuse to pay any tax to which he has not actually consented personally or by his representatives, and that rebellion upon this ground is justifiable. But, again, (3) we may go further and hold that no man ought to be compelled to submit to laws of any kind to which he has not similarly assented; and some would say that this is the only binding social contract, and that members of any society have a right to demand that they should be governed by no laws except those thus made, and to refuse obedience to other laws if this seems expedient. This principle, when applied to large communities, is thought to lead to Representative Government as the only one whose authority seems abstractly valid: and this in fact, is the form which the Individualistic Ideal has usually taken in its application to Politics: but it seems open to some of the objections previously urged against the general theory of Freedom as an absolute end, and also to others peculiar to this part of the subject. For, in the first place, if the principle be absolute, it ought to apply to all human beings alike: but if to avoid this absurdity we exclude children, an arbitrary line has to be drawn: and the exclusion of women, which even those who regard the suffrage as a natural right are often disposed to maintain, seems altogether indefensible. But, again, we must admit that the theory is very imperfectly realized (even as regards the male adults to whom its application has commonly been restricted) by Representative Government as commonly conceived and practised. For a Representative assembly is chosen only by a part of the nation, and each law is approved only by a part of the assembly: and it can hardly be said that a man has assented to a law passed, by a mere majority of an assembly against one member of which he has voted. In fact, as Mill and others have urged, the majority of a nation may be as tyrannical as any despot, and may encroach to any extent on the freedom of action of individuals.

But, again, the principle that the laws of any community ought to express the will of the majority of its members seems *primâ facie* incompatible with the view so vigorously maintained by Socrates and his most famous disciples, that laws ought to be made by people who understand law-making. For though the majority of a representative assembly in a particular country at a particular time may be more fit to make laws for their country than any set of experts otherwise selected, we certainly cannot tell *à priori* that this will be universally the case. Yet surely the Socratic proposition (which is merely a special application of the principle noticed in the latter part of the preceding chapter, 'that functions should be allotted to the fittest') has as much claim to be considered a primary intuition as the one we have been discussing. Indeed, the secular controversy between Aristocracy and Democracy seems ultimately reducible to a conflict between those two principles: a conflict of which it is impossible to find a solution, so long as the argument remains in the *à priori* region.

§ 3. However, to discuss this exhaustively would carry us too far beyond the range of Ethics proper: but we may perhaps conclude that it is impossible to elicit from Common Sense any clear and certain intuitions as to the principles on which an ideal constitution should be constructed. And there is an equal want of agreement as to the intrinsic lawfulness of introducing such a constitution in violation of the traditional and established order in any community. For some think that a nation has a natural right to a government approximately conformed to the ideal, and that it ought to be introduced by force. Others, however, hold that though the ideal polity may rightly be proclaimed and commended, and every means used to prepare the way for its introduction which the established government in any country permits; still, rebellion against this latter can never be justifiable. While others,—perhaps the majority,—would decide the question on grounds of expediency, balancing the advantages of improvement against the evils of disorder.

But further, as we saw, it is not so easy to say what the established government is. For sometimes there occurs a clear rupture of order in a society, and a triumph of Might over Right: and then a new order, springing out of and jurally rooted in disorder. An authority declared by law to be illegitimate issues ordinances and controls the administration of justice. The question then arises, how far obedience is due to such an authority. All are agreed that usurpation ought to be resisted; but as to the right behaviour towards an established government which has sprung from a successful usurpation, there is great difference of opinion. Some think that it should be regarded as legitimate, as soon as it is firmly established: others that it ought to be obeyed at once, but under protest, with the purpose of renewing the conflict on a favourable opportunity: others think that this latter is the right attitude at first, but that a usurping government, when firmly established, loses its illegitimacy gradually, and that it becomes, after a while, as criminal to rebel against it as it was originally to establish it. And this last seems, on the whole, the view of Common Sense; but it seems impossible to determine the point at which the metamorphosis is thought to take place[1], otherwise than by considerations of expediency.

---

[1] In discussing Justice, I did not notice this conflict of legalities: because (in modern times at least) it is but rarely that a change of government is accompanied by violent interference with the civil rights of the governed. Still, such an interference sometimes occurs: and then the determination of what I have called Conservative or Customary Justice becomes very perplexing. And sometimes the interference is only temporary, and the old order is afterwards restored: in which case the conflict of claims and expectations, arising out of

But again, it is only in the case of an absolute government, where customary obedience is unconditionally due to one or more persons, that the fundamental difficulties of ascertaining the legitimacy of authority are of the simple kind just discussed. In a constitutionally governed state numerous other moral disagreements arise. For, in such a state, while it is of course held that the sovereign is morally bound to conform to the constitution[1], it is still disputed whether the subjects' obligation to obedience is properly conceived as conditional upon this conformity: and whether they have the moral right (1) to refuse obedience to an unconstitutional command; and (2) even to inflict on the sovereign the penalty of rebellion for violating the constitution. Again, there is often no little difficulty in determining what the constitutional obligations really are. I do not mean merely a difficulty of erudition, capable of being removed by a completer knowledge of historical facts and documents; but a difficulty arising from uncertainty as to the principles on which these ought to be treated. For the various limitations of sovereign authority comprised in the constitution have often been originally concessions extorted by fear from a sovereign previously absolute; and it is doubted how far such concessions are morally binding on the sovereign from whom they were wrested, and still more how far they are binding on those who succeed. Or, *vice versâ*, a people may have allowed liberties once exercised to fall into disuse; and it is doubted whether it retains the right of reclaiming them. And, gene-

---

different established orders, is theoretically insoluble: only a rough practical compromise can be affected.

[1] It is perhaps hardly necessary that I should here notice the Hobbist doctrine, revived in a modified form by Austin, that "the power of the sovereign is incapable of [legal] limitation." For no one now maintains pure Hobbism: and Austin is as far as possible from meaning that there cannot be an express or tacit understanding between Sovereign and Subjects, the violation of which by the former may make it morally right for the latter to rebel. In fact, as used by him, Hobbes' doctrine reduces itself to the rather unimportant proposition that a sovereign will not be punished for unconstitutional conduct through the agency of his own law-courts, so long as he remains sovereign. I may take this opportunity of observing that Austin's definition of Law is manifestly unsuited for our present purpose: since a law, in his view, is not a command that ought to be obeyed, but a command for the violation of which we may expect a particular kind of punishment.

rally, when a constitutional rule has to be elicited from a comparison of precedents, it may be disputed whether a particular act of either party should be regarded as a constitutive precedent or as an illegitimate encroachment. And hence we find that in constitutional countries men's view of what their constitution traditionally is, has often been greatly influenced by their view of what it ideally ought to be: in fact, the two questions have rarely been kept quite distinct.

But even if we could ascertain clearly to what authority obedience is properly due, there remains the difficulty of defining the limits of such obedience. For no one in modern society maintains it to be due without qualification; we are always told that any authority ought to be disobeyed which commands immoral acts. But this is one of those tautological propositions, so common in popular morality, which convey no real information; the question is, what acts there are which do not cease to be immoral when they have been commanded by a rightful authority. There seems to be no clear principle upon which these can be determined. It has sometimes been said that the Law cannot override definite duties; but the obligation of fidelity to contract is peculiarly definite, and yet we do not consider it right to fulfil a contract of which the law has forbidden the execution. And, in fact, we do not find any practical agreement on this subject. For some would say that the duties of the domestic relations must yield to the duty of law-observance, and that (*e.g.*) a son ought not to aid a parent actively or passively in escaping the punishment of crime: while others would consider this rule too inhuman to be laid down, and others would draw the line between assistance and connivance. And similarly, when acts of extreme injustice are commanded by law: thus many have thought that laws could not make it right to deliver up a fugitive slave to his pursuers (and that without distinctly recognizing any defect of authority in the persons from whom the law emanated). And others would consider that a certain degree of inexpediency in a law made it right to disregard it: this, however, seems implicitly to admit that the duty of law-observance rests upon a utilitarian basis. Again, some jurists hold that we are not strictly bound to obey laws, when they command what is not otherwise a duty, or forbid what is not otherwise a sin; on the ground that in the case of duties prescribed only by positive laws, the alternatives of obeying or submitting to the penalty are morally open to us[1]. Others, however, think this principle too lax; and certainly if a wide-spread preference of penalty to obedience were shewn in the case of any particular law, the legislation in question would be thought to have failed. Nor, on the other hand, does there seem to be any agreement as to whether one is bound to submit to unjust penalties.

Since, then, on all these points there is found to be so much difference of opinion, it seems idle to maintain that there is any clear and precise axiom or first principle of Order, intuitively seen to be true by the common reason and conscience of mankind. There is, no doubt, a vague general instinct bidding us obey laws as such (even bad laws), which may be fairly said to rest on a universal *consensus* of civilized society: but when we try to state any explicit proposition corresponding to this general instinct, the *consensus* seems to abandon us, and we are drawn into endless controversies[2].

§ 4. We have next to treat of Good Faith, or Fidelity to Promises; which it is natural to consider in this place, because, as has been seen, the Duty of Law-observance has by some thinkers been based upon a prior duty of fulfilling a contract. The Social Contract however, as above examined, seems at best merely a convenient fiction, a logical artifice, by which the mutual jural relations of the members of a civilized community may be neatly expressed: and in stating the ethical principles of Common Sense, such a fiction would seem to be out of place. It must, however, be allowed that there has frequently been a close historical connexion between the Duty

---

[1] Cf. Blackstone, *Introduction*, § 2. "In relation to those laws which enjoin only positive duties, and forbid only such things as are not *mala in se*, but *mala prohibita* merely, without any intermixture of moral guilt, annexing a penalty to non-compliance, here I apprehend conscience is no further concerned, than by directing a submission to the penalty in case of our breach of those laws... the alternative is offered to every man, 'either abstain from this or submit to such a penalty.'"

[2] Into the ethical difficulties peculiar to some departments of Law (commonly so called), as (*e.g.*) International Law, I have not thought it worth while to enter.

of Law-observance and the Duty of Good Faith. In the first place, a considerable amount of Constitutional Law at least, in certain ages and countries, has been established or confirmed by compacts expressly made between different sections of the community; who agree that for the future government shall be carried on according to certain rules. The duty of observing these rules thus presents itself as a Duty of Fidelity to compact. Yet more is this the case, when the question is one of imposing not a law, but a law-giver; whose authority is strengthened by the enaction of an oath of allegiance from his subjects or a representative portion of them, or the holders of offices. Still, even in such cases, it can only be by a transparent fiction that the mass of the citizens can be regarded as bound by an engagement which only a few of them have actually taken.

We may begin our examination of the duty of Keeping Promises by noticing—what has been before mentioned—that some moralists have classified or even identified it with Veracity. From one point of view there certainly seems to be an analogy between the two; as we fulfil the obligations of Veracity and Good Faith alike by effecting a correspondence between words and facts—in the one case by making fact correspond with statement, and in the other by making statement correspond with fact. But the analogy is obviously superficial and imperfect; for we are not bound to make our actions correspond with our assertions generally, but only with our promises. If I merely assert my intention of abstaining from alcohol for a year, and then after a week take some, I am (at worst) ridiculed as inconsistent: but if I have pledged myself to abstain, I am blamed as untrustworthy. Thus the essential element of the Duty of Good Faith seems to be not conformity to my own statement, but <u>to the expectations that I have intentionally raised in others</u>: and thus it appears to come within our definition of Conservative Justice.

On this view, however, the question arises whether, when a promise has been understood in a sense not intended by the promiser, he is bound to satisfy expectations which he did not voluntarily create. It is, I think, clear to Common Sense that he is so bound in some cases, if the expectation was natural and such as most men would form under the circumstances: but this would seem to be one of the more or less indefinite duties of Justice, and not properly of Good Faith, as there has not been, strictly speaking, any promise at all. The normal effect of language is to convey the speaker's meaning to the person addressed (here the promiser's to the promisee), and we always suppose this to have taken place when we speak of a promise. If through any accident this normal effect is missed, we may say that there is no promise, or not a perfect promise.

The moral obligation, then, of a promise is perfectly constituted when it is understood by both parties in the same sense. And by the term 'promise' we include not words only, but all signs, and even tacit understandings not expressly signified in any way, if such clearly form a part of the engagement. The promiser is bound to perform what both he and the promisee understood to be undertaken.

§ 5. Is, then, this obligation intuitively seen to be independent and certain?

It is often said to be so: and perhaps we may say that it seems so to unreflective common sense. But reflection seems at least to disclose a considerable number of qualifications of the principle; some clear and precise, while others are more or less indefinite.

In the first place, thoughtful persons would commonly admit that the obligation of a promise is relative to the promisee, and may be annulled by him. And therefore if the promisee be dead, or otherwise inaccessible and incapable of granting release, there is constituted an exceptional case, of which the solution must cause some difficulty[1].

Secondly, a promise to do an immoral act is held not to be binding, for the prior obligation not to do the act is paramount: just as in law a contract to do what a man is not legally free to do, is invalid: otherwise one could evade any moral obligation by promising not to fulfil it, which is clearly absurd[2]. And the same principle is of course applicable to

[1] Vows to God constitute another exception: and it is thought by many that if these are binding, there must be some way in which God can be understood to grant release from them. But this it is beyond my province to discuss.

[2] The case is somewhat different when the act has become immoral after the

immoral omissions or forbearances to act: here, however, a certain difficulty arises from the necessity of distinguishing between different kinds or degrees of obligatoriness in duties; since it is clear that a promise may sometimes make it obligatory to abstain from doing what it would otherwise have been a duty to do. Thus it becomes my duty not to give money to a meritorious hospital if I have promised all I can spare to an undeserving friend; though apart from the promise it might have been my duty to prefer the hospital to the friend. We have, however, already seen the difficulty of defining the limits of strict duty in many cases: thus (*e.g.*) it might be doubted how far the promise of aid to a friend ought to override the duty of giving one's children a good education. The extent, therefore, to which the obligation of a promise overrides prior obligations is practically somewhat obscure; however clear the abstract principle for determining it may seem to be.

§ 6. Further qualifications of the duty of fidelity to promises the consideration of which is involved in more difficulty and dispute, are suggested when we examine more closely the conditions under which promises are made, and the consequences of executing them. In the first place, it is much disputed how far promises obtained by 'fraud or force' are binding. As regards fraud, if the promise was understood to be conditional on the truth of a statement which is found to be false, it is of course not binding, according to the principle I originally laid down. But a promise may be made in consequence of such a fraudulent statement, and yet made quite unconditionally. Even so, if it were clearly understood that it would not have been made but for the false statement[1], probably most persons would regard it as not binding. But the false statement may be only one consideration among others, and it may be of any degree of weight; and it seems doubtful whether most moral men would feel justified in breaking a promise, because a single fraudulent statement had been a part of the inducement to make it.

Or, again, there may have been no explicit assertion, but

promise was made: still, here also, the prior duty of abstaining from it would be universally held to prevail.

[1] What is here said of a 'statement' may be extended to any mode of producing a false impression.

only a suggestion of what is false : or no falsehood at all, stated or suggested, but only a suppression of truth. We ought also to consider the case in which the false impression has not been wilfully produced, but was either shared by the promisee or produced in some way unintentionally. Perhaps in this last case most would say that the bindingness of the promise is not affected, unless it was expressly conditional. But even on this point Common Sense seems doubtful; and, still more, how far a promise is binding if any kind of deception or concealment is shewn to have been used to obtain it. We may observe that certain kinds of concealment are even justified by the law: in most contracts of sale, for example, the law adopts the principle of 'caveat emptor,' and does not refuse to enforce the contract because the seller did not disclose defects in the article sold, unless by some words or acts he produced the belief that it was free from such defects. Still, this does not settle the moral question; on which we do not seem to find any clear intuition. The same may be said of promises obtained by illegal violence and intimidation.

§ 7. But, secondly, even if a promise has been made quite freely and fairly, circumstances may alter so much before the time comes to fulfil it, that the effects of keeping it may be quite other than those which were foreseen when it was made. In such a case probably all would agree that the promisee ought to release the promiser. But if he declines to do this, it seems difficult to decide how far the latter is bound. Some would say that he is in all cases : while others would consider that a considerable alteration of circumstances removed the obligation—perhaps adding that all engagements must be understood to be taken subject to a general understanding that they are only binding if material circumstances remain substantially the same. But such a principle very much impairs the theoretical definiteness of the duty.

This difficulty assumes a new aspect when we consider the case already noticed, of promises made to those who are now dead or temporarily out of the reach of communications. For then there is no means of obtaining release from the promise, while at the same time its performance may be really opposed to the wishes—or what would have been the wishes—of both parties. The difficulty is sometimes concealed by saying that it is our duty to carry out the 'intention' of the promise. For as so used the word Intention is, in common parlance, ambiguous: it may either mean the signification which the promisee attached to the terms employed, as distinct from any other signification which the common usage of words might admit: or it may include ulterior consequences of the performance of the promise, which he had in view in exacting it. Now we do not commonly think that the promiser is concerned with the latter. He certainly has not pledged himself to aim generally at the end which the promisee has in view, but only so far as some particular means are concerned: and if he considers these means not conducive to the end, he is not thereby absolved from his promise, under ordinary circumstances. But in the case supposed, when circumstances have materially changed, and the promise does not admit of revision, probably most persons would say that we ought to take into consideration the ulterior wishes of the promisee, and carry out what we sincerely think *would* have been his intention. But the obligation thus becomes very vague: since it is difficult to tell from a man's wishes under one set of circumstances what he would have desired under circumstances varying from these in a complex manner: and practically this view of the obligation of a promise generally leads to great divergence of opinion. Hence it is not surprising that some hold that even in such a case the obligation ought to be interpreted strictly: while others go to the other extreme, and maintain that it ceases altogether.

Under this head we may consider the undertaking of society to execute the testaments of dead persons: because, though there is here no express promise, there may be a sufficiently clear understanding to impose on society a duty of Good Faith. We have not now to discuss the political problem how far the right of bequest ought to be legally unrestricted in a well-ordered state: but rather whether, when a bequest of funds to certain public uses, under certain regulations and conditions, has once been legitimately made and carried into effect, the state has still a right to change the destination of the funds, at any subsequent period. There seem two distinct principles upon which it is sought to limit the obligation of a community in such cases. First it is said (as before) that when circumstances have materially changed, we ought to carry out what *would* have been the intentions of the testator under the changed state of things, rather than the prescriptions actually laid down by him. But secondly, it is sometimes doubted whether any obligation undertaken by the community, or any section of it which has a permanent existence, can last for ever; and whether such obligation does not naturally decay and come to an end in course of time. And so some have proposed that all such dispositions of property should be formally declared to be in force for a certain term of years only; after which time the community should enter into possession of the property. However, we do not doubt that there are some national contracts, the obligation of which has not this quality of becoming evanescent; and it is hard to see how these are to be distinguished from others, except on grounds of expediency. For example, we think ourselves bound to pay the interest on loans contracted by our forefathers: and most of us think that we are bound to observe their treaties also. And yet a nation is at least excused for repudiating a treaty, when it is humiliating and oppressive: and again, we do not think a state eternally bound to observe, as a part of its constitutional law, any compact that may have been made between previously divided or temporarily dissentient sections of itself; even though the compact may have been expressly announced as binding for ever, and though, from the nature of the case, it is impossible to obtain release from it. In short, it seems to be held that some special qualifications of the duty of keeping engagements are needed in the case of nations or other undying corporations: though we can hardly obtain from Common Sense any clear decision as to what these are.

But again, it was said that a promise cannot abrogate a prior obligation; and, as a particular application of this rule, it would be generally agreed that no promise can make it right to inflict harm on any one. On further consideration, however, it appears doubtful how far the persons between whom the promise passed are included in the scope of this prohibition. For, first, it does not seem to be commonly held that a man is as strictly bound not to injure himself as he is to avoid harming others; and so it is scarcely thought that a promise is not binding because it was a foolish one, and will entail an amount of pain or burden on the promiser out of proportion to the good done to the promisee. Still, if we take an extreme case, where the sacrifice is very disproportionate to the gain, many conscientious persons would think that the promise ought rather to be broken than kept. And, secondly, a different question arises when we consider the possibility of injuring the promisee by fulfilling the promise. For when it is said to be wrong to do harm to any one, we do not commonly mean only what he thinks harm, but what really is so, though he may think it a benefit; for it seems clearly a crime for me to give any one what I know to be poison, even though he may be stubbornly convinced that it is wholesome food. But now suppose that I have promised A to do something, which, before I fulfil the promise, I see reason to regard as likely to injure him. The circumstances may be precisely the same, and only my view of them have changed. If A takes a different view and calls on me to fulfil the promise, is it right to obey him? Surely no one would say this is an extreme case, such as that of the poison. But if the rule does not hold for an extreme case, where can we draw the line? at what point ought I to give up my judgment to A, unless my own conviction is weakened? Common Sense seems to give no clear answer.

§ 8. I have laid down that a promise is binding in so far as it is understood on both sides similarly. This understanding is ordinarily attained with sufficient clearness, as far as the apprehension of express words or signs is concerned. Still, even here obscurity and misapprehension sometimes occur: and in the case of the tacit understandings with which promises are often complicated, a lack of definite agreement is not improbable. It becomes, therefore, of practical importance to decide the question previously raised, What duty rests on the promiser of satisfying expectations which he did not intend to create? I called this a duty not so much of Good Faith as of Justice, which prescribes the fulfilment of natural and normal expectations. How then shall we determine what these are? The method by which we commonly ascertain them seems to be the following. We form the conception of an average or normal man, and consider what expectations he would form under the circumstances, inferring this from the beliefs and expectations which men generally entertain under similar circumstances. We refer, therefore, to the customary use of language, and customary tacit understandings current among persons, in the particular relations in which promiser and promisee stand. Such customary interpretations and understandings are of course not obligatory upon persons entering into an engagement: but they constitute a standard which we think we may presume to be known to all men, and to be accepted by them, except in so far as it is explicitly rejected. If one of the parties to an engagement has deviated from this common standard without giving express notice, we think it right that he should suffer any loss that may result from the misunderstanding. In legal contracts the usage of words has often by judicial interpretation been fixed and hardened into a signification very different from the ordinary: still, both parties are by law supposed to know this and to have used words accordingly. This criterion then is generally applicable: but if custom is ambiguous or shifting it cannot be applied; and then the just claims of the parties become a problem, the solution of which is very difficult, if not strictly indeterminate.

So far we have supposed that the promiser can choose his own words, and that if the promisee finds them ambiguous he can get them modified, or (what comes to the same thing) explained, by the promiser. But we have now to observe that in the case of promises made to the community, as a condition of obtaining some office or emolument, a certain unalterable form of words has to be used if the promise is made at all. Here the difficulties of moral interpretation are much increased. It may be said, indeed, that the promise ought to be interpreted in the sense in which its terms are understood by the community: and, no doubt, if their usage is quite uniform and unambiguous, this rule of interpretation is sufficiently obvious and simple. But since words are often used in different ways by different members of the same society, and especially with different degrees of strictness and laxity, it often happens that a promise to the community cannot strictly be said to be understood in any one sense: the question therefore arises, whether the promiser is bound to keep it in the sense in which it will be most commonly interpreted, or whether he may select any of its possible meanings. And if the formula is one of some antiquity, it is further questioned, whether it ought to be interpreted in the sense which its words would now generally bear, or in that which they bore when it was drawn up, or, if they were then ambiguous, in the sense which appears to have been attached to them by the government that imposed the promise. On all these points it is difficult to elicit any clear view from Common Sense. And the difficulty is increased by the fact that there are usually strong inducements to make these formal engagements, which cause even tolerably conscientious persons to take them in a strained and unnatural sense. When this has been done continually by many persons, a new general understanding grows up as to the meaning of the engagements: sometimes they come to be regarded as 'mere forms,' or, if they do not reach this point of degradation, they are at least understood in a sense differing indefinitely from their original one. The question then arises, how far this process of gradual illegitimate relaxation or perversion can modify the moral obligation of the promise for a thoroughly conscientious person. It seems clear that when the process is complete, we are right in adopting the new understanding as far as Good Faith is concerned, even if it palpably conflicts with the natural meaning of language; although it is always desirable in such cases that the form of the promise should be changed to correspond with the changed substance. Unfortunately, the process rarely is complete: there is almost always a portion of the community which understands the engagement in the original strict sense: very often the new understanding is half-esoteric, and confined to the minority of persons whose attention is especially drawn to the subject. Here, probably, most professed moralists would say that we are bound not to aid the process of illegitimate relaxation or alteration, though we may avail ourselves of its results when it is absolutely complete: but it seems doubtful whether we can give this as the decision of Common Sense.

To sum up: we seem able to state it as a generally accepted principle that a promise, express or tacit, is binding, if made by an individual, if the promiser has a clear belief as to the sense in which it was understood by the promisee, and if the latter is still in a position to grant release from it, but unwilling to do so, if it was not obtained by force or fraud, if it does not conflict with definite prior obligations, if we do not believe that its fulfilment will be harmful to the promisee, or will inflict a disproportionate sacrifice on the promiser, and if circumstances have not materially changed since it was made. For the principle thus qualified we may claim a clear *consensus*: but if any of the qualifications be omitted, the *consensus* seems to become evanescent, and our common moral perceptions fall into obscurity and disagreement.

CHAPTER VII.

THE CLASSIFICATION OF DUTIES.—VERACITY.

§ 1. It may easily seem that when we have discussed Benevolence, Justice, and the observance of Law and Contract, we have included in our view the whole sphere of social duty, and that whatever other maxims we find accepted by Common Sense must be subordinate to the principles which we have been trying to define.

For whatever we owe definitely to our fellow-men, besides the observance of special contracts, and of positive Law, seems —at least by a slight extension of common usage—to be naturally included under Justice: while the more indefinite obligations which we recognize seem to correspond to the goodwill which we think ought to exist among all members of the human family, together with the stronger affections appropriate to special relations and circumstances. And hence it may be thought that the best way of treating the subject would have been to divide Duty generally into Social and Self-regarding, and again to subdivide the former branch into the heads which I have discussed one by one; afterwards adding such minor details of duty as have obtained special names and distinct recognition. And this is perhaps the proper place to explain why I did not adopt this course. The division of duties into Social and Self-regarding, though obvious, and acceptable enough as a rough *primâ facie* classification, does not on closer examination seem exactly appropriate to the Intuitional Method. For these titles naturally suggest that the happiness or well-being, of the agent or of others, is always the end and final determinant of right action: whereas the Intuitional doctrine is, that at least certain kinds of conduct are prescribed absolutely, without reference to their ulterior consequences. And if a more general meaning be given to the terms, and by Social duties we understand those which consist in the production of certain effects upon others, while in the Self-regarding we aim at producing certain effects upon ourselves, the division is still an unsuitable one. For these consequences are not clearly recognized in the enunciation of common rules of morality: and in many cases we produce marked effects both on ourselves and on others, and it is not easy to say which (in the view of Common Sense) are most important: and again, this principle of division would sometimes make it necessary to cut in two the class of duties prescribed under some common notion; as the same rule may govern both our social and our solitary conduct. Take, for example, Courage. It seems clear that the prominence given to this Virtue in historic systems of morality has been due to the great social importance that must always attach to it, so long as communities of men are continually called upon to fight for their existence and well-being: but still the quality of bravery is the same essentially, whether it be exhibited for selfish or social ends.

It is no doubt true that when we examine with a view to definition the kinds of conduct commended or prescribed in any list of Virtues commonly recognized, we find, to a great extent, that the maxims we obtain are not absolute and independent: that the quality denoted by our term is only praiseworthy in so far as it promotes individual or general welfare, and becomes blameworthy—though remaining in other respects the same—when it operates adversely to these ends. We have already noticed this result in one or two instances, and it will be illustrated at length in the following chapters. But though this is the case to a great extent, it is not so altogether: and the exceptions are, for our present purpose, of special importance, because specially characteristic of the method that we call Intuitionism.

One of the most important of these exceptions is Veracity: and the affinity in certain respects of this duty—in spite of fundamental differences—to the duty of Good Faith or Fidelity to Promises renders it convenient to examine the two in immediate succession. Under either head a certain correspondence between words and facts is prescribed: and hence the questions that arise when we try to make the maxims precise are somewhat similar in both cases. For example, just as the duty of Good Faith did not lie in conforming our acts to the *admissible* meaning of certain words[1], but to the meaning which we knew to be put on them by the promisee; so the duty of Truthspeaking is not to utter words which *might*, according to common usage, produce in other minds beliefs corresponding to our own, but words which we believe will have this effect on the persons whom we address. And this is usually a very simple matter, as the natural effect of language is to convey our beliefs to other men, and we commonly know quite well whether we are doing this or not. A certain difficulty arises, as in the case of promises, from the use of set forms imposed either by law or by custom; to which most of the discussion of the similar difficulty in the preceding chapter applies *mutatis mutandis*. In the case of formulæ imposed by law—such (*e.g.*) as declarations of religious belief—it is doubtful whether we are to understand the terms in any sense which they commonly bear, or *ex animo imponentis*; and again, a difficulty is created by the gradual degradation or perversion of their meaning, which results from the strong inducements offered for their general acceptance; for thus they are continually strained and stretched until a new general understanding seems gradually to grow up as to the meaning of certain phrases; and it is continually disputed whether we may veraciously use the phrases in this new signification. A similar process continually alters the meaning of conventional expressions current in polite society. When a man declares that he 'has great pleasure in accepting' a vexatious invitation, or is 'the obedient servant' of one whom he regards as an inferior, he uses phrases which were probably once deceptive. If they are so no longer, Common Sense condemns as over-scrupulous the refusal to use them where it is customary to do so. But Common Sense seems doubtful and perplexed where the process

---

[1] The case where set forms are used being the *exceptio probans regulam*.

of degradation is incomplete, and there are still persons who may be deceived: as by the reply that one is 'not at home' to an inconvenient visitor.

However, apart from the use of conventional phrases, the rule 'to speak the truth' is not generally difficult of application in conduct. And many moralists have regarded this, from its simplicity and definiteness, as a quite unexceptionable instance of an ethical axiom. I think, however, that patient reflection will shew that this view is scarcely confirmed by the Common Sense of mankind.

§ 2. In the first place, it does not seem clearly agreed whether Veracity is an absolute and independent duty, or a special application of some higher principle. We find (*e.g.*) that Kant regards it as a duty owed to oneself to speak the truth, because 'a lie is an abandonment or, as it were, annihilation of the dignity of man.' And this seems to be the view in which lying is prohibited by the Code of Honour, except that it is not thought (by men of honour as such) that the dignity of man is impaired by *any* lying: but only that lying for selfish ends, especially under the influence of fear, is mean and base. In fact there seem to be circumstances under which the Code of Honour prescribes lying. Here, however, it may be said to be plainly divergent from the morality of Common Sense. Still, the latter does not seem to tell us clearly whether truth-speaking is absolutely a duty, needing no further justification: or whether it is rather a general right of each man to have truth spoken to him by his fellows, which right however may be forfeited or suspended under certain circumstances. Just as each man is thought to have a natural right to personal security generally, but not if he is himself attempting to injure others in life and property: so if we may even kill in defence of ourselves and others, it seems strange if we may not lie, if lying will defend us better. And again, just as the orderly and systematic slaughter which we call war is thought perfectly right under certain circumstances, though painful and revolting: so in the word-contests of the law-courts, the lawyer is commonly held to be justified in lying within strict rules and limits: for an advocate is thought to be over-scrupulous who refuses to say what he knows to be false, if he is instructed to say it[1]. Again, where deception is designed to benefit the person deceived, Common Sense seems to concede that it may sometimes be right: for example, most persons would not hesitate to speak falsely to an invalid, if this seemed the only way of concealing facts that might produce a dangerous shock: nor do I perceive that any one shrinks from telling fictions to children, on matters upon which it is thought well that they should not know the truth. But if the lawfulness of benevolent deception in any case be admitted, I do not see how we can decide when and how far it is admissible, except by considerations of expediency; that is, by weighing the gain of any particular deception against the imperilment of mutual confidence involved in any violation of truth. The much argued question of religious deception ('pious fraud') naturally suggests itself here. It seems clear, however, that Common Sense now pronounces against the broad rule, that falsehoods may rightly be told in the interests of religion. But there is a subtler form in which the same principle is still maintained by moral persons. It is sometimes said that the most important truths of religion cannot be conveyed into the minds of ordinary men, except by being enclosed, as it were, in a shell of fiction; so that by relating such fictions as if they were facts, we are really performing an act of substantial veracity[2].

Reflecting upon this argument, we see that it is not after all so clear wherein Veracity consists. For from the beliefs immediately communicated by any set of affirmations inferences are naturally drawn, and we may clearly foresee that they will be drawn. And though commonly we intend that both the beliefs immediately communicated and the inferences drawn from them should be true, and a person who always aims at this is praised as candid and sincere; still we find relaxation of the

---

[1] It can hardly be said that the advocate merely *reports* the false affirmations of others: since the whole force of his pleading depends upon his adopting them and working them up into a view of the case which, for the time at least, he appears to hold.

[2] While I write this (Aug., Sept., 1873) a certain religious school is publicly justifying itself in the manner above indicated for solemnly affirming a belief in the Fourth Commandment. It is urged that we may say that God created the world in 6 days and rested on the 7th, meaning that 1 : 6 is the divinely ordered proportion between rest and labour.

rule prescribing this intention claimed in two different ways by at least respectable sections of opinion. For first, as was just now observed, it is sometimes held that if a conclusion is true and important, and cannot be satisfactorily communicated otherwise, we may lead the mind of the hearer to it by means of fictitious premises. But the exact reverse of this is perhaps a commoner view: viz. that it is only an absolute duty to make our actual affirmations true: for it is said that though the ideal condition of human converse involves perfect sincerity and candour, and we ought to rejoice in exhibiting these virtues where we can, still in in our actual world concealment is frequently necessary to the well-being of society, and may be legitimately effected by any means short of actual falsehood. Thus it is not uncommonly said that in defence of a secret we may not *lie*[1], *i.e.* produce directly beliefs contrary to fact: but we may "turn a question aside," *i.e.* produce indirectly, by natural inference from our answer, a negatively false belief: or "throw the inquirer on a wrong scent," *i.e.* produce similarly a positively false belief. These two methods of concealment are known respectively as *suppressio veri* and *suggestio falsi*, and many think them legitimate under certain circumstances: while others say that if deception is to be practised at all, it is mere formalism to object to any one mode of effecting it more than another.

On the whole, then, reflection seems to shew that the rule of Veracity, as commonly accepted, cannot be elevated into a definite moral axiom: for there is no real agreement as to how far we are bound to impart true beliefs to others: and while it is contrary to Common Sense to exact absolute candour under all circumstances, we yet find no self-evident secondary principle, clearly defining when it is not to be exacted.

§ 3. There is, however, one method of exhibiting *à priori* the absolute duty of Truth, which we must not overlook; as, if it be valid, it would seem that the exceptions and qualifications above mentioned have been only admitted by Common Sense from inadvertence and shallowness of thought.

It is said that if it were once generally understood that lies were justifiable under certain circumstances, it would imme-

---

[1] Cf. Whewell, *Elements of Morality*, Book II. c. xv. § 299.

diately become quite useless to tell the lies, because no one would believe them; and that the moralist cannot lay down a rule which, if generally accepted, would be suicidal. To this there seem to be three answers. In the first place it is not necessarily an evil that men's confidence in each other's assertions should, *under certain peculiar circumstances*, be impaired or destroyed: it may even be the very result which we should most desire to produce: (*e.g.*) it is obviously a most effective protection for legitimate secrets that it should be universally understood and expected that those who ask questions which they have no right to ask will have lies told them: nor, again, should we be restrained from pronouncing it lawful to meet deceit with deceit, merely by the fear of impairing the security which rogues now derive from the veracity of honest men. No doubt the ultimate result of general unveracity under the circumstances would be a state of things in which such falsehoods would no longer be told: but unless this ultimate result is undesirable, the prospect of it does not constitute a reason why the falsehoods should not be told so long as they are useful. But, secondly, since the beliefs of men in general are not formed purely on rational grounds, experience shews that unveracity may long remain partially effective under circumstances where it is generally understood to be legitimate. We see this in the case of the law-courts. For though jurymen are perfectly aware that it is considered the duty of an advocate to state as plausibly as possible whatever he has been instructed to say on behalf of any criminal he may defend, still a skilful pleader can often produce an impression that he sincerely believes his client to be innocent: and it remains a question of casuistry how far this kind of hypocrisy is justifiable. But, finally, it cannot be assumed as certain that it is never right to act upon a principle of which the universal application would be an undoubted evil. This assumption may seem to be involved in what was previously admitted as an ethical axiom, 'that what is right for me must be right for all similar persons under similar circumstances[1].' But reflection will shew that there is a special case within the range of the axiom in which the universal 'all' is necessarily particularized into 'some': *i.e.*

[1] Cf. c. i., § 3.

where *my* circumstances include (1) the knowledge that the rule is not universally accepted; and (2) the conviction that my act will not tend to make it so, to any extent worth considering. And it can hardly be said that these conditions are impossible: at least so long as clear and consistent views of morality are only attained by a small minority in any society, and casuistical debates are for the most part confined within the same limited sphere. Hence the argument we are discussing certainly lacks demonstrative cogency: though it undoubtedly directs our attention to an important danger of unveracity, which constitutes a strong—but not formally conclusive—utilitarian ground for speaking the truth.

NOTE.—Mr Stephen (*Science of Ethics*, ch. v. § 33) explains the exceptions to the rule of truth-speaking as follows.

"The rule, 'Lie not,' is the external rule, and corresponds approximately to the internal rule, 'Be trustworthy.' Cases occur where the rules diverge, and in such cases it is the internal rule which is morally approved. Truthfulness is the rule because in the vast majority of cases we trust a man in so far as he speaks the truth; in the exceptional cases, the mutual confidence would be violated when the truth, not when the lie, is spoken."

This explanation seems to me for several reasons inadequate. (1) If we may sometimes lie to defend the life or secrets of others, it is paradoxical to say that we may not do so to defend our own; but a falsehood in selfdefence obviously cannot be justified as an application of the maxim "be trustworthy." (2) Even when the falsehood is in legitimate defence of others against attacks, we cannot say that the speaker manifests "trustworthiness" without qualification; for the deceived assailant trusted his veracity, otherwise he would not have been deceived: the question therefore is under what circumstances the confidence of A that I shall speak the truth may legitimately be disappointed in order not to disappoint the confidence of B that I shall defend his life and honour. This question Mr Stephen's explanation does not in any way aid us to answer.

CHAPTER VIII.

OTHER SOCIAL DUTIES AND VIRTUES.

§ 1. When we proceed to inquire how far the minor social duties and virtues recognized by Common Sense appear on examination to be anything more than special applications of the Benevolence—general or particular—discussed in chap. iv., the department of duty which most prominently claims our attention, is that which deals with the existence, and determines the legitimacy, of feelings antithetical to the benevolent.

For it seems that malevolent affections are as natural and normal to man as the benevolent: not indeed in the same sense normal, that is not at all times and towards all men (for man seems to have naturally some kindly feeling for any fellow-man, when there is no special cause operating to make him love or hate; though this is obscured and counteracted in the lower stages of social development by the habitual hostility between strange tribes and races): but still as arising from causes that continually occur, and, in the main, exemplifying a psychological law analogous to that by which the growth of benevolent feelings is explained. For just as we are apt to love those who are the cause of pleasure to us whether by voluntary benefits or otherwise: so by strict analogy we naturally dislike those who have done us harm, either consciously from malevolence or mere selfishness, or even unconsciously, as when another man is an obstacle to our attainment of a much-desired end. Thus we naturally feel ill-will to a rival who deprives us of an object of competition: and so in persons in whom the desire of superiority is strong, a certain dislike of any one who is more successful or prosperous than themselves is easily aroused: and however repulsive to our moral sense, seems as natural as any other malevolent emotion. And it is to be observed that each of the elements into which we can analyse malevolent affection finds its exact counterpart in the analysis of the benevolent: as the former includes a dislike of the presence of its object and a desire to inflict pain on it, and also a capacity of deriving pleasure from the pain thus inflicted[1].

If now we ask how far indulgence of malevolent emotions is right and proper, the answer of Common Sense is not easy to formulate. For some would say broadly that they ought to be repressed altogether or as far as possible. And no doubt we blame all envy (though sometimes to exclude it altogether requires a magnanimity which we praise): and we regard as virtues or natural excellences the *good-humour* which prevents one from feeling even pain to a material extent, much less resentment, from trifling annoyances inflicted by others, the *meekness* which does not resent even graver injuries, the *mildness* and *gentleness* which refrain from retaliating them, the *placability* which accords forgiveness rapidly and easily, and the *mercy* which spares even deserved punishment. And yet most moralists have allowed instinctive resentment for wrong to be legitimate and proper: and we all think that punishment ought to be inflicted for offences, and also that there is a righteous anger and a virtuous indignation.

As regards punishment we have already noticed the change that has taken place in the moral view of mankind. What seems now to be commonly held is this: that punishment is properly and intrinsically due in return for wrong-doing, but that the individual wronged ought not to take pleasure in inflicting it and ought not, generally speaking, to inflict it him-

---

[1] It is to be observed that men derive pleasure from the pains and losses of others, in various ways, without the specific emotion which I distinguish as malevolent affection: either (1) from the sense of power exercised—which explains much of the wanton cruelty of schoolboys, despots, &c.—or (2) from a sense of their own superiority or security in contrast with the failures and struggles of others, or (3) even merely from the excitement sympathetically caused by the manifestation or representation of any strong feeling in others; a real tragedy is interesting in the same way as a fictitious one. But these facts, though psychologically interesting, present no important ethical problems; since no one doubts that pain ought not to be inflicted from such motives as these.

self, but to leave it to society to enforce; and if in any case he must himself punish, he ought to do so as the organ of society, or at any rate to punish the act as abstractly wrong and not requite it as injury done to himself. And in accordance with this view it is stated generally that anger must be directed always against wrong acts as such, and not against the agent: for though the anger may prompt us to punish him, it ought never to overcome our kindly feeling towards him. And certainly if this state of mind is possible, it seems the simplest reconciliation of the general maxim of Benevolence with the admitted duty of inflicting punishment.

But some think that to retain a genuine kindly feeling towards a man, while we are gratifying a strong impulse of aversion to his acts by inflicting pain on him, requires a subtle complexity of emotion too far out of the reach of ordinary men to be prescribed as a duty: and that we must allow as right and proper a temporary suspension of benevolence towards wrong-doers until they have been punished. And others go even further and say that this is required in the interests of society, since the mere desire to realize Justice will not practically be strong enough to repress offences: and that it is as serious a mistake to attempt to substitute this for natural resentment as it would be to substitute prudence for natural appetite in eating and drinking, or mere dutifulness for filial affection. Others, again, make a distinction between Instinctive and Deliberate Resentment: saying that the former is legitimate in so far as it is required for the self-defence of individuals and the repression of mutual violence; but that deliberate resentment is not similarly needed, for if we act deliberately we can act from a better motive[1].

And even the rule of external duty, in respect of the actual infliction of punishment, is not easy to define. For it was said that punishment ought generally to be left to society (acting through its regular machinery of law-courts, judges, magistrates, &c.): but there are some acute injuries to individuals

---

[1] This last view does not differ much from Butler's (see Sermon VIII. *Upon Resentment*): but he recognizes that deliberate resentment "has in fact a good influence upon the affairs of the world;" though "it were much to be wished that men would act from a better principle".

which the law does not punish at all, or not adequately, or not in time; and there is no clear agreement as to our duty in relation to these. For the Christian code seems to prescribe a complete and absolute forgiveness of such offences, and many Christians in all periods of Christianity have endeavoured to carry out this rule: the majority, however, appear to understand these prescriptions as really relating to malevolent feeling and not to actual punishment for wrong. Others, again, seem to hold that we ought to bear without retaliation any injuries or insults inflicted on ourselves, but that we may rightly retaliate on behalf of friends or relatives who cannot defend themselves. Most, however, would probably say that acts of retaliation were permitted to private persons, not exactly as punishments, but in self-defence, and for the sake of others whom impunity might encourage the wrong-doer to attack. So that the question how far the precepts of Christianity are to be practically carried out seems to be determined by considerations of expediency; we are to forgive except when forgiveness is likely to be attended with harmful consequences.

On the whole we may perhaps sum up by saying that a superficial view of the matter naturally leads us to condemn sweepingly all malevolent feelings and the acts to which they prompt, as contrary to the general duty of benevolence: but that the common sense of reflective persons recognizes the necessity of relaxing this rule in the interests of society: only it is not clear as to the limits or principles of this relaxation, though inclined to let it be determined by considerations of expediency.

§ 2. The remaining virtues that are clearly and exclusively social, will be easily seen to have no independent maxims; the conduct in which they are respectively realized being merely the fulfilment, under special conditions, of the rules already discussed. We need not, then, enter upon an exhaustive examination of these minor virtues—for it is not our object to frame a complete glossary of ethical terms—: but for illustration's sake it may be well to discuss one or two of them; and I will select for examination Liberality with its cognate notions, partly on account of the prominence that it has had in the earlier ages of thought, and partly because of a certain complexity in the feelings with which it is usually regarded. Considered as a Virtue, Liberality seems to be merely Benevolence, as exhibited in the particular service of giving money, beyond the limits of strict duty as commonly recognized:—for in so far as it can be called a duty to be liberal, it is because in the performance of the more or less indefinite duties enumerated in chap. iv. we do not like exactness to be sought; a certain excess is needful if the duty is to be well done. And perhaps in the case of the poor this graceful excess is excluded by prudence: for though a poor man might make a great sacrifice in a small gift we should call this generous but scarcely liberal; Liberality appears to require an external abundance in the gift even more than a self-sacrificing disposition. It seems therefore to be possible only to the rich: and, as I have hinted, in the admiration commonly accorded to it there seems to be mingled an element which is not properly moral. For we are all apt to admire power, and we recognize the latent power of wealth gracefully exhibited in a certain degree of careless profusion when the object is to give happiness to others. Indeed the vulgar admire the same carelessness as manifested even in selfish luxury.

The sphere of Liberality, then, lies generally in the fulfilment of the indefinite duties of Benevolence. But there is a certain borderground between Justice and Benevolence where it is especially shewn; namely, in the full satisfaction of all customary expectations, even when indefinite and uncertain; as (*e.g.*) in the remuneration of services, in so far as this is governed by custom; and even where it is left entirely to free contract, and therefore naturally determined by haggling and bargaining (as market value generally), it is characteristic of a liberal man to avoid this haggling and to give somewhat higher remuneration than the other party might be induced to take, and similarly to take for his own services a somewhat lower payment than he might persuade the other to give. And again, since laws and promises and especially tacit understandings are sometimes doubtful and ambiguous, a liberal man will in such cases unhesitatingly adopt the interpretation which is least in his own favour, and pay the most that he can by any fairminded person be thought to owe, and exact the least that reasonably can be thought to be due to himself: that is, if the margin be, relatively to his resources, not considerable[1]. And of a man who does the opposite of all this we predicate Meanness; this being the vice antithetical to Liberality. Here again there seems no place for this particular vice if the amount at stake be considerable; for then we think it not mean to exact one's own rights to the full, and worse than mean to refuse another what he ought to have; in fact in such cases we think that any indefiniteness as to rights should be practically removed by the decision of a judge or arbitrator. The vice of meanness then is, we may say, bounded on the side of vice by injustice: the mean man is blamed not for violation of Justice, but because he chooses a trifling gain to himself rather than the avoidance of disappointment to others. And here, again, it should be observed, an element not strictly moral is included in the common disapprobation of meanness. For, as we have seen, a certain carelessness of money is admired as a sign of power and superiority: and the opposite habit is a symbol of inferiority. The mean man then is apt to be despised as having the bad taste to shew this symbol needlessly preferring a little gain to the respect of his fellow-men.

Meanness, however, has a wider sphere than Liberality, and refers not merely to the taking or refusing of money, but to taking advantages generally: in this wider sense the opposite virtue is Generosity.

In so far as the sphere of Generosity coincides with that of Liberality, the former seems partly to transcend the latter, partly to refer more to feelings than to outward acts, and to imply a completer triumph of unselfish over selfish impulses. In the wider sense it is strikingly exhibited in conflict and competition of all kinds. Here it is sometimes called Chivalry. Reflection shews us that the essence of this beautiful virtue is the realization of Benevolence under circumstances which make it peculiarly difficult and therefore peculiarly admirable. For Generosity or Chivalry towards adversaries or competitors seems to consist in shewing as much kindness and regard for their well-being as is compatible with the ends

---

[1] If the amount at stake is such as to constitute a real sacrifice, the conduct seems to be more than liberal, and (unless blamed as extravagant) is rather praised as generous or highminded.

and conditions of conflict: one prominent form of this being the endeavour to realize ideal justice in these conditions, not merely by observing all the rules and tacit understandings under which the conflict is conducted, but by resigning even accidental advantages. This latter is not of course considered a strict duty: nor is there even any agreement as to how far it is right and virtuous; for what some would praise and approve, others would regard as quixotic and extravagant.

To sum up, we may say that the terms Liberality and Generosity, so far as they are strictly ethical, denote the virtue of Benevolence (perhaps including Justice to some extent) as exhibited in special ways and under special conditions. And the examination of the other minor social virtues would evidently lead to similar general results: though it might not always be easy to agree on their definitions.

CHAPTER IX.

SELF-REGARDING VIRTUES.

§ 1. IN chap. iii. we noticed the difficulty of defining Wisdom from the point of view adopted in the present treatise: because Wisdom is the faculty and habit of choosing the best means to the best ends, and in different methods of Ethics different ends are regarded as absolutely best. As (*e.g.*) in Egoistic Hedonism (cf. Book III.) the end of Self-love is so regarded: whereas according to the present method it is held that Self-interest (or what may appear such) must always give way to Duty. Still, within the limits fixed by other duties, Common Sense considers, I think[1], that it is a duty to seek our own happiness, except in so far as we can promote the welfare of others by sacrificing it. This "due concern about our own interest or happiness" may be called the Duty of Prudence. It should, however, be observed that—since it is less evident that men do not adequately desire their own greatest good, than that their efforts are not sufficiently well directed to its attainment,—in conceiving Prudence as a Virtue or Excellence, attention is often fixed almost exclusively on its intellectual side. Thus regarded, Prudence may be said to be merely Wisdom made more definite by the acceptance of Self-interest

---

[1] Kant argues (*Metaph. of Ethics* § iv.) that as every one "inevitably wills" means to promote his own happiness this cannot be regarded as a duty. But, as I have before urged (Book I. ch. iv. § 1) a man does not "inevitably will" to do what he believes will be most conducive to his own *greatest* happiness.

The view in the text is that of Butler (Diss. 'Of the nature of Virtue'); who admits that "nature has not given us so sensible a disapprobation of imprudence and folly as of falsehood, injustice and cruelty"; but points out that such sensible disapprobation is for various reasons less needed in the former case.

as its sole ultimate end: the tendency to calculate carefully the best means to the attainment of our own interest, and resist all irrational impulses which may tend to perturb our calculations or prevent us from acting on them.

§ 2. There are, however, current notions of particular virtues, which would commonly be called Self-regarding; but yet with regard to which it is not quite clear whether they are merely particular applications of Prudence, or whether they have independent maxims. Of these Temperance, one of the four cardinal virtues anciently recognized, seems the most prominent. In its ordinary use, Temperance is the habit of controlling the principal appetites (or desires which have an immediate corporeal cause). The habit of moderating and controlling our desires generally is recognized by Common Sense as useful and desirable, but with less distinctness and emphasis.

All are agreed that our appetites need control: but in order to establish a maxim of Temperance, we have to determine within what limits, on what principle, and to what end they ought to be controlled. Now in the case of the appetites for food, drink, sleep, stimulants, &c., no one doubts that bodily health and vigour is the end naturally subserved by their gratification, and that the latter ought to be checked whenever it tends to defeat this end (including in the notion of health the most perfect condition of the mental faculties, so far as this appears to depend upon the general state of the body). And, further, the indulgence of a bodily appetite is manifestly imprudent, if it involves the loss of any greater gratification of whatever kind: and wrong if it interferes with the performance of duties; though it is perhaps doubtful how far this latter indulgence would commonly be condemned as 'intemperance.'

Some, however, deduce from the obvious truth, that the maintenance of bodily health is the chief natural end of the appetites, a more rigid rule of restraint, and one that goes beyond prudence. They say that this end ought to fix not only the negative but the positive limit of indulgence; that the pleasure derived from the gratification of appetite should never be sought *per se* (even when it does not impair health, or interfere with duty, or with a greater pleasure of a different kind);

but only in so far as such gratification is positively conducive to health. When we consider to what a marked divergence from the usual habits of the moral rich this principle would lead, we might be disposed to say that it is clearly at variance with Common Sense: but it is undeniable that it often meets with verbal assent.

There is, again, a third and intermediate view which accepts the principle that the gratification of appetite is not to be sought for its own sake, but admits other ends as legitimate besides the mere maintenance of health. *E.g.* Whewell[1] says, "The appétites…are to be indulged as subservient to the support of life, strength, and cheerfulness, and the cultivation of the social affections." We see that this rule need not be practically very austere, as there is scarcely any sensual pleasure that may not promote cheerfulness. And I think that some such principle is more or less consciously held by many. We certainly find that solitary indulgence in the pleasures of the table is very frequently regarded with something like moral aversion. And the banquets which are given and enjoyed by moral persons, are vaguely supposed to have for their end not the common indulgence of sensual appetites, but the promotion of conviviality and conversational entertainment. For it is generally believed that the enjoyment in common of a luxurious meal developes social emotions, and also stimulates the faculties of wit and humour and lively colloquy in general; and feasts which are obviously not contrived with a view to such convivial and colloquial gratifications seem to be condemned by refined persons. Still it would be going too far to state, as a maxim supported by Common Sense in respect of sensual pleasures generally, that they are never to be sought except they positively promote those of a higher kind.

§ 3. In the last section we have spoken chiefly of the appetites for food and drink. It is, however, in the case of the appetite of sex that the regulation morally prescribed most clearly and definitely transcends that of mere prudence: which is indicated by the special notion of Purity or Chastity[2].

---

[1] *Elements of Morality*, Bk. II. c. x.
[2] The notion of Chastity is nearly equivalent to that of Purity, only somewhat more external and superficial.

At first sight it may perhaps appear that the regulation of the sexual appetite prescribed by the received moral code merely confines its indulgence within the limits of the union sanctioned by law: only that here, as the natural impulse is peculiarly powerful and easily excited, it is especially necessary to prohibit any acts, internal as well as external, that tend even indirectly to the transgression of these limits. And this is to a great extent true: still on reflection it will appear, I think, that our common notion of purity implies a standard independent of law: for, first, conformity to this does not necessarily secure purity: and secondly, all illegitimate sexual intercourse is not thought to be impure[1], and it is only by inadvertence that the two notions are sometimes confounded. But it is not very clear what this standard is. For when we interrogate the moral consciousness of mankind, we seem to find two views, a stricter and a laxer, analogous to the two interpretations of Temperance last noticed. It is agreed that the sexual appetite ought never to be indulged for the sake of the sensual gratification merely, but as a means to some higher end: but some say that the propagation of the species is the only legitimate, as it is obviously the primary natural, end: while others regard the development of mutual affection in a union designed to be permanent as an end perfectly admissible and right. I need not point out that the practical difference between the two views is considerable; so that this question is one which it is necessary to raise and decide. But it may be observed that any attempt to lay down minute and detailed rules on this subject seems to be condemned by Common Sense as tending to defeat the end of purity; as such minuteness of moral legislation invites men in general to exercise their thoughts on this subject to an extent which is practically dangerous[2].

I ought to point out that the Virtue of Purity is certainly not merely self-regarding, and is therefore properly out of place

[1] In so far as mere illegitimacy of union is conceived to be directly and specially prohibited, and not merely from considerations of Prudence and Benevolence, it is regarded as a violation of Order rather than of Purity.

[2] It was partly owing to the serious oversight of not perceiving that Purity itself forbids too minute a system of rules for the observance of purity that the mediæval Casuistry fell into extreme, and on the whole undeserved, disrepute.

in this chapter: but the convenience of discussing it along with Temperance has led me to take it out of its natural order. Some, however, would go further, and say that it ought to be treated as a distinctly social virtue: for the propagation and rearing of children is one of the most important of social interests: and they would maintain that Purity merely connotes a sentiment protective of these important functions, supporting the rules which we consider necessary to secure their proper performance. But it seems clear that, though Common Sense undoubtedly recognizes this tendency of the sentiment of Purity to maintain the best possible provision for the continuance of the human race, it still does not regard that as the fundamental point in the definition of this rule of duty, and the sole criterion in deciding whether acts do or do not violate the rule.

There seem to be no similar difficulties or questions with respect to other desires. We recognize, no doubt, a general duty of self-control: but this is merely as a means to the end of acting rationally (whatever our interpretation of rational action may be); it only prescribes that we should yield to no impulse which prompts us to act in antagonism to ends or rules deliberately accepted. Further, there is a certain tendency among moral persons to the ascetic opinion that the gratification of merely sensual impulse is in itself somewhat objectionable: but this view does not seem to be taken by Common Sense in particular cases;—we do not (*e.g.*) commonly condemn the most intense enjoyment of muscular exercise, or warmth, or bathing. Indeed, the only other case, besides that of the appetites above discussed, in which the Common Sense of our age and country seems even tempted to regard as admirable the mere repression of natural impulses, is that of the promptings of pain and danger. We shall have occasion to discuss this in the next chapter.

CHAPTER X.

COURAGE, HUMILITY, &c.

§ 1. BESIDES the Virtue of Purity, which we found it convenient to discuss in the last chapter, there remain one or two prominent excellences of character which do not seem to be commonly admired and inculcated with any distinct reference either to individual or general happiness; and which, though in most cases obviously conducive to one or other of these ends, sometimes seem to influence conduct in a direction at variance with them.

For example, Courage is a quality which excites general admiration, whether it is shewn in self-defence, or in aiding others, or even when we do not see any benefit resulting from the particular exhibition of it. Again, in Christian societies, Humility (if believed sincere) often obtains unqualified praise, in spite of the loss that may evidently result from a man's underrating his own abilities. It will be well, therefore, to examine how far in either case we can elicit a clear and independent maxim defining the conduct commended under each of these notions.

To begin with Courage. We generally denote by this term a disposition to face danger of any kind without shrinking. We sometimes also call those who bear pain unflinchingly courageous: but this quality of character we more commonly distinguish as Fortitude. Now it seems plain that if we seek for a definition of *strict duty*, as commonly recognized, under the head either of Courage or of Fortitude, we can find none that does not involve a reference to other maxims and ends. For no one would say that it is our *duty* to face danger or to bear avoidable pain generally, but only if it meets us in the course of duty[1]. And even this needs further qualification: for as regards such duties as those (*e g.*) of general Benevolence, it would be commonly allowed that the agent's pain and danger are to be taken into account in practically determining their extent: thus one is not bound to attempt to save even the life of another if the risk of losing one's own is very great: and similarly for smaller services. On utilitarian principles it seems clear that we ought to endure any pain for the prevention of manifestly greater pain to another, or the attainment of an equivalent amount of positive good: and that we are bound to run any risk, if the chance of additional benefit to be gained for any one outweighs the chance of loss to ourselves if we fail. But it is doubtful whether the common estimate of the duty of Benevolence could be said to amount quite to this[2].

When, however, we consider Courage as an Excellence rather than a Duty, it seems to hold a more independent position in our moral estimation. And this view corresponds more completely than the other to the common application of the notion: as there are many acts of courage, which are not altogether within the control of the Will, and therefore cannot be regarded as strict duties. For (1) danger is frequently sudden and needs to be met without deliberation, so that our manner of meeting it can only be semi-voluntary. And (2) though naturally timid persons can perhaps with effort control fear as they can anger or appetite, if time be allowed for deliberation, and can prevent it from taking effect in dereliction of duty: still this result is not all that is required for the performance of such courageous acts as need more than ordinary energy—for the energy of the timid virtuous man is liable to be exhausted in the effort to control his fear: *e.g.* in battle he can perhaps stand still to be killed as well as the courageous man, but not charge with the same impetuosity or strike with the same vigour and precision[3].

---

[1] In the case of pain which cannot be avoided we consider that Fortitude will suppress outcries and lamentations: though in so far as these relieve the sufferer without annoying others, the duty seems doubtful.

[2] Cf. *ante*, c. iv. § 4.

[3] The above remarks apply in a less degree to the "moral courage" by which men face the pains and dangers of social disapproval in the performance

So far then as Courage is not completely voluntary, we have to consider whether it is a desirable quality rather than whether we are strictly bound to exhibit it. And here there seems no doubt that we commonly find it morally admirable without reference to any end served by it, and when the dangers which call it forth might be avoided without any dereliction of duty. At the same time we call a man foolhardy who runs unnecessarily into danger beyond a certain degree. Where then is the limit to be fixed? On utilitarian principles we should endeavour to strike as exact a balance as possible between the amount of danger incurred in any case and the probable benefit of cultivating and developing by practice a habit so frequently necessary for the due performance of important duties. This will obviously give a different result for different states of society and different callings and professions; as most people need this instinctive courage less in civilized societies than in semi-barbarous ones, and civilians less than soldiers. Perhaps the instinctive admiration of mankind for acts of daring does not altogether observe this limit: but we may say, I think, that in so far as it attempts to justify itself on reflection, it is commonly in some such way as this; and Common Sense does not seem to point to any limit depending on a different principle.

§ 2. As the Virtue of Courage is prominent in Pagan ethics, and in the Code of Honour which may be regarded as a sort of survival of the pagan view of morality; so Humility especially belongs to the ideal set before mankind by Christianity. The common account, however, of this virtue is somewhat paradoxical. For it is generally said that Humility prescribes a low opinion of our own merits: but if our merits are comparatively high, it seems strange to direct us to have a low opinion of them. It may be replied, that though our merits may be high when compared with those of ordinary men, there are always some to be found superior, and we can compare ourselves with these, and in the extreme case with ideal excellence, of which all fall far short; and that we ought to make this kind of comparison and not the other kind, and contemplate our

of what they believe to be duty: for the adequate accomplishment of such acts depends less on qualities not within the control of the will at any given time.

faults—of which we shall assuredly find a sufficiency—and not our merits. But surely in the most important deliberations which human life offers, in determining what kind of work we shall undertake and to what social functions we shall aspire, we must necessarily compare our qualifications carefully with those of other men, if we are to decide rightly. And it would seem just as irrational to underrate ourselves as to overrate; and though most men are more prone to the latter mistake, there are certainly some rather inclined to the former.

I think that if we reflect carefully on the common judgments in which the notion of Humility is used, we shall find that the quality commonly *praised* under this name (which is not always used eulogistically), is not properly regulative of the opinions we form of ourselves; for here as in other opinions we ought to aim at nothing but Truth: but tends to the repression of two different seductive emotions, one entirely self-regarding and internal, the other relating to others and partly taking effect in social behaviour. The internal duty relates to the emotion of self-admiration, which springs naturally from the contemplation of our own merits, and as it is highly agreeable, prompts to such contemplation. This admiring self-complacency is generally condemned: but not, I think, by an intuition that claims to be ultimate, as it is commonly justified by the reason that such self-admiration, even if well-grounded, tends to check our progress towards higher virtue. The mere fact of our feeling this admiration is thought to be evidence that we have not sufficiently compared ourselves with our ideal, or that our ideal is not sufficiently high: and it is thought to be indispensable to moral progress that we should have a high ideal and should continually contemplate it. At the same time, we obviously need some care in the application of this maxim. For all admit that self-respect is an important auxiliary to right conduct: and moralists continually point to the satisfactions of a good conscience as part of the natural reward which Providence has attached to virtue: yet it is difficult to separate the glow of self-approbation which attends the performance of a virtuous action from the complacent self-consciousness which Humility seems to exclude. Perhaps we may say that the feeling of self-approbation itself is natural and a legitimate pleasure, but that if prolonged and fostered it is liable to impede moral progress: and that what Humility prescribes is such repression of self-satisfaction as will tend on the whole to promote this end. On this view the maxim of Humility is clearly a dependent one: the end to which it is subordinate is progress in Virtue generally. As for such pride and self-satisfaction as are based not on our own conduct and its results, but on external and accidental advantages, these are condemned as involving a false and absurd view as to the nature of real merit.

But we not only take pleasure in our own respect and admiration, but still more, generally speaking, in the respect and admiration of others. The desire for this, again, is held to be to some extent legitimate, and even a valuable aid to morality: but as it is a dangerously seductive impulse, and frequently acts in opposition to duty, it is felt to stand in special need of self-control. Humility, however, does not so much consist in controlling this desire, as in repressing the claim for its satisfaction which we are naturally disposed to make upon others. We are inclined to demand from others 'tokens of respect,' some external symbol of their recognition of our elevated place in the scale of human beings; and to complain if our demands are not granted. Such claims and demands Humility bids us repress. It is thought to be our duty not even to exact, in many cases, the expression of reverence which others are strictly bound to pay. And yet here, again, there is a limit, in the view of Common Sense, at which this quality of behaviour passes over into a fault: for the omission of marks of respect is sometimes an insult which impulses commonly regarded as legitimate and even virtuous (sense of Dignity, Self-respect, Proper Pride, &c.) prompt us to repel. But the ascertainment of this limit involves complex difficulties, and I think it is quite impossible to claim a *consensus* for any mode of determining it.

CHAPTER XI.

REVIEW OF THE MORALITY OF COMMON SENSE.

§ 1. WE have now concluded such detailed examination of the morality of Common Sense as, on the plan laid down in chap. i., it seemed desirable to undertake. We have not discussed all the terms of our common moral vocabulary: but I believe that we have omitted none that are important either in themselves or relatively to our present inquiry. For of those that remain we may fairly say, that they manifestly will not furnish independent maxims: for a slight reflection shews that the conduct designated by them is either prescribed merely as a means to the performance of duties already discussed; or is really identical with the whole or part of some of these, viewed in some special aspect, or perhaps specialized by the addition of some peculiar circumstance or condition.

Let us now pause and survey briefly the process in which we have been engaged, and the results which we have elicited.

We started with admitting the point upon the proof of which moralists have often concentrated their efforts, the existence of apparently independent moral intuitions. It seemed undeniable that men judge acts to be right and wrong in themselves, without consideration of their tendency to produce the agent's happiness or that of others: and indeed without taking their consequences into account at all, except in so far as these are included in the common notion of the act. We saw, however, that in so far as these judgments are passed in particular cases, they seem to involve (at least for the more reflective part of mankind) a reference of the case to some general rule of duty: and that in the frequent cases of doubt or conflict of judgments as to the rightness of any action, appeal is commonly made to such rules or maxims, as the ultimately valid principles of moral cognition. In order, therefore, to throw the Morality of Common Sense into a scientific form, it seemed necessary to obtain as exact a statement as possible of these generally recognized principles. I did not think that I could dispense myself from this task by any summary general argument, based on the unscientific character of common morality. There is no doubt that the moral opinions of ordinary men are in many points loose, shifting, and mutually contradictory, but it does not follow that we may not obtain from this fluid mass of opinion, a deposit of clear and precise principles commanding universal acceptance. The question, whether we can do this or not, seemed to me one which should be put to the test of experiment: and it is partly in order to prepare materials for this experiment that the survey in the preceding eight chapters has been conducted. I have endeavoured to ascertain impartially, by mere reflection on our common moral discourse, what are the general principles or maxims, according to which different kinds of conduct are judged to be right and reasonable in different departments of life. I wish it to be particularly observed, that I have in no case introduced my own views, in so far as I am conscious of their being at all peculiar to myself. My sole object has been to make explicit the implied basis of our common moral reasoning: to formulate the ultimate enunciations of that Conscience or Moral Faculty which is thought to be a possession of ordinary men no less than of philosophers. I now wish to subject the results of this survey to a final examination, in order to decide whether these general formulæ possess the characteristics by which self-evident truths are distinguished from mere opinions.

§ 2. There seem to be four conditions, the complete fulfilment of which would establish an apparently self-evident proposition in the highest degree of certainty attainable: and which must be approximately realized by the premises of our reasoning in any department of enquiry, if that reasoning is to lead us cogently to true conclusions.

I. The terms of the proposition must be clear and precise. The rival originators of modern Methodology, Descartes and

Bacon, vie with each other in the stress that they lay on this point: and the latter's warning against the "notiones male terminatæ" of ordinary thought is peculiarly needed in ethical discussion. In fact my chief business in the preceding survey has been to free the common terms of Ethics, as far as possible, from objection on this score.

II. The self-evidence of the proposition must be ascertained by careful reflection. It is needful to insist on this, because most persons are liable to confound intuitions, on the one hand with mere impressions or impulses, which to careful observation do not present themselves as claiming objective validity; and on the other hand, with mere opinions, to which the familiarity that comes from frequent hearing and repetition often gives an illusory air of self-evidence which attentive reflection disperses. In such cases the Cartesian method of testing the ultimate premises of our reasonings, by asking ourselves if we clearly and distinctly apprehend them to be true, may be of real use; though it does not as Descartes supposed, afford a complete protection against error. A rigorous demand for self-evidence in our premises is a valuable protection against the misleading internal influence of our own irrational impulses: while at the same time it not only distinguishes as inadequate the mere external support of authority and tradition, but also excludes the more subtle and latent effect of these in fashioning our minds to a facile and unquestioning admission of common but unwarranted assumptions.

And we may observe that the application of this test is especially needed in Ethics. For, on the one hand, it cannot be denied that any strong sentiment, however purely subjective, is apt to transform itself into the semblance of an intuition; and it requires careful contemplation to detect the illusion. Whatever we desire we are apt to pronounce desirable: and we are strongly tempted to approve of whatever conduct gives us keen pleasure[1]. And on the other hand, among the rules of conduct to which we customarily conform, there are many which reflection shews to be really derived from some external authority: so that even if their obligation be un-

---

[1] Hence the practical importance of the Formal test of Rightness, on which Kant insists: cf. *ante*, ch. i. § 3.

questionable, it cannot be intuitively ascertained. This is of course the case with the Positive Law of the community to which we belong. There is no doubt that we ought,—at least generally speaking,—to obey this: but what it is we cannot of course ascertain by any process of abstract reflection, but only by consulting Reports and Statutes. Here, however, the sources of knowledge are so definite and conspicuous, that we are in no danger of confounding the knowledge gained from studying them with the results of abstract contemplation. The case is somewhat different with the traditional and customary rules of behaviour which exist in every society, supplementing the regulative operation of Law proper: here it is much more difficult to distinguish the rules which a moral man is called upon to define for himself, by the application of intuitively known principles, from those as to which some authority external to the individual is recognized as the final arbiter[1].

We may illustrate this by referring to two systems of rules which we have before[2] compared with Morality; the Law of Honour, and the Law of Fashion or Etiquette. I noticed that there is an ambiguity in the common terms 'honourable' and 'dishonourable'; which are no doubt sometimes used, like ethical terms, as implying an absolute standard. Still, when we speak of the Code of Honour we seem to mean rules of which the exact nature is to be finally determined by an appeal to the general opinion of well-bred persons: we admit that a man is in a sense 'dishonoured' when this opinion condemns him, even though we may think his conduct unobjectionable or even intrinsically admirable[3]. Similarly, when we consider from the point of view of reason the rules of Fashion or Etiquette, some may seem useful and commendable, some indifferent and arbitrary, some perhaps absurd and burdensome: but nevertheless we recognize that the final authority on matters of Etiquette is the custom of polite society; which feels itself under no obligation of reducing its rules to rational

---

[1] The final arbiter, that is, on the question what the rule is: of course the moral obligation to conform to any rule laid down by an external authority must rest on some principle which the individual's reason has to apply.

[2] Cf. Book I. ch. iii. § 2.

[3] Cf. *ante*, Book I. ch. iii. § 1.

principles. Yet it must be observed that each individual in any society commonly finds in himself a knowledge not obviously incomplete of the rules of Honour and Etiquette, and an impulse to conform to them without requiring any further reason for doing so. Each often seems to see at a glance what is honourable and polite just as clearly as he sees what is right: and it requires some consideration to discover that in the former cases custom and opinion are generally the final authority from which there is no appeal. And even in the case of rules regarded as distinctly moral, we can generally find an element that seems to us as clearly conventional as the codes just mentioned, when we contemplate the morality of other men, even in our own age and country. Hence we may reasonably suspect a similar element in our own moral code: and must admit the great importance of testing rigorously any rule which we find that we have a habitual impulse to obey; to see whether it really expresses or can be referred to a clear intuition of rightness.

III. The propositions accepted as self-evident must be mutually consistent. Here, again, it is obvious that any collision between two intuitions is a proof that there is error in one or the other, or in both. Still, we frequently find ethical writers treating this point very lightly. They appear to regard a conflict of ultimate rules as a difficulty that may be ignored or put aside for future solution, without any slur being thrown on the scientific character of the conflicting formulæ. Whereas such a collision is absolute proof that at least one of the formulæ needs qualification: and suggests a doubt whether the correctly qualified proposition will present itself with the same self-evidence as the simpler but inadequate one; and whether we have not mistaken for an ultimate and independent axiom one that is really derivative and subordinate.

IV. Since it is implied in the very notion of Truth that it is essentially the same for all minds, any defect in the universal acceptance of a proposition must *pro tanto* impair our confidence in its validity. And in fact 'universal' or 'general' consent has often been held to constitute by itself a sufficient proof of the most important beliefs; and is practically the only one upon which the greater part of mankind can rely. But a proposition accepted as true upon this ground alone is not scientifically known to the mind that so accepts it: scientific knowledge (strictly speaking) we only possess in the case of truths of which we can ourselves see the evidence. Still this does not impair, it rather exhibits and explains, the importance of the criterion of universal acceptance: for the persons who have thus seen the evidence for themselves are just those whose agreement constitutes the most (if not the only) valuable portion of the *consensus* of mankind in general. And it will be easily seen that this agreement must remain an indispensable negative condition of the certainty of our beliefs. For if I find any of my intuitions in direct conflict with an intuition of some other mind, there must be error somewhere: and if I have no more reason to suspect error in the other mind than in my own, reflective comparison between the two intuitions necessarily reduces me temporarily to a state of neutrality. And though the total result in my mind is not exactly suspense of judgment, but an alternation and conflict between positive affirmation by one act of thought and the neutrality that is the result of another; it is obviously something very different from scientific certainty.

Now if the account given of the Morality of Common Sense in the preceding chapters be in the main correct, it seems clear that, generally speaking, its principles do not fulfil the conditions just laid down. So long as they are left in the state of somewhat vague generalities, as we meet them in ordinary discourse, we are disposed to yield them unquestioning assent, and it may be fairly claimed that the assent is approximately universal. But as soon as we attempt to give them the definiteness which science requires, we find that we cannot do this without abandoning the universality of acceptance. We find, in some cases, that alternatives present themselves, between which it is necessary that we should decide; but between which we cannot pretend that Common Sense does decide, and which often seem equally or nearly equally plausible. In other cases the moral notion seems to resist all efforts to obtain from it a definite rule: in others it is found to comprehend elements which we have no means of reducing to a common standard. Even where we seem able to educe from Common Sense a more or less clear reply to the questions raised in the process of definition, the principle that results is qualified in so complicated a way that its self-evidence becomes dubious or vanishes altogether. And thus in each case what at first seemed like an intuition turns out to be either the mere expression of a vague impulse, needing regulation and limitation which it cannot itself supply, but which must be drawn from some other source: or a current opinion, the reasonableness of which has still to be shewn by a reference to some other principle.

In order that this result may be adequately exhibited, I must ask the reader to travel with me again through the series of principles elicited from Common Sense in the previous chapters, and to examine them from a somewhat different point of view. Before, our primary aim was to ascertain impartially what the deliverances of Common Sense actually are: we have now to ask how far these enunciations can claim to be classed as Intuitive Truths.

The reader should observe that throughout this examination a double appeal is made; on the one hand to his individual moral consciousness, and, on the other hand, to the Common Sense of mankind, as expressed generally by the body of persons on whose moral judgment he is prepared to rely. I ask him (1) whether he can state a clear, precise, self-evident first principle, according to which he is prepared to judge conduct under each head: and (2) if so, whether this principle is really that commonly applied in practice, by those whom he takes to represent Common Sense[1].

§ 3. If we begin by considering the duty of acting wisely, discussed in ch. iii. we may seem perhaps to have before us an axiom of undoubted self-evidence. For acting wisely appeared to mean taking the right means to the best ends; *i.e.* taking

---

[1] It has been fairly urged that I leave the determination of Common Sense very loose and indefinite: and if I were endeavouring to bring out a more positive result from this examination, I ought certainly to have discussed further how we are to ascertain the 'experts' on whose 'consensus' we are to rely, in this or any other subject. But my scientific conclusions are to so great an extent negative, I thought it hardly necessary to enter upon this discussion. I have been careful not to *exaggerate* the doubtfulness and inconsistency of Common Sense: should it turn out to be *more* doubtful and inconsistent than I have represented it, my argument will only be strengthened.

the means which reason indicates to the ends which Reason prescribes. And it is evident that it must be right to act reasonably. Equally undeniable is the immediate inference from, or negative aspect of, this principle; that it is wrong to act irrationally. This, taken in connexion with the empirical fact of impulses in our minds conflicting with Reason, gives—as another self-evident principle—the maxim of Temperance or Self-control in its widest interpretation; *i.e.* 'That Reason should never give way to Appetite or Passion[1].' And these principles have sometimes been enounced with no little solemnity as answering the fundamental question of Ethics and supplying the basis or summary of a doctrine of Practice.

But this statement of principles turns out to be one of those stages, so provokingly frequent in the course of ethical reflection, which, as far as practical guidance is concerned, are really brief circuits, leading us back to the point from which we started. Or rather, to prevent misapprehension, it should be observed that the maxims just given may be understood in two senses: in one sense they are certainly self-evident, because they are really identical propositions, slightly veiled: in another sense they include more or less distinctly a direction to an important practical duty, but as so understood they lose their self-evidence. For if the rules of wisdom and Self-control mean (1) that we ought always to do what we see to be reasonable, and (2) that we are not to yield to any impulse urging us in an opposite direction; they simply affirm that it is our duty (1) generally, and (2) under special temptations, to do what we see to be our duty: and do not even tend to remove our perplexities as to the method and principles by which duty is to be determined.

But if they are further understood (as they sometimes are understood) to prescribe the cultivation of a habit of acting rationally; that is, of referring each act to definitely conceived principles and ends, instead of allowing it to be determined by instinctive impulses; then I cannot see that the affirmation of

---

[1] In ch. ix. Temperance was regarded as subordinate to, or a special application of, Prudence or Self-love moralised: because this seemed to be on the whole the view of Common Sense, which in the preceding chapters I have been endeavouring to follow as closely as possible, both in stating the principles educed and in the order of their exposition.

this as an universal and absolute rule of duty is self-evidently true. For when Reason is considered not in the present as actually commanding, but as an End of which a fuller realization has to be sought in the future; the point of view from which its sovereignty has to be judged is entirely changed. The question is no longer whether the dictates of Reason ought always to be obeyed, but whether the dictation of Reason is always a Good; whether any degree of predominance of Reason over mere Impulse must necessarily tend to the perfection of the conscious self of which both are elements. And it is surely not self-evident that this predominance cannot be carried too far; and that Reason is not rather self-limiting, in the knowledge that rational ends are sometimes better attained by those who do not directly aim at them as rational. Certainly Common Sense is inclined to hold that in many matters instinct is a better spring of action than reason: thus it is commonly said that a healthy appetite is a better guide to diet than a doctor's prescription: and, again, that marriage is better undertaken as a consequence of falling in love than in execution of a tranquil and deliberate design: and we before observed (ch. iv.) that there is a certain excellence in services springing from spontaneous affection which does not attach to similar acts done from pure sense of duty. And in the same way experience seems to shew that many acts requiring promptitude and vigour are likely to be more energetic and effective, and that many acts requiring tact and delicacy are likely to be more graceful and pleasant to others, if they are done not in conscious obedience to the dictates of Reason but from other motives. It is not necessary here to decide how far this view is true: it suffices to say that we do not know intuitively that it is not true to some extent; that there may not be—to use Plato's analogy—*over-government* in the individual soul no less than in the state. The residuum, then, of clear intuition which we have so far obtained, is the practically tautological proposition that it is our duty to do what we judge to be our duty.

§ 4. Let us pass now to what I have called the duties of the Affections, the rules that prescribe either love itself in some degree, or the services that naturally spring from it in those relations where it is expected and desired. Here, in the first place, the question how far we are bound to render these services when we do not feel the affection, is answered differently in many cases by different persons, and no determination of the limit seems self-evident. And similarly if we ask whether affection itself is a duty; for on the one hand it is at least only partially within the control of the will, and in so far as it can be produced by voluntary effort, there is thought to be something unsatisfactory and unattractive in the result; and on the other hand, in certain relations it seems to be commonly regarded as a duty. On those points the doctrine of Common Sense is rather a rough compromise between conflicting lines of thought than capable of being deduced from a clear and universally accepted principle. And if we confine ourselves to the special relations where Common Sense admits no doubt as to the broad moral obligation of at least rendering such services as affection naturally prompts, still the recognized rules of external duty in these relations are, in the first place, wanting in definiteness and precision: and secondly, they do not, when rigorously examined, appear to be, or be referable to, any independent intuitions so far as the *particularity* of the duties is concerned. Let us take, for example, the duty of parents to children. We have no doubt about this duty as a part of the present order of society, by which the due growth and training of the rising generation is distributed among the adults. But when we reflect on this arrangement itself, we cannot say *intuitively* that it is the best possible. It may be plausibly maintained that children would be better trained, physically and mentally, if they were brought up under the supervision of physicians and philosophers, in large institutions maintained out of the general taxes. We cannot decide *à priori* which of these alternatives is preferable; we have to refer to psychological and sociological generalizations, obtained by empirical study of human nature in actual societies. If, however, we consider the duty of parents by itself, out of connexion with this social order, it is certainly not self-evident that we owe more to our own children than to others whose happiness equally depends on our exertions. To get the question clear, let us suppose that I am thrown with my family upon a desert island, where I find an abandoned orphan. Is it evident that I am less bound to provide this child, so far as lies in my power, with the means of subsistence, than I am to provide for my own children? According to some, my special duty to the latter would arise from the fact that I have brought them into being: but, if so, it would seem that on this principle I have a right to diminish their happiness, provided I do not turn it into a negative quantity; since, as without me they would not have existed at all, they can, as my children, have no claim upon me for more than an existence on the whole above zero in respect of happiness. We might even deduce a parental right (so far as this special claim is concerned) to extinguish children painlessly at any point of their existence, if only their life up to that point has been on the whole worth having; for how can persons who would have had no life at all but for me fairly complain that they are not allowed more than a certain quantity[1]? I do not mean to assert that these doctrines are even implicitly held by Common Sense: but merely to shew that here, as elsewhere, the pursuit of an irrefragable intuition may lead us unaware into a nest of paradoxes.

It seems, then, that we cannot, after all, say that the special duty of parents to children, considered by itself, possesses clear self-evidence: and it was easy to shew (cf. ch. iv.) that as recognized by Common Sense its limits are indeterminate.

The rule prescribing the duty of children to parents need not detain us; for to Common Sense it certainly seems doubtful whether this is not merely a particular case of gratitude; and we certainly have no clear intuition of what is due to parents who do not deserve gratitude. Again, the moral relation of husband and wife seems to depend chiefly upon contract and definite understanding. It is, no doubt, usually thought that Morality as well as law prescribes certain conditions for all connubial contracts: and in our own age and country it is held that they should be (1) monogamic and (2) permanent. But it seems clear that neither of these opinions would be maintained to be a primary intuition. Whether these or any other legal regulations of the union of the sexes can be deduced from some intuitive principle of Purity, we will presently consider:

[1] It may be noticed that a view very similar to this has often been maintained in considering what God is in justice bound to do for human beings in consequence of the quasi-parental relation in which he stands to them.

but as for such conjugal duties as are not prescribed by Law, probably no one at the present day would maintain that there is any such general agreement as to what these are, as would support the theory that they may be known *à priori*[1].

If, then, in these domestic relations, where the duties of affection are commonly recognized as so imperative and important, we can find no really independent and self-evident principles for determining them; I need not perhaps spend time in shewing that the same is the case in respect of the less intimate ties (of kindred, neighbourhood, &c.) that bind us to other human beings. Indeed, this was made sufficiently manifest in our previous discussion of those other duties.

No doubt there are certain obligations towards human beings generally which are, speaking broadly, unquestionable: as, for example, the negative duty of abstaining from causing pain to others against their will, except by way of deserved punishment (whether this is to be placed under the head of Justice or Benevolence); and of making reparation for any pain which we may have caused. Still, when we consider the extent of these duties and try to define their limits, it does not appear that Common Sense lays down an absolute and independent rule in either case. When we ask how far we may legitimately cause pain to other men (or other sentient beings) in order to obtain happiness for ourselves or third persons; or even to confer a greater good on the sufferer himself, if the pain be inflicted against his will; we do not seem able to obtain any clear and generally accepted principle for deciding this point, unless the Utilitarian formula be admitted as such. Again, as regards Reparation, there is, as we have seen, a fundamental doubt how far this is due for harm that has been involuntarily caused.

Similarly, all admit the general duty of rendering services to our fellow-men and especially to those who are in special need, and that we are bound to make sacrifices for them, when

---

[1] It is not irrelevant to notice the remarkable divergence of suggestions for the better regulation of marriage, to which reflective minds seem to be led when they are once set loose from the trammels of tradition and custom; as exhibited in the speculations of philosophers in all ages—especially of those (as *e.g.* Plato) to whom we cannot attribute any sensual or licentious bias.

the benefit that we thereby confer very decidedly outweighs the loss to ourselves; but when we ask how far we are bound to give up our own happiness in order to promote that of our fellows, Common Sense seems not distinctly to accept the Utilitarian principle, and yet not definitely to affirm any other.

And even the common principle of Gratitude, though its stringency is immediately and universally felt, seems yet essentially indeterminate: owing to the unsolved question whether the requital of a benefit ought to be proportionate to what it cost the benefactor, or to what it is worth to the recipient.

§ 5. When we pass to consider that element of Justice under which, as it seemed, the duty of Gratitude might be subsumed, the same difficulty recurs in a more complicated form. For here, too, we have to ask whether the Requital of Good Desert ought to be proportioned to the benefit rendered, or to the effort made to render it. And if we scrutinize closely the common moral notion of Retributive Justice, it appears, strictly taken, to imply the metaphysical doctrine of Free Will; since, according to this conception, the reasonableness of rewarding merit is considered solely in relation to the past, without regard to the future bad consequences to be expected from leaving merit without encouragement: and if every excellence in any one's actions or productions seems referable ultimately to causes other than himself, the individual's claim to requital, from this point of view, appears to vanish. On the other hand it is obviously paradoxical in estimating Desert to omit the moral excellences due to transmission and education: or even intellectual excellences, since good intention without foresight is commonly held to constitute a very imperfect merit. Even if we cut through this speculative difficulty by leaving the ultimate reward of real Desert to Divine Justice; we still seem unable to find any clear principles for framing a scale of merit. And much the same may be said, *mutatis mutandis*, of the scale of Demerit which Criminal Justice seems to require.

And even if these difficulties were overcome, we should still be only at the commencement of the perplexities in which the determination of Justice is involved. For the examination of the contents of this notion, which we conducted in ch. v., furnished us not with a single definite principle, but with a whole swarm of principles, which are unfortunately liable to come into conflict with each other; and of which even those, that when singly contemplated have the air of being self-evident truths, do not certainly carry with them any intuitively ascertainable definition of their mutual boundaries and relations. Thus, for example, in constructing an ideally perfect distribution of the means of happiness, it seems necessary to take into account the notion (as I called it) of Fitness, which, though often confounded with Desert, seems essentially distinct from it. For the social 'distribuend' includes not merely the means of obtaining pleasurable passive feelings, but also functions and instruments, which are important sources of happiness, but which it is obviously reasonable to give to those who can perform and use them. And even as regards the material means of comfort and luxury—wealth, in short—we do not find that the same amount produces the same result of happiness in every case: and it seems reasonable that the means of refined and varied pleasure should be allotted to those who have the corresponding capacities for enjoyment[1]. And yet these may not be the most deserving, so that this principle may clearly conflict with that of requiting Desert.

And either principle, as we saw, is liable to come into collision with the widely-accepted doctrine that the proper ultimate end of Law is to secure the greatest possible Freedom of action to all members of the community: and that all that any individual, strictly speaking, owes to any other is non-interference, except so far as he has further bound himself by free contract. But further, when we come to examine this principle in its turn, we find that, in order to be at all capable of affording a practical basis for social construction, it needs limitations and qualifications which make it look less like an independent principle than a *medium axioma* of Utilitarianism: and that it cannot without a palpable strain be made to cover the most important rights which positive law secures. For example, the

---

[1] For example, many hold that wealth is, roughly speaking, rightly distributed when cultivated persons have abundance and the uncultivated a bare subsistence, since the former are far more capable of deriving happiness from wealth than the latter.

justification of permanent appropriation is surely rather that it supplies the only adequate motive for labour than that it, strictly speaking, realizes Freedom: nor can the questions that arise in determining the limits of the right of property—such as whether it includes the right of bequest—be settled by any deductions from this supposed fundamental principle. Nor again, can even the enforcement of contracts be fairly said to be a realization of Freedom; for a man seems, strictly speaking, freer when no one of his volitions is allowed to cause an external control of any other. And if we disregard this as a paradoxical subtlety, we are met on the opposite side by the perplexity that if abstract Freedom is consistent with any engagement of future services, it must on the same grounds be consistent with such as are perpetual and unqualified, and so even with actual slavery. And this question becomes especially important when we consider that the duty of obeying positive laws has by many been reconciled with the abstract right of Freedom, by supposing a 'tacit compact' or understanding between each individual and the rest of his community. This Compact, however, seems on examination too clearly fictitious to be put forward as a basis of moral duty: as is further evident from the indefinitely various qualifications and reservations with which the 'understanding' has by different thinkers been supposed to be 'understood.' Hence many who maintain the 'Birthright of Freedom' consider that the only abstractly justifiable social order is one in which no laws are imposed without the *express* consent of those who are to obey them. But we found it impossible really to construct society upon this basis: and such Representative Governments as have actually been established only appear to realize this idea by means of rather sweeping limitations and rather transparent fictions. It was manifest, too, that the maximum of what I have called Constitutional Freedom, *i.e.* the most perfect conformity between the action of a government and the wishes of the majority of its subjects, need by no means result in the maximum of Civil Freedom being established in the society so governed.

But even if we could delineate to our satisfaction an ideal social order, including an ideal form of government, we have still to reconcile the duty of realizing this with the conformity due to the actual order of society. For we have a strong conviction that positive laws ought, generally speaking, to be obeyed: and, again, our notion of Justice seemed to include a general duty of satisfying the expectations generated by custom and precedent. Yet if the actual order of society deviates very much from what we think ought to exist, the duty of conforming to it seems to become obscure and doubtful. And apart from this we cannot say that Common Sense regards it as an axiom that Laws ought to be obeyed. Indeed, all are agreed that they ought to be disobeyed when they command what is wrong: though we do not seem able to elicit any clear general view as to what remains wrong after it has been commanded by the sovereign. And, again, the positive laws that ought to be obeyed as such, must be the commands issued by a (morally) rightful authority: and though these will ordinarily coincide with the commands legally enforced, we cannot say that this is always the case; for the courts may be temporarily subservient to a usurper; or, again, the sovereign hitherto habitually obeyed may be one against whom it has become right to rebel (since it is generally admitted that this is sometimes right). We require, then, principles for determining when usurpation becomes legitimate and when rebellion is justifiable: and we do not seem able to elicit these from Common Sense—except so far as it may be fairly said that on this whole subject Common Sense inclines more to the Utilitarian method than it does in matters of private morality.

Still less can we state the general duty of satisfying 'natural expectations'—*i.e.* such expectations as an average man would form under given circumstances—in the form of a clear and precise moral axiom. No doubt a just man will generally satisfy customary claims: but it can hardly be maintained that the mere existence of a custom renders it clearly obligatory that any one should conform to it who has not already promised to do so: especially since bad customs can only be abolished by individuals venturing to disregard them.

§ 6. We have still to examine (whether as a branch of Justice or under a separate head) the duty of fulfilling express promises and distinct understandings. The peculiar confidence which moralists have generally felt in this principle is strikingly illustrated by those endeavours to extend its scope which we have just had occasion to notice: and it certainly seems to surpass in simplicity, certainty, and definiteness the moral rules that we have hitherto discussed. Here, then, if anywhere, we seem likely to find one of those ethical axioms of which we are in search. Now we saw that the notion of a Promise requires several qualifications not commonly noticed to make it precise: but this is no reason why we may not construct with it an intuitive principle, such as when enunciated and understood will obtain universal acceptance. For similarly the uninstructed majority of mankind could not define a circle as a figure bounded by a line of which every point is equidistant from the centre: but nevertheless, when the definition is explained to them, they will accept it as expressing the perfect type of that notion of roundness which they have long had in their minds. And the same potential universality of acceptance may, I think, be fairly claimed for the propositions that the promise which the Common Sense of mankind recognizes as binding must be understood by promiser and promisee in the same sense at the time of promising, and that it is relative to the promisee and capable of being annulled by him, and that it cannot override determinate[1] prior obligations.

But the case is different with the other qualifications which we had to discuss. When once the question of introducing these has been raised, we see that Common Sense is clearly divided as to the answer. If we ask (*e.g.*) how far a promise is binding if it was made in consequence of false statements, on which, however, it was not understood to be conditional? or if important circumstances were concealed, or the promiser was in any way led to believe that the consequences of keeping the promise would be different from what they turn out to be? or if the promise was given under compulsion? or if circumstances have materially altered since it was given, and we find that the results of fulfilling it will be different from what we foresaw when we promised? or even if it be only our knowledge of consequences which has altered, and we now see that fulfilment will entail on us a sacrifice out of proportion to the benefit re-

[1] I refer later (p. 360) to the difficulty before noticed in respect of such prior obligations as are not strictly determinate.

ceived by the promisee? or perhaps that it will even be injurious to him though he may not think so? different conscientious persons would answer these and other[1] questions (both generally and in particular cases) in different ways: and though we could perhaps obtain a decided majority for some of these qualifications and against others, there would not in any case be a clear *consensus* either way. And, moreover, the mere discussion of these points seems to make it plain that the confidence with which the "unsophisticated conscience" asserts unreservedly "that promises ought to be kept," is due to inadvertence; and that when the qualifications to which we referred are fairly considered, this confidence inevitably changes into hesitation and perplexity. It should be added, that some of these qualifications themselves suggest a reference to the more comprehensive principle of Utilitarianism, as one to which this particular rule is naturally subordinate.

Again, reflection upon the place of this duty in a classified system of moral obligations tends to confirm our distrust of the ordinary enunciations of Common Sense in respect of it. For, as was seen, Fidelity to promises is very commonly ranked with Veracity; as though the mere fact of my having said that I would do a thing were the ground of my duty to do it. But on reflection we perceive that the obligation must be regarded as contingent on the reliance that another has placed on my assertion: that, in fact, the breach of duty is constituted by the disappointment of expectations voluntarily raised. And when we see this we become less disposed to maintain the absoluteness of the duty: it seems now to depend upon the amount of harm done by disappointing expectations; and we shrink from saying that the promise ought to be kept, if the keeping it would involve an amount of harm that seems decidedly to outweigh this.

The case of Veracity we may dismiss somewhat more briefly, as here it was still more easy to show that the common enunciation of the unqualified duty of Truth-speaking is made without full consideration, and cannot approve itself to the reflective

[1] I have omitted as less important the special questions connected with promises to the dead or to the absent, or where a form of words is prescribed, which were discussed in ch. vi.

mind as an absolute first principle. For, in the first place, we found no clear agreement as to the fundamental nature of the obligation; or as to its exact scope, *i.e.* whether it is our actual affirmation as understood by the recipient which we are bound to make correspondent to fact (as far as we can), or whatever inferences we foresee that he is likely to draw from this, or both. To realize perfect Candour and Sincerity, we must aim at both: and we no doubt admire the exhibition of these virtues: but few will maintain that they ought to be exhibited under all circumstances. And, secondly, it seems to be admitted by Common Sense, though vaguely and reluctantly, that the principle, however defined, is not of universal application: as we do not think that truth ought always to be told to children, or madmen, or invalids, or by advocates: and we are not sure that we are bound to tell it to enemies or robbers, or even to persons who ask questions which they know they have no right to ask (if a mere refusal to answer would practically reveal an important secret). And when we consider the limitations generally admitted, it seems still more plain than in the last case, that they are very commonly determined by utilitarian reasonings, implicit or explicit.

§ 7. If, then, the prescriptions of Justice, Good Faith, and Veracity, as laid down by Common Sense, appear so little capable of being converted into first principles of scientific Ethics, it seems scarcely necessary to inquire whether such axioms can be extracted from the minor maxims of social behaviour, such as the maxim of Liberality or the rules restraining the Malevolent Affections: or, again, from such virtues as Courage and Humility, which we found it difficult to class as either social or self-regarding. Indeed, it was made plain in ch. ix. that as regards the proper regulation of resentment, Common Sense can only be saved from inconsistency or hopeless vagueness by adopting the 'interest of society' as the ultimate standard: and in the same way we cannot definitely distinguish Courage from Foolhardiness except by a reference to the probable tendency of the daring act to promote the well-being of the agent or of others, or to some definite rule of duty prescribed under some other notion. Similarly the duties of Temperance, Self-control, and other cognate virtues, are only clear and definite in so far as they are conceived as subordinate either to Prudence (as is ordinarily the case), or to Benevolence or some definite rule of social duty, or at least to some end of which the conception involves the notion of duty supposed to be already determinate, as 'furtherance of moral progress[1].' Certainly the authority of Common Sense cannot be fairly claimed for any more strict regulation even of the bodily appetites for food and drink.

In the case, however, of the sexual appetite, a special regulation certainly seems to be prescribed on some independent principle under the notion of Purity or Chastity. In ch. ix., where we examined this notion, we were met by the fact that Common Sense is not only not explicit, but actually averse to explicitness, on this subject. As my aim in the preceding chapters was to give, above all things, a faithful exposition of the morality of Common Sense, I allowed my inquiry to be checked by this (as it seemed) clearly recognizable sentiment. But when it becomes our primary object to test the intuitive evidence of the moral principles commonly accepted, it seems necessary to override this aversion: for we can hardly ascertain whether we have what can properly be called knowledge as to the acts allowed and forbidden under this notion and its opposite, without subjecting it to the same close scrutiny that we have endeavoured to give to the other leading notions of Ethics. Here the briefest account of such a scrutiny will be sufficient. I am aware that in giving even this I cannot but cause a certain disgust in the mind of a reader trained in good moral habits: but I trust I may claim the same indulgence as is commonly granted to the physiologist, who also has to direct the student's attention to objects which a healthy mind is naturally disinclined to contemplate.

What, then, is the conduct which Purity forbids (for the principle is more easily discussed in its negative aspect)? As the normal and obvious end of sexual intercourse is the propagation of the species, some have thought that all indulgence of appetite, except as a means to this end, should be prohibited. But this doctrine would lead to a restriction of conjugal intercourse far too severe for Common Sense. Shall we say, then,

---

[1] It was this conception that seemed to give the true standard of Humility, considered as a purely internal duty.

that Purity forbids such indulgence except under the conditions of conjugal union defined by Law? But this answer, again, further reflection shews to be unsatisfactory. For, first, we should not, on consideration, call a conjugal union impure, *merely* because the parties had wilfully omitted to fulfil legal conditions, and had made a contract which the law declined to enforce. We might condemn their conduct, but we should not apply to it this notion. And, secondly, we feel that positive law may be unfavourable to Purity, and that in fact Purity, like Justice, is something which the law ought to maintain, but does not always. We have to ask, then, what kind of sexual relations we are to call essentially impure, whether countenanced or not by Law and Custom? There appear to be no distinct principles, having any claim to self-evidence, upon which the question can be answered so as to command general assent. It would be difficult even to state such a principle for determining the degree of consanguinity between husband and wife which constitutes a union incestuous; although the aversion with which such unions are commonly regarded is the most intense of moral sentiments : and the difficulty becomes indefinitely greater when we consider the *rationale* of prohibited degrees of affinity. Again, probably few would stigmatize a legal polygynous connexion as impure, however they might disapprove of the law and of the state of society in which such a law was established : but if legal Polygyny is not impure, is Polyandry, when legal and customary—as is not unfrequently the case among the lower races of man—to be so characterized? and if not, on what rational principle can the notion be applied to institutions and conduct? Again, where divorce by mutual consent, with subsequent marriage, is legalized, we do not call this an offence against Purity : and yet if the principle of free change be once admitted, it seems paradoxical to distinguish purity from impurity merely by less rapidity of transition[1]; and to condemn as impure even 'Free Love,' in so far as it is earnestly advocated as a means to a completer harmony of sentiment between men and women, and not to mere sensual license.

[1] It should be observed that I am not asking for an exact quantitative decision, but whether we can really think that the decision depends upon considerations of this kind.

Shall we, then, fall back upon the presence of mutual affection (as distinguished from mere appetite) as constituting the essence of pure sexual relations? But this, again, while too lax from one point of view, seems from another too severe for Common Sense: as we do not condemn marriages without affection as impure, although we disapprove of them as productive of unhappiness. Such marriages, indeed, are sometimes stigmatized as "legalized prostitution," but the phrase is felt to be extravagant and paradoxical; and it is even doubtful whether we do disapprove of them under all circumstances; as (e g.) in the case of royal alliances.

Again, how shall we judge of such institutions as those of Plato's Commonwealth, establishing community of women and children, but at the same time regulating sexual indulgence with the strictest reference to social ends? Our habitual standards seem inapplicable to such novel circumstances.

The truth seems to be, that reflection on the current sexual morality discovers to us two distinct grounds for it, which we may distinguish as external and internal: first and chiefly, the maintenance of a certain social order, believed to be most conducive to the prosperous continuance of the human race: and, secondly, the protection of habits of feeling in individuals believed to be generally most important to their perfection or their happiness. We commonly conceive that both these ends are to be attained by the same regulations: and in an ideal state of society this would perhaps be the case: but in actual life there is frequently a partial separation and incompatibility between them. But further, if the repression of sexual license is prescribed merely as a means to these ends, it does not, after all, seem that we can affirm *à priori* that it is always a necessary means in either case. Such a belief seems to be a mere 'anticipatio mentis,' invalid without empirical confirmation. We cannot be certain, without induction from extensive and careful sociological observation, that a certain amount of sexual license will be incompatible with the maintenance of population in sufficient numbers and good condition. And if we consider the matter in its relation to the individual's perfection, it is certainly clear that he misses the highest and best development of his emotional nature, if his sexual relations are of a merely sensual kind: but we can hardly know *à priori* that this lower kind of relation interferes with the development of the higher (nor indeed does experience seem to shew that this is universally the case). And this latter line of argument has a further difficulty. For the common opinion that we have to justify does not merely condemn the lower kind of development in comparison with the higher, but in comparison with none at all. Since we do not positively blame a man for remaining celibate (though we perhaps despise him somewhat unless the celibacy is adopted as a means to a noble end); it is difficult to shew why we should condemn—in its bearing on the individual's emotional perfection solely—the imperfect development afforded by merely sensual relations.

Much more might be said to exhibit the perplexities in which the attempt to define the rule of Purity or Chastity involves us. But I do not desire to extend the discussion beyond what is necessary for the completion of my argument. It seems to me that the conclusion announced in § 2 of this chapter has now been sufficiently justified. We have examined the moral notions that present themselves with a *primâ facie* claim to furnish independent and absolute rules of morality: and we have in each case found that from such regulation of conduct as the Common Sense of mankind really supports, no proposition can be elicited which, when fairly contemplated, even appears to have the characteristic of a scientific axiom. It is therefore scarcely needful to proceed to a systematic examination of the manner in which Common Sense provides for the co-ordination of these principles. In fact, this question seems to have been already discussed as far as is profitable: for the attempt to define each principle singly has inevitably led us to consider their mutual relations: and it was in the cases where two moral principles came into collision that we most clearly saw the vagueness and inconsistency with which the boundaries of each are determined by Common Sense. For example, the distinction between perfectly stringent moral obligations, and such laxer duties as may be modified by a man's own act, is often taken: and it is one which, as we saw, is certainly required in formulating the Common Sense view of the effect of a promise in creating new obligations: but it is one which we cannot apply with any practical precision, because of the high degree of indeterminateness which we find in the common notions of duties to which the highest degree of stringency is yet commonly attributed.

It only remains to guard my argument from being understood in a more sweeping sense than it has been intended or is properly able to bear. Nothing that I have said even tends to shew that we have not distinct moral impulses, claiming authority over all others, and prescribing or forbidding kinds of conduct as to which there is a rough general agreement, at least among educated persons of the same age and country. It is only maintained that the objects of these impulses do not admit of being scientifically determined by any reflective analysis of common sense. The notions of Benevolence, Justice, Good Faith, Veracity, Purity, &c. are not necessarily emptied of significance for us, because we have found it impossible to define them with precision. The main part of the conduct prescribed under each notion is sufficiently clear: and the general rule prescribing it need not lose its force because there is in each case a margin of conduct involved in obscurity and perplexity, or because the rule does not on examination appear to be absolute and independent. In short, the Morality of Common Sense may still be perfectly adequate to give practical guidance to common people in common circumstances: but the attempt to elevate it into a system of scientific Ethics brings its inevitable imperfections into prominence without helping us to remove them[1].

[1] It should be observed that the more positive treatment of Common-sense Morality, in its relation to Utilitarianism, to which we shall proceed in ch. iii. of the following book, is intended as an indispensable supplement of the negative criticism which has just been completed.

CHAPTER XII.

MOTIVES OR SPRINGS OF ACTION CONSIDERED AS SUBJECTS OF MORAL JUDGMENT.

§ 1. IN the first chapter of this third Book I was careful to point out that motives, as well as intentions, form part of the subject-matter of our common moral judgments: and indeed in our notion of 'conscientiousness' the habit of reflecting on motives, and judging them to be good or bad, is a prominent element. It is necessary, therefore, in order to complete our examination of the Intuitional Method, to consider this comparison of motives, and ascertain how far it can be made systematic, and pursued to conclusions of scientific value. And this seems a convenient place for treating of this part of the subject: since it has been maintained by an important school of English moralists that Desires and Affections rather than Acts are the proper subjects of the ethical judgment: and it is natural to fall back upon this view when systematic reflection on the morality of Common Sense has shewn us the difficulty of obtaining a precise and satisfactory determination of rightness and wrongness in external conduct.

To avoid confusion, it should be observed that the term 'motive' is commonly used in two ways. It is sometimes applied to those among the foreseen consequences of any act which the agent desired in willing: and sometimes to the desire, or conscious impulse itself. The two meanings are in a manner correspondent, as, where impulses are different, there must always be some sort of difference in their respective objects. But for our present purpose it is more convenient to take the latter meaning: as it is our own impulsive nature that we have practically to deal with, in the way of controlling, resisting, indulging the different impulses; and therefore it is the ethical value of these that we are primarily concerned to estimate: and we often find that two impulses, which would be placed very far apart in any psychological list, are directed towards an end materially identical, though regarded from a different point of view in each case. As (*e.g.*) both appetite and Rational self-love may impel a man to seek a particular sensual gratification; though in the latter case it is regarded under the general notion of pleasure, and as forming part of a sum called Happiness. In this chapter then I shall use the term Motive to denote the desires of particular results, believed to be attainable as consequences of our voluntary acts, by which we are stimulated to will those acts[1].

The first point to notice in considering the ethical result

[1] In Green's *Prolegomena to Ethics*, Book II. chaps. i. and ii. a peculiar view is taken of "motives, of that kind by which it is the characteristic of moral or human action, to be determined." Such motives, it is maintained, must be distinguished from desires in the sense of "mere solicitations of which a man is conscious;" they are "constituted by the reaction of the man's self upon these, and its identification of itself with one of them." In fact the "direction of the self-conscious self to the realization of an object" which I should call an act of will, is the phenomenon to which Green would restrict the term "desire in that sense in which desire is the principle and notion of an improbable human action."

The use of terms here suggested appears to me inconvenient, and the psychological analysis implied in it to a great extent erroneous. I admit that in certain simple cases of choice, where the alternatives suggested are each prompted by a single definite desire, there is no psychological inaccuracy in saying that in willing the act to which he is stimulated by any such desire the agent "identifies himself with the desire." But in more complex cases the phrase appears to me incorrect, as obliterating important distinctions between the two kinds of psychical phenomena which are usually and conveniently distinguished as "desires" and volitions. In the first place as I have before pointed out (ch. i. § 2 of this Book), it often happens that certain foreseen consequences of volition, which as foreseen are undoubtedly *willed* and—in a sense—*chosen* by the agents, are not objects of desire to him at all, but even possibly of aversion—aversion, of course, overcome by his desire of other consequences of the same act. In the second place, it is specially important, from an ethical point of view, to notice that, among the various desires or aversions aroused in us by the complex foreseen consequences of a contemplated act, there are often impulses with which we do not identify ourselves, but which we even try to suppress as far as possible: though as it is not possible to suppress them completely—especially if we do the act to which they prompt—we cannot say that they do not operate as motives.

of a comprehensive comparison of motives is, that the issue in any internal conflict is not usually thought to be between positively good and bad, but between better and less good, more or less estimable or elevated motives. The only kind of motive which (if any) we commonly judge to be *intrinsically bad*, apart from the circumstances under which it operates, is malevolent affection; that is, the desire, however aroused, to inflict pain or harm on some other sentient being. And it is perhaps doubtful (as we saw in ch. 8), whether even this impulse ought to be pronounced absolutely bad. Butler allows it to be legitimate in the forms of Instinctive Resentment: and a more sustained and deliberate malevolence is commonly approved as Righteous Indignation: and if it be said that this Indignation ought to be directed against the act and not the agent, it may be fairly questioned whether it is within the capacity of human nature to maintain this distinction clearly[1]. At any rate there is no other motive except deliberate malevolence which Common Sense condemns as absolutely bad. The other motives that are commonly spoken of in 'dyslogistic' terms seem to be most properly called (in Bentham's language) 'Seductive' rather than bad. That is, they prompt to forbidden conduct with conspicuous force and frequency: but when we consider them carefully we find that there are certain limits, however narrow, within which their operation is legitimate.

If then all kinds of motives, with one doubtful exception, are, considered abstractly, at least indifferent and allowable, it remains for the moralist to determine their comparative goodness or rank in the scale of impulses.

A distinguished living writer[2] maintains that whenever two different springs of action come into conflict, their comparative goodness is recognized by immediate intuition: and that such intuitions are the ultimate premises upon which all valid moral reasoning depends. I will give in his own words his very clear and complete exposition of this doctrine.

[1] Perhaps we may distinguish between the impulse to inflict pain and the desire of the antipathetic pleasure which the agent will reap from this infliction, and approve the former in certain circumstances, but condemn the latter absolutely.

[2] The Rev. J. Martineau: in a review of Whewell's *Elements of Morality*.

"We think that, in common with the inferior animals, we are created with certain determinate propensities to particular ends, or with provisions for the development of such propensities: that in the lower animals, these operate singly and successively, each taking its turn for the command and guidance of the creature, and none of them becoming objects of reflection; that in us also this instinctive impulse is the original type of activity, and would perhaps become permanent in a solitary human being, or in a mind with only one propension at a time: but that with us the same occasion calls up simultaneously two or more springs of action; that immediately on their juxta-position we intuitively discern the higher quality of one than another, giving it a divine and authoritative right of preference; that when the whole series of springs of action has been experienced, the feeling or 'knowledge with ourselves' of their relative rank constitutes the individual conscience: that all human beings, when their consciousness is faithfully interpreted, as infallibly arrive at the same series of moral estimates as at the same set of rational truths: that it is no less correct therefore to speak of a universal conscience than of a universal reason in mankind: and that on this community of nature alone rests the possibility of ethical science." If then a table of springs of action be drawn up in the order of their natural ranks, "the obligatory value of every action is found by the following rule: 'every action is *right* which, in the presence of a lower principle, follows a higher; every action is *wrong* which, in the presence of a higher principle, follows a lower.'"

Mr Martineau has not, as far as I am aware, anywhere put forward such a table or scale of motives. But the English moralists of the last century who adopted the Emotional (as distinct from the Rational) form of Intuitionism were naturally led to arrangement of impulses on a principle similar to his. A rudimentary classification of this sort was attempted by Shaftesbury: and his disciple, Hutcheson, developed this into a more complete and elaborate system, to which I shall presently refer. I have before[1] argued that it is incorrect to regard this comparison of *motives* as the normal form of our

[1] Cf. *ante* p. 201.

common moral judgments, nor do I see any ground for holding it to be the original form. I think that in the normal development of man's moral consciousness, both in the individual and in the race, moral judgments are first passed on outward acts, and that motives do not come to be considered till later; just as external perception of physical objects precedes introspection. At the same time, in my view, it does not therefore follow that the comparison of motives is not the final and most perfect form of the moral judgment. It might approve itself as such by the systematic clearness and mutual consistency of the results to which it led, when pursued by different thinkers independently: and by its freedom from the puzzles and difficulties to which other developments of the Intuitional Method seem to be exposed.

It appears, however, on examination that, on the one hand, many (if not all) of the difficulties which have emerged in the preceding discussion of the commonly received principles of conduct are reproduced in a different form when we try to arrange Motives in order of excellence: and on the other hand, such a construction presents difficulties peculiar to itself, and the attempt to solve these exhibits greater and more fundamental differences among Intuitive moralists, as regards Rank of Motive, than we found to exist as regards Rightness of Conduct.

§ 2. In the first place, it has to be decided whether we are to include in our list the Moral Sentiments, or Impulses towards different kinds of virtuous conduct. Hutcheson certainly gives some of these a place in his scale, as (*e.g.*) Candour, Veracity, Fortitude; and it is *primâ facie* necessary to include them, as such sentiments are observable as distinct and independent impulses in most well-trained minds, and we sometimes recognize their existence in considerable intensity, as when we speak of a man being 'enthusiastically brave,' or intensely veracious,' or 'having a passion for justice.' At the same time their admission places us in the following dilemma. Either the objects of these impulses are represented by the very notions that we have been examining—in which case, after we have decided that any impulse is better than its rival, all the perplexities set forth in the previous chapters will recur, before we can act on our decision; for what avails it to recognize the superiority of the impulse to do justice, if we do not know what it is just to do?—or if in any case the object which a moral sentiment prompts us to realize is conceived more simply, without the qualifications which a complete reflection on Common Sense forced us to recognize—then, as the previous investigation shews, we shall certainly not find agreement as to the relation between this and other impulses. For example a dispute, whether the impulse to speak the truth ought or ought not to be followed, will inevitably arise when Veracity seems opposed either to the general good, or to the interests of some particular person; that is, when it conflicts with 'particular' or 'universal' benevolence. Now, we find that Hutcheson places these latter impulses in a higher rank than Veracity and the others above mentioned: but this view, which coincides practically with Utilitarianism[1], would certainly not be accepted by Intuitional moralists generally.

Mr Martineau seems disposed to escape all perplexity of this kind by denying the independent existence of the moral impulses proper. He says that "when we have run over in fancy all the sorts of *natural* good appropriate to the appetites, the understanding, the imagination, the affections, we come to a stop, and can form no notion of an intrinsic lot of good, over and above these, under the name of *moral* good. Between Virtue and a good dinner, or Virtue and a full purse, we never experienced a rivalry," &c. But this only brings out more impressively the extreme divergence of the results to which his method leads as used by different thinkers. For moralists of a Stoical cast (such as Kant) regard all actions as bad—or not good—which are not done from pure love of virtue, or choice of Right as Right. While Hutcheson, who represents the opposite pole of Intuitional Ethics, equally distinguishes the love of Virtue as a separate impulse; but treats it as at once coordinate in rank and coincident in its effects with Benevolence. I have before argued that it is not really in accordance with Common Sense to regard the predominance of this motive as an absolutely essential characteristic of right or even of Virtuous Conduct: but it

[1] The difference between such a system as Hutcheson's and modern Utilitarianism is chiefly that the latter values the result attained, and the former the feeling that prompts to its attainment.

appears to me still more paradoxical not to recognize the love of virtue as a distinct impulse, the play of which is attended with its own peculiar satisfaction. And surely we must similarly recognize the more special impulses corresponding to particular virtues; and consider their rank in any scale of motives.

So, again, we may observe how widely moralists diverge in estimating the ethical value of Self-love. For Butler seems to regard it as one of two superior and naturally authoritative impulses, the other being Conscience: nay, in a passage before quoted, he even concedes that it would be reasonable for Conscience to yield to it, if the two could possibly conflict. Other moralists (and Butler elsewhere) appear to place this among virtuous impulses under the name of Prudence: though perhaps among these they usually rank it rather low, and would have it yield, in case of conflict, to nobler virtues. Others, again, exclude it from Virtue altogether: *e.g.* Kant, in one of his treatises[1], says that the end of Self-love, one's own happiness, cannot be an end for the Moral Reason; that the force of the reasonable Will, in which Virtue consists, is always exhibited in resistance to natural egoistic impulses.

§ 3. But even if we put out of sight the Moral sentiments and Self-love, it is still scarcely possible to frame a scale of motives arranged in order of merit, for which we could claim anything like a clear consent, even of cultivated and thoughtful persons. On one or two points, indeed, we seem to be generally agreed; *e.g.* that the bodily appetites are inferior to the benevolent affections and the intellectual desires; and perhaps that all impulses tending primarily to the well-being of the individual are lower in rank than those which we class as extra-regarding or disinterested. But beyond a few general statements of this kind, it is very difficult to proceed. For example, when we compare personal affections with the love of knowledge or of beauty, or the passion for the ideal in any form, much doubt and divergence of opinion become manifest. Indeed, we should hardly agree on the relative rank of the benevolent affections taken by themselves; for some would

[1] The *Metaphysische Anfangsgründe der Tugendlehre*: but it ought to be observed that the ethical view briefly expounded in the *Kritik der reinen Vernunft* appears to have much more affinity with Butler's.

prefer the more intense, though narrower, while others would place the calmer and wider feelings in the highest rank. Or again, since Love, as we saw[1], is a complex emotion, and commonly includes, besides the desire of the good or happiness of the beloved, a desire for union or intimacy of some kind; some would consider an affection more elevated in proportion as the former element predominated, while others would regard the latter as at least equally essential to the highest kind of affection. And, in fact, in the love of God, which many consider to be the most elevated of all emotions, the former element can hardly be included at all; for we can scarcely wish to make God better or happier.

Again, we may notice the love of Fame and the love of Power as important and widely operative motives, which would be ranked very differently by different persons: for some would place the former "spur that the clear spirit doth raise" among the most elevated impulses after the moral sentiments; while others think it degrading to depend for one's happiness on the breath of popular favour. And similarly as regards the love of Power; for the effects of this impulse are of nearly all degrees of goodness and badness, and we seem inclined to praise or blame it according to its varying effects.

Hitherto I have assumed it to be a simple matter to ascertain by what motives one's actions are determined. But a consideration of the last-mentioned impulse, as treated by different writers, shews that this is sometimes very difficult. For while some scarcely recognize the love of Power at all, as distinct from the desire of Fame or of Superiority, others trace its operation in almost every exercise of choice. Hobbes, for example, regards the benevolent impulse as being really the love of power in disguise: and Dugald Stewart considers that Avarice is a particular manifestation of it, and that the love of knowledge, of property, and of liberty, may be to some extent resolved into it. My own reflection seems to show at least a partial truth in this view of Stewart's, and even in the paradox of Hobbes: though in all these cases we can trace other elements in combination with the love of power, and it is often difficult to say how many such there are and

[1] Cf. *ante*, ch. iv. § 2.

which predominates. For the more we contemplate the actual promptings that precede any volition, the more we seem to find complexity of motive the rule rather than the exception, at least in the case of educated persons. And this much increases the difficulties of determining right conduct by comparison of motives. In the first place, in the obscurity of introspective analysis, we may easily miss some element, or mistake the predominant motive. But, secondly, from this composition of impulses there results a fundamental perplexity as to the principles on which our decision is to be made, even supposing that we have a clear view of the relative worth of the elementary impulses. For the compound will generally contain nobler and baser elements, and we can hardly get rid of the latter; for—as I have before said—though we may frequently suppress and expel a motive by firmly resisting it, it does not seem possible to exclude it if we do the act to which it prompts. Suppose, then, that we are impelled in one direction by a combination of high and low motive, and in another by an impulse that ranks between the two in the scale, how shall we decide which course to follow? Such a case is by no means uncommon: *e.g.* an injured man may be moved by an impulse of pity to spare his injurer, while a regard for justice and a desire of revenge combined impel him to inflict punishment. Or, again, a Jew of liberal views might be restrained from eating pork by a desire not to shock the feelings of his friends, and might be moved to eat it by the desire to vindicate true religious liberty combined with a liking for pork. How are we to deal with such a case as this? For it will hardly be suggested that we should estimate the relative proportions of the different motives and decide accordingly; even if the values of the different motives could be reduced to a common standard. And if it be said that the highest motive present, however feeble compared with others, should always prevail, and that we need only attend to that: then this mode of determining right conduct seems practically to pass over and resolve itself into some other method. For if several virtuous impulses, prompting to realize particular rules or qualities of conduct, are admitted as distinct and independent, these will naturally occupy the highest rank: and if not, then Rational Benevolence, or some similar principle, within the range of which all actions may be comprehended. And thus, when a conflict occurs between motives inferior to these, the inferior will naturally carry up the case, so to say, into the court of the higher motive; so that the practical issue will, after all, depend upon the determination of the object of the higher motive, whether it be conformity to moral rules or universal happiness and the means to this. And, in fact, such a reference seems continually to occur in our psychical experience; our lower impulses, bodily appetites, &c., when they conflict with some higher principle, continually impel us to justify them by considerations of their tendency to promote individual or general good. And thus our estimate of the value of all motives below the highest turns out to have little practical application, as the final decision as to the rightness of conduct will depend, after all, upon some quite different consideration.

But finally, even if we could satisfactorily arrange the relative rank of all concrete motives, it would still (as we have seen) be opposed to Common Sense to hold that the higher ought always to prevail over the lower. Indeed it would lead to the conclusion that we ought to substitute the higher for the lower wherever this is possible, and so to that suppression of natural impulses in favour of Reason, which we commonly regard as a Stoical extravagance. Whereas Common Sense seems rather to shrink from expelling any normal impulse—except perhaps malevolence—from human nature altogether, holding that the operation of each within due limits is necessary to the perfection of human life. And these limits, within which the higher motive ought not to supplant the lower, seem only to be determined by comparing the respective *effects* of different combinations and harmonies of motives: and thus we are brought back to that judgment of actions in their external aspect as right and wrong (or good and bad), for which this comparison of motives was proposed as a substitute.

CHAPTER XIII.

PHILOSOPHICAL INTUITIONISM.

§ 1. Is there, then, no possibility of attaining, by a more profound and discriminating examination of our common moral thought, to real ethical axioms—intuitive propositions of real clearness and certainty?

This question leads us to the examination of that third phase of the intuitive method, which was called Philosophical Intuitionism[1]. For we conceive it as the aim of a philosopher, as such, to do somewhat more than define and formulate the common moral opinions of mankind. His function is to tell men what they ought to think, rather than what they do think: he is expected to transcend Common Sense in his premises, and is allowed a certain divergence from Common Sense in his conclusions. It is true that the limits of this deviation are firmly, though indefinitely, fixed: the truth of a philosopher's premises will always be tested by the acceptability of his conclusions: if in any important point he be found in flagrant conflict with common opinion, his method will be declared invalid. Still, though he is expected to establish and concatenate at least the main part of the commonly accepted moral rules, he is not necessarily bound to take them as the basis on which his own system is constructed. Rather, we should expect that the history of Moral Philosophy—so far at least as those whom we may call orthodox thinkers are concerned—would be a history of attempts to enunciate, in full breadth and clearness, those primary intuitions of Reason, by the scientific appli-

[1] Cf. *ante*, Book I. ch. viii. § 4.

cation of which the common moral thought of mankind may be at once systematized and corrected.

And this is to some extent the case. But Moral Philosophy, or philosophy as applied to Morality, has had other tasks to occupy it, even more profoundly difficult than that of penetrating to the fundamental principles of Duty. In modern times especially, it has admitted the necessity of demonstrating the harmony of Duty with Interest; that is, with the Happiness or Good of the agent on whom the duty in each case is imposed. It has also undertaken to determine the relation of Right or Good generally to the world of actual existence; a task which could hardly be satisfactorily accomplished without an adequate explanation of the existence of Evil. It has further been distracted by questions which, in my view, are of psychological rather than ethical importance, as to the 'innateness' of our notions of Duty, and the origin of the faculty that furnishes them. With their attention concentrated on these difficult subjects, each of which has been mixed up in various ways with the discussion of fundamental moral intuitions, philosophers have too easily been led to satisfy themselves with ethical formulæ which implicitly accept the morality of Common Sense *en bloc*, ignoring its defects; and merely express a certain view of the relation of this morality to the individual mind or to the universe of actual existence. Perhaps also they have been hampered by the fear (not, as we have seen, unfounded) of losing the support given by 'general assent' if they set before themselves and their readers too rigid a standard of scientific precision. Still, in spite of all these drawbacks, we find that philosophers have provided us with a considerable number of comprehensive moral propositions, put forward as certain and self-evident, and such as at first sight may seem well adapted to serve as the first principles of scientific morality.

§ 2. But here a word of caution seems required, which has been somewhat anticipated in earlier chapters, but on which it is particularly needful to lay stress at this point of our discussion: against a certain class of sham-axioms, which are very apt to offer themselves to the mind that is earnestly seeking for a philosophical synthesis of practical rules, and to delude the unwary with a tempting aspect of clear self-evidence. These are principles which appear certain and self-evident because they are substantially tautological: because, when examined they are found to affirm no more than that it is right to do that which is, in a certain department of life, under certain circumstances and conditions—right to be done. One important lesson which the history of moral philosophy teaches is that, in this region, even powerful intellects are liable to acquiesce in tautologies of this kind; sometimes expanded into circular reasonings, sometimes hidden in the recesses of an obscure notion, often lying so near the surface that, when once they have been exposed, it is hard to understand how they could ever have presented themselves as important.

Let us turn, for illustration's sake, to the time-honoured Cardinal Virtues. If we are told that the dictates of Wisdom and Temperance may be summed up in clear and certain principles, and that these are respectively,

(1) It is right to act rationally:
(2) It is right that the Lower parts of our nature should be governed by the Higher,

we do not at first feel that we are not obtaining valuable information. But when we find (cf. *ante*, ch. xi. § 2) that "acting rationally" is merely another phrase for "doing what we see to be right," and, again, that the "higher part" of our nature to which the rest are to submit is explained to be Reason, so that "acting temperately" is only "acting rationally" under the special condition of non-rational impulses needing to be resisted, the tautology of our "principles" is obvious. Similarly when we are asked to accept as the principle of Justice "that we ought to give every man his own," the definition seems plausible—until it appears that we cannot define "his own" except as equivalent to "that which it is right he should have."

The definitions quoted may be found in modern writers: but it seems worthy of remark that throughout the ethical speculation of Greece[1], such universal affirmations as are presented

---

[1] I am fully sensible of the peculiar interest and value of the ethical thought of ancient Greece. Indeed through a large part of the present work the influence of Plato and Aristotle on my treatment of this subject has been greater than that of any modern writer. But I am here only considering the value of

to us concerning Virtue or Good conduct seem almost always to be propositions which can only be defended from the charge of tautology, if they are understood as definitions of the problem to be solved, and not as attempts at its solution. For example, we come to the study of Plato and Aristotle, expecting to find that they as constructive moralists have supplied the scientific knowledge on ethical matters of which Socrates proclaimed the absence; knowledge, that is, of the Good and Bad in human life. And as to what this is, they seem to be in the main agreed. It is true that Plato wishes us to understand that he has attained a knowledge of absolute abstract Good, of which the good that can be realized in the concrete life of men and communities is but an imperfect copy: and so far he is at issue with Aristotle. Still it is only with this latter, the good in human life, that we are now concerned: and both philosophers are agreed that this is chiefly Virtue, or (as Aristotle more precisely puts it) the *exercise* of Virtue. Therefore at least the practical part of ethical science must consist in the knowledge of Virtue. How, then, can we ascertain the kind of conduct which is properly to be called Virtuous? It seems that Plato can tell us no more of each virtue in turn than that it consists in (1) the knowledge of what is Good in certain circumstances and relations, and (2) such a harmony of the different elements of man's appetitive nature, that their resultant impulse may be always in accordance with this knowledge. But it is just this knowledge (or at least its principles and method) that we are expecting him to give us: and to explain to us instead the different exigencies under which we need it, in no way satisfies our expectation. Nor, again, does Aristotle bring us much nearer such knowledge by telling us that the Good in conduct is to be found somewhere between different kinds of Bad. This at best only indicates the *whereabouts* of Virtue: it does not give us a method for finding it.

On the Stoic system[1], as constructed by Zeno and Chrysippus, the general principles for determining what ought to be done, which the ancient systems profess to supply.

[1] The following remarks apply less to *later* Stoicism—especially the Roman Stoicism which we know at first hand in the writings of Seneca and Marcus Aurelius; in which the relation of the individual man to Humanity generally is more prominent than it is in the earlier form of the system.

it is perhaps unfair to pronounce decisively, from the accounts given of it by adversaries like Plutarch, and such semi-intelligent expositors as Cicero, Diogenes Laertius, and Stobæus. But, as far as we can judge of it, we must pronounce the exposition of its general principles a complicated enchainment of circular reasonings, by which the inquirer is continually deluded with an apparent approach to practical conclusions, and continually led back to the point from which he set out.

The fundamental formula of Stoicism, the primary intuition upon which the system was based, seems to have been that declaring 'Life according to Nature' to be the ultimate end of action. The spring of the motion that sustained this life was in the vegetable creation a mere unfelt impulse: in animals it was impulse accompanied with sensation: in man it was the direction of Reason, which in him was naturally supreme over all merely blind irrational impulses. What then does Reason direct? 'To live according to Nature' is one answer: and thus we get the circular exposition of ethical doctrine in its simplest form. Sometimes, however, we are told that it is 'Life according to Virtue': which leads us into the circle already noticed in the Platonic-Aristotelian philosophy; as Virtue, by the Stoics also, is only defined as knowledge of Good and Bad in different circumstances and relations. Indeed, this latter circle is given by the Stoics more neatly and perfectly: for with Plato and Aristotle Virtue was not the *sole*, but only the *chief* content of the notion Good, in its application to human life: but in the view of Stoicism the two notions are absolutely coincident. The result, then, is that Virtue is knowledge of what is good and ought to be sought or chosen, and of what is bad and ought to be shunned or rejected: while at the same time there is nothing good or properly choice-worthy, nothing bad or truly formidable, except Virtue and Vice respectively. But if Virtue is thus declared to be a science that has no object except itself, the notion is inevitably emptied of all practical content. In order, therefore, to avoid this result and to reconcile their system with common sense, the Stoics explained that there were other things in human life which were in a manner preferable, though not strictly good, including in this class the primary objects of men's normal impulses. On what principle then are we to select these objects when our impulses are conflicting or ambiguous? If we can get an answer to this question, we shall at length have come to something practical. But here again the Stoic could find no other general answer except either that we were to choose what was Reasonable, or that we were to act in accordance with Nature: each of which answers is liable to bring us back into the original circle at a different point[1].

In Butler's use of the Stoic formula, this circular reasoning seems to be avoided: but it is so only so long as the intrinsic reasonableness of right conduct is ignored or suppressed. Butler assumes with his opponents that it is reasonable to live according to Nature, and argues that Conscience or the faculty that imposes moral rules is naturally supreme in man. It is therefore reasonable to obey Conscience. But are the rules that Conscience lays down merely known to us as the dictates of arbitrary authority, and not as in themselves reasonable? This would give a surely dangerous absoluteness of authority to the possibly unenlightened conscience of any individual: and Butler is much too cautious to do this: in fact, in more than one passage of the *Analogy*[2] he expressly adopts the doctrine of Clarke, that the true rules of morality are essentially reasonable. But if Conscience, is, after all, Reason applied to Practice, then Butler's argument seems to bend itself into the old circle: 'it is reasonable to live according to Nature, and it is natural to live according to Reason.'

In the next chapter I shall have to call attention to another logical circle into which we are liable to slide, if we refer to the Good or Perfection, whether of the agent or of others, in giving

---

[1] It should be observed that in determining the particulars of external duty the Stoics to some extent used the notion 'nature' in a different way: they tried to discover and realize the end or Design of the 'nature' or constitution of the particular things (especially human beings) that make up the Universe. But since in their view the whole course of the Universe was both perfect and completely predetermined, it was impossible for them to obtain from any observation of actual existence a clear and consistent principle for preferring and rejecting alternatives of conduct: and in fact their most characteristic practical precepts shew a curious collision between the tendency to accept what was customary as 'natural,' and the tendency to reject what seemed arbitrary as unreasonable.

[2] Cf. *Anal.* Pt. II. ch. i. and ch. viii.

an account of any special virtue; unless we are careful, in explaining Good or Perfection, not to use the general notion of virtue (which is commonly regarded as an important element of either). Meanwhile I have already given, perhaps, more than sufficient illustration of one of the most important dangers that beset the student of Ethics. In the laudable attempt to escape from the doubtfulness, disputableness, and apparent arbitrariness of current moral opinions, he is liable to take refuge in principles that are incontrovertible but tautological and insignificant.

§ 3. Can we then, between this Scylla and Charybdis of ethical inquiry, avoiding on the one hand doctrines that merely bring us back to common opinion with all its imperfections, and on the other hand doctrines that lead us round in a circle, find any way of obtaining self-evident moral principles of real significance? It would be disheartening to have to regard as altogether illusory the strong instinct of Common Sense that points to the existence of such principles, and the deliberate convictions of the long line of moralists who have enunciated them. At the same time, the more we extend our knowledge of man and his environment, the more we realize the vast variety of human natures and circumstances that have existed in different ages and countries, the less disposed we are to believe that there is any definite code of absolute rules, applicable to all human beings without exception. And we shall find, I think, that the truth lies between these two conclusions. There are certain absolute practical principles, the truth of which, when they are explicitly stated, is manifest; but they are of too abstract a nature, and too universal in their scope, to enable us to ascertain by immediate application of them what we ought to do in any particular case; particular duties have still to be determined by some other method.

One such principle was given in ch. i. § 3 of this Book; where I pointed out that whatever action any of us judges to be right for himself, he implicitly judges to be right for all similar persons in similar circumstances. Or, as we may otherwise put it, 'if a kind of conduct that is right (or wrong) for me is not right (or wrong) for some one else, it must be on the ground of some difference between the two cases, other than the fact that I and he are different persons[1].' A corresponding proposition may be stated with equal truth in respect of what ought to be done *to*—not *by*—different individuals. These principles have been most widely recognized, not in their most abstract and universal form, but in their special application to the mutual relations of two (or more) similarly situated individuals: as so applied, they appear in what is popularly known as the Golden Rule, 'Do to others as you would have them do to you.' This formula is obviously unprecise in statement; for one might wish for another's co-operation in sin, and be willing to reciprocate it. Nor is it even true to say that we ought to do to others only what we think it right for them to do to us; for no one will deny that there may be differences in the circumstances—and even in the natures—of two individuals, A and B, which would make it wrong for A to treat B in the way in which it is right for B to treat A. In short the self-evident principle strictly stated must take some such negative form as this; 'it cannot be right for A to treat B in a manner in which it would be wrong for B to treat A, merely on the ground that they are two different individuals, and without there being any difference between the natures or circumstances of the two which can be stated as a reasonable ground for difference of treatment.' Such a principle manifestly does not give complete guidance—indeed its effect, strictly speaking, is merely to throw a definite *onus probandi* on the man who applies to another a treatment of which he would complain if applied to himself; but Common Sense has amply recognized the practical importance of the maxim: and its truth, so far as it goes, is certainly self-evident.

A somewhat different application of the same fundamental principle that individuals in similar conditions should be treated similarly finds its sphere in the ordinary administration of Law, or (as we say) of 'Justice.' Accordingly in § 2 of ch. v. of this Book I drew attention to 'impartiality in the

[1] The possibility of conflict between this principle and the maxim of Prudence will be considered later. Here I will only say that the fact that I recognize as possible a conflict between the two does not prevent me from regarding either as self-evident when contemplated by itself. This statement applies equally to the possibility of conflict between Prudence and Benevolence.

application of general rules,' as an important element in the common notion of Justice; indeed, there ultimately appeared to be no other element which could be intuitively known with perfect clearness and certainty. Here again it must be plain that this precept of impartiality is insufficient for the complete determination of just conduct, as it does not help us to decide what kind of rules should be thus impartially applied; though all admit the importance of excluding from government, and human conduct generally, all conscious partiality and 'respect of persons.'

The principle just discussed, which seems to be more or less clearly implied in the common notion of 'fairness' or 'equity,' is obtained by considering the similarity of the individuals that make up a Logical Whole or Genus. There are others, no less important, which emerge in the consideration of the similar parts of a Mathematical or Quantitative Whole. Such a Whole is presented in the common notion of the Good—or, as is sometimes said, 'good on the whole'—of any individual human being. The proposition 'that one ought to aim at one's own good' is sometimes given as the maxim of Rational Self-love or Prudence. As so stated it may seem tautological; since we may define 'good' as 'what one ought to aim at.' But if we say 'one's good on the whole,' the addition at least suggests a principle which, when explicitly stated, is not tautological; though, like those just discussed, it is merely negative and regulative. I have already referred to this principle[1] as that ' of impartial concern for all parts of our conscious life':—we might express it concisely by saying 'that Hereafter *as such* is to be regarded neither less nor more than Now.' It is not, of course, meant that the good of the present may not reasonably be preferred to that of the future on account of its greater certainty: or again, that a week ten years hence may not be more important to us than a week now, through an increase in our means or capacities of happiness. All that the principle affirms is that the mere difference of priority and posteriority in time is not a reasonable ground for having more regard to the consciousness of one moment than to that of

---

[1] Cf. *ante*, note to p. 120.

another. The form in which it practically presents itself to most men is 'that a smaller present good is not to be preferred to a greater future good' (allowing for difference of certainty): since Prudence is generally exercised in restraining a present desire (the object or satisfaction of which we commonly regard as *pro tanto* 'a good'), on account of the remoter consequences of gratifying it. The commonest view of the principle would no doubt be that the present *pleasure* or *happiness* is reasonably to be foregone with the view of obtaining greater pleasure or happiness hereafter: but the principle need not be restricted to a hedonistic application; it is equally applicable to any other interpretation of 'one's own good,' in which good is conceived as a mathematical whole, of which the integrant parts are realized in different parts or moments of a lifetime. And therefore it is perhaps better to distinguish it here from the principle 'that Pleasure is the sole Ultimate Good,' which does not seem to have any logical connexion with it.

So far we have only been considering the 'good on the whole' of a single individual: but just as this notion is constructed by comparison and integration of the different 'goods' that succeed one another in the series of our conscious states, so we have formed the notion of Universal Good which includes the goods of all individual human—or sentient—existences. And here again, just as in the former case, by considering the relation of the integrant parts to the whole and to each other, I obtain the self-evident principle that the good of any one individual is of no more importance, from the point of view (if I may so say) of the Universe, than the good of any other; unless, that is, there are special grounds for believing that more good is likely to be realized in the one case than in the other. And as rational beings we are bound to aim at good generally,—so far as we recognize it as attainable by our efforts—not merely at this or that part of it; we can only evade the conviction of this obligation by denying that there is any such universal good.

This, then, I hold to be the abstract principle of the duty of Benevolence, so far as it is cognizable by direct intuition; that one is morally bound to regard the good of any other individual as much as one's own, except in so far as we judge it to be less, when impartially viewed, or less certainly knowable or attainable. I before observed that the duty of Benevolence as recognized by common sense seems to fall somewhat short of this. But I think it may be fairly urged in explanation of this that *practically* each man, even with a view to universal Good, ought chiefly to concern himself with promoting the good of a limited number of human beings, and that generally in proportion to the closeness of their connexion with him. I think that a 'plain man,' in this age and country at least, if his conscience were fairly brought to consider the hypothetical question, whether it would be morally right for him to seek his own happiness on any occasion if it involved a certain sacrifice of the greater happiness of some other human being, —without any counterbalancing gain to any one else—would answer unhesitatingly in the negative.

I have tried to shew how in the principles of Prudence, Justice and Rational Benevolence as commonly recognized there is at least a self-evident element, immediately cognizable by abstract intuition; depending in each case on the relation which individuals and their particular ends bear to the wholes of which they are parts. I regard the apprehension, with more or less distinctness, of these abstract truths, as the permanent basis of the common conviction that the fundamental precepts of morality are essentially reasonable. No doubt by loose thinkers these principles are often placed side by side with other precepts to which custom and general consent have given a merely illusory air of self-evidence: but the distinction between the two kinds of maxims appears to me to become manifest by merely reflecting upon them. I know by direct reflection that the propositions 'I ought to speak the truth,' 'I ought to keep my promises'—however true they may be— are not self-evident to me; they present themselves as propositions requiring rational justification of some kind. On the other hand, the propositions, 'I ought not to prefer a present lesser good to a future greater good,' and 'I ought not to prefer my own lesser good to the greater good of another[1]' do present

[1] To avoid misapprehension I should state that in these propositions the consideration of the different degrees of *certainty* of present and future, Self and Other, respectively is supposed to have been fully taken into account *before* the future or alien Good is judged to be greater.

themselves as self-evident; as much (*e.g.*) as the mathematical axiom that 'if equals be added to equals the wholes are equal.'

It is on account of the fundamental and manifest importance, in my view, of the distinction above drawn between (1) the moral maxims which reflection shews not to possess ultimate validity, and (2) the moral maxims which are or involve genuine ethical axioms, that I refrained at the outset of this investigation from entering at length into the psychogonical question as to the origin of apparent moral intuitions. For no psychogonical theory has ever been put forward professing to discredit the propositions that I regard as really axiomatic, by shewing that the causes which produced them were such as had a tendency to make them false: while as regards the former class of maxims, a psychogonical proof that they are untrustworthy when taken as absolutely and without qualification true is, in my view, superfluous: since direct reflection shews me that they have no claim to be so taken. On the other hand, so far as psychogonical theory represents moral rules as, speaking broadly and generally, means to the ends of individual and social Good or well-being, it obviously tends to give a general support to the conclusions to which the preceding discussion has brought us by a different method: since it leads us to regard other moral rules as subordinate to the principles of Prudence and Benevolence. It may, however, be thought that in exhibiting this aspect of the morality of Common Sense, psychogonical theory leads us to define in a particular way the general notion of 'good' or 'well-being,' regarded as a result which morality has a demonstrable natural tendency to produce. This question will be most conveniently considered in subsequent chapters[1].

§ 4. I should, however, rely less confidently on the conclusions set forth in the preceding section, if they did not appear to me to be in substantial agreement—in spite of superficial differences—with the doctrines of those moralists who have been most in earnest in seeking among commonly received moral rules for genuine intuitions of the Practical Reason. I have already pointed out[2] that in the history of English Ethics

---

[1] Cf. *post* ch. xiv. § 1: and Book iv. ch. iv.
[2] Cf. *ante* Book i. ch. viii. pp. 98, 99.

the earlier intuitional school shew, in this respect, a turn of thought on the whole more philosophical than that which the reaction against Hume rendered prevalent. Among the writers of this school there is no one who shews more earnestness in the effort to penetrate to really self-evident principles than Clarke[1]. Accordingly, I find that Clarke lays down, in respect of our behaviour towards our fellow-men, two fundamental "rules of righteousness[2]": the first of which he terms Equity, and the second Love or Benevolence. The Rule of Equity he states thus: "Whatever I judge reasonable or unreasonable that another should do for me: that by the same judgment I declare reasonable or unreasonable that I should *in the like case* do for him[3]"—which is, of course, the 'Golden Rule' precisely stated. The obligation to "Universal Love or Benevolence" he exhibits as follows:—

"If there be a natural and necessary difference between Good and Evil: and that which is Good is fit and reasonable, and that which is Evil is unreasonable, to be done: and that which is the Greatest Good is always the most fit and reasonable to be chosen: then...every rational creature ought in its sphere and station, according to its respective powers and faculties, to do all the Good it can to its fellow-creatures: to which end, universal Love and Benevolence is plainly the most certain, direct, and effectual means[4]."

Here the mere statement that a rational agent is bound to

---

[1] In drawing attention to Clarke's system, I ought perhaps to remark that his anxiety to exhibit the parallelism between ethical and mathematical truth (on which Locke before him had insisted) renders his general terminology inappropriate and occasionally leads him into downright extravagances. *E.g.* it is patently absurd to say that "a man who wilfully acts contrary to Justice wills things to be what they are not and cannot be": nor are "Relations and Proportions" or "fitnesses and unfitnesses of things" very suitable designations for the matter of moral intuition. But for the present purpose there is no reason to dwell on these defects.

[2] Clarke's statement of the "Rule of Righteousness with respect to ourselves" I pass over, because it is, as he states it, a derivative and subordinate rule. It is that we should preserve our being, be temperate, industrious, &c., *with a view to the performance of Duty:* which of course supposes Duty (*i.e.* the ultimate and absolute rules of Duty) already determined. I may observe that the reasonableness of Prudence or Self-love is only recognized by Clarke indirectly; in a passage which I quoted before (p. 116).

[3] *Boyle Lectures* (1705), &c. pp. 86, 87.   [4] *l.c.* p. 92.

aim at universal good is open to the charge of tautology, since Clarke defines 'Good' as 'that which is fit and reasonable to be done.' But Clarke obviously holds that each individual 'rational creature' is capable of receiving good in a greater or less degree, such good being an integrant part of universal good. This indeed is implied in the common notion, which he uses, of 'doing Good to one's fellow-creatures,' or, as he otherwise expresses it, 'promoting their welfare and happiness.' And thus his principle is implicitly what was stated above, that the good or welfare of any one individual must as such be an object of rational aim to any other reasonable individual no less than his own similar good or welfare.

It should be observed however that the proposition that Universal Benevolence is the right means to the attainment of universal good, requires the qualification given in ch. v, that the end may not always be best attained by directly aiming at it. Rational Benevolence, like Rational Self-Love, may be self-limiting; may direct its own partial suppression in favour of other impulses.

§ 5. Among modern moralists other than English, Kant would be generally admitted to have been especially careful and rigorous in separating the purely rational element of the moral code. Now we have already noticed that his fundamental principle of duty is the 'formal' rule of "acting on a maxim that one can will to be law universal"; which is an immediate practical corollary from the principle that I first noticed in the preceding section. And we find that when he comes to consider the ends at which virtuous action is aimed, the only really ultimate end which he lays down is the object of Rational Benevolence as commonly conceived—the happiness of other men[1]. Owing, however, to the error before pointed out[2] of exaggerating the efficacy of his formal principle in determining right conduct, he makes an unsuccessful attempt to exhibit the duty of Benevolence as an immediate deduction

---

[1] Kant no doubt gives the agent's own Perfection as another absolute end; but when we come to examine his notion of perfection, we find that it is not really determinate without the statement of other ends of reason, for the accomplishment of which we are to perfect ourselves.

[2] Cf. § 3 of ch. i. of this book.

from this formula; when considered in combination with the desire for the kind services of others which (as he assumes) the exigencies of life must arouse in every man. The maxim, he says, "that each should be left to take care of himself without either aid or interference," is one that we might indeed *conceive* existing as a universal law: but it would be impossible for us to *will* it to be such. "A will that resolved this would be inconsistent with itself, for many cases may arise in which the individual thus willing needs the benevolence and sympathy of others[1]." Similarly elsewhere[2] he explains at more length that the Self-love which necessarily exists in every one involves the desire of being loved by others and receiving aid from them in case of need. We thus necessarily constitute ourselves an end for others, and claim that they shall contribute to our happiness: and so, according to his fundamental principle, we must recognize the duty of making *their* happiness *our* end.

Now I cannot regard this reasoning as strictly cogent. In the first place, that every man in need wishes for the aid of others is an empirical proposition which Kant cannot know *à priori*. We can certainly conceive a man in whom the spirit of independence and the distaste for incurring obligations should be so strong that he would choose to endure any privations rather than receive aid from others. But even granting that every one, in the actual moment of distress, must necessarily wish for the assistance of others; still a strong man, after balancing the chances of life, may easily think that he and such as he have more to gain, on the whole, by the general adoption of the egoistic maxim; benevolence being likely to bring them more trouble than profit.

In other passages, however, Kant reaches the same conclusion by a different line of argument. He lays down that, as all action of rational beings is done for some end, there must be some absolute end, corresponding to the absolute rule before given that imposes on our maxims the form of universal law. This absolute end, prescribed by Reason necessarily and *à priori* for all rational beings as such, can be nothing but Reason itself, or the Universe of Rationals; for what the rule inculcates is, in

---

[1] *Grundlegung*, p. 50 (Rosenkrantz).
[2] *Metaph. Anfangsgr. d. Tugendlehre*, Einleit. § 8. Cf. also § 30.

fact, that we should act as rational units in a universe of rational beings (and therefore on principles conceived and embraced as universally applicable). Or again, we may reach the same result negatively. For all particular ends at which men aim are constituted such by the existence of some particular object. Now we cannot tell *à priori* that any one of these special impulses forms part of the constitution of all men: and therefore we cannot state it as an absolute dictate of Reason that we should aim at any such special object. If, then, we thus exclude all particular empirical ends, there remains only the principle that "all Rational beings as such are ends to each:" or, as Kant sometimes puts it, that "humanity exists as an end in itself."

Now, says Kant, so long as I confine myself to mere non-interference with others, I do not positively make Humanity my end; my aims remain selfish, though restricted by this condition of non-interference with others. My action, therefore, is not truly virtuous; for Virtue is exhibited and consists in the effort to realize the end of Reason in opposition to mere selfish impulses. Therefore "the ends of the subject, which is itself an end, must of necessity be my ends, if the representation of Humanity as an end in itself is to have its full weight with me[1]," and my action is to be truly rational and virtuous.

Here, again, I can hardly accept the form of Kant's argument. In the first place, the conception of "humanity as an end in itself" is perplexing: because by an End we commonly mean something to be realized, whereas "humanity" is, as Kant says, "a self-subsistent end." Indeed, there seems to be a sort of paralogism in the deduction of the principle of Benevolence by means of this conception. For the humanity which Kant maintains to be an end in itself is Man (or the aggregate of men) *in so far as rational*. But the subjective ends of other men, which Benevolence directs us to take as our own ends, would seem, according to Kant's own view, to depend upon and correspond to their *non-rational* impulses—their empirical desires and aversions. It is hard to see why, if man *as a rational being* is an absolute end to other rational beings, they must therefore adopt his subjective aims as determined by his non-

[1] *Grundlegung*, p. 59.

rational impulses. And, as I have before argued[1], the rational end or good of the individual cannot be identified with the object of his actual desires, even if we add the qualification 'so far as these desires are mutually consistent.'

The nature of Ultimate Good will be further considered in the next chapter. Meanwhile I observe that by whatever arguments it is reached, Kant's conclusion is in substantial agreement with the view of the duty of Rational Benevolence that I gave in § 3. He regards it as evident *à priori* that each rational agent is bound to aim at the happiness of all other rational beings no less than its own: nay, in his view, it can only be stated as a *duty* for me to seek my own happiness in so far as I consider it a part of Universal Happiness.

I must now point out—if it has not long been apparent to the reader—that the self-evident principles laid down in § 3 do not specially belong to Intuitionism in the restricted sense which, for clear distinction of methods, I gave to this term at the outset of our investigation. The axiom of Prudence, as I have given it, is the self-evident principle on which, according to me, Rational Egoism is based; it makes explicit the ground on which Butler, Reid and their followers have attributed "reasonableness" and "authority" to self-love[2]. Again, the axiom of Justice or Equity as above stated—'that similar cases ought to be treated similarly'—belongs in all its applications to Utilitarianism as much as to any system commonly called Intuitional: while the axiom of Rational Benevolence is, in my view, required as a rational basis for the Utilitarian system.

§ 6. We seem then to have arrived, in our search for really clear and certain ethical intuitions, at the fundamental maxim of Utilitarianism. It must be admitted indeed that the thinkers who in recent times have taught this latter system, have not, for the most part, expressly tried to exhibit the truth of their first principle by means of any such procedure as that above given. Still, whenever they do offer any "considerations

[1] Book I. ch. ix. § 3.
[2] On the relation of Rational Self-love to Rational Benevolence—which I regard as the profoundest problem of Ethics—my final view is given in the last chapter of this treatise.

capable of determining the reason to give assent[1] to the principle of utility," their reasoning seems to involve some such procedure, or at least to be logically incomplete without it. To illustrate this, let us consider the considerations of this kind that Mill offers in ch. iv. of his *Utilitarianism*.

"The only proof capable of being given that an object is visible, is that people actually see it. The only proof that a sound is audible, is that people hear it: and so of the other sources of our experience. In like manner, I apprehend, the sole evidence it is possible to produce that anything is desirable, is that people do actually desire it...... No reason can be given why the general happiness is desirable, except that each person, so far as he believes it to be attainable, desires his own happiness. This, however, being a fact, we have not only all the proof which the case admits of, but all which it is possible to require, that happiness is a good: that each person's happiness is a good to that person, and the general happiness, therefore, a good to the aggregate of persons." He then goes on to shew that pleasure, and pleasure alone, is what all men actually do desire.

Now it must be borne in mind that it is as a "standard of right and wrong," or "directive rule of conduct," that the utilitarian principle is put forward by Mill. Hence, in giving as a statement of this principle that "the general happiness is *desirable*," he must be understood to mean (and his whole treatise shews that he does mean) that it is what each individual *ought* to desire, or at least—in the stricter sense of 'ought'—to aim at realizing in action[2]. But this proposition is not established by Mill's reasoning, even if we grant that what is actually desired may be legitimately inferred to be in this sense desirable. For an aggregate of actual desires, each directed towards a different part of the general happiness, does not constitute an actual desire for the general happiness, ex-

---

[1] Cf. Mill, *Utilitarianism*, ch. i. p. 6.

[2] It has been suggested that I have overlooked a confusion in Mill's mind between two possible meanings of the term 'desirable,' (1) what can be desired and (2) what ought to be desired. I intended to shew by the two first sentences of this paragraph that I was aware of this confusion, but thought it unnecessary for my present purpose to discuss it.

isting in any individual; and Mill would certainly not contend that a desire which does not exist in any individual can possibly exist in an aggregate of individuals. There being therefore no actual desire—so far as this reasoning goes—for the general happiness, the proposition that the general happiness is desirable cannot be in this way established. In fact there is a gap in the expressed argument, which must, I think, have been consciously or unconsciously filled in Mill's mind by what I have above tried to exhibit as the intuition of Rational Benevolence.

Utilitarianism is thus presented as the final form into which Intuitionism tends to pass, when the demand for really self-evident first principles is rigorously pressed. In order, however, to make this transition logically complete, we require to interpret 'Universal Good' as 'Universal Happiness.' And this interpretation cannot, in my view, be justified by arguing, as Mill does, from the psychological fact that Happiness is the sole object of men's actual desires, to the ethical conclusion that it alone is desirable or good: because in Book I. ch. iv. of this treatise I have attempted to shew that Happiness or Pleasure is not the only object that each for himself actually desires. The identification of Ultimate Good with Happiness is properly to be reached, I think, by a more indirect mode of reasoning; which I will endeavour to explain in the next Chapter.

CHAPTER XIV.

ULTIMATE GOOD.

§ 1. At the outset of this treatise[1] I noticed that there are two forms in which the object of ethical inquiry is considered; it is sometimes regarded as a Rule or Rules of Conduct, 'the Right,' sometimes as an end or ends, 'the Good.' I shall presently explain why, in my view, the distinction between these two notions is to be treated as ultimate and irreducible: for the present, it is enough to say that in the moral consciousness of modern Europe the two notions are *prima facie* distinct; since while it is thought that the obligation to obey moral rules is absolute, it is not commonly held that the whole Good of man lies in such obedience; this view, we may say, is respectfully repudiated as a Stoical paradox. The 'Summum Bonum' of man is rather regarded as an ulterior result, the connexion of which with his Right Conduct is indeed certain, but less cognizable by us than the Rightness of Conduct itself: in fact this connexion is frequently conceived as supernatural, and so beyond the range of independent ethical speculation. But now, if the conclusions of the preceding chapters are to be trusted, it would seem (1) that most of the commonly received maxims of Duty—even of those which at first sight appear absolute and independent—are found when closely examined to contain an implicit subordination to the more general principles of Prudence and Benevolence: and (2) that no principles except these—and the formal principle of Justice or Equity, which is included in Universal Benevolence, as commonly conceived[2]—can be admitted as at once intuitively clear and certain. While again

---

[1] Cf. Bk. I. ch. i. § 2.

[2] My own exact view of the relation of Justice to Rational Benevolence will be given later (Book IV. ch. 1. § 2).

these principles themselves, so far as they are immediately known by abstract intuition, can only be stated as precepts to seek (1) one's own good on the whole, and (2) the good of any other no less than one's own, in so far as it is no less an element of universal good. It appears then that we are after all brought round again to the old question with which ethical speculation in Europe began, 'What is the Ultimate Good for man?' When however we examine the controversies to which this question originally led, we see that the investigation which has brought us round to it has at any rate shewn us the necessity of excluding the chief answer that orthodox Greek moralists generally gave to it. It will not do for us to say that 'General Good' consists in general Virtue; that is, in such prescriptions and prohibitions as make up the morality of Common Sense. This would obviously involve us in a logical circle; if we are right in holding that the exact determination of these prescriptions and prohibitions must depend on the definition of this General Good.

It may be thought, perhaps, that this argument applies only to morality considered as a code of rules; and that it may be evaded by adopting the view of what I have called 'Æsthetic Intuitionism' and regarding Virtues as excellences of conduct clearly discernible by trained insight, although their nature does not admit of being stated in definite formulæ. But it will be seen on closer inspection that our notions of special virtues do not really become more independent by becoming more indefinite: they still contain, though perhaps more latently, the same reference to 'Good' or 'Wellbeing' as an ultimate standard. This appears clearly when we consider any virtue in relation to the cognate vice—or at least *non-virtue*—into which it tends to pass over when pushed to an extreme, or exhibited under inappropriate conditions. For example, Common Sense may seem to regard Liberality, Frugality, Courage, Placability as intrinsically desirable: but when we consider their relation respectively to Profusion, Meanness, Foolhardiness, Weakness, we find that Common Sense draws the line in each case not by immediate intuition, but by reference either to some definite maxim of duty, or to the general notion of 'Good' or Wellbeing: and similarly when we ask at what point Candour, Generosity, Humility, cease to be virtues by becoming 'excessive.' Other qualities commonly admired such as Energy, Zeal, Self-control, Thoughtfulness are obviously regarded as virtues only when they are directed to good ends. In short, the only so-called Virtues which can be thought to be essentially and always such, and incapable of excess, are such qualities as Wisdom, Universal Benevolence, and (in a sense) Justice; of which the notions manifestly involve this notion of Good, supposed already determinate. Wisdom is insight into Good and the means to Good; Benevolence is exhibited in doing Good: Justice (when so regarded) lies in distributing Good (or evil) impartially according to right rules. If then we are asked what is this Good which it is excellent to know, to bestow on others, to distribute impartially, it would be absurd to reply that it is just this knowledge, this beneficent impulse, this impartial distribution. I conclude therefore that however prominent Virtue may properly be made in a popular description of the Good or Desirable life, we cannot, without manifest divergence from Common Sense, introduce it in a scientific explanation of the nature of Ultimate Good.

And if this be true of Virtue, it seems to be yet more evidently true of most of the other graces and gifts, bodily or mental, which make up the common notion of human Excellence or Perfection. Although the goodness of such gifts and skills may be recognized and admired instinctively, reflection shews us that they are conceived as essentially relative to some Good which they contribute to produce and maintain. Thus, though from a practical point of view I fully recognize the importance of urging that men should aim at an ideal of character, and consider action in its effects on character, I cannot therefore infer that virtues or talents, faculties, habits, or dispositions of any kind, are the constituents of Ultimate Good. Indeed it seems to me that the opposite is implied in the very conception of a faculty or disposition; it can only be defined as a tendency to act or feel in a certain way under certain conditions; and such a tendency is obviously not valuable in itself but for the acts and feelings in which it takes effect, or for the ulterior consequences of these—which consequences, again, cannot be regarded as Ultimate Good, so long as they are merely conceived as modifications of faculties, dispositions, &c. When, therefore, I say that effects on character are important, it is a summary way of saying that by the laws of our mental constitution the present act or feeling is a cause tending to modify importantly our acts and feelings in the indefinite future: the comparatively permanent result supposed to be produced in the mind or soul, being a tendency that will shew itself in an indefinite number of particular acts and feelings, may easily be more important than a single act or the transient feeling of a single moment: but its comparative permanence is no ground for regarding it as a constituent of ultimate good; as it is as permanently conducive to something else that we value it. The skill of a chess-player is permanent as compared with the games in which it is exhibited: but it would be paradoxical to say that the games are desirable for the sake of the skill and not the skill for the sake of the amusement; and the same thing is true, *mutatis mutandis*, of all the elements of our common notion of perfection of intellect or character.

Have we then simply to fall back on the other answer which Greek speculation brought out in continually sharper antithesis to the view that Ultimate Good was Virtue; and say that it is Pleasure or Happiness? Perhaps the majority of mankind would affirm this without hesitation; and accordingly in my examination of the common rules of morality I have sometimes stated 'general happiness' as the end or standard to which the rule was found implicitly to refer[1]. But more often it has seemed to me more correct to give the reference vaguely to 'good' (or sometimes 'expediency') or wellbeing; recognizing that there are many persons who are not prepared to interpret these wider notions in terms of Pleasure. It remains, then, to ask, what we can say of Good or Wellbeing, if we are not to say that it is Happiness, nor yet Perfection of Character?

§ 2. In ch. ix. of Book I. we were led to the conclusion that none of the comparatively permanent things which we commonly judge to be good could, on reflection, be maintained to be ultimately good and desirable for man, except some quality of human existence itself: and if, on the grounds above stated,

---

[1] I have done this (*e.g.*) in the case of Benevolence; and elsewhere where *pain* or *pleasure* of any kind seemed clearly to come within the purview of Common Sense.

Goodness of character is excluded, the only alternative seems to be to say that what is ultimately Good, must be Good or desirable Conscious Life.

And we may limit the notion yet further: for when we reflect upon Conscious Life, it becomes evident that we can attach no intrinsic value to the merely corporeal side of our organic life, the movements in the particles of organized matter which we suppose to be inseparable concomitants of our ever-varying conscious states. That these movements, considered in themselves, should be of one kind rather than another, or that they should be continued for a longer rather than a shorter period, is in itself quite indifferent to us. If therefore a certain quality of human Life is that which is ultimately desirable, it must be human Life regarded on its psychical side, or, briefly, Consciousness.

I cannot therefore accept a view of the wellbeing or welfare of human beings—as of other living things—which is suggested by current zoological conceptions and apparently maintained with more or less definiteness by influential writers; according to which, when we attribute goodness or badness to the manner of existence of any living organism, we should be understood to attribute to it a tendency either (1) to self-preservation or (2) to the preservation of the community or race to which it belongs —so that what "Wellbeing" adds to mere "Being" is just promise of future being. It appears to me that this doctrine needs only to be distinctly contemplated in order to be rejected. If all life were as little desirable as some portions of it have been, in my own experience and in that (I believe) of all or most men, I should judge all tendency to the preservation of it to be unmitigatedly bad. Actually, no doubt, as I am not a pessimist, I regard what is preservative of life as generally good, and what is destructive of life as bad: and I quite admit that a most fundamentally important part of the function of morality consists in maintaining such habits and sentiments as are necessary to the continued existence, in full numbers, of a society of human beings under their actual conditions of life. But this is not because the mere existence of human organisms, even if prolonged to eternity, appears to me in any way desirable; it is only assumed to be so because it is supposed to be accompanied by Consciousness on the whole desirable; it is therefore this Desirable Consciousness which we must regard as ultimate Good.

At this point it seems that many utilitarians would consider that no further establishment of their fundamental principle is required; that when we have limited the application of the notion Good to Consciousness, we have really identified it with Happiness; that to say that all other things called good are only means to the end of making consciousness intrinsically better or more desirable, is in fact saying that they are means to the end of happiness. But very important distinctions remain to be considered. In the first place, it is not a sufficient account of the elements of happiness to say that they are "desirable feelings": it is essential, as I before explained, to state that the desirability of each feeling is only directly cognizable by the sentient individual at the time of feeling it, and that therefore this particular judgment of the sentient individual must be taken as final[1] on the question how far each element of feeling has the quality of Ultimate Good. Now no one, I conceive, would estimate in any other way the desirability of feeling considered merely as feeling: but our conscious experience includes other psychical phenomena besides feelings; it includes Cognitions and Volitions, and it is not obvious that the desirability of these is to be estimated by the standard above stated. I think, however, that when we reflect on a cognition as a transient fact of an individual's psychical experience,—distinguishing it on the one hand from the feeling that normally accompanies it, and on the other hand from that relation of the knowing mind to the object known which is implied in the term "true" or "valid cognition[2]";—it is seen to be an element of consciousness quite neutral in respect of desirability: and similarly as regards Volition. It is no doubt true that in ordinary thought consciousness, active and passive, is judged to

[1] Final, that is, so far as the quality of the present feeling is concerned. I have pointed out that so far as any estimate of the desirability or pleasantness of a feeling involves comparison with feelings only represented in idea, it is liable to be erroneous through imperfections in the representation.

[2] The term "cognition" without qualification more often implies what is signified by "true" or "valid": but for the present purpose it is necessary to eliminate this implication.

be preferable on other grounds than its pleasantness: but the explanation of this seems to be (as was suggested in Book II. ch. ii. § 2) that what in such cases we really prefer is no longer the present consciousness itself, but either effects on future consciousness more or less distinctly foreseen, or else something in the conditions or concomitants of the present consciousness.

Thus for example, we may prefer the mental state of apprehending truth to the state of half-reliance on generally accredited fictions[1], although, if the fiction be pleasant, the former state may be more painful than the latter; and such preference may be independent of any effect which we expect either state to have upon our subsequent consciousness. Here, on my view, the real object of preference is not the consciousness of knowing truth, considered merely as consciousness, because the element of pleasure or satisfaction in this is more than outweighed by the concomitant pain; but the relation between the mind and something else, which, as the very notion of 'truth' implies, is whatever it is independently of our cognition of it, and which I therefore call objective. This may become more clear if we imagine ourselves learning afterwards that what we took for truth is not really such: for in this case we should certainly feel that our preference had been mistaken; whereas if our choice had really been between two elements of transient consciousness, its reasonableness could not be affected by any subsequent discovery.

Similarly, a man may prefer freedom and penury to a life of luxurious servitude, not because the pleasant consciousness of being free outweighs in prospect all the comforts and securities that the other life would afford, but because he has a predominant aversion to that relation between his will and the will of another which we call slavery: or, again, a philosopher may choose what he conceives as 'inner freedom'—the consistent self-determination of the will—rather than the gratifications of appetite; though recognizing that the latter are more desirable, considered merely as transient feelings. Here, too, he may perhaps be led to regard his preference as mistaken, if he be afterwards persuaded that there is no such thing as Freedom; that we are all slaves of circumstances, destiny, &c.

[1] Cf. Lecky, *History of European Morals*, pp. 52 seqq.

So again, one may believe that what pleases one most among works of art is not really the most beautiful, and may prefer the contemplation of the latter to that of the former, as a more elevated exercise of taste.

§ 3. In this way it is possible to hold that the objective relations of conscious minds which we call cognition of Truth, contemplation of Beauty, Freedom of action, &c., are Good, independently of the pleasures that we derive from them; so that the principle of Rational Benevolence, which was stated in the last chapter as an indubitable intuition of the practical Reason, would not direct us to the pursuit of universal happiness alone, but of Truth, Freedom, Beauty as well, as ends ultimately desirable for mankind generally. And this view though not, I think, the prevailing one, is undoubtedly widely accepted among cultivated persons.

I think, however, that this view ought not to commend itself to the sober judgment of reflective persons. In order to shew this, I must ask the reader to use the same twofold procedure that I before requested him to employ in considering the absolute and independent validity of common moral precepts. I appeal firstly to his intuitive judgment after due consideration of the question when fairly placed before it: and secondly to a comprehensive comparison of the ordinary judgments of mankind. As regards the first argument, to me at least it seems clear that these objective relations of the conscious subject, when distinguished from the consciousness accompanying and resulting from them, are not ultimately and intrinsically desirable; any more than material or other objects are, when considered apart from any relation to conscious existence. Admitting that we have actual experience of such preferences as have just been described, of which the ultimate object is something that is not merely consciousness: it still seems to me that when (to use Butler's phrase) we "sit down in a cool hour," we can only justify to ourselves the importance that we attach to any of these objects by considering its conduciveness, in one way or another, to the happiness of conscious (or sentient) beings.

The second argument, that refers to the common sense of mankind, obviously cannot be made completely cogent; since, as above stated, several cultivated persons do habitually judge that knowledge, art, &c., are ends independently of the pleasure derived from them. But we may urge not only that all these elements of "ideal good" are productive of pleasure in various ways; but also that they seem to obtain the commendation of Common Sense, roughly speaking, in proportion to the degree of this productiveness. This seems obviously true of Beauty; and will hardly be denied in respect of any kind of social ideal: it is paradoxical to maintain that any degree of Freedom, or any form of social order, would still be commonly regarded as desirable even if we were certain that it had no tendency to promote the general happiness. The case of Knowledge is rather more complex; but certainly Common Sense is most impressed with the value of knowledge, when its 'fruitfulness' has been demonstrated. It is, however, aware that experience has frequently shewn how knowledge, long fruitless, may become unexpectedly fruitful, and how light may be shed on one part of the field of knowledge from another apparently remote: and even if any particular branch of scientific pursuit could be shewn to be devoid of even this indirect utility, it would still deserve some respect on utilitarian grounds; both as furnishing to the inquirer the refined and innocent pleasures of curiosity, and because the intellectual disposition which it exhibits and sustains, is likely on the whole to produce fruitful knowledge. Still in cases approximating to this latter, Common Sense is somewhat disposed to complain of the misdirection of valuable effort; so that the meed of honour commonly paid to Science seems to be graduated, though perhaps unconsciously, by a tolerably exact utilitarian scale. Certainly the moment the legitimacy of any branch of scientific inquiry is seriously disputed, as in the recent case of vivisection, the controversy on both sides is generally conducted on an avowedly utilitarian basis.

At the same time it must be allowed that we find in Common Sense an aversion to admit Happiness (when explained to mean a sum of pleasures) to be the sole ultimate end and standard of right conduct. But this, I think, can be fully accounted for by the following considerations.

I. The term Pleasure is not commonly used so as to include clearly *all* kinds of consciousness which we desire to retain or reproduce: in ordinary usage it suggests too prominently the coarser and commoner kinds of such feelings; and it is difficult even for those who are trying to use it scientifically to free their minds altogether from the associations of ordinary usage, and to mean by Pleasure only Desirable Consciousness or Feeling of whatever kind. Again, our knowledge of human life continually suggests to us instances of pleasures which will inevitably involve as concomitant or consequent either a greater amount of pain or a loss of more important pleasures: and we naturally shrink from including even hypothetically in our conception of ultimate good these—in Bentham's phrase—"impure" pleasures; especially since we have, in many cases, moral or æsthetic instincts warning us against such pleasures.

II. We have seen[1] that many important pleasures can only be felt on condition of our experiencing desires for other things than pleasure. Thus the very acceptance of Pleasure as the ultimate end of conduct involves the practical rule that it is not always to be made the conscious end. Hence, even if we are considering merely the good of one human being taken alone, excluding from our view all effects of his conduct on others, still the reluctance of Common Sense to regard pleasure as the sole thing ultimately desirable may be justified by the consideration that human beings tend to be less happy if they are exclusively occupied with the desire of happiness. *E.g.* (as was before shewn) we shall miss the valuable pleasures which attend the exercise of the benevolent affections if we do not experience genuinely disinterested impulses to procure happiness for others (which are, in fact, implied in the notion of 'benevolent affections').

III. But again, I hold as was expounded in the preceding chapter, that disinterested benevolence is not only thus generally in harmony with rational Self-love, but also in another sense and independently rational: that is, Reason shews me that if my happiness is desirable and a good, the equal happiness of any other person must be equally desirable. Now, when Happiness is spoken of as the sole ultimate good of man, the idea most commonly suggested is that each individual is to seek his own happiness at the expense (if necessary) or, at any rate, to

---

[1] Book I. ch. iv., cf. Book II. ch. iii.

the neglect of that of others: and this offends both our sympathetic and our rational regards for others' happiness. It is, in fact, rather the end of Egoistic than of Universalistic Hedonism, to which Common Sense feels an aversion. And certainly one's individual happiness is, in many respects, an unsatisfactory mark for one's supreme aim, apart from any direct collision into which the exclusive pursuit of it may bring us with rational or sympathetic Benevolence. It does not possess the characteristics which, as Aristotle says, we "divine" to belong to Ultimate Good: being (so far, at least, as it can be empirically foreseen) so narrow and limited, of such necessarily brief duration, and so shifting and insecure while it lasts. But Universal Happiness, desirable consciousness or feeling for the innumerable multitude of living beings, present and to come, seems an End that satisfies our imagination by its vastness, and sustains our resolution by its comparative security.

It may, however, be said that the individual who prefers another's happiness to his own, on the ground that it is reasonable to do so, must regard the realization of Reason, and not happiness, as his own Good—since we have defined Good to be what a man may reasonably desire—; and that if it be a Good for him to act on this preference he must recognize it as a Good for others; so that there will be two incommensurable ultimate Goods for each and all, Conformity to Reason and Happiness. Here we must carefully distinguish a mere question of words from a question of ethical principle. The latter it will be perhaps easier to raise clearly by asking (1) whether real self-sacrifice—the sacrifice of one's own 'good on the whole' to that of others—is conceivable; and (2) whether, if so, what appears to be real self-sacrifice is under any circumstances dictated by the moral Reason and Conscience of mankind. It seems to me clear that Common Sense answers these questions in the affirmative; while at the same time holding—as Butler interprets it—that "self love" no less than Conscience is "reasonable" and therefore a ruling principle in the nature of man, which must somehow be reconciled with conscience if action in conformity with man's rational nature is to be really possible. I follow Butler in recognizing this Dualism of the Practical Reason, which I regard as an irreducible result of ethical reflection: and I consider that the best mode of recognizing it is to adopt as final the distinction in ordinary use between the terms Right and Good, and say that, in the case supposed, self-sacrifice is judged to be morally Right, though—*ex vi termini*—it is not judged to be Good on the whole for the self-sacrificing individual. My object in thus distinguishing the terms is not in any way to obscure the apparent conflict of Practical Reason with itself; but rather to assist in making clear wherein it consists: i.e. in the inevitable twofold conception of a human individual as a whole in himself, and a part of a larger whole. There is something that it is reasonable for him to desire, when he considers himself as an independent unit, and something again which he must recognize as reasonably to be desired, when he takes the point of view of a larger whole; the former of these objects I call his own Ultimate "Good," and the latter Ultimate Good taken universally; while to the sacrifice of the part to the whole, which is from the point of view of the whole reasonable, I apply the different term "right," to avoid confusion[1].

The fact that, in the earlier age of ethical thought which Greek philosophy represents, men sometimes judged an act to be 'good' for the agent, and what he for his own sake would reasonably desire to do, even while recognizing that its consequences would be on the whole painful to him,—as (*e.g.*) a heroic exchange of a life full of happiness for a painful death at the call of duty—should be explained, I think, in two ways combined: partly, in my opinion, it is to be attributed to a certain confusion of thought between the two points of view just distinguished, and partly to a faith deeply rooted in the moral consciousness of mankind, that there cannot be really and ultimately any conflict between the two kinds of reasonableness[2]. But when 'Reasonable Self-love' has been clearly distinguished from Conscience, as it is by Butler and his fol-

[1] This 'Dualism of the Practical Reason' will be further discussed in the concluding chapter of the treatise.

[2] We may illustrate this double explanation by a reference to some of Plato's dialogues, such as the *Gorgias*, where the ethical argument has a singularly mixed effect on the mind. Partly, it seems to us more or less dexterous sophistry, playing on a confusion of thought latent in the common notion of good: partly a noble and stirring expression of a profound moral faith.

lowers, we find it is naturally understood to mean desire for one's own Happiness: so that in fact the interpretation of 'one's own good,' which was almost peculiar in ancient thought to the Cyrenaic and Epicurean heresies, is adopted by some of the most orthodox of modern moralists. Indeed it often does not seem to have occurred to these latter that this notion can have any other interpretation[1]. If, then, when any one hypothetically concentrates his attention on himself, Good is naturally and almost inevitably conceived to be Pleasure, we shall hardly conclude that the Good of any number of similar beings, whatever their mutual relations may be, can be something essentially different in quality.

IV. But lastly, from the universal point of view no less than from that of the individual, it seems true that Happiness is likely to be better attained if the extent to which we set ourselves consciously to aim at it be carefully restricted. And this not only because action is likely to be more effective if our effort is temporarily concentrated on the realization of more limited ends—though this is no doubt an important reason:—but also because the fullest development of happy life for each individual seems to require that he should have other external objects of interest besides the happiness of other conscious beings. And thus we may conclude that the pursuit of the ideal objects before mentioned, Truth, Freedom, Beauty, &c., *for their own sakes*, is indirectly and secondarily, though not primarily and absolutely, rational; on account not only of the happiness that will result from their attainment, but also of that which springs from their disinterested pursuit. While yet if we ask for a final criterion of the comparative value of the different objects of men's enthusiastic pursuit, and of the limits within which each may legitimately engross the attention of mankind, we shall none the less conceive it to depend upon the degree in which they respectively conduce to Happiness.

If, however, this view be rejected, it remains to consider whether we can frame any other coherent account of Ultimate Good. If we are not to systematize human activities by taking Universal Happiness as their common end, on what other prin-

---

[1] Cf. Stewart, *Philosophy of the Active and Moral Powers*, Bk. II. c. i.

ciples are we to systematize them? It should be observed that these principles must not only enable us to compare among themselves the values of the different non-hedonistic ends which we have been considering, but must also provide a common standard for comparing these values with that of Happiness; unless we are prepared to adopt the paradoxical position of rejecting happiness as absolutely valueless. For we have a practical need of determining not only whether we should pursue Truth rather than Beauty, or Freedom or some ideal constitution of society rather than either, or perhaps desert all of these for the life of worship and religious contemplation; but also how far we should follow any of these lines of endeavour, when we foresee among its consequences the pains of human or other sentient beings, or even the loss of pleasures that might otherwise have been enjoyed by them[1].

I have failed to find and am unable to construct any systematic answer to this question deserving of serious consideration: and hence I am finally led to the conclusion (which at the close of the last chapter seemed to be premature) that the Intuitional method rigorously applied yields as its final result the doctrine of pure Universalistic Hedonism[2].

[1] The controversy on vivisection, to which I referred just now, affords a good illustration of the need that I am pointing out. I do not observe that any one in this controversy has ventured on the paradox that the pain of sentient beings is not *per se* to be avoided.

[2] I have before noticed (Bk. II. ch. iii., note) the metaphysical objection taken by certain writers to the view that Happiness is Ultimate Good; on the ground that Happiness (=sum of pleasures) can only be realized in successive parts, whereas a "Chief Good" must be "something of which some being can be conceived in possession"—something, that is, which he can have all at once. On considering this objection it seemed to me that, in so far as it is even plausible, its plausibility depends on the exact form of the notion 'a Chief Good' (or 'Summum Bonum'), which is perhaps inappropriate as applied to Happiness. I have therefore in this chapter used the notion of 'Ultimate Good': as I can see no shadow of reason for affirming that that which is Good or Desirable *per se*, and not as a means to some further end, must *necessarily* be capable of being possessed all at once. I can understand that a man may aspire after a Good of this latter kind: but so long as Time is a necessary form of human existence, it can hardly be surprising that human good should be subject to the condition of being realized in successive parts.

BOOK IV.

UTILITARIANISM.

BOOK IV.

CHAPTER I.

THE MEANING OF UTILITARIANISM.

§ 1. THE term Utilitarianism is, at the present day, in common use, and is supposed to designate a doctrine or method with which we are all familiar. But on closer examination, it appears to be applied to several distinct theories, having no necessary connexion with one another, and not even referring to the same subject-matter. It will be well, therefore, to define, as carefully as possible, the doctrine that is to be denoted by the term in the present book: at the same time distinguishing this from other doctrines to which usage would allow the name to be applied, and indicating, so far as seems necessary, its relation to these.

By Utilitarianism is here meant the ethical theory, that the conduct which, under any given circumstances, is objectively right, is that which will produce the greatest amount of happiness on the whole; that is, taking into account all whose happiness is affected by the conduct. It would tend to clearness if we might call this principle, and the method based upon it, by some such name as "Universalistic Hedonism:" and I have therefore sometimes ventured to use this term, in spite of its cumbrousness.

The first doctrine from which it seems necessary to distinguish this, is that of Egoistic Hedonism, expounded and discussed in Book II. of this treatise. The difference, however, between the propositions (1) that each ought to seek his own happiness, and (2) that each ought to seek the happiness of all, is so obvious and glaring, that instead of dwelling upon it we seem rather called upon to explain how the two ever came to be confounded, or in any way included under one notion. This question, and the general relation between the two doctrines, were briefly discussed in a former chapter[1]. Among other points it was there noticed that the confusion between these two ethical theories was partly assisted by the confusion with both of the psychological theory that in voluntary actions every agent does, universally or normally, seek his own individual happiness or pleasure. Now there seems to be no *necessary* connexion between this latter proposition and any ethical theory: but in so far as there is a natural tendency to pass from psychological to ethical Hedonism, the transition must be—at least primarily—to the Egoistic phase of the latter. For clearly, from the fact that every one actually does seek his own happiness we cannot conclude, as an immediate and obvious inference, that he ought to seek the happiness of other people[2].

Nor, again, is Utilitarianism, as a doctrine of Duty and Virtue, necessarily connected with the theory (belonging to what may be called ethical psychology) that the moral sentiments are derived, by "association of ideas" or otherwise, from experiences of the non-moral pleasures and pains resulting to the agent or to others from different kinds of conduct. An Intuitionist might accept this theory, so far as it is capable of scientific proof, and still hold that these moral sentiments, being found in our present consciousness as independent impulses, ought to possess the authority that they seem to

---

[1] B. I. ch. vi. It may be worth while to notice, that in Mill's well-known treatise on Utilitarianism this confusion, though expressly deprecated, is to some extent encouraged by the author's treatment of the subject. On p. 9, we find stated as the first principle of Utilitarianism "that actions are right and wrong in proportion as they tend to promote happiness." Now this statement does not distinguish Egoistic from Universalistic Hedonism: and the argument as continued for several pages would apply equally well to either system. It is not till we come to p. 16, that we are informed that "the standard is not the agent's own happiness, but the greatest amount of happiness altogether." Hence it is hardly surprising that the most thoughtful opponents of Utilitarianism have often failed to distinguish properly between the two doctrines.

[2] I have already criticised (B. III. ch. xiii.) the mode in which Mill attempts to exhibit this inference.

claim over the more primary desires and aversions from which they have sprung: and an Egoist on the other hand might fully admit the altruistic element of the derivation, and still hold that these and all other impulses (including even Universal Benevolence) are properly under the rule of Rational self-love: and that it is really only reasonable to gratify them in so far as we may expect to find our private happiness in such gratification. In short, what is often called the "utilitarian" theory of the origin of the moral sentiments cannot by itself provide a proof of the ethical doctrine to which I in this treatise restrict the term Utilitarianism. I think, however, that this psychological theory has an important though subordinate place in the establishment of Ethical Utilitarianism, the precise nature of which I shall hereafter examine[1].

Finally, the doctrine that Universal Happiness is the ultimate *standard* must not be understood to imply that Universal Benevolence is the only right or always best *motive* of action. For, as we have before observed, it is not necessary that the end which gives the criterion of rightness should always be the end at which we consciously aim: and if experience shews that the general happiness will be more satisfactorily attained if men frequently act from other motives than pure universal philanthropy, it is obvious that these other motives are reasonably to be preferred on Utilitarian principles.

§ 2. Let us now examine the principle itself somewhat closer. I have already attempted (B. II. ch. i.) to render the notion of Greatest Happiness as clear and definite as possible; and the results there obtained are of course as applicable to the discussion of Universalistic as to that of Egoistic Hedonism. We shall understand, then, that by Greatest Happiness is meant the greatest possible surplus of pleasure over pain, the pain being conceived as balanced against an equal amount of pleasure, so that the two contrasted amounts annihilate each other for purposes of ethical calculation. And of course, here as before, the assumption is involved that all pleasures included in our calculation are capable of being compared quantitatively with one another and with all pains; that every such feeling has a certain intensive quantity, positive or negative (or, per-

[1] Cf. *post*, ch. iv.

haps, zero), in respect of its desirableness, and that this quantity may be to some extent known: so that each may be at least roughly weighed in ideal scales against any other. This assumption is involved in the very notion of Maximum Happiness; as the attempt to make 'as great as possible' a sum of elements not quantitatively commensurable would be a mathematical absurdity. Therefore whatever weight is to be attached to the objections brought against this assumption (which was discussed in ch. iii. of Book II.) must of course tell against the present method.

We have next to consider who the "all" are, whose happiness is to be taken into account. Are we to extend our concern to all the beings capable of pleasure and pain whose feelings are affected by our conduct? or are we to confine our view to human happiness? The former view is the one adopted by Bentham and Mill, and (I believe) by the Utilitarian school generally: and is obviously most in accordance with the universality that is characteristic of their principle. It is the Good *Universal*, interpreted and defined as 'happiness' or 'pleasure,' at which a Utilitarian considers it his duty to aim: and it seems arbitrary and unreasonable to exclude from the end, as so conceived, any pleasure of any sentient being.

It must, however, be admitted that by giving this extension to the notion, we considerably increase the scientific difficulties of the hedonistic comparison, which have already been pointed out (B. II. ch. iii.). For if it be difficult to compare the pleasures and pains of other men accurately with our own, a comparison of either with the pleasures and pains of the inferior animals is obviously still more obscure. Practically, Utilitarians have always concerned themselves almost entirely with *human* happiness: apparently assuming the comparative inferiority in intensity of the pleasure of other sentient beings. But even if we limit our attention to human beings, the extent of the subjects of happiness is not yet quite determinate. In the first place, it may be asked, How far we are to consider the interests of posterity when they seem to conflict with those of existing human beings? Perhaps, however, it is clear that the time at which a man exists cannot affect the value of his happiness from a universal point of view; and that the interests of posterity must concern a Utilitarian as much as those of his contemporaries, except in so far as the effect of his actions on posterity—and even the existence of human beings to be affected—must necessarily be more uncertain. But a further question arises when we consider that we can to some extent influence the number of future human (or sentient) beings. We have to ask how, on Utilitarian principles, this influence is to be exercised. Here, again, it seems clear that, supposing the average happiness enjoyed to remain the same, Utilitarianism directs us to make the number enjoying it as great as possible. But if we foresee as possible that an increase in numbers will be accompanied by a decrease in average happiness, or *vice versâ*, a difficulty arises which has not only never been formally noticed, but which seems to have been substantially overlooked by many Utilitarians. For example, political economists of the school of Malthus often appear to assume that no increase of numbers can be right which involves any decrease in average happiness. But if we take Utilitarianism to prescribe, as the ultimate end of action, happiness on the whole, and not any individual's happiness, unless considered as an element of the whole, it would follow that, if the additional population enjoy on the whole positive happiness, we ought to weigh the amount of happiness gained by the extra number against the amount lost by the remainder. So that, strictly conceived, the point up to which, on Utilitarian principles, population ought to be encouraged to increase, is not that at which average happiness is the greatest possible, but that at which the product formed by multiplying the number of persons living into the amount of average happiness reaches its maximum[1].

It may be well here to make a remark which has a wide application in Utilitarian discussion. The conclusion just given wears a certain air of absurdity to the view of Common Sense; because its show of exactness is grotesquely incongruous with our consciousness of the inevitable inexactness of all such cal-

---

[1] I do not mean to deny that the assumptions required to throw the Malthusian argument into a strictly utilitarian form are such as Malthusians generally would reject, if explicitly stated: I merely urge that the necessity of making them is often overlooked.

culations in actual practice. But, that our practical Utilitarian reasonings must necessarily be rough, is no reason for not making them as accurate as the case admits; and we shall be more likely to succeed in this if we keep before our mind as distinctly as possible the strict type of the calculation that we should have to make, if all the relevant considerations could be estimated with mathematical precision.

There is one more point that remains to be noticed. It is evident that there may be many different ways of distributing the same quantum of happiness among the same number of persons; in order, therefore, that the Utilitarian criterion of right conduct may be as complete as possible, we ought to know which of these ways is to be preferred. This question is often ignored in expositions of Utilitarianism. It has perhaps seemed somewhat idle, as suggesting a purely abstract and theoretical perplexity, that could have no practical exemplification; and no doubt, if all the consequences of actions were capable of being estimated and summed up with mathematical precision, we should probably never find the excess of pleasure over pain exactly equal in the case of two competing alternatives of conduct. But the very indefiniteness of all hedonistic calculations, which was sufficiently shewn in Book II., renders it by no means unlikely that there may be no *cognizable* difference between the quantities of happiness involved in two sets of consequences respectively; the more rough our estimates necessarily are, the less likely we shall be to come to any clear decision between our alternatives. In all such cases, therefore, it becomes practically important to ask whether any mode of distributing a given quantum of happiness is better than any other. Now the Utilitarian formula seems to supply no answer to this question: at least we have to supplement the principle of seeking the greatest happiness on the whole by some principle of Just or Right distribution of this happiness. The principle which most Utilitarians have either tacitly or expressly adopted is that of pure equality—at any rate so far as the persons among whom happiness is to be distributed do not include the agent[1]—as given in Bentham's formula,

---

[1] Utilitarians have not usually considered very closely the question *how far* it is right for A to sacrifice his own happiness for that of B: and probably most

"everybody to count for one, and nobody for more than one." And this principle is obviously the simplest, and the only one which does not need a special justification; for, as we saw, it must be reasonable to treat any one man in the same way as any other, if there be no reason apparent for treating him differently[1].

of them would consider it extravagant to demand that the agent should give no preference to himself, in the case supposed in the text.

[1] It should be observed that the question here is as to the distribution of *Happiness*, not the *means of happiness*.

CHAPTER II.

THE PROOF OF UTILITARIANISM.

In Book II., where we discussed the method of Egoistic Hedonism, we did not take occasion to examine any proof of its first principle: and in the case of Universalistic Hedonism also, what chiefly concerns us is not how its principle is to be proved to those who do not accept it, but <u>what</u> consequences are logically involved in its acceptance. At the same time it is important to observe that the principle of aiming at universal happiness is more generally felt to require some proof, or at least (as Mill puts it) some "considerations determining the mind to accept it," than the principle of aiming at one's own happiness. From the point of view, indeed, of abstract philosophy, I do not see why the Egoistic principle should pass unchallenged any more than Universalistic. Apart from the aversion, already noticed, which many minds have to Egoism as base and despicable, which leads them to cling eagerly to that state of choice in which they prefer something else to their own feelings, and refuse to acquiesce in any other attitude[1], I do not see why the axiom of Prudence should not be questioned on a ground similar to that on which Egoists refuse to admit the axiom of Rational Benevolence. If the Utilitarian has to answer the question, 'Why should I sacrifice my own happiness for the greater happiness of another?' it must surely be admissible to ask the Egoist, 'Why should I sacrifice a present pleasure for a greater one in the future? Why should I concern myself about my own future feelings any more than about the feelings of

---

[1] I have before suggested a Utilitarian explanation of this. Cf. B. III. ch. xiv. § 3.

other persons?' And this question, we may observe, lies especially obvious to those who adopt the views of the extreme empirical school of psychologists, although these views are commonly supposed to have a close affinity with Egoistic Hedonism. If the Ego is merely a system of coherent phenomena, if the permanent identical 'I' is not a fact but a fiction, as Hume and his followers maintain; why should one part of the series of feelings into which the Ego is resolved be concerned with another part of the same series, any more than with any other series?

However, I do not press this question now; since it undoubtedly seems to Common Sense paradoxical to ask for a reason why one should seek one's own happiness on the whole; nor do I myself require such a reason. Arguments for conforming to the commonly received rules of morality are not, perhaps, held to be equally superfluous: indeed we find that utilitarian reasons are continually given for this and that particular moral maxim. Still the fact that certain rules are commonly received as binding renders it generally unnecessary to prove their authority to the Common Sense that receives them: while for the same reason a Utilitarian who claims to supersede them by a higher principle is naturally challenged, by Intuitionists no less than by Egoists, to demonstrate the legitimacy of his claim. To this challenge Utilitarians often reply by saying that it is impossible to "prove" a first principle; and this is of course true, if by proof we mean a process which exhibits the principle in question as an inference from premises upon which it remains dependent for its certainty; for these premises, and not the inference drawn from them, would then be the real first principles. Nay, if Utilitarianism is to be *proved* to a man who already holds some other moral principles,—whether he be an Intuitional moralist, who regards as final the principles of Truth, Justice, Obedience to authority, Purity, &c., or an Egoist who regards his own interest as the ultimately reasonable end of his conduct—; the process must be one which establishes a conclusion actually *superior* in validity to the premises from which it starts. For the Utilitarian prescriptions of duty are *primâ facie* in conflict, at certain points and under certain circumstances, both with

Intuitional rules, and with the dictates of Rational Egoism; so that Utilitarianism, if accepted at all, must be accepted as overruling Intuitionism and Egoism. At the same time, if the other principles are not throughout taken as valid, the so-called proof does not seem to be addressed to the Intuitionist or Egoist at all. How shall we deal with this dilemma? How is such a process (certainly somewhat different from ordinary proof) possible or conceivable? Yet there certainly seems to be a general demand for it. Perhaps we may say that what is needed is a line of argument which on the one hand allows the validity, to a certain extent, of the principles already accepted, and on the other hand shews them to be imperfect,—not absolutely and independently valid, but needing qualification and completion.

Such a line of argument, addressed to Egoism, was given in ch. xiii. of the foregoing book. It should be observed that the applicability of this argument depends on the manner in which the Egoistic first principle is formulated. If the Egoist strictly confines himself to stating his conviction that he ought to take his own happiness or pleasure as his ultimate end, there seems no opening for any line of reasoning to lead him to Universalistic Hedonism as a first principle[1]; it cannot be proved that the difference between his own happiness and another's happiness is not *for him* all-important. In this case all that the Utilitarian can do is to effect as far as possible a reconciliation between the two principles; by expounding to the Egoist the *sanctions* of rules deduced from the Universalistic principle—, *i.e.* the pleasures and pains that may be expected to accrue to the Egoist himself from their observation and violation respectively. It is obvious that such an exposition has no tendency to make him accept the greatest happiness of the greatest number as his ultimate end; but only as a means to the end of his own happiness. It is therefore totally different from a *proof* (as above explained) of Universalistic Hedonism. When, however, the Egoist puts forward, implicitly or explicitly, the proposition that his happiness or pleasure is Good, not only *for him*

[1] It is to be observed that he may be led to it in other ways than that of argument: *i.e.* by appeals to his sympathies, or to his moral or quasi-moral sentiments.

but from the point of view of the Universe,—as (*e.g.*) by saying that 'nature designed him to seek his own happiness',—it then becomes relevant to point out to him that *his* happiness cannot be a more important part of Good, taken universally, than the equal happiness of any other person. And thus, starting with his own principle, he may be brought to accept Universal happiness or pleasure as that which is absolutely and without qualification Good or Desirable: as an end, therefore, to which the action of a reasonable agent as such ought to be directed.

This, it will be remembered, is the reasoning[1] that I used in ch. xiii. of the preceding book in exhibiting the principle of Rational Benevolence as one of the few Intuitions which stand the test of rigorous criticism. It should be observed, however, that as addressed to the Intuitionist, this reasoning only shews the Utilitarian first principle to be *one* moral axiom: it does not prove that it is *sole* or *supreme*. The premises with which the Intuitionist starts commonly include other formulæ held as independent and self-evident. Utilitarianism has therefore to exhibit itself in the twofold relation above described, at once positive and negative, to these formulæ. The Utilitarian must, in the first place, endeavour to shew to the Intuitionist that the principles of Truth, Justice, &c. have only a dependent and subordinate validity: arguing either that the principle is really only affirmed by Common Sense as a general rule admitting of exceptions and qualifications, as in the case of Truth, and that we require some further principle for systematizing these exceptions and qualifications; or that the fundamental notion is vague and needs further determination, as in the case of Justice; and further, that the different rules are liable to conflict with each other, and that we require some higher principle to decide the issue thus raised; and again, that the rules are differently formulated by different persons, and that these differences admit of no Intuitional solution, while they shew the vagueness and ambiguity of the common moral notions to which the Intuitionist appeals.

[1] I ought to remind the reader that the argument in ch. xiii. only leads to the first principle of Utilitarianism, if it be admitted that Happiness would be the only thing ultimately and intrinsically Good or desirable. I afterwards in ch. xiv. endeavoured to bring Common Sense to this admission.

This part of the argument I have perhaps sufficiently developed in the preceding book. But this line of reasoning taken by itself is, though effective, incomplete and scarcely adapted to produce perfect conviction. It has to be supplemented by developing the positive relation that exists between Utilitarianism and the Morality of Common Sense: by shewing how Utilitarianism sustains the general validity of the current moral judgments, and thus gives them a further justification, supplementing the defects which reflection finds in the intuitive recognition of their stringency; and at the same time affords a principle of synthesis, and a method for binding the unconnected and occasionally conflicting principles of common moral reasoning into a complete and harmonious system. If systematic reflection upon the morality of Common Sense thus exhibits the Utilitarian principle as that to which Common Sense naturally appeals for that further development of its system which this same reflection shews to be necessary; the proof of Utilitarianism seems as complete as it can be made. And since, further, it is of the utmost importance in considering the method of Utilitarianism to determine exactly its relation to the commonly received rules of morality; it will be proper to examine this relation at some length in the following chapter.

CHAPTER III.

RELATION OF UTILITARIANISM TO THE MORALITY OF COMMON SENSE.

§ 1. It has been before observed (B. I. c. vi.) that the two sides of the double relation in which Utilitarianism stands to the Morality of Common Sense have been respectively prominent at two different periods in the history of English ethical thought. Since Bentham we have been chiefly familiar with the negative or aggressive aspect of the former method. But when Cumberland, replying to Hobbes, put forward the general tendency of the received moral rules to promote the "common Good[1] of all Rationals" his aim was simply Conservative: it never occurs to him to consider whether these rules as commonly formulated are in any way imperfect, and whether there are any discrepancies between such common moral opinions and the conclusions of Rational Benevolence. So in Shaftesbury's system the "Moral" or "Reflex Sense" is supposed to be always pleased with that "balance" of the affections which tends to the good or happiness of the whole, and displeased with the opposite. In Hume's treatise this coincidence is drawn out more in detail, and with a more definite assertion that the perception of utility[2] (or the re-

---

[1] It ought to be observed that Cumberland does not adopt a hedonistic interpretation of Good. Still, I have followed Hallam in regarding him as the founder of English Utilitarianism: since it seems to have been by a gradual and half-unconscious process that 'Good' came to have the definitely hedonistic meaning which it has implicitly in Shaftesbury's system, and explicitly in that of Hume.

[2] I should point out that Hume uses "utility" in a narrower sense than that which Bentham gave it, and one more in accordance with the usage of ordinary language. He distinguishes the "useful" from the "immediately agreeable":

verse) is in each case the source of the moral likings (or aversions) which are excited in us by different qualities of human character and conduct. And we may observe that the most penetrating among Hume's contemporary critics, Adam Smith, admits unreservedly the objective coincidence of Rightness or Approvedness and Utility: though he maintains, in opposition to Hume, that "it is not the view of this utility or hurtfulness, which is either the first or the principal source of our approbation or disapprobation." After stating Hume's theory that "no qualities of the mind are approved of as virtuous, but such as are useful or agreeable either to the person himself or to others, and no qualities are disapproved of as vicious but such as have a contrary tendency;" he remarks that "Nature seems indeed to have so happily adjusted our sentiments of approbation and disapprobation to the conveniency both of the individual and of the society, that after the strictest examination it will be found, I believe, that this is universally the case."

And no one can read the *Inquiry into the First Principles of Morals* (the best, as it seemed to himself, of Hume's philosophical compositions) without being convinced of this at least, that if a list were drawn up of the qualities of character and conduct that are directly or indirectly productive of pleasure to ourselves or to others, it would include all that are commonly known as virtues. Whatever be the origin of our notion of moral goodness or excellence, there is no doubt that "Utility" is a general characteristic of the dispositions to which we apply it: and that, so far, the Morality of Common Sense may be truly represented as at least unconsciously Utilitarian. But it may still be objected, that this coincidence is merely general and qualitative, and that it breaks down when we attempt to draw it out in detail, with the quantitative precision which Bentham introduced into the discussion. And no doubt there is a great

---

so that while recognizing "utility" as the main ground of our moral approbation of the more important virtues, he holds that there are other elements of personal merit which we approve because they are "immediately agreeable", either to the person possessed of them or to others. It appears, however, more convenient to use the word in the wider sense in which it has been current since Bentham.

difference between the assertion that virtue is always productive of happiness, and the assertion that the right action is under all circumstances that which will produce the greatest possible happiness on the whole. But it must be borne in mind that Utilitarianism is not concerned to prove the absolute coincidence in results of the Intuitional and Utilitarian methods. Indeed, if it could succeed in proving as much as this, its success would be almost fatal to its claims; as the adoption of the Utilitarian principle would then become a matter of complete indifference. Utilitarians are rather called upon to shew a natural transition from the Morality of Common Sense to Utilitarianism, somewhat like the transition in special branches of practice from trained instinct and empirical rules to the technical method that embodies and applies the conclusions of science: so that Utilitarianism may be presented as the scientifically complete and systematically reflective form of that regulation of conduct, which through the whole course of human history has always tended substantially in the same direction. For this purpose it is not necessary to prove that existing moral rules are *more* conducive to the general happiness than any others: but only to point out in each case some manifest felicific tendency which they possess.

Hume's dissertation, however, incidentally exhibits much more than a simple and general harmony between the moral sentiments with which we commonly regard actions and their foreseen pleasurable and painful consequences. And, in fact, the Utilitarian argument cannot be fairly judged unless we take fully into account the cumulative force which it derives from the complex character of the coincidence between Utilitarianism and Common Sense.

It may be shewn, I think, that the Utilitarian estimate of consequences not only supports broadly the current moral rules, but also sustains their generally received limitations and qualifications: that, again, it explains anomalies in the Morality of Common Sense, which from any other point of view must seem unsatisfactory to the reflective intellect; and moreover, where the current formula is not sufficiently precise for the guidance of conduct, while at the same time difficulties and perplexities arise in the attempt to give it additional precision, the

Utilitarian method solves these difficulties and perplexities in general accordance with the vague instincts of Common Sense, and is naturally appealed to for such solution in common moral discussions. It may be shewn further, that it not only supports the generally received view of the relative importance of different duties, but is also naturally called in as arbiter, where rules commonly regarded as co-ordinate come into conflict: that, again, when the same rule is interpreted somewhat differently by different persons, each naturally supports his view by urging its Utility, however strongly he may maintain the rule to be self-evident and known *à priori*: that where we meet with marked diversity of moral opinion on any point, in the same age and country, we commonly find manifest and impressive utilitarian reasons on both sides: and that finally the remarkable discrepancies found in comparing the moral codes of different ages and countries are for the most part strikingly correlated to differences in the effects of actions on happiness, or in men's foresight of, or concern for, such effects. Most of these points are noticed by Hume, though in a somewhat casual and fragmentary way: and many of them have been incidentally illustrated in the course of the examination of Common Sense Morality, with which we were occupied in the preceding book. But considering the importance of the present question, it may be well to exhibit in systematic detail the cumulative argument which has just been summed up, even at the risk of repeating to some extent the results previously given.

§ 2. We may begin by replying to an objection which is frequently urged against Utilitarianism. How, it is asked, if the true ground of the moral goodness or badness of actions lies in their utility or the reverse, can we explain the broad distinction drawn by Common Sense between the moral and other parts of our nature? Why is the excellence of Virtue so strongly felt to be different, not merely in kind but in degree, from the excellence of a machine, a fertile field, or a navigable river? It might be answered, in the first place, that as the *natural* (non-moral) feelings excited in us by human beings are generally very different from those caused by inanimate objects, it is to be expected that our judgment of goodness or badness should be accompanied by different sentiments in the two cases; just as the beauty of a woman affects a man quite differently from the beauty of a landscape. But in the case of strictly moral judgments there is a further difference of a fundamental kind. As we saw (B. III. ch. ii.), qualities that are, in the strictest sense of the term, Virtuous, are always such as we conceive capable of being immediately realized by voluntary effort, at least to some extent; that is, the only obstacle to virtuous action is absence of adequate motive. Hence we expect that the judgments of moral goodness or badness, passed either by the agent himself or by others, will—by the fresh motive which they supply on the side of virtue—have an immediate practical effect in causing actions to be at least externally virtuous: and the habitual consciousness of this will account for almost any difference between moral sentiments and the pleasure and pain that we derive from the contemplation of extra-human utilities and inutilities. To this it is replied, that among the tendencies to strictly voluntary actions there are many not commonly regarded as virtuous, which are yet not only useful but on the whole *more* useful than many virtues. "The selfish instinct that leads men to accumulate confers ultimately more advantage on the world than the generous instinct that leads men to give....... It is scarcely doubtful that a modest, diffident, and retiring nature, distrustful of its own abilities, and shrinking with humility from conflict, produces on the whole less benefit to the world than the self-assertion of an audacious and arrogant nature, which is impelled to every struggle, and developes every capacity. Gratitude has no doubt done much to soften and sweeten the intercourse of life, but the corresponding feeling of revenge was for centuries the one bulwark against social anarchy, and is even now one of the chief restraints to crime. On the great theatre of public life, especially in periods of great convulsions where passions are fiercely roused, it is neither the man of delicate scrupulosity and sincere impartiality, nor yet the single-minded religious enthusiast, incapable of dissimulation or procrastination, who confers most benefit on the world. It is much rather the astute statesman, earnest about his ends, but unscrupulous about his means, equally free from the trammels of conscience and from the blindness of zeal, who governs because he partly yields to the passions and the prejudices of his time. But......it has scarcely yet been contended that the delicate conscience which in these cases impairs utility constitutes vice[1]."

These objections are forcibly urged; but they are not very difficult to answer, it being always borne in mind that the present argument does not aim at proving an exact coincidence between Utilitarian inferences and the intuitions of Common Sense, but rather seeks to represent the latter as inchoately and imperfectly Utilitarian.

In the first place, we must carefully distinguish between the recognition of goodness in dispositions, and the recognition of rightness in conduct. An act that a Utilitarian must condemn as likely to do more harm than good may yet shew a disposition or tendency that will on the whole produce more good than harm. This is eminently the case with scrupulously conscientious acts. However true it may be that unenlightened conscientiousness has impelled men to fanatical cruelty, mistaken asceticism, and other infelicific conduct; I suppose no Intuitionist would maintain that carefulness in conforming to the received moral rules has not, on the whole, a tendency to promote happiness. It may be observed, however, that when we perceive the effects of a disposition generally felicific to be in any particular case adverse to happiness, we often apply to it, as so operating, some term of condemnation: thus we speak, in the case above noticed, of 'over-scrupulousness' or 'fanaticism.' But in so far as we perceive that the same disposition would generally produce good results, it is not inconsistent still to regard it, abstracting from the particular case, as a good element of character. Secondly, although, in the view of a Utilitarian, only the useful is praiseworthy, he is not bound to maintain that it is necessarily worthy of praise in proportion as it is useful. From a Utilitarian point of view, as has been before said, we must mean by calling a quality 'deserving of praise', that it is expedient to praise it, with a view to its future production: accordingly, in dis-

---

[1] Lecky, *Hist. of Eur. Mor.*, c. i. pp. 38, 41 seqq.

tributing our praise of human qualities, on utilitarian principles, we have to consider primarily not the usefulness of the quality, but the usefulness of the praise: and it is obviously not expedient to encourage by praise qualities which are likely to be found in excess rather than in defect. Hence (*e.g.*) however necessary self-love or resentment may be to society, it is quite in harmony with Utilitarianism that they should not be recognized as virtues by Common Sense, in so far as it is reasonably thought that they will always be found operating with at least sufficient intensity. We find, however, that when self-love comes into conflict with impulses seen to be on the whole pernicious, it is praised as Prudence: and that when a man seems clearly deficient in resentment, he is censured for tameness: though as malevolent impulses are much more obviously productive of pain than pleasure, it is not unnatural that their occasional utility should be somewhat overlooked. The case of Humility and Diffidence may be treated in a somewhat similar way. As we saw[1], it is only inadvertently that Common Sense praises the tendency to underrate one's own powers: on reflection every one admits that it cannot be good to be in error on this or any other point. But the desires of Superiority and Esteem are so strong in most men, that arrogance and self-assertion are both much commoner than the opposite defects, and at the same time are faults peculiarly disagreeable to others: so that humility gives us an agreeable surprise, and hence Common Sense may naturally overlook the more latent and remote bad consequences of undue self-distrust.

We may observe further that the perplexity which we seemed to find in the Morality of Common Sense, as to the relation of moral excellence to moral effort, is satisfactorily explained and removed when we adopt a Utilitarian point of view: for on the one hand it is easy to see how certain acts—such as kind services—are likely to be more felicific when performed without effort, and from other motives than regard for duty: while on the other hand a person who in doing similar acts achieves a triumph of duty over strong seductive inclinations, exhibits thereby a character which we recognize as felicific in a

[1] B. III. ch. x.

more general way, as tending to a general performance of duty in all departments. So again, there is a simple and obvious utilitarian solution of another difficulty which I noticed, as to the choice between Subjective and Objective rightness in the exceptional case in which alone the two can be presented as alternatives; *i.e.* when we are considering whether we shall influence another to act contrary to his conviction as to what is right. A utilitarian would decide the question by weighing the external felicific consequences of the particular right act against the infelicific results to be apprehended hereafter from the moral deterioration of the person whose conscientious convictions were overborne by other motives: unless the former effects were very important he would certainly regard the danger to character as the greater: but if the other's mistaken sense of duty threatened to cause a grave disaster, he would not hesitate to overbear it by any motives which it was in his power to apply. And in practice I think that the Common Sense of mankind would come to similar conclusions by more vague and unconscious modes of reasoning.

In order, however, to form a precise estimate of the extent to which Utilitarianism agrees or disagrees with Common Sense, it seems best to examine the more definite judgments of right and wrong in conduct, under the particular heads represented by our common notions of virtues and duties. It should be observed that there are some among these notions, the examination of which cannot really affect our decision of the present question; since any adequately precise definitions of them involve, implicitly or explicitly, the notion of 'good' or 'right' supposed already determinate; so that they can neither be used to determine these fundamental conceptions, nor to oppose a Utilitarian interpretation of them. For example, we saw this to be the case with the chief of the intellectual excellences discussed in B. III. c. iii. Wisdom, as commonly conceived, is not exactly the faculty of choosing the right means to the end of universal happiness; rather, as we saw, its notion involves an uncritical synthesis of the different ends and principles that are distinguished and separately examined in the present treatise. But if its import is not distinctly Utilitarian, it is certainly not anything else as distinct from Utilitarian: if we can only define it as the faculty or habit of choosing the right or best means to the right or best end, for that very reason our definition leaves it quite open to us to give the notions 'good' and 'right' a Utilitarian import.

§ 3. Let us then consider first the group of virtues and duties discussed in Book III. c. iv., under the head of Benevolence. Here we naturally begin by noticing the obvious point of coincidence between the Intuitional and Utilitarian systems. For though Benevolence would perhaps be more commonly defined as a disposition to promote the Good of one's fellow-creatures, rather than their Happiness (as definitely understood by Utilitarians); still, as the chief element in the common notion of good (besides happiness) is moral good or Virtue[1], if we can shew that the other virtues are—speaking broadly— all qualities conducive to the happiness of the agent himself or of others, it is evident that Benevolence, whether it prompts us to promote the virtue of others or their happiness, will aim directly or indirectly at the Utilitarian end[2].

Nor, further, does the comprehensive range which Utilitarians give to Benevolence, in stating as their ultimate end the greatest happiness of all sentient beings, seem to be really opposed to Common Sense; for in so far as certain Intuitional moralists restrict the scope of the direct duty of Benevolence to human beings, and regard our duties to brute animals as merely indirect and derived "from the duty of Self-culture," they rather than their Utilitarian opponents appear paradoxical. And if, in laying down that each agent is to consider all other happiness as equally important with his own, Utilitarianism goes decidedly beyond the standard of duty commonly prescribed under the head of Benevolence, it yet can scarcely be said to conflict with Common Sense on this point. For the practical application of this theoretical impartiality of Utilitarianism is limited by several important considerations. In the first place, generally speaking, each man is far better able to provide for his own happiness than for that of any other person, from his more intimate knowledge of his own desires

[1] B. III. ch. iv. § 1.
[2] It will be seen that I do not here assume in their full breadth the conclusions of ch. xiv. of the preceding book.

and needs, and his greater opportunities of gratifying them. And besides, it is under the stimulus of self-interest—at least as expanded into *domestic* interest—that the active energies of most men are most easily and thoroughly drawn out: and if this were removed, general happiness would be diminished by a serious loss of those means of happiness which are obtained by labour; and also, to some extent, by the diminution of the labour itself. For these reasons it would not under actual circumstances promote the universal happiness if each man were to concern himself with the happiness of others as much as with his own. While if I consider the duty abstractly and ideally, even Common-Sense morality seems to bid me "love my neighbour as myself."

It might indeed be plausibly objected, on the other hand, that under the notions of Generosity, Self-sacrifice, &c., Common Sense praises (though it does not prescribe as obligatory) a suppression of egoism beyond what Utilitarianism approves: for we perhaps admire as virtuous a man who gives up his own happiness for another's sake, even when the happiness that he confers is clearly less than that which he resigns, so that there is a diminution of happiness on the whole. But (1) it seems very doubtful whether we do altogether approve such conduct when the disproportion between the sacrifice and the benefit is obvious and striking: and (2) a spectator is often unable to judge whether happiness is lost on the whole, as (*a*) he cannot tell how far he who makes the sacrifice is compensated by sympathetic and moral pleasure, and (*b*) the remoter felicific consequences flowing from the moral effects of such a sacrifice on the agent and on others have to be taken into account: while (3) even if there be a loss in the particular case, still our admiration of self-sacrifice will admit of a certain Utilitarian justification, because such conduct shews a disposition far above the average in its general tendency to promote happiness, and it is perhaps this disposition that we admire rather than the particular act.

It has been said[1], however, that the special claims and duties belonging to special relations, by which each man is

---

[1] Cf. J. Grote, *Utilitarianism*, ch. v.

connected with a few out of the whole number of human beings, are expressly ignored by the rigid impartiality of the Utilitarian formula: and hence that, though Utilitarianism and Common Sense may agree in the proposition that all right action is conducive to the happiness of some one or other, and so far beneficent, still they are irreconcileably divergent on the radical question of the *distribution* of beneficence.

Here, however, it seems that even fair-minded opponents have scarcely treated the Utilitarian argument fairly. They have attacked Bentham's well-known formula, "every man to count for one, nobody for more than one," on the ground that the general happiness will be best attained by inequality in the distribution of each one's services. But it is just because it will be best attained in this way that Utilitarianism necessarily prescribes this way of aiming at it. And the reasons why it is, generally speaking, conducive to the general happiness that each individual should distribute his beneficence in the channels marked out by commonly recognized ties and claims, are tolerably obvious.

For first, in the chief relations discussed in ch. iv. of Book III.—the domestic, and those constituted by consanguinity, friendship, previous kindnesses, and special needs,—the services which Common Sense prescribes as duties are commonly prompted by natural affection, while at the same time they tend to develope and sustain such affection. Now the subsistence of benevolent affections among human beings is itself an important means to the Utilitarian end, because (as Shaftesbury and his followers forcibly urged) the most intense and highly valued of our pleasures are derived from such affections; for both the emotion itself is highly pleasurable, and it imparts this quality to the activities which it prompts and sustains, and the happiness thus produced is continually enhanced by the sympathetic echo of the pleasures conferred on others. And again, where genuine affection subsists, the practical objections to spontaneous beneficence, which were before noticed, are much diminished in force. For such affection tends to be reciprocated, and the kindnesses which are its outcome and expression commonly win a requital of affection: and in so far as this is the case, they have less tendency to weaken the springs of activity in the person benefited; and may even strengthen them by exciting other sources of energy than the egoistic—personal affection, and gratitude, and the desire to deserve love, and the desire to imitate beneficence. And hence it has been often observed that the injurious effects of almsgiving are at least much diminished if the alms are bestowed with unaffected sympathy and kindliness, and in such a way as to elicit a genuine response of gratitude. And further, the beneficence that springs from affection is less likely to be frustrated from defect of knowledge: for not only are we powerfully stimulated to study the real conditions of the happiness of those whom we love, but also such study is rendered more effective from the sympathy which naturally accompanies affection.

On these grounds the Utilitarian will evidently approve of the cultivation of affection and the performance of affectionate services. It may be said, however, that what we ought to approve is not so much affection for special individuals, but rather a feeling more universal in its scope—charity, philanthropy, or (as it has been called) the 'Enthusiasm of Humanity.' And certainly all special affections tend occasionally to come into conflict with the principle of promoting the general happiness: and Utilitarianism must therefore prescribe such a culture of the feelings as will, as far as possible, counteract this tendency. And no doubt some speculative persons have thought the existing relations of human beings highly unfavourable to this culture; and have desired instead some approximation to Plato's ideal of a "communion of wives and children and property, in which the private and the individual should be altogether banished from life." But this view is opposed to the results of psychological experience as commonly interpreted: for it seems rather that most persons are only capable of strong affections towards a few human beings in certain close relations, especially the domestic: and that if these are suppressed, what they will feel towards their fellow-creatures generally will be, as Aristotle says, "but a watery kindliness" and a very feeble counterpoise to self-love: and thus that such specialized affections as the present organization of society normally produces afford the best means of developing in most persons a more extended benevolence, to the degree to which they are capable of feeling it.

Besides, as each person is for the most part, from limitation either of power or knowledge, not in a position to do much good to more than a very small number of persons; it seems, on this ground alone, desirable that his chief benevolent impulses should be correspondingly limited.

And this leads us to consider, secondly, the reasons why, affection apart, it is conducive to the general happiness that prior claims should be commonly recognized as attaching to special relations; so as to modify that impartial universality in the distribution of beneficence which Utilitarianism *primâ facie* inculcates. For clearness' sake it seems best to take this argument separately, though it cannot easily be divided from the former one, because the services in question are often such as cannot so well be rendered without affection. In such cases, as we saw[1], Common Sense regards the affection itself as a duty, in so far as it is capable of being cultivated: but still prescribes the performance of the services even if the affection be unhappily absent. Indeed we may properly consider the services to which we are commonly prompted by the domestic affections, and also those to which we are moved by gratitude and pity, as an integral part of the system of mutual aid by which the normal life and happiness of society is maintained, under existing circumstances; being an indispensable supplement to the still more essential services which are definitely prescribed by Law, or rendered on commercial terms as a part of an express bargain. As political economists have explained, the means of happiness are immensely increased by that complex system of co-operation which has been gradually organized among civilized men: and while it is thought that under such a system it will be generally best on the whole to let each individual exchange such services as he is disposed to render for such return as he can obtain for them by free contract; still there are many large exceptions to this general principle. Of these the most important is constituted by the case of children. It is necessary for the well-being of mankind that in each generation children should be produced in adequate numbers, neither too many nor too few; and that, as they cannot be left to provide for themselves, they should

[1] B. III. c. iv. § 1.

be adequately nourished and protected during the period of infancy; and further, that they should be carefully trained in good habits, intellectual, moral and physical: and it is commonly believed that the best or even the only known means of attaining these ends in even a tolerable degree is afforded by the existing institution of the Family, resting as it does on a basis of legal and moral rules combined. For Law fixes a minimum of mutual services and draws the broad outlines of behaviour for the different members of the family, imposing[1] on the parents lifelong union and complete mutual fidelity and the duty of providing for their children the necessaries of life up to a certain age; in return for which it gives them the control of their children for the same period, and sometimes lays on the latter the burden of supporting their parents when aged and destitute: so that Morality, in inculcating a completer harmony of interests and an ampler interchange of kindnesses, is merely filling in the outlines drawn by Law. We found, however, in attempting to formulate the different domestic duties as recognized by Common Sense, that there seemed to be in most cases a large vague margin with respect to which *consensus* could not be affirmed, and which, in fact, forms an arena for continual disputes. But we have now to observe that it is just this margin which furnishes the most striking evidence of the latent Utilitarianism of common moral opinion: for when the question is once raised as to the precise mutual duties of husbands and wives, or of parents and children, each disputant commonly supports his view by a forecast of the effects on human happiness to be expected from the general establishment of any proposed rule; this seems to be the standard to which the matter is, by common consent, referred.

Similarly the claim to services that arises out of special need (which natural sympathy moves us to recognize) may obviously be rested on an utilitarian basis: indeed the proper fulfilment of this duty seems so important to the well-being of society, that it has in modern civilized communities generally been brought to some extent within the sphere of Govern-

---

[1] Strictly speaking, of course, the Law of modern states does not enforce this, but only refuses to recognize connubial contracts of any other kind: but the social effect is substantially the same.

mental action. We noticed that the main utilitarian reason why it is not right (for example) for every rich man to distribute his superfluous wealth among the poor, is that the happiness of all is on the whole most promoted by maintaining in adults generally, (except married women), the expectation that each will be thrown on his own resources for the supply of his own wants. But if I am made aware that, owing to a sudden calamity that could not have been foreseen, another's resources are manifestly inadequate to protect him from pain or serious discomfort, the case is altered; my theoretical obligation to consider his happiness as much as my own becomes at once practical; and I am bound to make as much effort to relieve him as will not entail a greater loss of happiness to myself or others. If, however, the calamity is one which might have been foreseen and averted by proper care, my duty becomes more doubtful: for then by relieving him I seem to be in danger of encouraging improvidence in others. In such a case a Utilitarian has to weigh this indirect evil against the direct good of removing pain and distress: and it is now more and more generally recognized that the question of providing for the destitute has to be treated as a utilitarian problem of which these are the elements; whether we are considering the minimum that should be secured to them by law, or the proper supplementary action of private charity.

Poverty, however, is not the only case in which it is conducive to the general happiness that one man should render unbought services to another. In any condition or calling a man may find himself unable to ward off some evil or to realize some legitimate or worthy end without assistance of such kind as he cannot purchase on the ordinary commercial terms; assistance which, on the one hand, will have no bad effect on the receiver, from the exceptional nature of the emergency, while at the same time it may not be burdensome to the giver. Here, again, some jurists have thought that where the service to be rendered is great, and the burden of rendering it very slight, it might properly be made matter of legal obligation: so that (e.g) if I could save a man from drowning by merely holding out a hand, I should be legally punishable if I omitted the act. But, however this may be, the moral rule condemning the refusal of aid in such emergencies is obviously conducive to the general happiness.

Further, besides these, so to say, *accidentally* unbought services, there are some for which there is normally no market-price; such as counsel and assistance in the intimate perplexities of life, which one is only willing to receive from genuine friends. It much promotes the general happiness that such services should be generally rendered. On this ground, as well as by the emotional pleasures which directly spring from it, we perceive Friendship to be an important means to the Utilitarian end. At the same time we feel that the charm of Friendship is lost if the flow of emotion is not spontaneous and unforced. The combination of these two views seems to be exactly represented by the sympathy that is not quite admiration with which Common Sense regards all close and strong affections; and the regret that is not quite disapproval with which it contemplates their decay.

In all cases where it is conducive to the general happiness that unbought services should be rendered, Gratitude (if we mean by this a settled disposition to repay the benefit in whatever way one can on a fitting opportunity) is enjoined by Utilitarianism no less than by Common Sense; for one can hardly expect that any kind of onerous services will be adequately rendered unless there is a general disposition to requite them. In fact we may say that a general understanding that all services which it is expedient that A should render to B will be in some way repaid by B, is a natural supplement of the more definite contracts by which the main part of the great social interchange of services is arranged. Indeed the one kind of requital merges in the other, and no sharp line can be drawn between the two: we cannot always say distinctly whether the requital of a benefit is a pure act of gratitude or the fulfilment of a tacit understanding[1]. There is, however, a certain difficulty in this view of gratitude as analogous to the fulfilment of a bargain. For it may be said that of the services peculiar to friendship, disinterestedness is an indispensable characteristic; and that in all cases bene-

---

[1] Sometimes such unbargained requital is even legally obligatory: as when children are bound to repay the care spent on them by supporting their parents in decrepitude.

fits conferred without expectation of reward have a peculiar excellence, and are indeed peculiarly adapted to arouse gratitude; but if they are conferred in expectation of such gratitude, they lose this excellence; and yet, again, it would be very difficult to treat as a friend one from whom gratitude was not expected. This seems, at first sight, an inextricable entanglement: but here, as in other cases, an apparent ethical contradiction is found to reduce itself to a psychological complexity. For most of our actions are done from several different motives, either coexisting or succeeding one another in rapid alternation: thus a man may have a perfectly disinterested desire to benefit another, and one which might possibly prevail over all conflicting motives if all hope of requital were cut off, and yet it may be well that this generous impulse should be sustained by a vague trust that requital will not be withheld. And in fact the apparent puzzle really affords another illustration of the latent Utilitarianism of Common Sense. For, on the one hand, Utilitarianism prescribes that we should render services whenever it is conducive to the general happiness to do so, which may often be the case without taking into account the gain to oneself which would result from their requital: and on the other hand, since we must conclude from the actual selfishness of average men that such services would not be adequately rendered without expectation of requital, it is also conducive to the general happiness that men should recognize a moral obligation to repay them.

We have discussed only the most conspicuous of the duties of affection: but it is probably obvious that similar reasonings would apply in the case of the others.

In all cases there are three distinct lines of argument which tend to show that the commonly received view of special claims and duties arising out of special relations, though *primâ facie* opposed to the impartial universality of the Utilitarian principle, is really maintained by a well-considered application of the latter. First, morality is here in a manner protecting the normal channels and courses of natural benevolent affections; and the development of such affections seems of the highest importance to human happiness, both as a direct source of pleasure, and as an indispensable preparation for a more enlarged "altruism.". And again, the mere fact that such affections are normal, causes an expectation of the services that are their natural expression; and the disappointment of such expectations is inevitably painful. While finally, apart from these considerations, we can shew in each case strong utilitarian reasons why, generally speaking, services should be rendered to the persons commonly recognized as having such claims rather than to others.

We may add, in conclusion, that all the difficulties of determining the limits of these duties, and their relative importance, which the Intuitional method raised and failed to overcome, are removed, in theory at least, by the Utilitarian synthesis. For each of the preceding arguments has shewn us different kinds of pleasures gained and pains averted by the fulfilment of the claims in question. There are, first, those in the causing or averting of which the service consists: secondly, it prevents the pain and secondary harm of disappointed expectation: thirdly, we have to reckon the various pleasures connected with the exercise of natural benevolent affections, especially when reciprocated, including the indirect effects on the agent's character of maintaining such affections. All these different pleasures and pains combine differently, and with almost infinite variation as circumstances vary, into utilitarian reasons for each of these claims; none of these reasons being absolute and conclusive, but each having its own weight, while liable to be outweighed by others.

§ 4. I pass to consider another group of duties, often contrasted with those of Benevolence, under the comprehensive notion of Justice.

"That Justice is useful to society," says Hume, "it would be a superfluous undertaking to prove:" what he endeavours to shew at some length is, "that public utility is the *sole* origin of Justice:" and it is the same question of origin which has chiefly occupied the attention of Mill[1]. Here, however, we are not so much concerned with the growth of the sentiment of Justice from experiences of utility, as with the Utilitarian basis of the mature notion; while at the same time if the analysis previously given be correct, the Justice that is commonly demanded and inculcated is something more complex than these

[1] *Utilitarianism*, ch. v.

writers have recognized. What Hume (*e.g.*) means by Justice is rather what I should call Order, understood in its widest sense: the observance of the actual system of rules, whether strictly legal or customary, which bind together the different members of any society into an organic whole, checking malevolent or otherwise injurious impulses, distributing the different objects of men's clashing desires, and exacting such positive services, customary or contractual, as are commonly recognized as matters of debt. And though there have rarely been wanting plausible empirical arguments for the revolutionary paradox quoted by Plato, that "laws are imposed in the interest of rulers," it remains true that the general conduciveness to social happiness of the habit of Order or Law-observance, is, as Hume says, too obvious to need proof; indeed it is of such paramount importance to a community, that even where particular laws are clearly injurious, it is almost always expedient to observe them, apart from any penalty which their breach might entail on the individual. We saw, however, that Common Sense sometimes bids us refuse obedience to bad laws, because "we ought to obey God rather than men" (though there seems to be no clear intuition as to the kind or degree of badness that justifies resistance); and further allows us, in special emergencies, to violate rules generally good, for "necessity has no law," and "salus populi suprema lex."

These and similar common opinions seem at least to suggest that the limits of the duty of Law-observance are to be determined by utilitarian considerations. While, again, the Utilitarian view gets rid of the difficulties in which the attempt to define intuitively the truly legitimate source of legislative authority involved us[1]; at the same time that it justifies to some extent each of the different views current as to the intrinsic legitimacy of governments. For, on the one hand, it finds the moral basis of law-observance in the effects rather than the causes of the laws that exist; so that, generally speaking, obedience will seem due to any *de facto* government that is not governing very badly. On the other hand, in so far as laws originating in a particular way are likely to be (1) better, or (2) more readily observed, it is a Utilitarian duty

[1] Cf. Bk. III. ch. vi. §§ 2, 3.

to aim at introducing this mode of origination: and thus in a certain stage of social development it may be right that a 'representative system' should be popularly demanded, or possibly (in extreme cases) even introduced by force: while, again, there is expediency in maintaining an ancient mode of legislation, because men readily obey such: and loyalty to a dispossessed government may be on the whole expedient, even at the cost of some temporary suffering and disorder, in order that ambitious men may not find usurpation too easy. Here, as elsewhere, Utilitarianism at once supports the different reasons commonly put forward as absolute, and also brings them theoretically to a common measure, so that in any particular case we have a principle of decision between conflicting political arguments.

As was before said, this Law-observance, in so far at least as it affects the interests of other individuals, is what we frequently mean by Justice. It seems however[1], that the notion of Justice, exhaustively analysed, includes several distinct elements combined in a somewhat complex manner: we have to inquire, therefore, what latent utilities are represented by each of these elements.

Now, first, a constant part of the notion, which appears in it even when the Just is not distinguished from the Legal, is impartiality or the negation of arbitrary inequality. This impartiality, as we saw[2] (whether exhibited in the establishment or in the administration of laws), is merely a special application of the wider maxim that it cannot be right to treat two persons differently if their cases are similar in all material circumstances. And this maxim obviously belongs to Utilitarianism no less than to all other systems of Ethics. At the same time, since this negative criterion is clearly inadequate for the complete determination of what is just in laws, or in conduct generally; when we have admitted this, it still remains to ask, "What are the inequalities in laws, and in the distribution of pleasures and pains outside the sphere of law, which are not arbitrary and unreasonable? and to what general principles can they be reduced?"

Here in the first place we may explain, on utilitarian principles, why apparently arbitrary inequality in a certain part of

[1] Cf. Bk. III. ch. v.   [2] Bk. XIII. § 3.

the conduct of individuals[1] is not regarded as injustice or even—in some cases—as in any way censurable. For freedom of action is an important source of happiness to the agents, and a socially useful stimulus to their energies: hence it is obviously expedient that a man's free choice in the distribution of wealth or kind services should not be restrained by the fear of legal penalties, or even of social disapprobation, beyond what the interests of others clearly require; and therefore, when distinctly recognized claims are satisfied, it is *pro tanto* expedient that the mere preferences of an individual should be treated by others as legitimate grounds for inequality in the distribution of his property or services. Nay, as we have before seen, it is within certain limits expedient that each individual should practically regard his own unreasoned impulses as reasonable grounds of action : as in the rendering of services prompted by such affections as are normally and properly spontaneous and unforced.

Passing to consider the general principles upon which 'just claims' as commonly recognized appear to be based, we notice that the grounds of a number of such claims may be brought under the general head of 'normal expectations: but that the stringency of such obligations varies much in degree, according as the expectations are based upon definite engagements, or on some vague mutual understanding, or are merely such as an average man would form from past experience of the conduct of other men. In these latter cases Common Sense appeared to be somewhat perplexed as to the validity of the claims. But for the Utilitarian the difficulty has ceased to exist. He will hold any disappointment of expectations to be *pro tanto* an evil, but a greater evil in proportion to the previous security of the expectant individual, from the greater shock thus given to his reliance on the conduct of his fellow-men generally: and many times greater in proportion as the expectation is generally recognized as normal and reasonable, as in this case the shock extends to all who are in any way cognisant of his disappointment. The importance to mankind of being able to rely on each other's actions is so great, that in ordinary cases of absolutely definite engagements there is scarcely any advantage that can

[1] Cf. *ante*, p. 266 note.

counterbalance the harm done by violating them. Still, we found[1] that several exceptions and qualifications to the rule of Good Faith were more or less distinctly recognized by Common Sense: and most of these have a utilitarian basis, which it does not need much penetration to discern. To begin, we may notice that the superficial view of the obligation of a promise which makes it depend on the assertion of the promiser, and not, as Utilitarians hold, on the expectations produced in the promisee, cannot fairly be attributed to Common Sense: for we all condemn a breach of promise much more strongly when others have acted in reliance on it, than when its observance did not directly concern others, and its breach only causes the indirect evil of a bad precedent; as when a man breaks a pledge of total abstinence. We see, again, how a material change of circumstances[2] diminishes the utilitarian reasons for keeping a promise; for whatever expectations may be disappointed in that case, they are at least not those which the promise originally created. It is obvious, too, that it is not advantageous to the community that men should be able to rely on the performance of promises procured by fraud or unlawful force: indeed the chief utilitarian ground for not repudiating such promises is, that persons cognisant of the repudiation might not know or might insufficiently consider the special circumstances of the case, and so might be demoralised by the example[3]. We saw, again[4], that when the performance would be injurious to the promisee, Common Sense is disposed to admit that its obligation is superseded, and is so far in harmony with Utilitarianism. And even when it is only the promiser who would be injured, still, if the harm be extreme, Common Sense is at least doubtful whether the promise should be kept. And similarly for the other qualifications and exceptions: they all turn out to be as clearly utilitarian, as the general utility of keeping one's word is plain and manifest.

---

[1] Bk. III. ch. vi.   [2] Cf. *ante*, Bk. III. ch. vi. § 7.

[3] There is another reason of a different kind in the case where the lawbreaker is too strong to be put down, so that the law-abiding part of society has to reckon with him as a permanent hostile power, and establish (as diplomatists say) a *modus vivendi* with him.

[4] Cf. Bk. III. ch. vi. § 9.

But further, the expediency of satisfying natural and normal expectations, even when they are not based upon a definite contract, is obvious; it will clearly conduce to the tranquillity of social existence, and to the settled and well-adjusted activity on which social happiness greatly depends, that such expectations should be as little as possible baulked. And here Utilitarianism relieves us of the difficulties which beset the common view of just conduct as something absolutely precise and definite. For in this vaguer region we cannot draw a sharp line between valid and invalid claims; 'injustice' shades gradually off into mere 'hardship.' Hence the Utilitarian view that the disappointment of natural expectations is an evil, but an evil which must sometimes be incurred for the sake of a greater good, is that to which Common Sense is practically forced, though unable to reconcile it with the theoretical absoluteness of Intuitive Morality.

The gain of recognizing the relativity of this obligation will be still more felt, when we consider what I distinguished as Ideal Justice, and examine the general conceptions of this which we find expressed or latent in current criticisms of the existing order of Society.

We saw that there were two competing views of an ideally just social order, or perhaps we may say two extreme types between which the looser notions of ordinary men seem to fluctuate: which I called respectively the Individualistic and the Socialistic. According to the former view an ideal system of Law ought to aim at Freedom, or perfect mutual non-interference of all the members of the community, as an absolute end. Now the general utilitarian reasons for leaving each rational adult free to seek happiness in his own way are obvious and striking: for, generally speaking, each is best qualified to provide for his own interests, since even when he does not know best what they are and how to attain them, he is at any rate most keenly concerned for them: and again, the consciousness of freedom and concomitant responsibility increases the average effective activity of men: and besides, the discomfort of constraint is directly an evil and *pro tanto* to be avoided. Still, we saw[1] that the attempt to

[1] Bk. III. ch. v. § 1.

construct a consistent code of laws, taking Maximum Freedom (instead of Happiness) as an absolute end, must lead to startling paradoxes and insoluble puzzles: and in fact the practical interpretation of the notion 'Freedom,' and the limits within which its realization has been actually sought, have always—even in the freest societies—been more or less consciously determined by considerations of expediency. So that we may fairly say that in so far as Common Sense has adopted the Individualistic ideal in politics, it has always been as subordinate to and limited by the Utilitarian first principle[1].

It seems, however, that what we commonly demand or long for, under the name of Ideal Justice, is not so much the realization of Freedom, as the distribution of good and evil according to Desert: indeed it is as a means to this latter end that Freedom is often advocated; for it is said that if we protect men completely from mutual interference, each will reap the good and bad consequences of his own conduct, and so be happy or unhappy in proportion to his deserts. In particular, it has been widely held that if a free exchange of wealth and services is allowed, each individual will obtain from society, in money or other advantages, what his services are really worth. We saw, however, that the price which an individuual obtains under a system of perfect free trade, for wealth or services exchanged by him, may for several reasons be not proportioned to the social utility of what he exchanges: and if we inquire how far and why Common Sense admits this proportion as legitimate, the answer seems to be that it does admit it to some extent, under the influence of utilitarian considerations correcting the spontaneous utterances of our common moral sentiments.

To take a particular case: if a moral man were asked how far A is justified in taking advantage in bargaining of the ignorance of B, probably his first impulse would be to condemn such a procedure altogether. But reflection, I think, would shew him that such a censure would be too sweeping: that it would be contrary to Common Sense to "blame A for having, in negociating with a stranger B, taken advantage of B's

---

[1] In another work (*Principles of Political Economy*, Bk. III. ch. ii.) I have tried to shew that complete *laisser faire*, in the organization of industry, tends in various ways to fall short of the most economic production of wealth.

ignorance of facts known to himself, provided that A's superior knowledge had been obtained by a legitimate use of diligence and foresight, which B might have used with equal success.... What prevents us from censuring in this and similar cases is, I conceive, a more or less conscious apprehension of the indefinite loss to the wealth of the community that is likely to result from any effective social restrictions on the free pursuit and exercise" of economic knowledge. And for somewhat similar reasons of general expediency, if the question be raised whether it is fair for a class of persons to gain by the unfavourable economic situation of any class with which they deal, Common Sense at least hesitates to censure such gains—at any rate when such unfavourable situation is due "to the gradual action of general causes, for the existence of which the persons who gain are not specially responsible[1]".

And, to speak more generally, the principle of 'requiting desert', so far as Common Sense really accepts it as practically applicable to the relations of men in society, is quite in harmony with Utilitarianism, if only we give the notions of 'good' and 'ill' desert a Utilitarian interpretation: to which Common Sense when dealing practically with particulars, seems at least to offer no obstacle. It is obviously the best encouragement to the production of general happiness that we should reward and punish men according as their conduct is felicific or the reverse; only the Utilitarian scale of rewards will not be determined entirely by the magnitude of the services performed, but partly also by the difficulty of inducing men to perform them. But this latter element seems to be always taken into account (though perhaps unconsciously) by Common Sense: for, as we have been led to notice[2], we do not commonly recognize merit in right actions, if they are such as men are naturally inclined to perform rather too much than too little. Again, in spite of the opposition between the Intuitional principle that ill-desert lies in wrong intention, and the Utilitarian view of punishment as purely preventive, we find that in the actual administration of criminal justice, Common Sense is

---

[1] The quotations are from my *Principles of Political Economy*, Book III. ch. ix.: where these questions are discussed at somewhat greater length.

[2] Cf. *ante*, § 2 and Bk. III. ch. ii. § 1.

forced, however reluctantly, into practical agreement with Utilitarianism. After a civil war it demands the execution of the most purely patriotic rebels; and after a railway accident it clamours for the severe punishment of unintentional neglects, which, except for their consequences, would have been regarded as very venial. And it is often curious in such cases to observe the sophistries by which Common Sense tries to persuade itself that there has been wilful wrong-doing.

If, however, in any distribution of pleasures and privileges, or of pains and burdens, considerations of desert do not properly come in (*i.e.* if the good or evil to be distributed have no relation to any conduct on the part of the persons who are to receive it); or if it is practically impossible to take them into account; then Common Sense seems to fall back on simple equality as the principle of just apportionment[1]. Now we saw that the Utilitarian formula does not strictly include any principle for distributing the happiness which it directs us to make as great as possible. Still, in the case supposed, Equality is the only mode of distribution that is not arbitrary and so unreasonable; and thus this mode of apportioning the means of happiness is likely to produce more happiness on the whole; partly because men have a disinterested aversion to unreason; but still more because they have an aversion to any kind of inferiority to others, which is much intensified when the inferiority seems unreasonable. This latter feeling is so strong that it often prevails in spite of obvious claims of desert; and it may even be expedient that it should so prevail within limits.

For, finally, it must be observed that Utilitarianism furnishes us with a common standard to which the different elements included in the notion of Justice may be reduced. Such a standard is imperatively required: as these different elements are continually liable to conflict with each other. The issue, for example, in practical politics between Conservatives and Reformers often represents such a conflict: the question is, whether we ought to do a certain violence to expec-

---

[1] I have before observed that it is quite in harmony with Utilitarian principles to recognize a sphere of private conduct within which each individual may distribute his wealth and kind services as unequally as he chooses, without incurring censure as unjust.

tations arising naturally out of the existing social order, with the view of bringing about a distribution of the means of happiness more in accordance with ideal justice. Here, if my analysis of the common notion of Justice be sound, the attempt to extract from it a clear decision of such an issue must necessarily fail: as the conflict is, so to say, permanently latent in the very core of Common Sense. But the Utilitarian will merely use this notion of Justice as a guide to different kinds of utilities; and in so far as these are incompatible, he will balance one set of advantages against the other, and decide according to the preponderance.

§ 5. The duty of Truth-speaking is sometimes taken as a striking instance of a moral principle not resting on a Utilitarian basis. But a careful study of the qualifications with which the common opinion of mankind actually inculcates this duty seems to lead us to an opposite result: for not only is the general utility of truth-speaking so manifest as to need no proof, but wherever this utility seems to be absent, or outweighed by particular bad consequences, we find that Common Sense at least half admits an exception to the rule. For example, if a man be pursuing criminal ends, it is *primâ facie* injurious to the community that he should be aided in his pursuit by being able to rely on the assertions of others. So far deception seems legitimate as a protection against crime: but when we consider the bad effects on habit, and through example, of even a single act of unveracity, the case is seen to be, on Utilitarian principles, doubtful: and this is just the view of Common Sense. Again, though it is generally a man's interest to know the truth, there are exceptional cases in which it is injurious to him; as when an invalid hears bad news; and here, too, Common Sense is disposed to suspend the rule. Again, we found it difficult to define exactly wherein Veracity consists; for we may either require truth in the spoken words, or in the inferences which the speaker foresees will be drawn from them, or in both. Perfect Candour, no doubt, would require it in both: but in the various circumstances where this seems inexpedient, we often find Common Sense at least half-willing to dispense with one or other part of the double obligation. Thus we found a respectable school of thinkers maintaining that a religious truth may properly be communicated by means of a historical fiction: and, on the other hand, the unsuitability of perfect frankness to our existing social relations is recognized in the common rules of politeness, which impose on us not unfrequently the necessity of suppressing truths and suggesting falsehoods. I would not say that in any of these cases Common Sense pronounces quite decidedly in favour of unveracity: but then neither is Utilitarianism decided, as the importance of maintaining a general habit of truth-speaking is so great, that it is not easy to say positively that it is outweighed by even strong special reasons for violating the rule.

When we pass to consider the different views as to the legitimacy of Malevolent impulses, out of which we found it hard to frame a consistent doctrine for Common Sense, we find them exactly correspondent to different forecasts of the consequences of gratifying such impulses. *Primâ facie*, the desire to injure any one in particular is inconsistent with a deliberate purpose of benefiting as much as possible people in general; accordingly, we find that what I may call Superficial Common Sense passes a sweeping condemnation on such desires. But a study of the actual facts of society shews that resentment plays an important part in that repression of injuries which is necessary to social well-being: accordingly, the reflective moralist shrinks from excluding it altogether. It is evident, however, that personal ill-will is a very dangerous means to the general happiness: for its direct end is the exact opposite of happiness; and though the realization of this may in certain cases be the least of two evils, still the impulse if encouraged is likely to prompt to the infliction of pain beyond the limits of just punishment, and to have an injurious reaction on the character of the angry person, and even, through sympathy, upon others. Accordingly, the moralist is disposed to prescribe that indignation be directed always against acts, and not against persons; and it seems clear that if indignation so restricted would be efficient in repressing punishment, this is the state of mind most conducive to the general happiness. But it is doubtful whether human nature is capable of maintaining this distinction, or whether, if it could be maintained, the more refined aversion would by itself be sufficiently efficacious: accordingly, Common Sense is reluctant to condemn personal ill-will if directed against wrong-doers.

It would be tedious—and seems unnecessary for the reasons before given—to go through a similar discussion of the minor social virtues with their vaguer maxims. Nor is it needful to shew that Temperance, Self-control, and what are called the Self-regarding virtues generally, are 'useful' to the individual who possesses them. If it is not quite clear, in the view of Common Sense, to what end that regulation and government of appetites and passions, which moralists have so much inculcated and admired, is to be directed; at least there seems no obstacle in the way of our defining this end as Happiness. And even in the ascetic extreme of Self-control, which has sometimes led to the repudiation of sensual pleasures as radically bad, we may trace an unconscious Utilitarianism. For the ascetic condemnation has always been chiefly directed against those pleasures, in respect of which men are especially liable to commit excesses dangerous to health; and free indulgence in which, even when it keeps clear of injury to health, is thought to interfere with the development of other faculties and susceptibilities which are important sources of happiness.

§ 6. An apparent exception to this statement may seem to be constituted in the case of the sexual appetite, by the regulation prescribed under the notion of Purity or Chastity. And there is no doubt that under this head we find condemned, with special vehemence and severity, acts of which the immediate effect is pleasure not obviously outweighed by subsequent pain. But a closer examination of this exception transforms it into an important contribution to the present argument: as it shews a specially complex and delicate correspondence between moral sentiments and social utilities.

In the first place, the peculiar intensity and delicacy of the moral sentiments that govern the relations of the sexes are thoroughly justified by the vast importance to society of the end to which they are obviously a means: the maintenance, namely, of the permanent unions which are thought to be necessary for the proper rearing and training of children. Hence the first and fundamental rule in this department is that which directly secures conjugal fidelity. But, secondly, the utility of protecting marriage indirectly, by condemning all extra-nuptial intercourse of the sexes, is easy to expound: for otherwise men would not have adequate motives to incur the restraints and burdens which marriage entails; and the youth of both sexes would form habits of feeling and conduct tending to unfit them for marriage; and, again, if such intercourse were fertile, it would be attended with those bad effects on the succeeding generation, which it seems the object of permanent unions to prevent; while if it were sterile, the future of the human race would, as far as we can see, be still more profoundly imperilled.

But, further, it is only on Utilitarian principles that we can account for the anomalous difference which the morality of Common Sense has always made between the two sexes as regards the simple offence of unchastity. For the offence is commonly more deliberate in the man, who has the additional guilt of soliciting and persuading the woman; in the latter, again, it is far more often prompted by some motive that we rank higher than mere lust: so that, according to the ordinary canons of Intuitional Morality, it ought to be more severely condemned in the man. The actual inversion of this result can only be justified by taking into account the greater interest that society has in maintaining a high standard of female chastity. For the degradation of this standard must strike at the root of family life, by impairing men's security in the exercise of their parental affections: but there is no corresponding consequence of male unchastity, which may therefore prevail to a considerable extent without imperilling the very existence of the family, though it impairs its well-being.

At the same time the condemnation of unchastity in men, by the common moral sense of Christian countries at the present day, is sufficiently clear and explicit: though we recognize the existence of a laxer code—the morality, as it is called, of 'the world'—which treats it as indifferent, or very venial. But the very difference between the two codes gives a kind of support to the present argument; as it corresponds to easily explained differences of insight into the consequences of maintaining certain moral sanctions. For partly it is thought by 'men of the world' that men cannot practically be restrained from sexual indulgence, at least at the period of life when the passions are strongest: and hence that it is expedient to tolerate such kind and degree of illicit sexual intercourse as is not directly dangerous to the well-being of families. Partly, again, it is maintained by some, in bolder antagonism to Common Sense, that the existence of a certain limited amount of such intercourse (with a special class of women, carefully separated, as at present, from the rest of society) is scarcely a real evil, and may even be a positive gain in respect of general happiness; for continence is perhaps somewhat dangerous to health, and in any case involves a loss of pleasure considerable in intensity; while at the same time the maintenance of as numerous a population as is desirable in an old society does not require that more than a certain proportion of the women in each generation should become mothers of families; and if some of the surplus thus left make it their profession to enter into casual and temporary sexual relations with men, there is no necessity that their lives should compare unfavourably in respect of happiness with those of other women in the less favoured classes of society.

This view has perhaps a superficial plausibility: but it ignores the essential fact that it is only by the present severe enforcement against unchaste women of the penalties of social contempt and exclusion, resting on moral disapprobation, that the class of courtezans is kept sufficiently separate from the rest of female society to prevent the contagion of unchastity from spreading; and that the illicit intercourse of the sexes is restrained within such limits as not to interfere materially with the due development of the race. This consideration is sufficient to decide a Utilitarian to support generally the established rule against this kind of conduct, and therefore to condemn violations of the rule as on the whole infelicific, even though they may perhaps appear to have this quality only in consequence of the moral censure attached to them[1]. Further, the 'man

---

[1] It is obvious that so long as the social sanction is enforced, the lives of the women against whom society thus issues its ban must tend to be unhappy from disorder and shame, and the source of unhappiness to others; and also that the breach by men of a recognized and necessary moral rule must tend to have injurious effects on their moral habits generally.

of the world' ignores the vast importance to the human race of maintaining that higher type of sexual relations which is not, generally speaking, possible, except where a high value is set upon chastity in both sexes. From this point of view the Virtue of Purity may be regarded as providing a necessary shelter under which that intense and elevated affection between the sexes, which is most conducive both to the happiness of the individual and to the well-being of the family, may grow and flourish.

And in this way we are able to explain what must have perplexed many reflective minds in contemplating the commonsense regulation of conduct under the head of Purity: viz. that on the one hand the sentiment that supports these rules is very intense, so that the subjective difference between right and wrong in this department is marked with peculiar strength: while on the other hand it is found impossible to give a clear definition of the conduct condemned under this notion. For the impulse to be restrained is so powerful and so sensitive to stimulants of all kinds, that in order that the sentiment of purity may adequately perform its protective function, it is necessary that it should be very keen and vivid; and that the aversion to impurity should extend far beyond the acts that primarily need to be prohibited, and include in its scope everything (in dress, language, social customs, &c.) which may tend to excite lascivious ideas. But it is not necessary that a clear and precise theoretical line should be drawn between right and wrong in this matter. Here, as in other cases, it is sufficient for practical purposes if the main central portion of the region of duty be strongly illuminated, while the margin is left somewhat obscure. And, in fact, the detailed regulations which it is important to society to maintain depend so much upon habit and association of ideas, that they must vary to a great extent from age to age and from country to country.

§ 7. The preceding survey has supplied us with several illustrations of the manner in which Utilitarianism is normally introduced as a method for deciding between different conflicting claims, in cases where common sense leaves their relative importance obscure,—as (*e.g.*) between the different duties of the affections, and the different principles which analysis shews to be involved in our common conception of Justice—: and we have also noticed how, when a dispute is raised as to the precise scope and definition of any current moral rule, the effects of different acceptations of the rule on general happiness or social wellbeing are commonly regarded as the ultimate grounds on which the dispute is to be decided. In fact these two arguments practically run into one; for it is generally a conflict between maxims that impresses men with the need of giving each a precise definition. It may be urged that the consequences to which reference is commonly made in such cases are rather effects on 'social wellbeing' than on 'general happiness' as understood by Utilitarians; and that the two notions ought to be carefully distinguished. I admit this: but in the last chapter of the preceding book I have tried to shew that Common Sense is unconsciously utilitarian in its practical determination of those very elements in the notion of Ultimate Good or Wellbeing which at first sight least admit of a hedonistic interpretation. We may now observe that this hypothesis of 'Unconscious Utilitarianism' explains the different relative importance attached to particular virtues by different classes of human beings, and the different emphasis with which the same virtue is inculcated on these different classes by mankind generally. For such differences ordinarily correspond to variations either real or apparent in the Utilitarian importance of the virtues under different circumstances. Thus we have noticed the greater stress laid on chastity in women than in men: courage, on the other hand, is more valued in the latter, as they are more called upon to cope energetically with sudden and severe dangers. And for similar reasons a soldier is expected to shew a higher degree of courage than (*e.g.*) a priest. Again, though we esteem candour and scrupulous sincerity in most persons, we scarcely look for them in a diplomatist who has to conceal secrets, or in a tradesman describing his goods (for purchasers can find out the defects of what they buy). And we may explain the more lenient view commonly taken of bad faith in international, as compared with civic, relations, by reference to the smaller degree of mutual confidence already established in the former, in consequence of which the breach of a contract gives much less shock to expectation.

Finally, when we compare the different moral codes of different ages and countries, we see that the discrepancies between any two correspond, at least to a great extent, to differences either in the actual effects of actions on happiness, or in the extent to which such effects are foreseen or regarded as important by the community in which the code is maintained. Several instances of this have already been noticed: and the general fact, which has been much dwelt upon by Utilitarian writers, is also admitted and even emphasized by their opponents. Thus Dugald Stewart[1] lays stress on the extent to which the moral judgments of mankind have been modified by "the diversity in their physical circumstances," the "unequal degrees of civilization which they have attained," and "their unequal measures of knowledge or of capacity." He points out, for instance, that theft is regarded as a very venial offence in the South Sea Islanders, because little or no labour is there required to support life; that the lending of money for interest is commonly reprehended in societies where commerce is imperfectly developed, because the 'usurer' in such communities is commonly in the odious position of wringing a gain out of the hard necessities of his fellows; and that where the legal arrangements for punishing crime are imperfect, private murder is either justified or regarded very leniently. Many other examples might be added to these if it were needful. But I conceive that few persons who have studied the subject will deny that there is a certain degree of correlation between the variations in the moral code from age to age, and the variations in the real or perceived effects on general happiness of actions prescribed or forbidden by the code. And in proportion as the apprehension of consequences becomes more comprehensive and exact, we may trace not only change but progress in the moral code handed down from age to age: progress which consists in a gradually closer approximation to a perfectly enlightened Utilitarianism. Only we must distinctly notice another important factor in the progress, which Stewart has not mentioned: the extension, namely, of the capacity for sympathy in an average member of the community. The im-

---

[1] *Active and Moral Powers*, B. II. ch. iii.

perfection of earlier moral codes is at least as much due to defectiveness of sympathy as of intelligence; often, no doubt, the ruder man did not perceive the effects of his conduct on others; but often, again, he perceived them more or less, but felt little or no concern about them. Thus it happens that changes in the conscience of a community often correspond to changes in the extent and degree of the sensitiveness of an average member of it to the feelings of others. Of this it is perhaps needless to give particular examples, as the moral revolution wrought by Christianity is one vast and complex illustration of it.

I am not maintaining that this correlation between the development of current morality, and the changes in the consequences of conduct as sympathetically forecast, is perfect and exact. On the contrary, the history of morality shews us many striking evidences of what, from the Utilitarian point of view, we should consider partial aberrations of the moral sense. But even in these instances we can often discover a germ of unconscious Utilitarianism; the aberration is either an exaggeration of an obviously useful sentiment, or the extension of it by mistaken analogy to cases to which it does not properly apply, or perhaps the survival of a sentiment which once was useful but has now ceased to be so.

Further, it must be observed that I have carefully abstained from asserting that the perception of the rightness of any kind of conduct has always—or even ordinarily—been derived by conscious inference from a perception of consequent advantages. This is perhaps the hypothesis most naturally suggested by such a survey as the preceding; but the evidence of history does not seem to support it. On the contrary, we seem to find, that, as we retrace the stream of ethical thought, the Utilitarian basis of current morality, which I have endeavoured to exhibit in the present chapter, is less and less distinctly apprehended by the common moral consciousness. Thus (*e g.*) Aristotle sees that the sphere of the Virtue of Courage ($ἀνδρεία$), as recognized by the Common Sense of Greece, is restricted to dangers in war. We can now explain this limitation by a reference to the utilitarian importance of this kind of courage, at a period of history when the individual's happiness was bound up more completely than it now is with the welfare of his state, while the very existence of the latter was more frequently imperilled by hostile invasions: but this explanation lies quite beyond the range of Aristotle's own reflection. We can of course obtain no direct historical evidence as to the origin of our moral notions and sentiments: the whole question belongs to those obscure regions of hypothetical history where conjecture has free scope: but we do not find that, as our retrospect approaches the borders of this realm, the connexion historically traceable in men's minds, between accepted moral rules and foreseen effects on general happiness, becomes more clearly marked. The admiration felt by early man for beauties or excellences of character seems to have been as direct and unreflective as his admiration of any other beauty: and the stringency of law and custom in primitive times presents itself as sanctioned by divine rather than by human displeasure. It is therefore not as the mode of regulating conduct with which mankind began, but rather as that to which we can now see that human development has been always tending, as the adult and not the germinal form of Morality, that Utilitarianism may most plausibly claim the acceptance of Common Sense.

CHAPTER IV.

THE METHOD OF UTILITARIANISM.

§ 1. IF the view maintained in the preceding chapter as to the general Utilitarian basis of the Morality of Common Sense may be regarded as sufficiently established, we are now in a position to consider more closely to what method of determining right conduct the acceptance of Utilitarianism will practically lead. The most obvious method, of course, is that of Empirical Hedonism, discussed in Book II. ch. iii.; according to which we have in each case to compare all the pleasures and pains that can be foreseen as probable results of the different alternatives of conduct presented to us, and to adopt the alternative which seems likely to lead to the greatest happiness on the whole.

In Book II., however, it appeared that even the more restricted application of this method, which we there had to consider, was involved in much perplexity and uncertainty. Even when an individual is only occupied in forecasting his own pleasures, it seems difficult or impossible for him to avoid errors of considerable magnitude; whether in accurately comparing the pleasantness of his own past feelings, as represented in memory, or in appropriating the experience of others, or in arguing from the past to the future. And these difficulties are obviously much increased when we have to take into account all the effects of our actions on all the sentient beings who may be affected by them. At the same time, in Book II. we could not find any satisfactory substitute for this method of empirical comparison. It did not appear reasonable to take refuge in the uncriticised beliefs of men in general as to the sources of happiness: indeed, it seemed impossible to extract any clear and definite *consensus* of opinion from the confused and varying utterances of Common Sense on this subject. Nor again could it be shewn that the individual would be more likely to attain the greatest happiness open to him by practically confining his efforts to the realization of any scientifically ascertainable physical or psychical conditions of happiness: nor did it seem possible to infer on empirical grounds that the desired result would be secured by conformity to the accepted principles of morality. But when we consider these latter in relation, not to the happiness of the individual, but to that of human (or sentient) beings generally, it is clear from the preceding chapter that the question of harmony between Hedonism and Intuitionism presents *primâ facie* an entirely different aspect. Indeed from the considerations that we have just surveyed it is but a short and easy step to the conclusion that in the morality of Common Sense we have ready to hand a body of Utilitarian doctrine; that the "rules of morality for the multitude" are to be regarded as "positive beliefs of mankind as to the effects of actions on their happiness[1]," so that the apparent first principles of Common Sense may be accepted as the "middle axioms" of Utilitarian method; direct reference being only made to utilitarian considerations, in order to settle points upon which the verdict of Common Sense is found to be obscure and conflicting. On this view the traditional controversy between the advocates of Virtue and the advocates of Happiness would seem to be at length harmoniously settled.

And the arguments for this view which have been already put forward are certainly strengthened by the probability of the hypothesis, now widely accepted by naturalists and sociologists, that the moral sentiments are historically derived from experiences of pleasure and pain. The hypothesis, in its completest form, would seem to be this; that the experience of each member of the human community impresses itself on the consciousness of others, partly by their direct sympathy with his pleasures and pains, and partly through their regard for his gratitude and resentment, goodwill and

---

[1] Cf. J. S. Mill, *Utilitarianism*, ch. ii. Mill, however, only affirms that the "rules of morality for the multitude" are to be accepted by the philosopher provisionally, until he has got something better.

hatred, and their consequences; that these impressions are retained and accumulated, and confirmed and kept from divergence by the mutual sympathy of all; that their effects are transmitted from generation to generation, partly by physical inheritance, and partly by tradition from parents to children, and imitation of adults by the young; and that thus common likings or (aversions) for conduct that affects pleasurably (or painfully) the community generally or some part of it, are gradually developed, till they become what we now know as the moral sentiments. This theory does not, in my view, account adequately for the actual results of the faculty of moral judgment and reasoning, so far as I can examine them by reflection on my own moral consciousness: for this, as I have before said, does not yield any apparent intuitions that stand the test of rigorous examination except such as, from their abstract and general character, have no cognizable relation to particular experiences of any kind. But that the theory gives a partially true explanation of the historical origin of particular moral sentiments and habits and commonly accepted rules, I see no reason to doubt; and I regard it as furnishing a valuable supplement to the arguments of the preceding chapter that tend to exhibit the morality of common sense as unconsciously or 'instinctively' utilitarian.

But it is one thing to hold that the current morality expresses, half consciously and half unconsciously, the results of human experience as to the effects of actions: it is quite another thing to accept this morality *en bloc*, so far as it is clear and definite, as the best guidance we can get to the attainment of maximum general happiness. However attractive this simple reconciliation of Intuitional and Utilitarian methods may be, it is not, I think, really warranted by the evidence. In the first place, I hold that in a complete view of the development of the moral sense a more prominent place should be given to the effect of sympathy with the impulses that prompt to actions, as well as with the feelings that result from them. It may be observed that Adam Smith[1] assigns to this operation of sympathy,—the echo (as it were) of each agent's

---

[1] *Theory of Moral Sentiments*, B. I.

passion in the breast of unconcerned spectators,—the first place in determining our approval and disapproval of actions[1]: sympathy with the effect of conduct on others he treats as a merely secondary factor, correcting and qualifying the former. Without going so far as this, I think that there are certainly many cases where the resulting moral consciousness would seem to indicate a balance or compromise between the two kinds of sympathy; and the compromise may easily be many degrees removed from the rule which Utilitarianism would prescribe. For though the passions and other active impulses are doubtless themselves influenced, no less than the moral sentiments, by experiences of pleasure and pain; still this influence is not sufficient to make them at all trustworthy guides to general, any more than to individual, happiness—as some of our moral sentiments themselves emphatically announce. But even if we consider our common moral sentiments as entirely due to the accumulated and transmitted experiences of primary and sympathetic pains and pleasures; it is obvious that the accuracy with which impulses thus produced will guide us to the general happiness must depend upon the accuracy with which the whole sum of pleasurable and painful consequences to sentient beings, resulting from any course of action, has been represented in the consciousness of an average member of the community. And it is seen at a glance that this representation has been always liable to errors of great magnitude, from causes that were partly noticed in the previous chapter, when we were considering the progress of morality. We have to allow, first, for limitation of sympathy; since in every age and country

---

[1] This operation of sympathy is strikingly illustrated in the penal codes of primitive communities, both by the mildness of the punishments inflicted for homicide, and by the startling differences between the penalties allotted to the same crime according as the criminal was taken in the act or not. "It is curious to observe," says Sir H. Maine (*Ancient Law*, ch. x.), "how completely the men of primitive times were persuaded that the impulses of the injured person were the proper measure of the vengeance he was entitled to exact, and how literally they imitated the probable rise and fall of his passions in fixing the scale of punishment." And even in more civilized societies there is a very common feeling of uncertainty as to the propriety of inflicting punishment for crimes committed long ago, which seems traceable to the same source.

the sympathy of an average man with other sentient beings, and even his egoistic regard for their likings and aversions, has been much more limited than the influence of his actions on the feelings of others. We must allow further for limitation of intelligence: for in all ages ordinary men have had a very inadequate knowledge of natural sequences; so that such indirect consequences of conduct as have been felt have been frequently traced to wrong causes, and been met by wrong moral remedies, owing to imperfect apprehension of the relation of means to ends. We must allow again for the influences of false religions; for whenever the fictitious pleasures and displeasures of deities have constituted an important part of the represented consequences of conduct, the resulting moral sentiments are liable to have been perverted to a corresponding extent. This suggests a further deflection, due to the sensibilities of religious teachers influencing the code of duty accepted by their followers, in points where these sensibilities were not normal and representative, but exceptional and idiosyncratic[1].

On the other hand, we must suppose that these deflecting influences have been more or less limited and counteracted by the struggle for existence in past ages among different human races and communities; since so far as any moral habit or sentiment was unfavourable to the preservation of the social organism, it would be a disadvantage in the struggle for existence, and would therefore tend to perish with the community that adhered to it. But we have no reason to suppose that this force would be adequate to prevent any material tendencies to the divergence of positive morality from a Utilitarian ideal. For (1) imperfect morality would be only one disadvantage among many, and not, I conceive, the most important, unless the imperfection were extreme,—especially in the earlier stages of social and moral development, in which the struggle

---

[1] No doubt this influence is confined within strict limits: no authority can permanently impose on men regulations flagrantly infelicific: and the most practically originative of religious teachers have produced their effect chiefly by giving new force and vividness to sentiments already existing (and recognized as properly authoritative) in the society upon which they acted. Still, it might have made a great difference to the human race if (*e.g.*) Mohammed had been fond of wine, and indifferent to women.

for existence was most operative: and (2) as before noticed, a morality perfectly preservative might still be imperfectly felicific, and so require considerable improvement from a Utilitarian point of view[1]. Further, analogy would lead us to expect that however completely adapted the moral instincts of a community may be at some particular time to its conditions of existence, any rapid change of circumstances would tend to derange the adaptation, from survival of instincts formerly useful, which thus suddenly become useless or pernicious. And indeed, apart from any apparent changes in external circumstances, it might result from the operation of some law of human development, that the most completely organized experience of human happiness in the past would guide us but imperfectly to the right means of making it a maximum in the future. For example, a slight decrease in the average strength of some common impulse might render the traditional rules and sentiments, that regulate this impulse, infelicific on the whole. And if, when we turn from these abstract considerations to history, and examine the actual morality of other ages and countries, we find that, considered as an instrument for producing general happiness, it continually seems to exhibit imperfections arising from these or other causes; there is surely a strong presumption that there are similar imperfections to be discovered in our own moral code, though habit and familiarity prevent them from being obvious.

Finally, we have to observe that the discrepancies which we find when we compare the moralities of different ages and countries, exist to some extent side by side in the morality of any one society at any given time. We discover on examination that there is scarcely any department of conduct in reference to which some respectable section of the community is not found to diverge from the received moral code, both in a positive and a negative direction. It has already been observed that whenever such divergent opinions are entertained by a minority so large, that we cannot fairly regard the dogma of the majority as the plain utterance of Common Sense, an appeal is necessarily made to some higher principle, and very

---

[1] On this point I shall have occasion to speak further in the next section.

commonly to Utilitarianism. But a smaller minority than this, particularly if composed of persons of enlightenment and special acquaintance with the effects of the conduct judged, may reasonably inspire us with distrust of Common Sense: just as in the more technical parts of practice we prefer the judgment of a few trained experts to the instincts of the vulgar. And so we seem to be forced back on the method of pure empirical Utilitarianism, which, so far as we find it applicable, must practically tend to submerge the Intuitional method, however we may still maintain the general harmony between the two. Yet again, a contemplation of these divergent codes and their relation to the different circumstances in which men live, suggests a conclusion profoundly opposed to the convictions of Common Sense, and yet quite in harmony with the general reasoning by which it is proposed to reconcile Intuitional and Utilitarian Ethics; namely, that Common-Sense morality is really only adapted for ordinary men in ordinary circumstances—although it may still be expedient that these ordinary persons should regard it as absolutely and universally prescribed, since any other view of it may dangerously weaken its hold over their minds. In this case we must use the Utilitarian method to ascertain how far persons in special circumstances require a morality more specially adapted to them than Common Sense is willing to concede: and also how far men of peculiar physical or mental constitution ought to be exempted from ordinary rules, as has sometimes been claimed for men of genius, or men of intensely emotional nature, or men gifted with more than usual prudence and self-control.

In examining this question, it is important to notice, that besides the large amount of divergence that exists between the moral instincts of different classes and individuals, there is often a palpable discrepancy between the moral instincts of any class or individual, and such Utilitarian reasonings as their untrained intellects are in the habit of conducting. There are many things in conduct which many people think right but not expedient, or at least which they would not think expedient if they had not first judged them to be right; in so far as they reason from experience only, their conclusions as to what conduces to the general happiness are opposed to their moral intuitions. It may be said that this results generally from a hasty and superficial consideration of expediency; and that the discrepancy would disappear after a deeper and completer examination of the consequences of actions. And I do not deny that this would often turn out to be the case: but as we cannot tell *à priori* how far it would be so, this only constitutes a further argument for a comprehensive and systematic application of a purely Utilitarian method.

We must conclude, then, that we cannot take the moral rules of Common Sense as expressing the *consensus* of competent judges, up to the present time, as to the kind of conduct which is likely to produce the greatest amount of happiness on the whole. It would rather seem that it is the unavoidable duty of a systematic Utilitarianism to make a thorough revision of these rules, in order to ascertain how far the causes previously enumerated (and perhaps others) have actually operated to produce a divergence between Common Sense and a perfectly Utilitarian code of morality.

§ 2. But in thus stating the problem we are assuming that the latter term of this comparison can be satisfactorily defined and sufficiently developed; that we can frame with adequate precision a system of rules, constituting the true moral code for human beings as deduced from Utilitarian principles. And this seems to be commonly assumed by the school whose method we are now examining. But when we set ourselves in earnest to the construction of such a system, we find it beset with serious difficulties. For, passing over the uncertainties involved in hedonistic comparison generally, let us suppose that the *quantum* of happiness that will result from the establishment of any plan of behaviour among human beings can be ascertained with sufficient exactness for practical purposes; and that even when the plan is as yet constructed in imagination alone. It still has to be asked, What is the nature of the human being for whom we are to construct this hypothetical scheme of conduct? For humanity is not something that exhibits the same properties always and everywhere: whether we consider the intellect of man or his feelings, or his physical condition and circumstances, we find them so different in different ages and countries, that it seems *primâ facie* absurd to lay down a set of ideal Utilitarian rules for mankind generally. It may be said that these differences after all relate chiefly to details; and that there is in any case sufficient uniformity in the nature and circumstances of human life always and everywhere to render possible an outline ideal of behaviour for mankind at large. But it must be observed, that it is with details that we are now principally concerned; for the previous discussion has sufficiently shewn that the conduct approved by Common Sense has a *general* resemblance to that which Utilitarianism would prescribe; but we wish to ascertain more exactly how far the resemblance extends, and with what delicacy and precision the current moral rules are adapted to the actual needs and conditions of human life.

Suppose, then, that we contract the scope of the investigation, and only endeavour to ascertain the rules appropriate to men as we know them, in our own age and country. But the men whom we know are beings who recognize more or less definitely a certain moral code: and it is obvious that this element of their actual nature must not be included in our conception of them as beings for whom a code is yet to be constructed *de novo*. If, however, we take an actual man—let us say, an average Englishman—and abstract his morality, what remains is an entity so purely hypothetical, that it is not clear what practical purpose can be served by constructing a system of moral rules for a community of such beings. No doubt if we might assume that the scientific deduction of such a system would ensure its general acceptance; if we could reasonably expect to convert all mankind at once to Utilitarian principles, or even all educated and reflective mankind, so that all preachers and teachers should take universal happiness as the goal of their efforts as unquestioningly as physicians take the health of the individual body; and if we could be sure that men's moral habits and sentiments would adjust themselves at once and without any waste of force to these changed rules, then perhaps in framing the Utilitarian code we might fairly leave existing morality out of account. But since we are not warranted in making these suppositions; since we have to take the moral habits, impulses, and tastes of men as a material given us to work upon no less than the rest of their nature, and as something which, as it only partly results from reasoning in the past, so can only be partially modified by any reasoning which we can now apply to it; then surely the solution of the hypothetical Utilitarian problem above stated will not give us the result which we practically require.

It will perhaps be said, "No doubt such an ideal Utilitarian morality can only be gradually, and perhaps after all imperfectly, introduced; but still it will be useful to work it out as a pattern to which we may approximate." But, in the first place, it is not yet proved that we can approximate to it. It is always possible that an existing moral rule, though not the ideally best even for such beings as existing men under the existing circumstances, is yet the best that they can be got to obey: and that it would be futile to propose any other; or even harmful, as it might tend to impair old moral habits without effectively replacing them by new ones. And secondly, we may fairly ask, Why should we try to approximate to just this pattern? for such an attempt only seems to be the best means of promoting human happiness if we make the assumption that man cannot be importantly improved, in his capacities for happiness and his power of attaining it, except so far as his morality is concerned; that the other elements of his nature and condition must be taken as substantially unchangeable. But if this is not the case; if, on the contrary, the state of men's knowledge and intellectual faculties, and the range of their sympathies, and the direction and strength of their prevailing impulses, and their relations to the external world and to each other, are continually being altered, and such alteration is to some extent under our control: then the endeavour gradually to approximate to a morality constructed on the supposition that the non-moral part of existing human nature is constant, may lead us quite wrong. In short, the Utilitarian is placed in this dilemma:—The nature of man, intellectual and impulsive, and the conditions of his life, are continually being changed, and it seems illegitimate to assume them constant, unless we are confining our attention to the present or proximate future; while again, if we are considering them in the present or proximate future, we must take into account men's moral habits and sentiments, as a part of their nature only somewhat more modifiable than the rest.

At this point certain thinkers of the evolutionist school would suggest that these difficulties of Utilitarian method should be avoided by adopting, as the *practically* ultimate end and criterion of morality, "health" or "efficiency" of the social organism, instead of Happiness. This view is maintained, for instance, in Mr Stephen's *Science of Ethics*[1]; and deserves careful examination. We have first to get the meaning of the terms clear. As I understand Mr Stephen, he means by "health" that state of the social organism which tends to its preservation under the conditions of its existence, as they are known or capable of being predicted; and he means the same by "efficiency"; since the work for which, in his view, the social organism has to be "efficient" is simply the work of living, the function of "going on and still to be." It is necessary to state this distinctly; because "efficiency" might be understood to imply some 'task of humanity' which the social organism has to execute, beyond the task of merely living; and similarly "health" might be taken to mean a state tending to the preservation not of existence merely, but of *desirable* existence—desirability being interpreted in some non-hedonistic[2] manner: and in this case an examination of either term would lead us again over the ground traversed in the discussion on Ultimate Good in ch. xiv. of the preceding Book[3]. But I do not understand that any such implications were in Mr Stephen's mind; and they certainly would not be in harmony with the general drift of his argument. If then we take "health" and "efficiency" to mean merely that state or internal condition of

---

[1] See especially chap. ix., Pars. 12—15.

[2] It is obvious that if 'desirability,' in the above definition, were interpreted hedonistically, the term "health" would merely give us a new name for the general problem of utilitarian morality; not a new suggestion for its solution.

[3] The notions of "social welfare" or "wellbeing," which Mr Stephen elsewhere uses, are still more obviously ambiguous: I have therefore avoided them: but I do not think that Mr Stephen means by them any more than what I understand him to mean by "health" or "efficiency"—*i.e.* that state of the social organism which tends to its preservation under the conditions of its existence.

an organism in which it tends to be preserved, we may make the issue clearer by asking whether if Happiness be admitted to be the really ultimate end in a system of morality, it is nevertheless reasonable to take Preservation as the practically ultimate "scientific criterion" of moral rules.

My reasons for answering this question in the negative are two-fold. In the first place I know no adequate grounds for supposing that if we aim exclusively at the preservation of the social organism we shall secure the maximum attainable happiness of its individual members: indeed, so far as I know, of two social states which equally tend to be preserved one may be indefinitely happier than the other. As has been before observed[1], a large part of the pleasures which cultivated persons value most highly—æsthetic pleasures—are derived from acts and processes that have no material tendency to preserve the individual's life[2]: and the statement remains true if we substitute the social organism for the individual. And I may add that much refined morality is concerned with the prevention of pains which have no demonstrable tendency to the destruction of the individual or of society. Hence, while I quite admit that the maintenance of preservative habits and sentiments is the most indispensable function of utilitarian morality—and perhaps almost its sole function in the earlier stages of moral development, when to live at all was a difficult task for human communities—I do not therefore think it reasonable that we should be content with the mere securing of existence for humanity generally, and should confine our efforts to promoting the increase of this security, instead of seeking to make the secured existence more desirable.

But, secondly, I do not see on what grounds Mr Stephen holds that the criterion of "tendency to the preservation of the social organism" is necessarily capable of being applied with greater precision than that of "tendency to general happiness," even so far as the two ends are coincident: and that the former "satisfies the conditions of a scientific criterion." I should

---

[1] Bk. II. ch. vi. § 3.

[2] I do not mean to assert that 'play' in some form is not necessary for physical health: but there is a long step from the encouragement of play, so far as salutary, to the promotion of social culture.

admit that this would probably be the case, if the Sociology that we know were a science actually constructed, and not merely the sketch of a possible future science: but Mr Stephen has himself told us that sociology at present "consists of nothing more than a collection of unverified guesses and vague generalisations, disguised under a more or less pretentious apparatus of quasi-scientific terminology." This language is stronger than I should have ventured to use; but I agree generally with the view that it expresses; and it appears to me that if Mr Stephen holds this view, he ought to maintain the practical superiority of the evolutional to the utilitarian criterion by some special arguments more positive than a mere statement of the defects of the latter. Such special arguments, however, I am unable to find.

Holding this view of the present condition of Sociology, I consider that, from the utilitarian point of view, there are equally decisive reasons against the adoption of any such notion as "development" of the social organism—instead of mere preservation—as the practically ultimate end and criterion of morality. On the one hand, if by "development" is meant an increase in "efficiency" or preservative qualities, this notion is only an optimistic specialisation of that just discussed (involving the—I fear—unwarranted assumption that the social organism tends to become continually more efficient); so that no fresh arguments need be urged against it. If, however, something different is meant by development—as (e.g.) a disciple of Mr Spencer might mean an increase in "definite coherent heterogeneity," whether or not such increase was preservative—then I know no scientific grounds for concluding that we shall best promote general happiness by concentrating our efforts on the attainment of this increase. I do not say that it is impossible that every increase in the definite coherent heterogeneity of a society of human beings may be accompanied or followed by an increase in the aggregate happiness of the members of the society: but I do not perceive that Mr Spencer, or any one else, has even attempted to furnish the kind of proof which this proposition requires[1].

[1] It may be observed that the increased heterogeneity which the development of modern industry has brought with it, in the form of a specialisation of

Still less can I agree with Mr Spencer[1] in thinking that it is possible—in the present condition of our sociological knowledge—to construct the final perfect form of society, towards which the process of human history is tending; and to determine the rules of mutual behaviour which ought to be, and will be, observed by the members of this perfect society. Granting that we can conceive as possible a human community which is from a utilitarian point of view perfect; and granting also Mr Spencer's definition of this perfection—viz. that the voluntary actions of all the members cause "pleasure unalloyed by pain anywhere" to all who are affected by them[2];—it still seems to me quite impossible to forecast the nature and relations of the persons composing such a community with sufficient clearness and certainty to enable us to define even in outline their moral code. Even if it were otherwise, even if we could construct scientifically Mr Spencer's ideal morality, I do not think such a construction would be of much avail in solving the practical problems of actual humanity. For a society in which—to take one point only—there is no such thing as punishment, is necessarily a society with its essential structure so unlike our own, that it would be idle to attempt any close imitation of its rules of behaviour. It might possibly be best for us to conform approximately to some of these rules; but this we could only know by examining each particular rule in detail; we could have no general grounds for concluding that it would be best for us to conform to them as far as possible. For even supposing that this ideal society is ultimately to be realized, it must at any rate be separated

industrial functions which tends to render the lives of individual workers narrow and monotonous, has usually been regarded by philanthropists as seriously infelicific; and as needing to be counteracted by a general diffusion of the intellectual culture now enjoyed by the few—which, if realized, would tend *pro tanto* to make the lives of different classes in the community *less* heterogeneous.

[1] I refer especially to the views put forward by Mr Spencer in the concluding chapters of his *Data of Ethics*.

[2] This definition, however, does not seem to me admissible, from a utilitarian point of view: since a society in this sense perfect might not realize the maximum of possible happiness; it might still be capable of a material increase of happiness through pleasures involving a slight alloy of pain, such as Mr Spencer's view of perfection would exclude.

from us by a considerable interval of evolution; hence it is not unlikely that the best way of progressing towards it will be some other than the apparently directest way, and that we shall reach it more easily if we begin by moving away from it. Whether this is so or not, and to what extent, can only be known by carefully examining the effects of conduct on actual human beings, and inferring its probable effects on the human beings whom we may expect to exist in the proximate future.

To sum up: I hold that the utilitarian, in the existing state of our knowledge, cannot possibly construct a morality *de novo* either for man as he is (abstracting his morality), or for man as he ought to be and will be. He must start, speaking broadly, with the existing social order, and the existing morality as a part of that order: and in deciding the question whether any divergence from this code is to be recommended, must consider chiefly the immediate consequences of such divergence, upon a society in which such a code is conceived generally to subsist. No doubt a thoughtful and well-instructed Utilitarian may see dimly a certain way ahead, and his attitude towards existing morality may be to some extent modified by what he sees. He may discern in the future certain evils impending, which can only be effectually warded off by the adoption of new and more stringent views of duty in certain departments: while, on the other hand, he may see a prospect of social changes which will render a relaxation of other parts of the moral code expedient or inevitable. But if he keeps within the limits that separate scientific prevision from fanciful Utopian conjecture, the form of society to which his practical conclusions relate will be one varying but little from the actual, with its actually established code of moral rules and customary judgments concerning virtue and vice.

CHAPTER V.

THE METHOD OF UTILITARIANISM CONTINUED.

§ 1. If, then, we are to regard the morality of Common Sense as a machinery of rules, habits, and sentiments, roughly and generally but not precisely or completely adapted to the production of the greatest possible happiness for sentient beings generally; and if, on the other hand, we have to accept it as the actually established machinery for attaining this end, which we cannot replace at once by any other, but can only gradually modify; it remains to consider the practical effects of the complex and balanced relation in which a scientific Utilitarian thus seems to stand to the Positive Morality of his age and country.

Generally speaking, he will clearly conform to it, and endeavour to promote its development in others. For, though the imperfection that we find in all the actual conditions of human existence—we may even say in the universe at large as judged from a human point of view—is ultimately found even in Morality itself, in so far as this is contemplated as Positive; still, practically, we are much less concerned with correcting and improving than we are with realizing and enforcing it. The Utilitarian must repudiate altogether that temper of rebellion against the established morality, as something purely external and conventional, into which the reflective mind is always apt to fall when it is first convinced that its rules are not intrinsically reasonable. He must, of course, also repudiate as superstitious that awe of it as an absolute or Divine Code which Intuitional moralists inculcate[1]. Still, he will naturally

---

[1] At the same time this sentiment, which Kant among others has expressed with peculiar force (*Kritik der prakt. Vern.* Beschluss), is in no way incompatible

contemplate it with reverence and wonder, as a marvellous product of nature, the result of long centuries of growth, shewing in many parts the same fine adaptation of means to complex exigencies as the most elaborate structures of physical organisms exhibit: he will handle it with respectful delicacy as a mechanism, constructed of the fluid element of opinions and dispositions, by the indispensable aid of which the actual *quantum* of human happiness is continually being produced; a mechanism which no 'politicians or philosophers' could create, yet without which the harder and coarser machinery of Positive Law could not be permanently maintained, and the life of man would become—as Hobbes forcibly expresses it—"solitary, poor, nasty, brutish, and short."

Still, as this actual moral order is admittedly imperfect, it will be the Utilitarian's duty to aid in improving it; just as the most orderly, law-abiding, member of a modern civilized society includes the reform of laws in his conception of political duty. We have therefore to consider by what method he will ascertain the particular modifications of positive morality which it would be practically expedient to attempt to introduce, at any given time and place. Here our investigation seems, after all, to leave Empirical Hedonism as the only method ordinarily applicable for the ultimate decision of such problems—at least until the science of Sociology shall have been really constructed. It is no doubt true that changes in morality might be suggested—and have actually been proposed by persons seriously concerned to benefit their fellow-creatures—which even the imperfect sociological knowledge that we possess would lead us to regard as not merely infelicific but dangerous to the very existence of the social organism. But such changes for the most part involve changes in positive law as well; since most of the rules of which the observance is fundamentally important for the preservation of an organized community are either directly or indirectly maintained by legal sanctions: and it would be going too far beyond the line which, in my view, separates ethics from politics, to discuss changes of this kind in the present book. The rules with which we have primarily to deal, in

with Utilitarianism; only it must not attach itself to any subordinate rules of conduct.

considering the utilitarian method of determining private duty, are rules supported by merely moral sanctions; and the question of maintaining or modifying such rules concerns, for the most part, the happiness rather than the existence of human society. The consideration of this question, therefore, from a utilitarian point of view, resolves itself into a comparison between the total amounts of pleasure and pain that may be expected to result respectively from maintaining any given rule as at present established, or endeavouring to introduce that which is proposed in its stead. That this comparison must generally be of a rough and uncertain kind, we have already seen; and it is highly important to bear this in mind: but yet we seem unable to find any substitute for it. It is not meant, of course, that each individual is left to his own unassisted judgment in dealing with such questions: there is a mass of traditional experience, which each individual imbibes orally or from books, as to the effects of conduct upon happiness; but the general formulæ in which this experience is transmitted are, for the most part, so indefinite, the proper range of their application so uncertain, and the observation and induction on which they are founded so uncritical, that they stand in continual need of further empirical verification; especially as regards their applicability to any particular case.

It is perhaps not surprising that some thinkers[1] of the Utilitarian school should consider that the task of hedonistic calculation which is thus set before the utilitarian moralist is too extensive: and should propose to simplify it by marking off a "large sphere of individual option and self-guidance," to which "ethical dictation" does not apply. I should quite admit that it is clearly expedient to draw a dividing line of this kind: but it appears to me that there is no simple general method of drawing it; that it can only be drawn by careful utilitarian calculation applied with varying results to the various relations and circumstances of human life. To attempt the required division by means of any such general formula as that 'the individual is not responsible to society for that part of his conduct which concerns himself alone and others only with their free consent' seems to me practically futile: since,

[1] For example, Mr Bain in 'Mind' (Jan. 1883, pp. 48, 49).

owing to the complex enlacements of interest and sympathy that connect the members of a civilized community, almost any material loss of happiness by any one individual is likely to affect some others without their consent to some not inconsiderable extent. And I do not see how it is from a utilitarian point of view justifiable to say broadly with J. S. Mill that such secondary injury to others, if merely "constructive or presumptive," is to be disregarded in view of the advantages of allowing free development to individuality; for if the injury feared is great, and the presumption that it will occur is shewn by experience to be strong, the definite risk of evil from the withdrawal of the moral sanction must, I conceive, outweigh the indefinite possibility of loss through the repression of individuality in one particular direction[1]. But further: even supposing that we could mark off the "sphere of individual option and self-guidance" by some simple and sweeping formula, still within this sphere the individual, if he wishes to guide himself reasonably on utilitarian principles, must take some account of all important effects of his actions on the happiness of others; and if he does this methodically, he must, I conceive, use the empirical method which we have examined in Book II. And—to prevent any undue alarm at this prospect—we may observe that every sensible man is commonly supposed to determine at least a large part of his conduct by what is substantially this method; it is assumed that, within the limits which morality lays down, he will try to get as much happiness as he can for himself and for other human beings, according to the relations in which they stand to him, by combining in some way his own experience with that of other men as to the felicific and infelicific effects of actions. And it is actually in this way that each man usually deliberates (*e.g.*) what profession to choose for himself, or what mode of education for his children, whether to aim at marriage or remain single, whether to settle in town or country, in England or abroad, &c. No doubt there are, as we saw[2], other ends besides Happiness, such as Knowledge, Beauty, &c.,

---

[1] It may be observed that Mill's doctrine is certainly opposed to common sense: since (*e.g.*) it would exclude from censure almost all forms of sexual immorality committed by unmarried and independent adults.

[2] Cf. B. III. c. xiv.

commonly recognized as unquestionably desirable, and therefore largely pursued without consideration of ulterior consequences: but when the pursuit of any of these ends involves an apparent sacrifice of happiness in other ways, the practical question whether under these circumstances such pursuit ought to be maintained or abandoned seems always decided by an application, however rough, of the method of pure empirical Hedonism.

And in saying that this must be the method of the Utilitarian moralist, I only mean that no other can normally be applied in reducing to a common measure the diverse elements of the problems with which he has to deal. Of course, in determining the nature and importance of each of these diverse considerations, the utilitarian art of morality will lay various sciences under contribution. Thus, for example, it will learn from Political Economy what effects a general censure of usurers, or of landowners who take the full advantages of unrestricted competition in determining rents, or the ordinary commendation of liberality in almsgiving, is likely to have on the wealth of the community; it will learn from the physiologist the probable consequences to health of a general abstinence from alcoholic liquors or any other restraint on appetite proposed in the name of Temperance; more generally, it will learn from the experts in any science how far knowledge is likely to be promoted by investigations offensive to any prevalent moral or religious sentiment. But how far the increase of wealth or of knowledge, or even the improvement of health, should under any circumstances be subordinated to other considerations, I know no scientific method of determining other than that of empirical Hedonism. Nor, as I have said, does it seem to me that any other method has ever been applied or sought by the common sense of mankind, for regulating the pursuit of what our older moralists called 'Natural Good,'—*i.e.* of all that is intrinsically desirable *except* Virtue or Morality,—within the limits fixed by the latter; the Utilitarian here only performs somewhat more consistently and systematically the reasoning processes which are generally admitted to be properly decisive of the questions that this pursuit raises. His distinctive characteristic, as a Utilitarian, is that he has to apply the same method to the criticism and correction of the limiting morality itself. The particulars of this criticism will obviously vary with the almost infinite variations in human nature and circumstances: the construction of a detailed system of Utilitarian casuistry, even if limited to our own age and country, would carry us far beyond the limits of the present treatise. I here only propose to discuss the general points of view which a Utilitarian critic must take, in order that no important class of relevant considerations may be omitted.

§ 2. Let us first recall the distinction previously noticed[1] between duty as commonly conceived,—that to which a man is bound or obliged—, and praiseworthy or excellent conduct; since, in considering the relation of Utilitarianism to the moral judgments of Common Sense, it will be convenient to begin with the former element of current morality, as the more important and indispensable; the *ensemble* of rules imposed by common opinion in any society, which form a kind of unwritten legislation, supplementary to Law proper, and enforced by its own penalties, the disfavour and contempt of society. This legislation, as it does not emanate from a definite body of persons acting in a corporate capacity, obviously cannot be altered by any formal deliberations and resolutions of the persons on whose *consensus* it rests; any change in it must therefore result from the private action of individuals, whether determined by impulse and sentiment or (as we at present suppose) by Utilitarian considerations. As we shall presently see, the practical Utilitarian problem is liable to be complicated by the conflict and divergence which is found to some extent in all societies between the moral opinions of different sections of the community: but however far this divergence goes there is always a considerable body of moral law common to the diverging codes: and it will be convenient to confine our attention to this in the first instance. Let us suppose then that after considering the consequences of any rule of duty, really supported by 'Common Consent,' a Utilitarian comes to the conclusion that a different rule would be more conducive to the general happiness, if similarly established in a society remaining in other respects the same as at present—or in one slightly different (in so far as our forecast of social changes can be made sufficiently

[1] Cf. especially Bk. III. c. ii.

clear to furnish any basis for practice). And first we will suppose that this new rule differs from the old one not only positively but negatively; that it does not merely go beyond and include it, but actually conflicts with it. Before he can decide that it is right for him (*i.e.* conducive to the general happiness) to support the new rule against the old, by example and precept, he ought to estimate the force of certain disadvantages necessarily attendant upon such innovations, which may conveniently be arranged under the following heads.

In the first place, as his own happiness is a part of the universal end at which he aims, he must consider the importance to himself, and to others connected with him, of the penalties of social disapprobation which he will incur: and he must further take into account, besides the immediate pain of this disapprobation, its indirect effect in diminishing his power of serving society and promoting the general happiness in other ways. The prospect of such pain and loss is, of course, not decisive against the innovation; since it must to some extent be regarded as the regular price that has to be paid for the advantage of this kind of reform in current morality. But here, as in many Utilitarian calculations, everything depends on the quantity of the effects produced; which in the case supposed may vary very much, from slight distrust and disfavour to severe condemnation and social exclusion. It often seems that by attempting change prematurely an innovator may incur the severest form of the moral penalty, whereas if he had waited a few years he would have been let off with the mildest. For the hold which a moral rule has over the general mind commonly begins to decay from the time that it is seen to be opposed to the calculations of expediency: and it may be better for the community as well as for the individual that it should not be openly attacked, until this process of decay has reached a certain point.

It is, however, of more importance to point out certain general reasons for doubting whether an apparent improvement will really have a beneficial effect on others. It is possible that the new rule, though it would be more felicific than the old one, if it could get itself equally established, may be not so likely to be adopted, or if adopted, not so likely to be obeyed, by the mass of the community in which it is proposed to innovate. It may be too subtle and refined, or too complex and elaborate: it may require a greater intellectual development, or a higher degree of self-control, or a different quality or balance of feelings, than is to be found in an average member of the community. Nor can it be said in reply, that by the hypothesis the innovator's example must be good to whatever extent it operates, since *pro tanto* it tends to substitute a better rule for a worse. For experience seems to shew that an example of this kind is more likely to be potent negatively than positively; that here, as elsewhere in human affairs, it is easier to pull down than to build up; easier to weaken or destroy the restraining force that a moral rule, habitually and generally obeyed, has over men's minds, than to substitute for it a new restraining habit, not similarly sustained by tradition and custom. Hence the effect of an example intrinsically good may be on the whole bad, owing to its destructive operation being more vigorous than its constructive. And again, such destructive effect must be considered not only in respect of the particular rule violated, but of all other rules. For just as the breaking of any positive law has an inevitable tendency to encourage lawlessness generally, so the violation of any generally recognized moral rule seems to give a certain aid to the forces that are always tending towards moral anarchy in any society.

Nor must we neglect the reaction which any breach with customary morality will have on the agent's own mind. For the regulative habits and sentiments which each man has received by inheritance or training constitute an important force impelling his will, in the main, to conduct such as his reason would dictate; a natural auxiliary, as it were, to Reason in its conflict with seductive passions and appetites; and it may be practically dangerous to impair the strength of these auxiliaries. On the other hand, it would seem that the habit of acting rationally is the best of all habits, and that it ought to be the aim of a reasonable being to bring all his impulses and sentiments into more and more perfect harmony with Reason. And indeed when a man has earnestly accepted any moral principle, those of his pre-existing regulative habits and sentiments that are not supported by deductions from this principle tend naturally to decay and disappear; and it would perhaps be scarcely worth while to take them into account, except for the support that they derive from the sympathy of others.

But this last is a consideration of great importance. For the moral impulses of each individual commonly draw the large part of their effective force from the sympathy of other human beings. I do not merely mean that the pleasures and pains which each derives sympathetically from the moral likings and aversions of others are important as motives to felicific conduct no less than as elements of the individual's happiness: I mean further that the direct sympathetic echo in each man of the judgments and sentiments of others concerning conduct sustains his own similar judgments and sentiments. Through this twofold operation of sympathy it becomes practically much easier for most men to conform to a moral rule established in the society to which they belong than to one made by themselves. And any act by which a man weakens the effect on himself of this general moral sympathy tends *pro tanto* to make the performance of duty more difficult for him. On the other hand, we have to take into account—besides the intrinsic gain of the particular change—the general advantage of offering to mankind a striking example of consistent Utilitarianism; since, in this case as in others, a man gives a stronger proof of genuine conviction by conduct in opposition to public opinion than he can by conformity. In order, however, that this effect may be produced, it is almost necessary that the non-conformity should not promote the innovator's personal convenience; for in that case it will almost certainly be attributed to egoistic motives, however plausible the Utilitarian deduction of its rightness may seem.

The exact force of these various considerations will differ indefinitely in different cases; and it does not seem profitable to attempt any general estimate of them: but on the whole, it would seem that the general arguments which we have noticed constitute an important check upon Utilitarian innovations on Common Sense morality, of the negative or destructive kind.

If now we consider such innovations as are merely positive and supplementary, and consist in adding a new rule to those already established by Common Sense; it will appear that there is really no collision of methods, so far as the Utilitarian's own observance of the new rule is concerned. For, as every such rule is, *ex hypothesi*, believed by him to be conducive to the common good, he is merely giving a special and stricter interpretation to the general duty of Universal Benevolence, where Common Sense leaves it loose and indeterminate. Hence the restraining considerations above enumerated do not apply to this case. And whatever it is right for him to do himself, it is obviously right for him to approve and recommend to other persons in similar circumstances. But it is a different question whether he ought to seek to impose his new rule on others, by express condemnation of all who are not prepared to adopt it; as this involves not only the immediate evil of the annoyance given to others, but also the further danger of weakening the general good effect of his moral example, through the reaction provoked by this aggressive attitude. On this point his decision will largely depend on the prospect, as far as he can estimate it, that his innovation has of meeting with support and sympathy from others.

It should be observed, however, that a great part of the reform in popular morality, which a consistent Utilitarian will try to introduce, will probably lie not so much in establishing new rules (whether conflicting with the old or merely supplementary) as in enforcing old ones. For there is always a considerable part of morality in the condition of receiving formal respect and acceptance, while yet it is not really sustained by any effective force of public opinion: and the difference between the moralities of any two societies is often more strikingly exhibited in the different emphasis attached to various portions of the moral code in each, than in disagreement as to the whole sum of rules which the code should include. In the case we are considering, it is chiefly conduct which shews a want of comprehensive sympathy or of public spirit, to which the Utilitarian will desire to attach a severer condemnation than is at present directed against it. There is much conduct of this sort, of which the immediate effect is to give obvious pleasure to individuals, while the far greater amount of harm that it more remotely and indirectly causes is but dimly recognized by Common Sense. Such conduct, therefore, even when it is allowed to be wrong, is very mildly treated by common opinion; especially when it is prompted by some impulse not self-regarding. Still, in all such cases, we do not require the promulgation of any new moral doctrine, but merely a bracing and sharpening of the moral sentiments of society, to bring them into harmony with the greater comprehensiveness of view and the more impartial concern for human happiness which characterize the Utilitarian system.

§ 3. We have hitherto supposed that the innovator is endeavouring to introduce a new rule of conduct, not for himself only, but for others also, as more conducive to the general happiness than the rule recognized by Common Sense. It may perhaps be thought that this is not the issue most commonly raised between Utilitarianism and Common Sense: but rather whether exceptions should be allowed to rules which both sides agree to be generally valid. For no one doubts that it is, *generally speaking,* conducive to the common happiness that men should be veracious, faithful to promises, obedient to law, disposed to satisfy the normal expectations of others, having their malevolent impulses and their sensual appetites under strict control: but it is thought that an exclusive regard to pleasurable and painful consequences would frequently admit exceptions to rules which Common Sense imposes as absolute. Here, however, we must observe that the admission of an exception on general grounds is merely the establishment of a more complex and delicate rule, instead of one that is broader and simpler; for if it is conducive to the general good that the exception be admitted in one case, it will be equally so in all similar cases. Let us take an illustration of some present interest. Suppose a Utilitarian is asked how he voted in the recent election (1874). If he wishes to conceal his vote he may easily think it expedient and right to answer falsely: for the Utilitarian reasons against falsehood generally are, (1) the immediate harm done by misleading a particular individual, and (2) the tendency which each falsehood has to diminish the mutual confidence that men ought to have in each other's assertions. But in this exceptional case it may be expedient that the questioner should be misled; and, in so far as the falsehood tends to produce a general distrust of all affirmations about voting, it only furthers the end for which voting has been made secret. It is evident, however, that if these reasons are valid for any person, they are valid for all persons; in fact, that they establish the expediency of a new general rule in respect of truth and falsehood, more complicated than the old one; a rule which the Utilitarian, as such, desires to be universally obeyed.

There are, of course, some kinds of moral innovation which, from the nature of the case, are not likely to occur frequently; as where Utilitarian reasoning leads a man to take part in a political revolution, or to support a public measure in opposition to what Common Sense regards as Justice or Good Faith. Still, in such cases a Utilitarian usually proceeds on general principles, which he would desire all persons in similar circumstances to carry into effect.

We have, however, to consider another kind of exceptions, differing fundamentally from this, which Utilitarianism seems to admit; where the agent does not think it expedient that the rule on which he himself acts should be universally adopted, and yet maintains that his individual act is right, as producing a greater balance of pleasure over pain than any other conduct open to him would produce.

And certainly we cannot argue that, because a large aggregate of acts would cause more harm than good, therefore any single act of the kind will produce this effect. It may even be a straining of language to say that it has a *tendency* to produce it: no one (*e.g.*) would say that because an army walking over a bridge would break it down, therefore the crossing of a single traveller has a tendency to destroy it. And just as a prudent physician in giving rules of diet recommends an occasional deviation from them, as more conducive to the health of the body than absolute regularity; so there may be rules of social behaviour of which the general observance is necessary to the well-being of the community, while yet a certain amount of non-observance is rather advantageous than otherwise.

Here, however, we seem brought into conflict with Kant's fundamental principle, that a right action must be one of which the agent could "will the maxim to be law universal[1]": and yet this was accepted as a self-evident truth. But, as was before[2] noticed in the particular case of veracity, we must admit an application of this principle, which importantly modifies its practical force: we must admit the case where the belief that the action will not be widely imitated is an essential qualification of the maxim. In fact, the Kantian principle, as accepted by me, means no more than that an act, if right for any individual, must be right on general grounds and therefore for some class of persons; it does not prevent us from defining this class by the above-mentioned characteristic of believing that the act will remain an exceptional one. Of course if this belief turns out to be erroneous, serious harm may possibly result; but this is no more than may be said of many other Utilitarian deductions. Nor is it difficult to find instances of conduct which Common Sense holds to be legitimate solely on the ground that we have no fear of its being too widely imitated. Take, for example, the case of Celibacy. A universal refusal to propagate the human species would be the greatest of conceivable crimes from a Utilitarian point of view;—that is, according to the commonly accepted belief in the superiority of human happiness to that of other animals;—and hence the principle in question, applied without the qualification above given, would make it a crime in any one to choose celibacy as the state most conducive to his own happiness. But Common Sense (in the present age at least) regards such preference as within the limits of right conduct; because there is no fear that population will not be sufficiently kept up, as in fact the tendency to propagate is thought to exist rather in excess than otherwise.

In this case it is a non-moral impulse on the average strength of which we think we may reckon: but there does not appear to be any formal or universal reason why the same procedure should not be applied by Utilitarians to an actually existing moral sentiment. Thus there would be a discrepancy between Utilitarianism and Common Sense morality of a very curious kind; as it is the very firmness with which the latter is es-

---

[1] Cf. B. III. c. i. and c. xiii.
[2] B. III. c. vii. § 3.

tablished which becomes the rational ground for relieving the individual of its obligations. We are supposed to see that the happiness of the community will be enhanced (just as the excellence of a metrical composition is) by a slight admixture of irregularity along with a general observance of received rules; and to justify the irregular conduct of a few individuals, on the ground that the supply of regular conduct from other members of the community may reasonably be expected to be adequate.

It does not seem to me that this reasoning can be shewn to be necessarily unsound, as applied to human society as at present constituted: but the cases in which it could really be thought to be applicable, by any one sincerely desirous of promoting the general happiness, must certainly be rare. For it should be observed that it makes a fundamental difference whether the sentiment in mankind generally, on which we rely to sustain sufficiently a general rule while admitting exceptions thereto, is moral or non-moral; because a moral sentiment is inseparable from the conviction that the conduct to which it prompts is objectively right—i.e. right whether or not it is thought or felt to be so—for oneself and all similar persons in similar circumstances; it cannot therefore coexist with approval of the contrary conduct in any one case, unless this case is distinguished by some material difference other than the mere non-existence in the agent of the ordinary moral sentiment against his conduct. Thus, assuming that general unveracity and general celibacy would both be evils of the worst kind, we may still all regard it as legitimate for men in general to remain celibate if they like, on account of the strength of the natural sentiments prompting to marriage, because the existence of these sentiments in ordinary human beings is not affected by the universal recognition of the legitimacy of celibacy: but we cannot similarly all regard it as legitimate for men to tell lies if they like, however strong the actually existing sentiment against lying may be. If therefore we were all enlightened Utilitarians, it would be impossible for any one to justify himself in making false statements while admitting it to be inexpedient for persons similarly conditioned to make them; as he would have no ground for believing that persons similarly conditioned would act differently from himself. The case, no doubt, is different in a society as actually constituted; it is conceivable that the practically effective morality in such a society, resting on a basis independent of utilitarian or any other reasonings, may not be materially affected by the particular act or expressed opinion of a particular individual: but the circumstances are, I conceive, very rare, in which a really conscientious person could feel so sure of this as to conclude that by approving a particular violation of a rule, of which the *general* (though not *universal*) observance is plainly expedient, he will not probably do harm on the whole. Especially as all the objections to innovation, noticed in the previous section, apply with increased force if the innovator does not even claim to be introducing a new and better general rule.

It appears to me, therefore, that the cases in which practical doubts are likely to arise, as to whether exceptions should be permitted from ordinary rules on Utilitarian principles, will mostly be those which I discussed in the first paragraph of this section: where the exceptions are not claimed for a few individuals, on the mere ground of their probable fewness, but either for persons generally under exceptional circumstances, or for a class of persons defined by exceptional qualities of intellect, temperament or character. Here the Utilitarian may have no doubt that in a community consisting generally of enlightened Utilitarians, these grounds for exceptional ethical treatment would be regarded as valid; but he may, as I have said, doubt whether the more refined and complicated rule which recognizes such exceptions is adapted for the community in which he is actually living; and whether the attempt to introduce it is not likely to do more harm by weakening current morality than good by improving its quality. Supposing such a doubt to arise, either in a case of this kind, or in one of the rare cases referred to in the preceding paragraph, it becomes obviously necessary that the Utilitarian should consider carefully the extent to which his advice or example are likely to influence persons to whom they would be dangerous: and it is evident that the result of this consideration may depend largely on the degree of publicity which he gives to either advice or example. Thus, on Utilitarian principles, it may be right to do and privately recommend, under certain circumstances, what it would not be right to advocate openly; it may be right to teach openly to one set of persons what it would be wrong to teach to others; it may be conceivably right to do, if it can be done with comparative secrecy, what it would be wrong to do in the face of the world; and even, if perfect secrecy can be reasonably expected, what it would be wrong to recommend by private advice or example. These conclusions are all of a paradoxical character[1]: there is no doubt that the moral consciousness of a plain man broadly repudiates the general notion of an esoteric morality, differing from that popularly taught; and it would be commonly agreed that an action which would be bad if done openly is not rendered good by secrecy. We may observe however that there are strong utilitarian reasons for maintaining generally this latter common opinion; for it is obviously advantageous, generally speaking, that acts which it is expedient to repress by social disapprobation should become known, as otherwise the disapprobation cannot operate; so that it seems inexpedient to support by any moral encouragement the natural disposition of men in general to conceal their wrong doings; besides that the concealment would in most cases have importantly injurious effects on the agent's habits of veracity. Thus the Utilitarian conclusion, carefully stated, would seem to be this; that the opinion that secrecy may render an action right which would not otherwise be so should itself be kept comparatively secret; and similarly it seems expedient that the doctrine that esoteric morality is expedient should itself be kept esoteric. Or if this concealment be difficult to maintain, it may be desirable that Common Sense should repudiate the doctrines which it is expedient to confine to an enlightened few. And thus a Utilitarian may reasonably desire, on Utilitarian principles, that some of his conclusions should be rejected by mankind generally; or even that the vulgar should keep aloof from his system as a whole, in so far as the inevitable indefiniteness and complexity of its calculations render it likely to lead to bad results in their hands.

[1] In particular cases, however, they seem to be admitted by Common Sense to a certain extent. For example, it would be commonly thought wrong to express in public speeches disturbing religious or political opinions which may be legitimately published in books.

Of course, as I have said, in an ideal community of enlightened Utilitarians this swarm of perplexities and paradoxes would vanish; as in such a society no one can have any ground for believing that other persons will act on moral principles different from those which he adopts. And any enlightened Utilitarian must of course desire this consummation; as all conflict of moral opinion must *pro tanto* be regarded as an evil, as tending to impair the force of morality generally in its resistance to seductive impulses. Still such conflict may be a necessary evil in the actual condition of civilized communities, in which there are so many different degrees of intellectual and moral development.

We have thus been led to the discussion of the question which we reserved in the last section; viz. how Utilitarianism should deal with the fact of divergent moral opinions held simultaneously by different members of the same society. For it has become plain that though two different kinds of conduct cannot both be right under the same circumstances, two contradictory opinions as to the rightness of conduct may possibly both be expedient; it may conduce most to the general happiness that A should do a certain act, and at the same time that B, C, D should blame it. The Utilitarian of course cannot really join in the disapproval, but he may think it expedient to leave it unshaken; and at the same time may think it right, if placed in the supposed circumstances, to do the act that is generally disapproved. And so generally it may be best on the whole that there should be conflicting codes of morality in a given society at a certain stage of its development. And, as I have already hinted, the same general reasoning, from the probable origin of the moral sense and its flexible adjustment to the varying conditions of human life, which furnished a presumption that Common-Sense morality is roughly coincident with the code which a perfectly enlightened Utilitarian would lay down for human beings as now constituted, may be applied in favour of these divergent codes: it may be said that these, too, form part of the complex adjustment of man to his circumstances, and that they are needed to supplement and qualify the morality of Common Sense.

However paradoxical this doctrine may appear, we can find

cases where it seems to be implicitly accepted by Common Sense; or at least where it is required to make Common Sense consistent with itself. Let us consider, for example, the common moral judgments concerning rebellions. It is commonly thought, on the one hand, that these abrupt breaches of order are sometimes morally necessary; and, on the other hand, that they ought always to be vigorously resisted, and in case of failure punished by extreme penalties inflicted at least on the ring-leaders; for otherwise they would be attempted under circumstances where there was no sufficient justification for them: but it seems evident that, in the actual condition of men's moral sentiments, this vigorous repression requires the support of a strong body of opinion condemning the rebels as wrong, and not merely as mistaken in their calculations of the chances of success. And, for similar reasons, it may possibly be best on the whole that some of those special relaxations of certain moral rules, that were before noticed in certain professions and sections of society, should continue to exist, while at the same time they should continue to be disapproved by the rest of the society. The evils, however, which must spring from this permanent conflict of opinion are so grave, that it seems improbable that an enlightened Utilitarian will not in most cases attempt to remove it; by either openly maintaining the need of a relaxation of the ordinary moral rule under the special circumstances in question; or, on the other hand, endeavouring to get the ordinary rule recognized and enforced by all conscientious persons in that section of society where its breach has become habitual. And of these two courses it seems that he will in most cases adopt the latter; since the rule is most commonly found on examination to have been relaxed rather for the convenience of individuals, than in the interest of the community at large.

§ 4. Finally, let us consider the general relation of Utilitarianism to that part of common morality which extends beyond the range of strict duty; that is, to the Ideal of character and conduct which in any community at any given time is commonly admired and praised as the sum of Excellences or Perfections. To begin, it must be allowed that this distinction between Excellence and Strict Duty does not seem properly admissible in Utilitarianism, for a Utilitarian must hold that it is always wrong and irrational for a man to do anything else than what he believes most conducive to Universal Happiness; and it is not possible for him to do more. Still, it seems practically expedient, on various grounds, to retain this double view of felicific conduct. In the first place, some excellences are only partially and indirectly within the control of the will, and we require to distinguish the realization of these in conduct from the performance of Duty proper, which is always something that can be done at any moment. Secondly, even in the case of strictly voluntary conduct, the distinction between a part that is praiseworthy and admirable and a part that is merely right is—if I may so say—*secondarily* reasonable on Utilitarian principles, though it is not so *primarily*: because, as it is natural to us to compare any individual's character or conduct, not with our highest ideal—Utilitarian or otherwise—but with a certain average standard; so it seems ultimately conducive to the general happiness that such natural sentiments of admiration should be encouraged and developed. For the recognition of excellence in ourselves, and still more in others, is directly an important source of happiness, as it is commonly attended with a peculiar pleasurable emotion of a highly refined kind: and again, the attractive force of the excellence thus exhibited, the desire of imitation which it arouses in others, is a powerful stimulus to right action, which we cannot afford to spare. Further, these emotions naturally tend to inspire disinterested personal affections of a pure and elevated kind, which are again directly an important source of happiness and a valuable aid to the fulfilment of duty. Moreover, our nature seems to require the double stimulus of praise and blame from others, in order to the best performance of duty that we can at present attain; so that the 'social sanction' would be less effective if it became purely penal. Indeed, since the pains of remorse and disapprobation are in themselves to be avoided, it is plain that the Utilitarian construction of a Jural morality is essentially self-limiting; that is, it prescribes its own avoidance of any department of conduct in which the addition that can be made to happiness through the enforcement of rules sustained by social penalties appears doubtful or inconsiderable. In such departments, however, the æsthetic phase of morality may still reasonably find a place; we may properly admire and praise where it would be inexpedient to judge and condemn. We may conclude, then, that it is reasonable for a Utilitarian to praise any conduct more felicific in its tendency than what an average man would do under the given circumstances:—being aware of course that the limit down to which praiseworthiness extends must be relative to the particular state of moral progress reached by mankind generally in his age and country; and that it is desirable to make continual efforts to elevate this standard. Similarly, the Utilitarian will praise the Dispositions or permanent qualities of character of which felicific conduct is conceived to be the result, and the Motives that are conceived to prompt to it when it would be a clear gain to the general happiness that they should become more frequent: and, as we have seen[1], he may without inconsistency admire the Disposition or Motive if it is of a kind which it is generally desirable to encourage, even while he disapproves of the conduct to which it has led in any particular case.

Passing now to compare the contents of the Utilitarian Ideal of character with the virtues and other excellences recognized by Common Sense, we may observe, first, that general coincidence between the two on which Hume and others have insisted. No quality has ever been praised as excellent by mankind generally which cannot be shewn to have some marked felicific effect, and to be within proper limits obviously conducive to the general happiness. Still, it does not follow that such qualities are always fostered and encouraged by society in the proportion in which a Utilitarian would desire them to be: in fact, it is a common observation to make, in contemplating the morality of other societies, that some useful qualities are unduly neglected, while others are over-prized and even admired when they exist in such excess as to become, on the whole, infelicific. The consistent Utilitarian may therefore find it necessary to rectify the prevalent moral ideal in important particulars. And here it scarcely seems that he will find any such Utilitarian restrictions on innovation, as appeared to exist in the case of commonly received rules of duty. For the Common-Sense notions

[1] Cf. ch. iii. § 2 of this Book.

of the different excellences of conduct (considered as extending beyond the range of strict duty) are generally so vague as to offer at least no definite resistance to a Utilitarian interpretation of their scope: by teaching and acting upon such an interpretation a man is in no danger of being brought into infelicific discord with Common Sense: especially since the ideal of moral excellence seems to vary within the limits of the same community to a much greater extent than the code of strict duty. For example, a man who in an age when excessive asceticism is praised, sets an example of enjoying harmless bodily pleasures, or who in circles where useless daring is admired, prefers to exhibit and commend caution and discretion, at the worst misses some praise that he might otherwise have earned, and is thought a little dull or unaspiring: he does not come into any patent conflict with common opinion. And, if we may say more generally that an enlightened Utilitarian is likely to lay less stress on the cultivation of those negative virtues, tendencies to restrict and refrain, which are prominent in the Common-Sense ideal of character; and to set more value in comparison on those qualities of mind which are the direct source of positive pleasure to the agent or to others—some of which Common Sense scarcely recognizes as excellences,—he still will not carry this innovation to such a pitch as to incur general condemnation. For no enlightened Utilitarian can ignore the fundamental importance of these restrictive and regulative dispositions, or think that they are sufficiently developed in ordinary men at the present time, so that they may properly be excluded from moral admiration; though he may hold that they have been too prominent, to the neglect of other valuable qualities, in the common conception of moral Perfection. Nay, we may even venture to say that, under most circumstances, a man who earnestly and successfully endeavours to realize the Utilitarian Ideal, however he may deviate from the commonly-received type of a perfect character, is likely to win sufficient recognition and praise from Common Sense. For, whether it be true or not that the whole of morality has sprung from the root of sympathy, it is certain that self-love and sympathy combined are sufficiently strong in average men to dispose them to grateful admiration of any exceptional efforts to promote the common good, even though these efforts may take a somewhat novel form. To any exhibition of more extended sympathy or more fervent public spirit than is ordinarily shewn, and any attempt to develope these qualities in others, Common Sense is rarely unresponsive; provided, of course, that these impulses are accompanied with adequate knowledge of actual circumstances and insight into the relation of means to ends, and that they do not run counter to any recognized rules of duty[1]. And it seems to be principally in this direction that the recent spread of Utilitarianism has positively modified the ideal of our society, and is likely to modify it further in the future. Hence the stress which Utilitarians are apt to lay on social and political activity of all kinds, and the tendency which Utilitarian ethics have always shewn to pass over into politics. For one who values conduct in proportion to its felicific consequences, will naturally set a higher estimate on effective beneficence in public affairs than on the purest manifestation of virtue in the details of private life: while on the other hand an Intuitionist (though no doubt vaguely recognizing that a man ought to do all the good he can in public affairs) still commonly holds that virtue may be as fully and as admirably exhibited on a small as on a large scale. A sincere Utilitarian, therefore, is likely to be an eager politician: but, as I have already said, on what principles his political action ought to be determined, it scarcely lies within the scope of this treatise to investigate.

[1] We have seen that a Utilitarian may sometimes have to override these rules; but then the case falls under the head discussed in the previous section.

CONCLUDING CHAPTER.

THE MUTUAL RELATIONS OF THE THREE METHODS.

§ 1. In the greater part of the treatise of which the final chapter has now been reached, we have been employed in examining three methods of determining right conduct, which are for the most part found more or less vaguely combined in the practical reasonings of ordinary men, but which it has been my aim to develope as separately as possible. To attempt a complete synthesis of these different methods does not fall within the scope of the present work: at the same time it would hardly be satisfactory to conclude our analysis of them without discussing their mutual relations. Indeed we have already found it expedient to do this to a considerable extent, in the course of our examination of the separate methods. Thus in the present and preceding books we have directly or indirectly gone through a pretty full examination of the mutual relations of the Intuitional and Utilitarian methods. We have found that the common antithesis between Intuitionists and Utilitarians must be entirely discarded: since such abstract moral principles as we can admit to be really self-evident are not only not incompatible with a Utilitarian system, but even seem required to furnish a rational basis for such a system. Thus we have seen that the essence of Justice or Equity, (in so far as it is clear and certain), is that different individuals are not to be treated differently, except on grounds of universal application; which grounds, again, are given in the principle of Universal Benevolence, that sets before each man the happiness of all others as an object of pursuit no less worthy than his own; while, again, other time-honoured virtues seem to be fitly explained as special manifestations of impartial benevolence under various normal circumstances of human life, or else as habits and dispositions indispensable to the maintenance of prudent or beneficent behaviour under the seductive force of various non-rational impulses. And although there are other rules which our common moral sense when first interrogated seems to enunciate as absolutely binding; it has appeared that careful and systematic reflection on this very Common Sense, as expressed in the habitual moral judgments of ordinary men, results in exhibiting the real subordination of these rules to the fundamental principles above given. Then, further, this method of systematising particular virtues and duties receives very strong support from a comparative study of the history of morality; as the variations in the moral code of different societies at different stages correspond, in a great measure, to differences in the actual or believed tendencies of certain kinds of conduct to promote the general happiness—at least of certain portions of the human race: while, again, the most probable conjectures as to the pre-historic condition and original derivation of the moral faculty seem to be entirely in harmony with this view. No doubt, even if this synthesis of methods be completely accepted, there will remain some discrepancy in details between our particular moral sentiments and spontaneous judgments on the one hand, and the apparent results of special utilitarian calculations on the other; and we may often have some practical difficulty in balancing the latter against the more general utilitarian reasons for obeying the former: but there seems to be no longer any theoretical perplexity as to the principles for determining social duty.

It remains for us to consider the relation of the two species of Hedonism which we have distinguished as Universalistic and Egoistic. In ch. ii. of this book we have discussed the rational process (called by a stretch of language 'proof') by which one who holds it reasonable to aim at his own greatest happiness may be determined to take Universal Happiness instead, as his ultimate standard of right conduct. We have seen, however, that the application of this process requires that the Egoist should affirm, implicitly or explicitly, that his own greatest happiness is not merely the rational ultimate end for himself, but a part of Universal Good: and he may avoid the proof of Utilitarianism by declining to affirm this. And it may be observed that most Utilitarians, however anxious they have been to convince men of the reasonableness of aiming at happiness generally, have not commonly sought to attain this result by any logical transition from the Egoistic to the Universalistic principle. They have relied almost entirely on the Sanctions of Utilitarian rules; that is, on the pleasures gained or pains avoided by the individual conforming to them. Indeed, if an Egoist remains impervious to what we have called Proof, the only way of rationally inducing him to aim at the happiness of all, is to shew him that his own greatest happiness can be best attained by so doing: and even if he admits the self-evidence of the principle of Rational Benevolence, he may still hold that the ultimate validity of the maxim of Prudence is no less self-evident, and that a reconciliation of the two must be somehow found. This latter indeed (as I have before said) appears, to me, on the whole, the view of Common Sense: and it is that which I myself hold. It thus becomes needful to examine how far and in what way this reconciliation can be effected.

§ 2. Now, in so far as Utilitarian morality coincides with that of Common Sense—as we have seen that it does in the main—this investigation has been partly performed in ch. v. of B. II. It there appeared that while in any tolerable state of society the performance of duties towards others and the exercise of social virtues seem *generally* likely to coincide with the attainment of the greatest possible happiness in the long run for the virtuous agent, still the *universality* and *completeness* of this coincidence are at least incapable of empirical proof: and that, indeed, the more carefully we analyse and estimate the different sanctions—Legal, Social and Conscientious—considered as operating under the actual conditions of human life, the more difficult it seems to believe that they can be always adequate to produce this coincidence. The natural effect of this argument upon a convinced Utilitarian is merely to make him anxious to alter the actual conditions of human life: and it would certainly be a most valuable contribution to the actual happiness of mankind, if we could so improve the adjustment of the machine of Law in any society, and so stimulate and direct the common awards of praise and blame, and so develop and train the moral sense of the members of the community, as to render it clearly prudent for every individual to promote as much as possible the general good. However, we are not now considering what a consistent Utilitarian will try to effect for the future, but what a consistent Egoist is to do in the present. And, as things are, whatever difference exists between Utilitarian morality and that of Common Sense is of such a kind as to render the coincidence with Egoism still more improbable in the case of the former. For we have seen that Utilitarianism is more rigid than Common Sense in exacting the sacrifice of the agent's private interests where they are incompatible with the greatest happiness of the greatest number: and of course in so far as the Utilitarian's principles bring him into conflict with any of the commonly accepted rules of morality, the whole force of the Social Sanction operates to deter him from what he conceives to be his duty.

§ 3. There are however writers of the Utilitarian school, who seem to maintain or imply, that by due contemplation of the paramount importance of Sympathy as an element of human happiness we shall be led to see the coincidence of the good of each with the good of all. I may refer especially to Mill's treatise on Utilitarianism (ch. iii. *passim*): where however the argument is not easy to follow, from a confusion between three different objects of inquiry: (1) the actual effect of sympathy in inducing conformity to the rules of Utilitarian ethics, (2) the effect in this direction which it is likely to have in the future, (3) the value of sympathetic pleasures and pains as estimated by an enlightened Egoist. The first and third of these questions Mill did not clearly separate, owing to his psychological doctrine that our own pleasure is the sole object of our desires. But if my refutation of this doctrine[1] is valid, we have carefully to distinguish two ways in which sympathy operates: it no doubt generates sympathetic pleasures and pains, which must of course be taken into account in the calculations of Egoistic Hedonism: but it also causes impulses to altruistic action, of which the force is quite out of proportion to the sympathetic pleasure (or relief from pain) which such action

[1] Cf. B. i. c. iv. § 3.

seems likely to secure to the agent. So that even if the average man ever should reach such a pitch of sympathetic development, as never to feel prompted to sacrifice the general good to his own, still this will not prove that it is egoistically reasonable for him to behave in this way. Though certainly if we could only secure the actual result it would be comparatively unimportant for a Utilitarian to convince an Egoist of its reasonableness. But no one is likely to maintain that sympathy is now so far developed in most men as actually to produce this effect: and if we pass from considering what men actually do, to ask what enlightened self-interest would prescribe, it does not seem that Mill's argument affords even a probability that conduct so altruistic would be egoistically reasonable.

In saying this, I am as far as possible from any wish to depreciate the value of sympathy as a source of happiness even to human beings as at present constituted. Indeed I am of opinion that its pleasures and pains really constitute a great part of that internal reward of social virtue, and punishment of social misconduct, which in B. II. c. v. I roughly set down as due to the moral sentiments. For, in fact, though I can to some extent distinguish sympathetic from strictly moral feelings in introspective analysis of my own consciousness, I cannot say precisely in what proportion these two elements are combined. For instance: I seem able to distinguish the "sense of the ignobility of Egoism" of which I have before spoken—which, in my view, is the normal emotional concomitant or expression of the moral intuition that the Good of the whole is reasonably to be preferred to the Good of a part—from the jar of sympathetic discomfort which attends the conscious choice of my own pleasure at the expense of pain or loss to others; but I find it impossible to determine what force the former sentiment would have if actually separated from the latter; and what others communicate of their experience inclines me to think that the two kinds of feeling are very variously combined in different individuals. Perhaps, indeed, we may trace a general law of variation in the relative proportion of these two elements as exhibited in the development of the moral consciousness both in the race and in individuals; for it seems that at a certain stage of this development the mind is more susceptible to emotions connected with abstract moral ideas and rules presented as absolute; while after emerging from this stage and before entering it the feelings that belong to personal relations are stronger[1]. Certainly in a Utilitarian's mind sympathy tends to become a prominent element of all instinctive moral feelings that refer to social conduct; as in his view the rational basis of the moral impulse must ultimately lie in some pleasure won or pain saved for himself or for others; so that he never has to sacrifice himself to an impersonal Law, but always for some being or beings with whom he has at least some degree of fellow-feeling.

But besides admitting the actual importance of sympathetic pleasures to the majority of mankind, I should go further and maintain that, on empirical grounds alone, enlightened self-interest would direct most men to foster and develop their sympathetic susceptibilities to a greater extent than is now commonly attained. The effectiveness of Butler's famous argument against the vulgar antithesis between Self-love and Benevolence is undeniable: and it seems scarcely extravagant to say that, amid all the profuse waste of the means of happiness which men commit, there is no imprudence more flagrant than that of Selfishness in the ordinary sense of the term,—that excessive concentration of attention on the individual's own happiness which renders it impossible for him to feel any strong interest in the pleasures and pains of others. The perpetual prominence of self that hence results tends to deprive all enjoyments of their keenness and zest, and produce rapid satiety and *ennui:* the selfish man misses the sense of elevation and enlargement given by wide interests; he misses the more secure and serene satisfaction that attends continually on activities directed towards ends more stable in prospect than an individual's happiness can be; he misses the peculiar rich sweetness, depending upon a sort of complex reverberation of sympathy, which is always found in services rendered to those whom we love and who are grateful. He is made to feel in a thousand various ways, according to the degree of refinement which

---

[1] I do not mean to imply that the process of change is merely circular. In the earlier period sympathy is narrower, simpler, and more presentative; in the later it is more extensive, complex, and representative.

his nature has attained, the discord between the rhythms of his own life and of that larger life of which his own is but an insignificant fraction.

But allowing[1] all this, it yet seems to me to admit of no more doubt than the general uncertainty of hedonistic comparison necessarily involves, that the utmost development of sympathy, intensive and extensive, which is now possible to any but a very few exceptional persons, would not cause a perfect coincidence between Utilitarian duty and self-interest. Here it seems to me that what was said in B. II. ch. v. § 4, to shew the insufficiency of the Conscientious Sanction, applies equally, *mutatis mutandis*, to Sympathy. Suppose a man finds that a regard for the general good—Utilitarian Duty—demands from him a sacrifice, or extreme risk, of life. There are perhaps one or two human beings so dear to him that the remainder of a life saved by sacrificing their happiness to his own would be worthless to him from an egoistic point of view. But it is doubtful whether many men, "sitting down in a cool hour" to make the estimate, would affirm even this: and of course that particular portion of the general happiness, for which one is called upon to sacrifice one's own, may easily be the happiness of persons not especially dear to one. But again, from this normal limitation of our keenest and strongest sympathy to a very small circle of human beings, it results that the very development of sympathy may operate to increase the weight thrown into the scale against Utilitarian duty. There are very few persons, however strongly and widely sympathetic, who are so constituted as to feel for the pleasures and pains of mankind generally a degree of sympathy at all commensurate with their concern for wife or children, or lover, or bosom friend: and if any training of the affections is at present possible which would materially alter this proportion in the general distribution of our sympathy, it scarcely seems that

[1] I do not however think that we are justified in stating as *universally* true what has been admitted in the preceding paragraph. Some few thoroughly selfish persons appear at least to be happier than most of the unselfish; and there are other exceptional natures whose chief happiness seems to be derived from activity, disinterested indeed, but directed towards other ends than human happiness.

such a training is to be recommended as on the whole felicific[1]. And thus when Utilitarian Duty calls on us to sacrifice not only our own pleasures but the happiness of those we love to the general good, the very sanction on which Utilitarianism most relies must act powerfully in opposition to its precepts.

But even apart from these exceptional cases—which are yet sufficient to decide the abstract question—it seems that the course of conduct by which a man would most fully reap the rewards of sympathy (so far as they are empirically ascertainable) will often be very different from that to which a sincere desire to promote the general happiness would direct him. For the relief of distress and calamity is an important part of Utilitarian duty: but as the state of the person relieved is on the whole painful, it would appear that sympathy under these circumstances must be a source of pain rather than pleasure, in proportion to its intensity. It is probably true, as a general rule, that in the relief of distress other elements of the complex pleasure of benevolence decidedly outweigh this sympathetic pain:—for the effusion of pity is itself pleasurable, and we commonly feel more keenly that amelioration of the sufferer's state which is due to our exertions than we do his pain otherwise caused, and there is further the pleasure that we derive from his gratitude, and the pleasure that is the normal reflex of activity directed under a strong impulse towards a permanently valued end. Still, when the distress is bitter and continued, and such as we can only partially mitigate by all our efforts, the philanthropist's sympathetic discomfort must necessarily be considerable; and the work of combating misery, though not devoid of elevated happiness, will be much less happy on the whole than many other forms of activity; while yet it may be to just this work that Duty seems to summon us. Or again, a man may find that he can best promote the general happiness by working in comparative solitude for ends that he never hopes to see realized, or by working chiefly among and for persons for whom he cannot feel much affection, or by doing what must alienate

---

[1] To effect this we should probably require some such drastic treatment of human relations as that for which even the eloquence of Plato has failed to win approval. Cf. *Republic*, B. v.

or grieve those whom he loves best, or must make it necessary for him to dispense with the most intimate of human ties. In short, there seem to be numberless ways in which the dictates of that Rational Benevolence, which as a Utilitarian he is bound absolutely to obey, may conflict with that indulgence of kind affections which Shaftesbury and his followers so persuasively exhibit as its own reward.

§ 4. It seems then that we must conclude, from the arguments given in B. II. ch. v, supplemented by the discussion in the preceding section, that the inseparable connexion between Utilitarian Duty and the greatest happiness of the individual who conforms to it cannot be satisfactorily demonstrated on empirical grounds. Hence another section of the Utilitarian school has preferred to throw the weight of Duty on the Religious Sanction: and this procedure has been partly adopted by some of those who have chiefly dwelt on sympathy as a motive. From this point of view the Utilitarian Code is conceived as the Law of God, who is to be regarded as having commanded men to promote the general happiness, and as having announced an intention of rewarding those who obey his commands and punishing the disobedient. It is clear that if we feel convinced that an Omnipotent Being has, in whatever way, signified such commands and announcements, a rational egoist can want no further inducement to frame his life on Utilitarian principles. It only remains to consider how this conviction is attained. This is commonly thought to be either by supernatural Revelation, or by the natural exercise of Reason, or in both ways. As regards the former it is to be observed that—with a few exceptions—the moralists who hold that God has disclosed his law either to special individuals in past ages who have left a written record of what was revealed to them, or to a permanent succession of persons appointed in a particular manner, or to religious persons generally in some supernatural way, do not consider that it is the Utilitarian Code that has thus been revealed, but rather the rules of Common-Sense morality with some special modifications and additions. Still, as Mill has urged, in so far as Utilitarianism is more rigorous than Common Sense in exacting the sacrifice of the individual's happiness to that of mankind generally, it is strictly in accordance with the most characteristic teaching of Christianity. It seems, however, unnecessary to discuss the precise relation of different Revelational Codes to Utilitarianism, as it would be going beyond our province to investigate the grounds on which a Divine origin has been attributed to them.

In so far, however, as a knowledge of God's law is believed to be attainable by the Reason, Ethics and Theology seem to be so closely connected that we cannot sharply separate their provinces. For, as we saw[1], it has been widely maintained, that the relation of moral rules to a Divine Lawgiver is implicitly cognized in the act of thought by which we discern these rules to be binding. And no doubt the terms (such as 'moral obligation'), which we commonly use in speaking of these rules, are naturally suggestive of Legal Sanctions and so of a Sovereign by whom these are announced and enforced. Indeed many thinkers since Locke have refused to admit any other meaning in the terms Right, Duty, &c., except that of a rule imposed by a lawgiver. This view however seems opposed to Common Sense; as may be, perhaps, most easily shewn[2] by pointing out that the Divine Lawgiver is himself conceived as a Moral Agent; *i.e.* as prescribing what is right, and designing what is good. It is clear that in this conception at least the notions 'right' and 'good' are used absolutely; and that they are here used in a sense not essentially different from that which they ordinarily bear seems to be affirmed by the *consensus* of religious persons. Still, though Common Sense does not regard moral rules as being *merely* the mandates of an Omnipotent Being who will reward and punish men according as they obey or violate them; it certainly holds that this is a true though partial view of them, and perhaps that it may be intuitively apprehended. If then reflection leads us to conclude that the particular moral principles of Common Sense are to be systematized as subordinate to that preeminently certain and irrefragable intuition which stands as the first principle of Utilitarianism; then, of course, it will be the Utilitarian Code to which we shall believe the Divine Sanctions to be attached.

[1] Bk. III. ch. i. § 4.   [2] Cf. B 1. ch. iii. § 2.

Or, again, we may argue thus. If—as all Theologians agree—we are to conceive God as acting for some end, we must conceive that end to be Universal Good, and, if Utilitarians are right, Universal Happiness: and we cannot suppose that in a world morally governed it can be reasonable for us to act in conscious opposition to what we believe to be the Divine Design. Hence if in any case after calculating the consequences of two alternatives of conduct we choose that which seems likely to be less conducive to Happiness generally, we shall be acting in a manner for which we cannot but expect to suffer.

To this it has been objected, that observation of the actual world shews us that the happiness of sentient beings is so imperfectly attained in it, and with so large an intermixture of pain and misery, that we cannot really conceive Universal Happiness to be God's end, unless we admit that he is not Omnipotent. And no doubt the assertion that God is omnipotent will require to be understood with some limitation; but perhaps with no greater limitation than has always been implicitly admitted by thoughtful theologians. For these seem always to have allowed that some things are impossible to God: as, for example, to change the past. And perhaps if our knowledge of the Universe were complete, we might discern the *quantum* of happiness ultimately attained in it to be as great as could be attained without the accomplishment of what we should then see to be just as inconceivable and absurd as changing the past. This, however, is a view which it belongs rather to the theologian to develop. I should rather urge that there does not seem to be any other of the ordinary interpretations of Good according to which it would appear to be more completely realized in the actual universe. For the wonderful perfections of work that we admire in the physical world are yet everywhere mingled with imperfection, and subject to destruction and decay: and similarly in the world of human conduct Virtue is at least as much balanced by Vice as Happiness is by Misery. So that, if the ethical reasoning that led us to interpret Ultimate Good as Happiness is sound, there seems no argument from Natural Theology to set against it.

§ 5. If, then, we may assume the existence of such a Being, as God, by the *consensus* of theologians, is conceived to be, it seems that we may infer the existence of Divine—and of course adequate—sanctions to the code of social duty as constructed on a Utilitarian basis. It is, however, desirable, before we conclude, to examine carefully the validity of this assumption, in so far as it is supported on ethical grounds alone. For by the result of such an examination will be determined, as we now see, the very important question whether ethical science can be constructed on an independent basis; or whether it is forced to borrow a fundamental and indispensable premiss from Theology or some similar source[1]. In order fairly to perform this examination, let us reflect upon the clearest and most certain of our moral intuitions. I find that I undoubtedly seem to perceive, as clearly and certainly as I see any axiom in Arithmetic or Geometry, that it is 'right' and 'reasonable' for me to treat others as I should think that I myself ought to be treated under similar conditions, and to do what I believe to be ultimately conducive to universal Good or Happiness. But I cannot find inseparably connected with this conviction, and similarly attainable by mere reflective intuition, any cognition that there actually is a Supreme Being who will adequately[2] reward me for obeying these rules of duty, or punish me for violating them. Or, more generally, I do not find in my moral consciousness any intuition, claiming to be clear and certain, that the performance of duty will be adequately rewarded and its violation punished. I no doubt feel a strong sentiment, apparently inseparable from the strictly moral sentiments, prompting me to hope and long that it may be so:

[1] It is not necessary, if we are simply considering Ethics as a possible independent science, to throw the fundamental premiss of which we are now examining the validity into a Theistic form. Nor does it seem always to have taken that form in the support which Positive Religion has given to Morality. In the Buddhist creed this notion of the rewards inseparably attaching to right conduct seems to have been developed in a far more elaborate and systematic manner than it has in any phase of Christianity. But, as conceived by enlightened Buddhists, these rewards are not distributed by the volition of a Supreme Person, but by the natural operation of an impersonal Law.

[2] It may be well to remind the reader that by 'adequate' is here meant 'sufficient to make it the agent's interest to promote universal good;' not necessarily 'proportioned to Desert.'

nay more, my moral reason declares that in a certain sense it *ought* to be so—where 'ought' is not used in a strictly ethical meaning, but expresses the need that Practical Reason feels of obtaining this premiss, if it is to be made consistent with itself. For, if we find an ultimate and fundamental contradiction in our apparent intuitions of what is Reasonable in conduct, we seem forced to the conclusion that they were not really intuitions after all, and that the apparently intuitive operation of the Practical Reason is essentially illusory. Therefore it is, one may say, a matter of life and death to the Practical Reason that this premiss should be somehow obtained. And I cannot fall back on the resource of thinking myself under a moral necessity to regard all my duties *as if they were* commandments of God, although not entitled to hold speculatively that any such Supreme Being really exists. I am so far from feeling bound to believe for purposes of practice what I see no ground for holding as a speculative truth, that I cannot even conceive the state of mind which these words seem to describe, except as a momentary half-wilful irrationality, committed in a violent access of philosophic despair. Still it seems plain that in proportion as man has lived in the exercise of the Practical Reason—as he believed—and feels as an actual force the desire to do what is right and reasonable as such, his demand for the removal of conflict from the intuitions of his reason will be intense and imperious. Thus we are not surprised to find Socrates—the type for all ages of the man in whom this desire is predominant—declaring with simple conviction that 'if the Rulers of the Universe do not prefer the just man to the unjust, it is better to die than to live.' And we must observe that in the feeling that prompts to such a declaration the desire to rationalize one's own conduct is not the sole, nor perhaps always the most prominent, element: when a man passionately refuses to believe that the "Wages of Virtue" can "be dust," it is often less from any private reckoning about his own wages than from a disinterested aversion to a universe so fundamentally irrational that 'Good for the Individual' is *not* ultimately identified with 'Universal Good.'

To all this it may be replied that the existence of a desire for perfect rationality in human life, or in the world, does not

—any more than the existence of any other elevated desire—furnish a proof of the existence of their object; that, indeed, it can scarcely afford a strong presumption in favour of this conclusion, considering the large proportion of human desires that experience shews to be destined to disappointment. But it must be urged again that we do not fully conceive the argument in favour of the assumption that we are now considering, if we merely represent this as satisfying certain desires. We have rather to regard it as an hypothesis logically necessary to avoid a fundamental contradiction in one chief department of our thought. Whether this necessity constitutes a sufficient reason for accepting this hypothesis, is a question which I cannot here attempt adequately to discuss; as it could not be satisfactorily answered, without a general examination of the criteria of true and false beliefs. If we find that in other departments of our supposed knowledge propositions are commonly taken to be true, which yet seem to rest on no other grounds than that we have a strong disposition to accept them, and that they are indispensable to the systematic coherence of our beliefs; it will be difficult to reject a similarly supported assumption in ethics, without opening the door to universal scepticism. If on the other hand it appears that the edifice of physical science is really constructed of conclusions logically inferred from premises intuitively known; it will be reasonable to demand that our practical judgments should either be based on an equally firm foundation or should abandon all claim to philosophic certainty.

THE END.

CPSIA information can be obtained
at www.ICGtesting.com
Printed in the USA
BVHW061210020119
536873BV00022B/1162/P